Ariadne's
Thread

Ariadne's Thread

A Workbook of Goddess Magic

By
Shekhinah Mountainwater

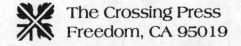

The Crossing Press
Freedom, CA 95019

Acknowledgments

To my mother, Frances, who gave me life and fed me on "mare's milk," folklore, and revolution.

To my daughter Freya, and my son Frey, and the years they danced and played inside the songs of my heart, contributing so greatly to my inspiration.

To Diane Stein, who recommended and acknowledged me and made a place for me in the circle.

Cover art by Monica Sjöö
Cover design by Anne Marie Arnold

Printed in the U.S.A.

Library of Congress Cataloging-in-Publication Data

Mountainwater, Shekhinah.
    Ariadne's thread : a workbook of goddess magic / by Shekhinah Mountainwater
       p. cm.
    ISBN 0-89594-476-6. ISBN 0-89594-475-8 (pbk.)
    1. Magic. 2. Goddess religion. 3. Ariadne (Greek mythology)-Cults. 4. Women—Religious life. I. Title.
BF1621. M68 1991
133.4'3—dc20   91-25382
                             CIP

CONTENTS

ARIADNE

In the deepening twilight
She stands
Just inside the entrance
To her cave,
Beckoning.

"Come," she softly calls
"Follow me."
"But I'm afraid," you tell her
"I fear I will be lost in there
"And they say that there are Minotaurs."

You peer into the labyrinth
Behind her
The twisting passages
Winding away
To nothing . . .

Out here the familiar world
Crashes on.
The Sea of Sexism,
the City of Doom.
She lifts her proud dark gaze in scorn
"'Tis *there* one meets the Minotaur."

In the shadow gleams her crescent crown
A snake stirs at her breast
And in her hand she holds the Thread
Unravelling a strand
And offering . . .

Will you come
Oh my sister
Will you come?

PROLOGUE

Who is Ariadne?

Ariadne is best known for providing guidance through the mysterious temple-maze of ancient Crete, where she presided as priestess. Her famous thread was the means by which seekers could find their way safely in and out again.

The maze or labyrinth can be understood on many levels. Patriarchal myth has taught us to view it as a frightening place, built to imprison the dangerous Minotaur, who fed upon innocent youths and maidens. The conquering hero Theseus, said to be the savior who liberated Crete from this scourge, was assisted by Ariadne and her magic ball of thread. She instructed him to place it on the ground upon entering the labyrinth, and the ball would roll and unwind of itself, leading him to the central chamber. To return he had only to pick up the thread and rewind it, following the strand back to the entrance. In the story Theseus successfully penetrated the maze and slew the monster, then fled Crete with Ariadne, his lover and promised bride, whom he later abandoned on a nearby island.

Stories such as these are curiously compelling, even when we don't fully comprehend them. This is because the images they contain are powerful, and resonate deeply within the psyche. The labyrinth, the thread, the priestess . . . these are very old ideas that go back and back into the shadows of prehistory. To unravel their meanings is a labyrinthine journey in itself.

In this first Theseus-strand, Ariadne is represented as priestess and princess, daughter of King Minos, a mortal woman of historic myth. Her primary role is as a supporter in the hero's journey, used when needed, discarded in the end.

In the next unravelling we discover Ariadne, still mortal, still human, but with a pivotal part to play in the historical shift on Crete from matriarchy to patriarchy. In June R. Brindel's account (*Ariadne*) we watch through Ariadne's eyes the crumbling of one age and the violent installation of another. Much like the parallel Arthurian saga as retold in *The Mists of Avalon* by Marion Zimmer Bradley, or Clysta Kinstler's *The Moon Under Her Feet*, which depicts a similar shift in the Middle East, we see women in key positions, struggling with or giving in to the men of the new order. In this view the maze is now a dance floor, fashioned by the clever magician Daedalus, where Ariadne performs the ritual movements of Cretan spring ceremonies. We see Minos deliberately rewriting the liturgies of these rites, changing the goddesses to gods, forcing the priestesses to mouth the new words before the people.

Robert Graves unwinds the next strand in *The White Goddess* and *The Greek Myths*. Here the labyrinth becomes the battleground where one hero/god slays another. Graves shows a mixed view of Ariadne as both mortal and divine, yet always through the eyes of men and their gods. As matriarchal princess, the human Ariadne is representative of the Triple Goddess, who weds the victorious hero, thus bestowing upon him the status of sacred king. Graves is well-known among scholars for his retelling of the many myths in which two gods must repeatedly overcome one another for the sake of the Goddess who is their Mother, Lover, and Destroyer. Graves tells us that the Minotaur is really the old matriarchal Moon-Bull, beloved of the Goddess, and sacrificed each year for the fertility of the earth. This tale of the dying and reviving gods, he explains, is the Perennial Theme of all true poetry and myth, and basis of much religious belief today.

In the end it is feminist scholars like Monica Sjöö, Barbara Mor, Barbara G. Walker, and Patricia Monaghan who take us back to the beginning. We come to see that Ariadne is the Goddess Herself. "Most Holy" and "High Fruitful Mother of the Barley" are the original meanings of Her beautiful name. Worshipped primarily by women, Her rites are peaceful, and concerned with the womanly cycles of body, mind and spirit. Like Persephone, the Dark Maiden, She is the cycle of growth and decay, the fate of the grain, giver of life, receiver of souls at death. The labyrinth is Her own body, the place of Her mysteries, the cave/womb of initiation. We find this spiralling labyrinth in pre-patriarchal cultures around the world, such as that of the Hopis in the American Southwest, or the ancient Celtic peoples of Britain. The stories always tell of a numinous woman who presides at these sacred sites. With her guidance the seeker travels through the labyrinth to the spirit world and back again, learning the lessons of ecstasy, transformation, and immortality.

The thread that guides us in and out is the same thread spun, woven and cut by the Goddesses of Fate, makers and unmakers of destiny. It is the same thread pulled from the body of Spider Woman in Hopi myth, with which She wove the universe, and which She attaches to the crown chakras of all Her children, to keep us connected to Her. It is the umbilical cord of birth and rebirth, from the womb to the tomb and back again.

The monster is not a monster, but only the still heart center of woman, that men have so long suppressed and feared. Like the wheeling of the heavens, the twisting of serpents, the convolutions of our brains, the labyrinth unfolds and folds again upon itself, and all the meanings we hear about it are true. Back and back it goes, taking us into history, into herstory, into myth, into time and death and birth, into the Goddess, and into our deepest Selves. And if we can keep our hold upon the thread, it will lead us back and out again, as we traverse corridor upon corridor, labyrinth upon labyrinth, outwards and outwards 'til we have found spiritual rebirth, and escaped at last the tangled web of patriarchy.

At the time of the writing of this prologue, war has just begun again on this planet, in the region of the Middle East. It is difficult not to be aware of this, as I ply words to paper and think upon ancient things. And I realize that the world in which Ariadne's original rites were practiced was a gentle world. No implements of war have been found amongst its ruins—only tools, art and pottery. Evidently there is a connection between Goddess-reverence and social peace. Perhaps this too is the lesson taught to us by Ariadne's thread . . .

GUIDELINES

For Students and Teachers

Ariadne's Thread began as a correspondence course called *The Mysteries of the Goddess, A Study in the Lore and Craft of Woman*, created in 1982-3. Until now it has only been shared privately, between myself and my students, with the exception of a few published excerpts. I feel that publication of this course presents some wonderful opportunities, not only as a continued study text for correspondence students, but as material for the independent student of women's spirituality, solitary magic-makers, and other teachers. *Ariadne's Thread* can serve as a complete or partial curriculum, be used for research, or simple personal enrichment. It can be read as a source of inspiration, a learning experience, or on a deeper level, as a process of spiritual initiation and social transformation. It is my hope that this book will be used in all these ways and will become a common resource for the women's spirituality movement as a whole. I would like to see those who have completed the course as students go on to teach and share it with other women. I envision the book as a tool for women's study groups and covens, a teaching aid for priestesses and leaders, as well as a magical resource for creating rituals, celebrating the holy days, and understanding Goddess ways.

The first thing I would suggest to both students and teachers is to look through the book and get a feeling for its shape and content. Note that each Cycle includes discussion and teachings, as well as projects and questions to ponder. In some, rituals are provided, in others there are projects to do, such as starting a magical journal, building an altar, and making calendars. Check to see what materials you may need, or what substitutes you may have on hand.

Ariadne's Thread has three main sections or Passages: Gathering, Spinning, and Weaving. In Gathering, the first Passage, we are introduced and prepared for the journey. We learn a little about altars and build a Goddess altar, then meet the Goddess in Her three aspects of Maiden, Mother and Crone. In the second Passage we start to Spin some of the reality we have learned in the first. We discover Goddess Time, make solar and lunar calendars, deepen with the holy days. We meet the Muse and hear her Perennial Theme of Birth and Life and Death, and learn of the correlations between Women's Mysteries and the Wheel of the Year. In the final Passage we become Weavers ourselves, as we discover and hone some of the skills and powers of magic: Divination, Ritual, Spells, Herbs, and the energies of Aphrodite,

Goddess of Love. In the end we turn to thoughts of community and the possibilities of personal and social transformation through use of our newfound awareness and skills.

Once you have an overview of what will be involved in the study, it's a good idea to make a time plan. Each study segment is a cycle, with a beginning, a middle and an end. First comes a period of reading and thinking about the material, then the activities or exercises, and finally a time of reflection and writing up the experience. These stages correspond very nicely with the phases of the moon, and I encourage you to set up your study plan in tune with Luna. The waxing or Maiden moon can be a time for investigation, reading, and discovery. The swelling or Mother moon can be the time for performing the rituals and doing the exercises. The waning or Crone moon can be a time of reflection and writing. Thirteen cycles makes thirteen moons, which means the course has the potential to be completed within one round of the sacred year.

MOON-SCHEDULE

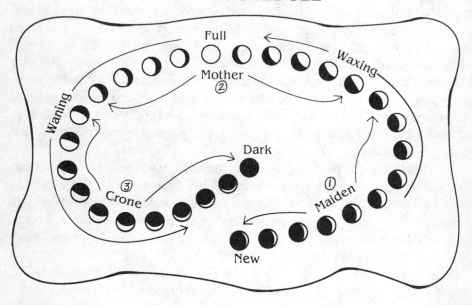

Thirteen moons or "a-year-and-a-day" is a classic span of time in the Old Religion, said to represent the temporal journey as well as the eternal. In a year and a day young novices would complete the first stages of initiation into the mysteries. These can be marked and acknowledged at the times of the eight great sabbats or solar holidays. Rituals for these have been provided in Cycle 8, The Goddess Year. The beginning and end of the course are also marked with ceremony: a Consecration

Ritual at the altar in Cycle 2, and an Initiation Rite to affirm completion after Cycle 13. Students who have completed the entire course are entitled to receive the Wise Woman Inscription (see example, page 379) and to use the letters W.W. after their names.

Magical studies, however, may not always conform neatly to preconceived schedules. Time-frames are helpful and stabilizing, but I have found that flexibility is important too. Some of the lessons may stir up the psyche, and this can bring changes outwardly as well as within. The Goddess teaches us in so many ways, and often life itself becomes the path of learning. You may need more time than one moon for a given lesson/cycle, in which case you can simply begin the next cycle at the waxing moon following completion of the last. Good magic is never rushed, but done from a deep and centered place. When it comes to spiritual growth, we all develop in our own time.

When you have devised a study plan, I suggest a ritual of some kind to affirm your commitment. It can be as simple as a silent promise between yourself and the Goddess, or a verbal one, spoken aloud at your altar. Women working together may wish to have a ceremony, light some candles, perhaps sign an agreement together. Solitary students can also write promises to themselves and to the Goddess. Students and teachers working by correspondence can benefit from a written contract. I have found that making a simple, yet formal statement helps to build trust and solidity, and ensures clarity so that there will be no misunderstandings or mistaken assumptions along the way. Basic commitments such as intentions to stay with the process until it is completed, respect and support for all involved, and honoring the sacredness of the teachings all help to make the course a success. If there is an energy exchange between teacher and student, or if there are any other responsibilities involved, it is a good idea to state these clearly. Most of all, it is important for each woman to have a say in what she would like to achieve.

Completion requires stability, motivation and dedication, as well as timing. Sometimes, even with the best of intentions, there are students who may not make it through all thirteen Cycles. If your life is full of other demands and pressures, you may need to take time out to rearrange your priorities. I have found that it is best to do this work when one is relatively settled and has access to some solitary time and space. For some of you it might work better to set smaller goals; perhaps do one passage, or a couple of Cycles. You can always come back to *the Thread*.

For Students

In olden times, the mysteries of woman were handed down by the crone-mothers to the maiden-daughters when their first bloods came. Learning and teaching were a personal exchange between women who loved and respected one another. Both learned and were transformed by the experience. This style of education is nearly lost today, but some of us are working to bring it back.

I have been teaching this way for many years now, working one-on-one as well as in circles of women. My offerings have been based not on coercion or credit, but on mutual desire. Students have come to me because they want to learn, and I have taught because I love to share the revelations and inspirations the Goddess has given me. I have learned a great deal in the process myself, and still feel there is endlessly more to discover. I have found that the teacher/student relationship can be an equal one, for each needs the other in order for the process of learning to happen. Instead of authority, punishment and rewards, it can be based on love, nurturance, inspiration, and genuine interest. Instead of measurements and judgments and grades as the goal, this approach offers a deepening of spirit and humanity, liberation and growth on many levels.

There is a kind of intimacy involved in this mode of education which flourishes in solitary study, in smaller groups, as well as in one-on-one exchanges. Because of this it is not always possible to duplicate the process in massive crowds of people. There is a premium on individual expression and personal worth, and each woman is given time to speak, to think, to search and communicate. And yet I wanted to find a way to reach more people, and make these teachings available on a larger scale. Thus the creation of the correspondence course, and now the book, *Ariadne's Thread*.

Around the world we now can find women studying the mysteries that have not been provided in patriarchal institutions. Some women are studying on their own, some with friends, some in circles, and some with teachers. Even in academia there are changes going on, and there is a new openness to alternative styles of education. We are discovering that there are many ways to reclaim what has been lost; the knowledge resides in books as well as teachers, in nature, in folklore, in mythology, in religious studies, in feminist works, in occult and mystical literature . . . but most of all it resides within ourselves.

This is perhaps the most important thing for you to remember when you embark upon the adventure of *Ariadne's Thread*—that you are a woman, and contain within your deep mind and cellular memory a heritage of wisdom. Hopefully, following the Thread through the Cycles will help to affirm the wonderful truth—that you are a miracle.

Whether you are studying this course within an academic structure or independently, it is essential to remember that it is a spiritual study and will have some requirements that differ from those usually associated with standard teachings. While a schedule is recommended, it is a flexible and non-linear one, designed to accommodate your personal pace and rhythms. I advise you to give yourself as much time as you need, and not to pressure yourself about achieving or completing. As the feminists say, it is the process, rather than the goal, that offers fulfillment. True, development and completion are the goals, but too much focus on these can inhibit your creative spirit. This is not a race for excellence and speed—it is a journey of the soul. Not only will it call upon you to think, but also to use your intuition, to examine your feelings and experiences, to open up psychically, to be honest about roles you have played and training you have had in the social system, to meet the challenges of new ideas and new ways of being, and to be flexible and willing to learn in ways you may not have done before.

You may find that some of the exercises are inappropriate, in which case, I hope you will feel free to invent and adapt. These are provided only as a service to those who need and want them, and not meant to be absolute. Many of you may already have altars, for example, in which case the work in Cycle 2, Altars, may need some modification. You could start a new Goddess altar just for the duration of this course, or you might want to cleanse and rededicate your current altar. Another example is in Cycle 4, The Mother Goddess, which suggests a ritual to be done alone, out in the wilderness. Someday I hope we can all have access to the wild land again, for our vision quests and our magic. Obviously, this is not always a safe or feasible undertaking nowadays, and the living room floor can be a reasonable substitute.

You may not always agree with everything I have written in the text. Again, feel free to disagree, adapt, modify to suit yourself. Know that the opinions expressed here are those of one passionate woman, offered in a spirit of sharing and not meant to be dogma. Ultimately, you are your own best teacher. The women's spirituality movement is marvelously individualistic and varied, and there is room for many kinds of ritual, many theologies, many approaches.

Of course there is another side to the coin of so much independence; it requires more from you than other paths that lay everything out for you and tell you how to think. The Goddess is a nurturing Mother and will cradle and coddle you for as long as you need this, but She is also a wise Crone who knows the time must come when you will take wing and find your own way. Witches tend to be very feisty and freedom-loving, and sometimes we have to be strong about meeting challenges on our own. Hopefully, this course will provide the support you need when you require guidelines, and the encouragement you need to develop your own.

Some of you may wish to get together with sisters and study the course together. *Ariadne's Thread* can easily be adapted to group process. Here too, you will need to do some long-term planning, so as to coordinate everyone's time and space. A firm commitment will help to keep the group together and ensure mutual sharing and completion. A group like this works best when kept to a minimum of three or a maximum of seven women who enjoy each other's company.

Again, it's a good idea to make a flexible time-plan. For those of you who have decided to study on your own, see the moon schedule suggested on page 6. For group study, I suggest at least two meetings for each cycle: one for reading aloud and discussing the text, the other for digesting your experiences after completing the exercises, and sharing the notes in your magical journals. Occasionally you can have additional meetings for planning and performing those rituals you would like to do together. In this case, your final meeting in the cycle can include discussion of the latest ritual. Everyone will need sufficient time between meetings to do the solitary work.

MOON-SCHEDULE

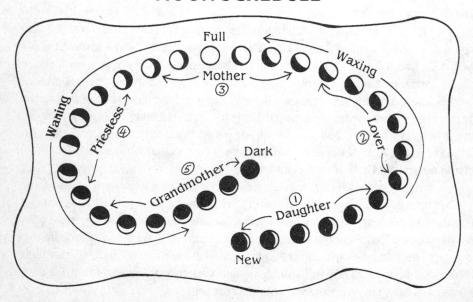

For group scheduling you can divide the lunar cycle up into five segments instead of three. In the place of Maiden, Mother, and Crone, these moontimes can be called Daughter, Lover, Mother, Priestess, and Grandmother. In the Daughter moon you can choose a day for the first meeting of the cycle. In the Lover moon, each member can do her solitary studies. The Mother moon period can be for either solitary or group exercises, depending on what everyone decides. Priestess moontime can be for solitary reflection and writing in your journals, and the fifth or Grandmother moon can be for the final meeting to share and digest the overall cycle's experience.

Please note that by marking off six moon-days per segment, I don't mean to imply that you would spend the entire time on these teachings. I understand that other parts of your life will flow in between the times that you will devote to the Thread. The idea is to offer flexible choices within the frame of a moon. You may find that you are too busy to accomplish everything within one moon cycle. In this case you may want to plan your schedule out over two moons or more. In any case, it's a good idea to do this work when your life is not too filled up with other commitments.

For your regular meetings I suggest three main sections: one for checking in and sharing your lives, one for discussing the material, and one for doing some group meditation or simple ritual. For this you can use the Rainbow Cone Meditation provided on page 29. Three hours is usually a good amount of time for covering everything. Figure about half an hour for check-in, an hour and a half for reading and discussion, and another half hour for meditation. This leaves an extra half hour for any business or planning you may need to do for future meetings and projects, and those little unexpected things that can come up in any group. Consider this arrangement as a general outline too, and be flexible. You may need to take more or less time for life-sharings at one meeting, or the material may demand an extra meeting, or your magic-making at the end could take more time.

I strongly urge you to use the rattle process for facilitation. This consists of passing a magical rattle, talking stick, crystal, or any other suitable object around the circle, so that each woman has some time to speak her heart and mind. She who holds the rattle holds the power, and when everyone takes her turn, a balance of power is achieved. It is also helpful when everyone in the group supports the woman holding the rattle, and gives her their complete and undivided attention. In this way we honor every sister in the circle, and everyone has an equal voice in the proceedings.

You can start each meeting with a brief centering meditation, then pass the rattle for initial check-in and life-sharings. During the second or study-section, have some rattle-passing and some open discussion. This format can provide good focus and communication, as well as some of the ambience needed for lively discussion.

If you do not have a teacher, you may decide that your group needs some leadership or facilitation from one woman to keep things flowing well. Some groups divide up these responsibilities, and women take turns at each meeting. Some groups choose one member to take care of such things as initiating transitions, watching the time, keeping the focus, bringing up topics that need to be discussed, and so on. I have found that the better a small group of women know one another, the less leadership is required, and vice versa. If you decide to choose one woman to be the ongoing facilitator throughout the course, I advise giving her some kind of energy or support in return. This ensures a balance of energy in the group, as well as providing acknowledgment and preventing burn-out for your facilitator. Obviously, group work presents its complications, but has the advantage of providing stimulation and support. Solitary work, on the other hand, can be less demanding, and give a student more time to explore her own journey. The fewer people involved, the less coordination of life-patterns is required.

If you are working alone, you can also have "meetings" with yourself and the Goddess. Set aside some special time when you know you will be undisturbed. Light a candle and some incense at your altar and ask the goddess to come share this time with you. For check-in, you can write down any life experiences, dreams, feelings or impressions you find relevant. Read the Cycle you are working on, write down any more thoughts or notes as they occur to you. At Mother moon, the bulk of your solitary meeting can consist of the ritual or other projects involved. At Crone time you can answer the questions and write down any other queries or conclusions that arise.

Working in tandem with one sister can also be a fine way to go. You could also set up a moon schedule, as described above, or perhaps a more spontaneous arrangement. Whether you work in pairs or in groups, make sure everyone has agreement on the procedure. One-on-one studies can offer the benefits of both group and solitary work, giving support and stimulation as well as more independence and free time for each woman.

Some of you may prefer to find a teacher, in which case scheduling and other arrangements would have to be worked out with her.

You can apply to study with me if you don't mind being on a waiting list for awhile. Also, I can recommend any teacher who has completed this course with me and received the Wise Woman certificate.

For Teachers

Among the legends of womanlore, there is the old Italian story of Aradia, daughter of the Goddess Diana. Aradia was said to have appeared to women during the Burning Times, when knowledge of the Goddess was considered dangerous, made illegal, and very hard to come by. Aradia (whose name is startlingly similar to Ariadne) would teach the women their heritage, show them how to do magic, make ceremony and give honor to the Goddess. Thus she became a symbol of sacred teachings, one of the few female avatars we can find in all the annals of spiritual literature.

Although we no longer live in the Burning Times, and women's knowledge is now becoming more available, there are still many forces of repression, and it can be difficult to find teachers. Therefore, a woman who can teach the mysteries is like Aradia, a gift to us all, and very much needed. It is my hope that those who have completed the study of *Ariadne's Thread* will feel encouraged and competent enough to pass the wisdom on to their sisters. As stated before, I will be happy to give my personal recommendation of those women who have completed with me and wish to become teachers. I also offer an informal correspondence exchange to women who want to teach with my guidance for back-up. You can offer this or an in-person arrangement with your own graduates as well.

Teaching the mysteries may be different from teaching math or science, but it is nevertheless a serious responsibility. Just as it is necessary for students to make firm commitments and plans, so it is for teachers. In fact, a teacher must be triply committed—to her student, to the Goddess, and to herself. While a student may come and go, a teacher must stay put and be willing to provide her services for the duration. While a student is responsible to show up for sessions, a teacher may also have to be the one to provide and arrange the space. While a student's main job is to study and learn, a teacher must be willing to teach as well as learn. While a student opens herself to a teacher's guidance, a teacher must offer information, support, insight, nurturance and understanding. At the same time she needs to have enough humility to allow for students' differing opinions and points of view, and the very real possibility that she does not know the answers to every question.

However weighty are the responsibilities involved, they are far surpassed, I feel, by the rewards. I can freely say after ten years of offering this course that, despite the hassles, it has been a wonderful experience. It is very much like watching the growth and flowering of your own child, to see women awakening to the Goddess without and within, learning magic, coming into their power, becoming a part of the wave for positive change in the world. Some of the women I have worked with have become good friends, and we have remained in contact over the years. Some have gone on to become priestesses and leaders in their own communities. Many have written to tell me how much they appreciate the teachings, and many have blessed me with their love. These are rewards that cannot be measured, but they are very precious.

On a more practical level, the correspondence course has helped to establish me as a priestess and given me some material support so that I could survive in the real world, doing the work I love. By asking for reasonable fees from students, I have been able to earn a portion of my income. This means that there is a strong potential for priestessing to become a viable field of work for women—work that is helpful, interesting, creative, and fulfilling. In a world where most women's jobs are oppressive and boring, such possibilities are important. If you decide to be a teacher of *Ariadne's Thread*, I encourage you to ask for some kind of energy in exchange.

Now I realize that this is a controversial subject, and there are those who feel that payment and spirituality do not mix. It's true that some spiritual teachers have become corrupt, and demanded too much of their students. Others have become teachers for the wrong reasons. A desire to "make money" has motivated them more than love for the work. But we must realize that at one time the holy people of our communities were always supported by those who benefited from their services. The people would bring the proverbial "bowl of rice" to the wise one's cave, vegetables from their gardens, sheep from the flocks. In this way they could give back, show their appreciation, and make it possible for the local shaman/healer to survive and attend to their spiritual needs.

Today it is not always practical to give back in the form of sheep or rice, but the principle remains the same. If women are to have opportunities to contribute in ways that are fulfilling and meaningful, then we who take the benefits must support them. Otherwise, what will sisters have to turn to but the same old stifling system that insists we must do something we hate to survive, preferably something that preserves the status quo, keeps us trapped and powerless, and props up somebody's hierarchy.

On the other hand, if you do ask for fees, there are a few responsibilities to keep in mind. We need to bring back the ethics of the ancient Goddess-centered marketplace, when women worked at the things they loved, all labor was equally valued, and all needs were met. It can happen if we are not greedy, but only ask for what we truly need, and always give of ourselves and our resources generously.

I do think it is possible to arrive at a happy medium when it comes to asking for payment for teachings, especially if we remember that the word "money" is descended from the name of Moneta, Roman Goddess of Abundance. When our symbol of exchange is a Goddess, it imparts a very different meaning to money. Instead of representing status or greed or "the root of all evil," money becomes a symbol of support, honest energy-exchange, and nurturance. Also, we can keep in mind the concept of the pentagram, which represents practicality and material things in some magical systems such as the tarot. The pentagram is made up of five elements: fire, water, spirit, air and earth. Earth is understood as matter or manifestation, and can also pertain to monetary concerns. When we can see this aspect as one-fifth of the whole, rather than being the whole, we can put money in perspective. While we need it for security and well-being, we also need the other four elements for completeness.

This pentagram awareness applies in all aspects of the teaching of *Ariadne's Thread.* The water or emotional element suggests love, compassion, supportiveness—all necessary gifts for students on a spiritual path. The air or mental element indicates thought, the sharing of ideas, help with decisions, answering questions, asking questions, offering advice and suggestions, interpretation of the material at hand, giving information as available, doing research, listening, giving clear and honest communication. The spirit element calls for psychic interaction, giving divinatory insight through tarot or any other medium of your choice, using your intuition, offering spiritual guidance when it is wanted, providing or suggesting rituals, prayers, maintaining a psychic link with your students. The fire element represents the energy you give and the actual hands-on work involved, whether it be typing letters, doing research, making plans, setting up a teaching space or a ceremony. The earth element, in addition to representing support, is also about structure, responsibility, and dependability.

Beyond all this, I think it is essential to give honor to your student. let her know that you value and respect her as an equal, and that you are there to help, not to control her or try to be an authority figure. Encourage her to be her own authority and to find the wisdom within. Invite her to share herself, her experience, her dreams, her hopes and fears and joys. Tell her about yourself, too, if she wants to know; don't be a "distant professional." If she makes mistakes or doesn't meet the schedule now and then, be patient. If she does something well, achieves growth or accomplishments, give her lots of appreciation. I like to give a small gift or some other tangible form of acknowledgment when a student completes a passage or has a birthday or a breakthrough. I sometimes send my students a crystal, charged up with appropriate thought-forms, to help them with a problem, or affirm their good work.

In this kind of study I don't think it's a good idea to give too much criticism, unless it is wanted. I usually tell students that I am not there to judge them or give them grades or tests; that I am there as a sister, to support their process. The Goddess and the course itself will offer tests enough, and I encourage students to be their own judges. I do offer to give an evaluation at the end of the course, if they ask for this, in which case I try to be loving, but honest. On the whole I feel it is up to them to put as much of themselves into the work as they choose, and that they will reap the benefits accordingly. Most students seem to do best if they can go at their own pace without pressure to "perform" or meet harsh deadlines and requirements, and if they are given lots of encouragement along the way.

Of course all of the above is subject to modification and your own preferences and style. With all of this giving and nurturance, it is also important to take care of yourself and honor your own ways. It's okay to be human, to make mistakes, and you don't have to be perfect or know everything. I think it's good to share your ideas and opinions about the material, and to speak freely on the issues you feel passionate about. This can be very beneficial when done in a spirit of free expression rather than authoritarianism.

It helps to set some boundaries right from the start. Let your students know what your own life schedule is like, and what kind of time and energy you can offer. If you are corresponding, you can also work by the moon cycle, as explained earlier. New lessons can go out during Maiden moon, and you can process assignments at the Crone's moon. The rest of the moon cycle can be for living your own life. Keep the work to a reasonable amount that provides what is needed, yet does not consume you. (I usually ask for a legible ten-page maximum from correspondence students.) Give yourself breaks so you have a chance to rest and recharge. Take only as many students as you can comfortably handle at one time. It is better to give quality time to fewer students than to go on overload and find yourself dashing through lessons. If more students want to sign up, you can refer them to other teachers, thus spreading all this good energy around and giving other sisters a chance, too. Or, if this is not an option, you can start a waiting list.

If a student is demanding too much, or reneging on her promises, or going off too far on a tangent, be honest and let her know how you feel about this. You also deserve to be treated with respect and consideration, and it should be mutual.

For all of you who are reading this, who wish to become students or teachers, I ask for the blessings of Aradia and Ariadne. May they shower you with their wisdom and help you to know your own. And may we all join together in the healing of this world by bringing back the lost mysteries of woman. So be it!

First Passage

GATHERING

Dear sisters
As you read these pages
I ask of you to read them well,
And greet all words as special sages
In meaning come with you to dwell . . .

Skim not upon the speedy surface
That slidy surface tales will tell,
But dive, my sisters, down to Her face
For deep within She spins her spell,
Take time to dream, reflect and ponder
Reading twice, or thrice . . . or more,
Meditate, be filled with wonder
Be washed on Her symbolic shore . . .

CYCLE 1

Entry

This book is like a cave in the body of the Goddess, and the turning of each page is like a turning in the passageways you will discover. I invite you to follow the thread of words I have woven here, perhaps to find new understanding, perhaps to rediscover what you already know. May your journey be blessed by the Goddess, and by your own desire to be with Her. May you find joy and healing and peace along the way, as well as insight, expansion, and liberation. If you think you might get lost, keep your hold upon the silver thread; in fact you can tie its end to a branch of this laurel tree, growing at the entrance. Remember, you can always wind it back and re-read what has gone before . . .

With the thread I also give you three laurel leaves to tuck into your pouch or pocket. The first is for Tenacity, that you may keep on 'til you have reached the Center, and then return again. May the Goddess Themis, the Steadfast One, walk beside you. The second leaf is for Remembrance, that you may keep with you all that you have found of use. Mnemosyne, Goddess of Memory, kisses your brow. And the third is for Open-Mindedness, that you may take nourishment from new ideas. I ask the Goddess Idea, she who births new concepts, to come and be with you.

And now, if you are ready my sister, take up the ball of thread and set it to rolling before you into the first passageway. I pray you will go safely and learn well, and have fun too. Welcome to the cave of initiation, the place of Women's Mysteries.

What are the mysteries of woman? In this day of technology and rational thinking such a phrase may sound fanciful, unreal. And yet, humans still persist in mystical and religious practices the world over. Despite the trend to ignore or deny spirituality, many people are accepting it as a basis for living. While some are reverting to familiar traditions, others are seeking alternatives. Witchcraft is such an alternative, now being practiced around the world by thousands of people.

The Craft is not for women exclusively; there are many male witches. However, there are mysteries that pertain specifically to women. It is the purpose of this course to awaken women to our own particular and ancient mystical knowledge.

Religion is a magic or science for dealing with our mysteries. There are many religions now accessible on the earth, but few have sacred traditions for women.

Those that do (such as Sufism and Islam) still promote a social order that keeps women under male authority.

A Women's Mystery system, therefore, is one that has been devised by and for women, that supports and enhances us. It provides female images and woman-identified rituals, symbols and concepts for interpreting and dealing with our special ways of being. We do have a female tradition, and though patriarchal religions have sought to crush it out of existence, there are still traces of it to be re-gathered. I have unearthed them in fairytales and folksongs, in Greek and Roman myth, in music and poetry and theater and dance, in the graphic arts, in my children, in other women, in Eastern spiritual thought, in the pagan roots of Christianity and Judaism, in feminist politics, in the Tarot and astrology, in meditation and visualization, in the New Sciences, in European Witchcraft, in Celtic culture, in Native American ceremony, in the many forms of Nature, in the experience of falling in love, in myself . . .

What, then, are the special ways of women? I have found in seeking to answer this question a bottomless well of possibility. I begin with the most obvious—our births and loves and deaths, our monthly blood-flows, our ability to sustain life through our wombs, hearts and breasts, our passions and sexuality, our mergings and separations, our aging and learning and growing. Then I came upon another layer: our sense of Self or identity, our ability to be inspired, our revelations or spiritual awakenings, our bonds with one another, out-of-body experiences . . . our psychic powers of divination, spell-casting, raising power. Our sense of life source or Goddess, our connections to the Earth, Moon and Stars . . . there are more Women's Mysteries than we can yet name.

Our mysteries are our passages or transformations, and they are the deep parts of our existence. Each of them, no matter how ordinary or extraordinary it may appear, has about it something numinous and sacred. It is the reclaiming and honoring of this sacredness that brings us back in touch with our power and the wonder of being women.

The passages of our lives, loves and deaths are deep and universal things. They are mysterious in that they are not entirely understood. Each time we go through them we learn more about them, and there is always more to be learned. They affect our values, our choices in work and play and relationship, our bodies, our feelings, our thoughts and actions. They can be intense, and sometimes frightening. No matter what our orientation, we all go through them and we all seek ways to cope with them. Some of us go to church, some go to a psychiatrist. Some repress and ignore the process, and some of us look to our sisters or within ourselves to find new and affirming rituals.

Passages are not to be simply understood as biological. They are concerned with the soul's experience, and the many symbolic levels of personal transformation. They usually occur on every level of our beings, including the biological, the psychological, the emotional and the spiritual. It is therefore a great healing to engage in observances of our Mysteries, for it gives us an opportunity to unify and bring together the scattered and severed parts of our Selves.

And where does the magic come in, you might ask. Magic is one of our mysteries; it is the unexplainable way we have of bringing things into being, just as the Goddess brings all of life into being. A Women's Mystery magical system gives us tools to work with that are of ourselves—female, dark, gentle, pulling, softly powerful, enfolding, deeply wise. Magic is invocation and banishing, drawing to us what we need, letting go of that which we do not . . . and when the word "magic" is spoken, the word "witchcraft" easily follows . . .

The word "witchcraft" calls up many images. It contains layers of meaning, the oldest of which imply wisdom, magic, and the ability to shape reality. The word "witch" is derived from the Anglo-Saxon "wic," which means to bend or shape; i.e., shape reality. Since the Burning Times, when witches were horribly persecuted, the word has been twisted into negative meanings. To complicate matters further, some have used the word to define innumerable destructive practices. Witches do not believe in the devil (a Christian god), nor do they seek to harm anyone. On the contrary: Witchcraft is a religion of love for people, nature, and our planet.

There *is* a dark side of the Craft, expressed through spells of banishment and binding, part of the province of the Crone. Some witches, in my opinion, have gone too far with this aspect, performing hexes or revengeful spells that harm and punish. While I agree that self-defense is sometimes necessary, and we must be able to protect ourselves psychically as well as on other planes, I also feel that there is a line between what is necessary and what serves to create more violence or harm than is warranted. Here is where we get into the ethics of the Craft, and we will be discussing this further.

I have chosen to reclaim the ancient word "witch" and to help return it to its former respectable place. Words shape reality according to the meanings we invest in them, and ancient words bring tradition and longevity, thereby lending more substance to the reality they generate. Besides, "witch" is a beautiful and powerful word, full of poetry and female qualities. A good witch, therefore, is one who practices the magic and religion of the ancient goddesses (and in some cases gods) and respects the seen and unseen forces of Nature.

There are other mystery systems offered by society today, but they are all either male-identified or neuter (which generally turns out to be male-oriented too, only more subtly). Patriarchal society is now on the path of self-destruction, precisely because it has repressed and lost the female powers.

We can, however, find a variety of pagan or nature-oriented teachings today. There is a revival happening, a return of practices that have developed out of Native American, East Indian, Celtic, Greek, African and other cultures. My own practices are influenced by some of these, as well as modern magical studies, current womanspirit trends, feminism, and my own intuitive inner sources.

When one studies alternative traditions, one is struck by some startling differences between these and the more publicized faiths. The first and most obvious is the presence of female deities, or at least a respectful acknowledgment of female forces. Practitioners of Islam, Christianity, and Judaism all envision their source as solely male. Buddhism addresses a great male teacher, while Hinduism places its male gods in a primary position. Significantly, the people whose cultures are shaped by these religions place women beneath or behind men in their social structures. While it is true that some women do rise to power in these societies, they are the exception, and often must do so at great cost to themselves.

The same studies which reveal past Goddess-worshipping cultures are also uncovering evidence of peaceful equalitarian societies. Women could own land or goods independently, be political or religious leaders, head their own families, and in general lead lives of choice and freedom. It is clear that the inward concepts of a people have much to do with the outer structures in which they live. Religions are the underpinnings of our world, the building blocks of belief. In developing female-oriented spirituality, we offer a healing that not only affirms woman, but also transforms society as a whole.

Another important difference can be seen in the way "pagans" organize themselves. There are no major leaders or central temples, and there is no one dogma or standardized set of rules. Power is seen as non-linear and cyclical, rather than hierarchical and rigid. People tend to cluster in small circles and develop bonds of trust and concepts of truth independently. This goes along with the idea that there are many goddesses, infinite varieties of form. It is a healthy move away from authoritarian, corporate systems that sap the power of the individual and place a few leaders at the top.

A third difference found in pagan mysticism is its value of pleasure, passion, and sensuality. You will find that the more familiar teachings impose rigid restrictions regarding these, or promote an amoral "anything goes" attitude. The witches support them as sacred and honor them with ritual. Pleasure and passion are understood as powerful life-forces, and expressions of the divine.

"For behold, all acts of love and pleasure
Are my rituals . . ."
    —The Charge of the Goddess

In patriarchy, passion often appears as a compulsive addiction, or a need to dominate or destroy, because it is the explosive reaction to suppression or guilt. In a nature-oriented society it arises as a desire for ecstatic union. Rituals for acknowledging pleasure and passion are part of the fabric of pagan life. Today's trends toward wholistic healing and sexual openness indicate a return cycle of reverence toward the body, the emotions and the self. Instead of the cross of self-negation and suffering, we are discovering the medicine wheel of harmony among all creatures; instead of obeying the command to reject the earth and our bodies as "illusion," we are learning the magic of taking responsibility for them and celebrating them. These are true signs of a renaissance that has at its core an essence which I believe is female.

The essential premise and basis for the teachings offered here is Goddess. Not only "The" Goddess, but Goddess, or goddess. After all, we don't say "The" God . . . we simply say "God." This implies an assumed reality, an Intelligence, or a Presence that we think of as here, with us. It implies a creative force that consciously makes each and every one of us. To transform the name to Goddess suggests femaleness in that Presence. If the life source is female, then we as women partake of Her divinity. When that divinity is named and envisaged only in male terms, where does that leave women? On the outside, looking in. We women need our own expressions of deity, our own female explanations for the way of things.

To invoke a deity is a magical act. It is the calling up of inner forces, shaped by the image they are conceived in and creating an effect or atmosphere. The intensity of devotion or feeling which accompanies such an act adds to its effectiveness. When done in trance states, these invocations set unconscious mental energies moving in desired patterns. Whole social orders and ethical systems grow out of these when many people do them together. After centuries of social conditioning, most people invoke automatically, without questioning, the deity of their culture. (How many times have you heard yourself cry out, "Oh my God!" even when you may profess that you do not believe in any deities . . .?) In a world where male invocation predominates, we can see that two main trends result: believers who maintain a repressive hierarchy of male-over-female, and non-believers who have severed themselves entirely from all spirituality. It is my feeling that female invocation would provide a healing alternative.

This is not an invective against men, nor an attempt to promote hatred of men. Women can share mysteries in common regardless of our orientation toward our brothers. Men belong to the Goddess too, if they only knew! Rather our work here is an expression *for* women.

It is now being discovered that goddesses were invoked in all parts of the world for thousands of years before patriarchy. Though she has been repressed, she has never really left us. Hindus still adore the Divine Kali and Shakti energy. Christians honor the Virgin Mary. Shintos in Japan still worship Amaterasu, Goddess of the Sun. Jews still invoke the Shekhinah at their Sabbaths and other celebrations. Goddess-worship has always been with us, and is now growing by leaps and bounds, in answer to the world's dire need. We are seeing a tremendous uprising, as the Goddess bestirs herself and the women awaken.

To invoke a female deity is to affirm the divinity of the female in ourselves. Practicing our magic is based on this essential invocation. It begins with meditation on the meaning and significance of the Great Goddess in our lives, in the universe, and deep within our selves. The ancients knew that worship was not an act of submission but an act of power. We are all goddesses in that we each have immortal energy, and the ability to manifest or create. Each of us is a little universe, birthing, growing and dying endlessly, containing within us the same elements we see in nature and the world around us.

There are qualities associated with the female and traditionally linked to concepts of the Goddess. These are many: the moon, psychic forces, fantasy, visualization, suction, the tides, menstruation, intuition, magic, weaving, spinning, nature, moistness, darkness of the womb, the tomb, the "other side" or the "underworld," dream states, circles and cycles, passion, softness, connectedness, right-brain functions, nurturance, poetry, art, the Muse, the wildness of untame Nature. Notice what all these qualities have in common—rejection or co-optation by a male-dominated society. Our values have been directed toward maleness: the sun, the intellect, "realism," logic, materialism, aggression, heroic bloodshed, pragmatism, linearity, hierarchy, competition, bright light or the "spiritual light," as opposed to spiritual darkness, hardness, rugged individualism, separateness, and so on . . . We live in a universe that has been arbitrarily halved, and are taught to favor only the "male" half.

How did things get so out of balance? It is as though the male ego feared to lose itself in the great Dark Mother, and so had to repress and control Her. But she is his source and his destiny, and provides necessary sustenance. Without her we become hyper-rational, efficient, sterile, unemotional, and warlike. In losing touch with the feminine nature, many people have lost touch with deep aspects of themselves, and can only make contact through rape or violence. This ranges from the most overt to the most subtle expressions—from nuclear poisoning, to pornography, or tales of bad witches. Many women conditioned to such a society have taken on its trappings also, having learned from role-models of aggression and submission. The time has come for a great healing of ourselves and our planet, which will touch women and men alike, though women are the vanguard of Goddess-awakening.

Now let us look more closely at these divisions we have come to know as "male" and "female." I have listed a number of these above; see if you can think of others in your own experience. As we set them beside one another, it becomes clear that our world has been divided into two sections, one headed "male" and the other "female." We are told that these are opposite "poles" of existence, mutually creating all that is. This model forms the basis for most of our social institutions. Notice that one tends to be placed above the other, to be seen as better, or more worthy of respect. Hence we are caught in the longtime "war between the sexes."

Theories have arisen in recent years under the name of "androgyny." According to these, all people are both male and female and need to affirm both sides in order to be whole and happy. For example, Carl Jung proposed that each woman has a man in her, called the "animus," and each man has a hidden woman called the "anima." These are understood as having behavioral traits such as those listed above. Therapies consist of integrating them into the personality, in order to achieve wholeness or "individuation." This is progress—a step in the right direction—for it begins to integrate the female, and therefore, women. However, I feel that it is still limited by its insistence on gender categories and socialized roles. As long as we create such a polarization, we will have a dualistic world divided against itself.

As a proponent of women's liberation and the practice of our Mysteries, I seek to develop an identity that is whole, yet wholly female. I believe our liberation lies in not having to define ourselves in terms of the male in any way. And yet, we need to integrate all of our qualities—the assertive as well as the receptive, the bright as well as the deep. In my quest to achieve this, I discovered that the five-element system of the Witch's Star or Pentagram can be a useful tool:

If we examine this Pentagram carefully, we can perceive that all the qualities named "male" and "female" can now be rearranged and listed according to the five elements of Air, Fire, Water, Earth, and Spirit. For the most part, "male" qualities can be placed under the headings of Air and Fire; "female" qualities under the headings of Earth, Water, and Spirit. For example, active Fire symbolizes assertiveness, strength, and courage, Air represents intelligence and reason. These qualities are usually assigned only to the male half of society. Watery qualities such as emotion, sensitivity, and vulnerability have most often been relegated to women. Heaven forbid we should cross these lines and allow women to become independent and strong, or allow men to become compassionate, sensitive, or nurturing. The five-element symbol system is a way out of these stereotypes, allowing us to express ourselves freely, according to our true natures, regardless of what gender we may be. Why is this so important? Because we create our reality out of the concepts we accept as true. Everyone, both men and women, has been restricted by gender roles, and the women's movement has much to do with freeing ourselves from these.

One of the ancient meanings of the five-pointed star is our own human form with head and four limbs. We *are* five-pointed stars or mini-universes (or goddesses) each containing within us the Air of our thoughts, the Fire of our actions, the Water of our emotions, the Earth of our bodies, and the Spirit of our psychic abilities and souls. A good exercise consists of taking the star position (either standing or lying down) with arms outstretched to either side, and legs apart. Imagine yourself whole and flowing through all the qualities that each point of the star represents. Thus we can begin to undo the restrictions imposed by socialized gender roles and affirm our potential in all areas.

Because of the greater value given to so-called male qualities, many of the "female" qualities have been demeaned or lost in our culture. It is more acceptable to be tough, competitive and fast-moving than to be gentle, cooperative, and slow. This is why you will notice that I seek to affirm the "female" qualities, often referred to as goddess energies. However, in keeping with our new Pentagram approach, it would be more accurate to call them Watery, Earthy, Psychic, Lunar, Receptive, Dark, and so on, and to consider the Goddess as She who contains all five arms of the Star. We need our darkness, our dreams, our sensitivity, our compassion urgently, for these are some of the lost aspects of ourselves, and of our magic. But we also need to be strong, independent, and free. With the Star it becomes easier to reclaim them all in our own image. In such a universe, both women and men can be free to be whatever they are naturally inclined to be, without guilt or false pride.

Myth-Making

Cultures are always built by the telling of stories. Within them are contained symbols and values that can be passed easily through the generations. Thousands of goddess tales are being unearthed and retold, and many new ones are being created. These tales are like threads with which we can weave our magic. In many stories the goddess is described in three phases—the Maiden, the Mother, and the Crone. This is a wonderful female trinity with infinite correspondences in life and nature. (See the Maiden-Mother-Crone table on the opposite page.) Cycles Three, Four, and Five will deal with each of these goddess-phases in turn.

Some of the old goddess tales were twisted to suit the takeover of male powers, in order to win converts to their new gods. For example, Pandora (All-Gifts) was originally a Great Mother Goddess, whose box (womb, cauldron, cave, cup) was a reservoir of beauty and life-sustaining gifts. Patriarchal myth tells us that Her box contained all manner of destructive demons, which once unleashed upon the world, brought evil and suffering to all. Eve was also a Mother Goddess, whose tree was the Tree of Life. The serpent was her own sensual wisdom, and the apple was her sacred fruit. Athene, whom we are told was born fully grown out of the head of Zeus, dressed in armor and ready for war, was originally the daughter of the matriarchal goddess Metis. (Meter, method, measure, matter, mother . . .) Both mother and daughter were worshipped by the Amazons at Lake Triton, and were born parthenogenetically— without sperm. The examples of mythic misogyny are endless. Medusa is another; the patriarchs would have us believe that one look upon her face would turn the

The Three-fold Goddess—Table of Correspondence

Maiden	Mother	Crone
young girl	mature woman	old woman
new moon	full moon	dark moon
birth	life	death
white magic (poetry)	red magic (healing)	black magic (spells)
beginning	middle	end
menstruation	lactation	menopause
creation	perpetuation	dissolution
play	nurturance	teaching
risk	protection	negotiation
flower	fruit	seed
planting	cultivating	harvest
spring	summer	winter
youth	maturity	old age
me	you	us
subjective	collective	objective
sky	earth	underworld
freedom	commitment	withdrawal
spontaneity	responsibility	reflection
power	love	wisdom
potential	fulfillment	completion
cardinal	fixed	mutable
daughter	mother	grandmother
sister	lover	friend

These are just some of the possible correspondences we can align with the aspects of goddess. Try making up some of your own. Remember, they are not rigid dogma, simply useful, flexible tools.

viewer to stone, because they did not wish us to know her true nature. One source reveals that the Medusae were a tribe of Amazon women; another that their snaky-haired masks were used over temple doorways to protect the Mysteries from irreverent intruders. Whenever we hear about a serpent in myth or fairy-tale, we can usually be sure that it hails back to an ancient Goddess and Her powers. The serpent, before the heyday of Freud and phallic symbols, meant transformation and kundalini energy.

As you can see, the tales we tell have a profound effect on the lives we live. This is just a small sampling of the knowledge to be gained from studying myths and legends. There will be more throughout the lessons, but I encourage you to pursue the topic on your own as well. Myths are seeds for planting in the fertile ground of our psyches. With them we can rewrite the scripts we live, gain deeper understanding of ourselves and one another, and create powerful spells.

Ethics

There are magical systems that do not have a Mystery base or a spiritual base. You may run across an advertisement, for instance, offering a "talisman that gives power to control others" for a generous fee. Or you can buy a series of books full of frightening, creepy stories of evil ghosts and witches. This sort of magic appeals to people who are looking for power or an easy way out of their problems. They are not seeking to understand the spiritual ramifications nor are they concerned with their connection with the universe, people and society. Such magic generally does not work, or if it does, can be dangerous. When we are wielding power it is essential that we have a philosophy, an ethical approach that keeps our motivations positive and helpful.

Knowledge *is* power, but it is also responsibility. The basic rule of magic is "An it harm none, do as thou wilt." (*An* means if in middle English.) This simple phrase contains profound wisdom. It means exactly what it says; do as you wish, but make sure no one is hurt by it. We have all heard tales about people who abuse magic or psychic powers. Some of this is propaganda for maintaining the current system. But some of it is also true. People who abuse any kind of energy will eventually have to face the consequences, whether it be drugs, sex, mental will, electricity, or nuclear energy. Traditionally, the Craft maintains that any energy sent into the universe will return to the sender three-fold. If our motives are life-supporting, our magic will benefit ourselves and others. This doesn't mean we should not protect ourselves, however. There will always be those who succumb to the temptation to use power to hurt or control others. In Cycle 10 you will find some methods of psychic self-protection. In the meantime, start thinking about your own motives and try to develop an ethical position on doing magic. This will be your foundation for safety, and will help to ensure that your experience will be fruitful and happy.

On Casting Circles

Many witches consider it of optimum importance to cast a circle, or, in other words, define a certain sacred space that holds power and protection. There are a number of ways to achieve this, from the most formal to the most spontaneous. Being of the spontaneous school myself, I tend to simply imagine that the circle is there, whenever I begin my ceremonies. When working in groups I always feel that the circle is cast by the simple act of holding hands and visualizing our connection. An ongoing group maintains a psychic circle even when they are not together, I have found. After many years of casting circles, magic-makers can find that they are automatically surrounded by them without even thinking about it.

If you feel a need to cast a more formal circle, however, please be free to honor this in yourself. There are a few methods provided in the Cycles, beginning with the Rainbow Cone Meditation here, which instructs you to simply visualize energy swirling around yourself and forming a cone of rainbow colors. In Cycle 2 there are instructions accompanying the blessing of the altar which you can always use and adapt to a variety of ceremonies. If you wish to invoke the seven directions, there is information provided on this in Cycle 10.

The Rainbow Cone Meditation

7. Violet	Crown
6. Indigo	Third Eye
5. Blue	Throat
4. Green	Heart
3. Yellow	Stomach
2. Orange	Sex
1. Red	Root

Sit comfortably on the floor, legs crossed, spine straight, hands relaxed. Close your eyes and breathe deeply, in and out, in and out. Weave your body in a circular motion, keeping your spine straight. Cleanse your body and your aura with purifying white light. Begin the Maaaa chant with a low note, imagining the color red swirling around and through your first or Root Chakra. Continue on up the scale and the chakras as shown in the illustration, using higher and higher notes as you go. Try to sustain your chanted notes as long as possible without straining. When you reach the violet and the Crown, let the energy come to a peak above your head, so that you are spinning inside a rainbow cone of power. Let the last note die down gradually, then feel the silence and the spin of energy for awhile. When it feels like the right moment, say one of the following invocations, or an invocation of your choice.

> I am one with thee, Goddess, and thou art one with me
> Thy power is my power
> Thy gifts course through me in poetry and beauty
> Thy breath is my breath
> My thoughts are of thee
> My eyes behold thee
> My ears hear thee
> My voice speaks and sings of thee
> My arms reach out to embrace thee
> My hands do thy work
> My heart loves through thee
> My stomach partakes of thee
> My womb and sex reveal thine inmost mystery
> My bowels know thee through death and rebirth
> My legs bend to kneel beside thee
> My feet walk and dance thy path.
>
> Let me be ever filled
> With thy glorious, divine life!

Here is a poetic chant I sometimes use to declare the casting of the circle:

> This is the inner circle
> This is our inner space
> Infinite space
> In which the soul floats free
> This is our circle
> Sacred sphere of energy
> Swirling swirling into orbit
> Turning, pulling, drawing, spinning
> Setting our spirits free
> Free to see
> Free to be
> That which we
> Will to be

So be it
And Blessed Be . . .

Or you can recite the famous Charge of the Goddess as an invocation:

Hear ye the words of the Star Goddess
The dust of whose feet are the hosts of heaven
She whose body encircles the universe:

I am the beauty of the green earth
And the white moon amongst the stars
And the mystery of the waters
And the desire in human hearts

Call unto your soul
Arise and come unto me
For I am the soul of nature
Who gives life to the universe

From me all things proceed
And unto me all things must return

Before my face, beloved of all
Let your divine innermost self be enfolded
In the rapture of the infinite

Let my worship be in the heart that rejoices
For behold, all acts of love and pleasure
Are my rituals

And therefore, let there be beauty
And strength and power
And compassion
Honor and pride
Mirth and reverence
Within you

And you who think to seek for me
Know your seeking and yearning
Shall avail you not, lest you know the mystery—
That if you seek me and find me not within you
You will never find me without

For behold, I have been with you from the beginning
And I am with you endlessly . . .

The charge is a witches' chant credited to Doreen Valiente. I have adapted it here for singing.

After you speak your invocation, send the energy you have raised back down through your body, then into the earth beneath you. This is what witches call grounding, and should always be done at the completion of any ceremony where energy is raised. After this, if you want to spend the time, you can add your own visualizations, spells, prayers, etc. When you feel complete, ground again, and open your eyes.

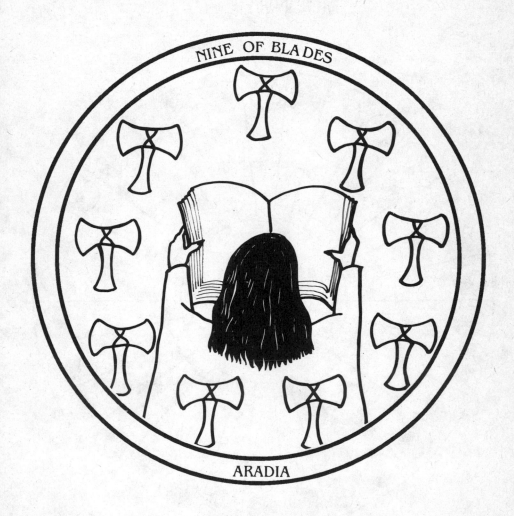

Aradia, Goddess of Sacred Teachings, gives us Study, Herstory, and Goddess Lore. She encourages us in learning the Mysteries, and developing Scholarship, Knowledge and Wisdom.

MOONWHEEL

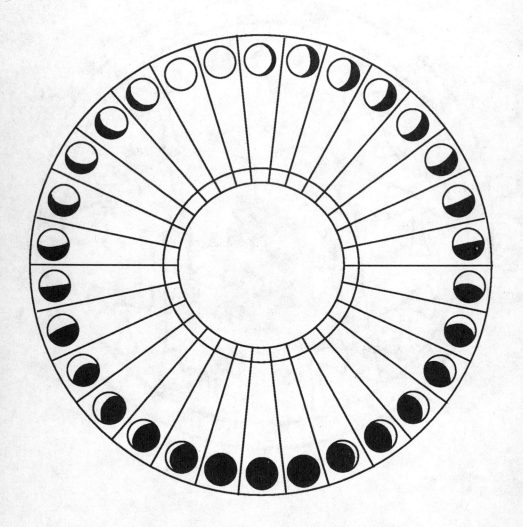

Moonwheel © 1989 Shekhinah Mountainwater

MOONCODE

To help keep track of your cycles, draw these symbols in red in
your moonwheel calendars . . . add your own designs, too!

Dark Moon:
Bleeding

Dark Moon w/Waning Crescent:
Heavy Bleeding

Full Moon:
Ovulating, Fertile

Dark Moon w/Waxing Crescent:
Light Bleeding

Waning Crescent:
Premenstrual

Crossed Moon:
Cramps, Pain

Waxing Crescent:
Post-Menstrual

Moondrop:
Discharge (can be combined)

Waning Quarter:
Early Flow

Flaming Moonboat:
Anger, Irritability

Waxing Quarter:
Late Flow

Morning Sickness

Spotted Moon:
Spotting

Sleeping Moonface:
Strong Dreams

Moonheart:
Passionate, Sexual

Mental Ups:
Intuitive   Intellectual

Baby Kicks:
(Quickening)

Dark Moonboat:
Emotional Ups

Feeling Heavy, Sluggish

Overturned Dark Moonboat:
Emotional Downs

Moonface:
Feeling Psychic

Pregnant

Moonboat:
Energy Ups

Heartmoon:
Lactating

Overturned Moonboat:
Energy Downs

Birthing, Creative

Menopause

Euphoria, Spaced Out

Suggested Projects

1. Make yourself a witch's journal, traditionally known as a *Book of Shadows*. The best book is your own book! Through the ages witches have kept these private pages for recording their spells, rituals, herbal recipes, prayers, and any other relevant magical material. This book will support your journey with *Ariadne's Thread*, providing a place to keep information that you wish to preserve for future use, and serving as a platform for exploring your thoughts and feelings, as well as your magical inventions and inspirations. Make your book special and beautiful, with plenty of lush empty pages that call to be filled. Decorate it with Goddesses, colors, symbols and other images meaningful to you. Cover it with attractive cloth or paper and attach ribbons for tying shut or marking your place. Make a title for the cover and/or first page such as _____'s *Book of Shadows*, or *My Journal of Magical Studies*. If you prefer, you can purchase a ready-made blank book and add your personal touches. There are some lovely ones available nowadays in most book and stationery stores. Some magical craftswomen make handbound journals, also.

2. When your book is ready, perform a ceremony to bless and consecrate it and keep it safe. (You may want to wait until you've completed Cycle 2 and have created your altar.) Make a large pentacle with yarn pinned in place to a cloth or small rug, or draw it on a large sheet of paper or cardboard. (A pentacle is a five-pointed star surrounded by an enclosing circle.) Place your magic book in the center of the star. Arrange appropriate objects at each of the points to represent the five elements. For example: a Goddess for Spirit, a bell for Air, incense for Fire, a crystal for Earth, a shell for Water. Flank the entire layout with two white candles. Light these and ask the Goddesses Ariadne, Mnemosyne, Idea and Themis to bless and protect your *Book of Shadows*. Ask the Muse to inspire your writings and drawings and any other creations, filling your mind with revelations, helping to speed your hand and pen along the pages. Hold the book against you and visualize its pages filled up with works of beauty and magic. Open to the first page and write a dedication to the purpose you wish the book to serve. Light the incense and pass the book through the smoke, chanting appropriate prayers. When you feel complete, replace your book in the center of the star, and leave it there for three days.

3. Witches' ethics are important for ensuring integrity, safety, and success in all magical undertakings. Study the statements on ethics in this Cycle, as well as those of other women you respect and trust. Develop a statement of ethics for yourself and write it up in your *Book of Shadows*. Address such issues as hexing, motivation, free will, banishing, binding, good and evil. Define and discuss at length the phrase "An it harm none, do as thou wilt," examining both its virtues and its limitations. Write

promises to yourself and to the Goddess to use your magic with harm to none and for the benefit of all concerned. Leave some pages blank after this writing, and add further discussion as you learn and grow in your ethical understanding.

4. Acquire or make yourself a magical moon calendar for keeping track of your study schedule, your bleeding cycles, and any other occurrences in your life that you find relevant. There are many ways to make moon calendars. The main thing is to show moontime, which doesn't always coincide exactly with regular, patriarchal dates. If you wish, you can use the Moonwheel provided on page 34 for a model, or as a calendar page for each lunar month. Have it enlarged or reduced, depending on how much information you wish to include. Then make plenty of copies, enough to last at least a year, with extras for future use or spares as needed. Smaller wheels can be mounted, thirteen at a time, on large sheets of cardboard, to make a year of moons. Larger wheels can be bound together in book fashion, like a regular calendar. Use a Witch's Almanac or other moon calendar (see source list on page 41) to find out moondates, moon phases, and where they coincide with patriarchal dates. Use the Moon Code on page 35 to help keep track of your bloods, energy, emotional or mental ups and downs, and any other significant matters. Mark the times when you plan to work with the *Thread*, and any other special times such as holy days, birthdays, rituals, and so on. More to come on moontime, solar time, and women's magical blood powers . . .

5. Make Your Own Rainbow Cone: Take a large piece of white, flexible cardboard and cut out a half-circle as shown. Draw six curving lines to make seven concentric semi-circles. (You can use varying sizes of dinner plates, bowls, and cups to trace your curved lines.) Color each curving stripe a color of the rainbow, as shown. Write in the names and the attributes of each chakra on its corresponding stripe: Red—Root Chakra, Grounding, Stability, Manifestation. Orange—Belly Chakra, Creativity, Fire, Blood, Womb-Powers. Yellow—Stomach Chakra, Influence, Power-from-Within, Survival. Green—Heart Chakra, Love, Compassion, Forgiveness, Emotions. Blue—Throat Chakra, Speech, Communication, Poetry, Truth. Indigo (Royal Blue)—Third Eye, Insight, Telepathy, Psychic Connection. Violet—Crown Chakra, Infinity, The Goddess, Out-of-Body, Union with All.

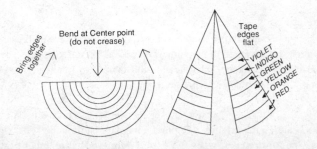

Once all is filled in, carefully bend your half-circle until the two straight edges meet. Overlap them a bit, and tape them firmly, front and back. (Use transparent tape so your colors will show through clearly.) Lo and behold, it's a cone! This cone can be kept nearby when you are doing the Rainbow Cone Meditation. It can help wonderfully to strengthen the ability of your inner eye to see vivid color.

6. Color Tarot Cards and Other Images: You will find a sprinkling of tarot drawings throughout *Ariadne's Thread*, as well as a number of other images. These are provided for the purpose of adding a visual dimension to the study process. You are invited to let your childself out to play in these parts of the book, and color in the images with your favorite pens, paints, pencils, or crayons. Tarot cards especially make excellent coloring meditations. Choose a card that goes with the material it illustrates, to catch a deeper glimpse beneath the message of the text.

Questions to Ponder

You will find sections like this one throughout the Cycles of *Ariadne's Thread*. These questions are designed to get your wheels turning, stimulate discussion, help you to look at issues, examine new ideas, and reflect on old ones. You can write your responses in your *Book of Shadows*, as well as any additional material that you find relevant.

1. Below are a few sample definitions of the word Witch. What does this word mean to you? Do you feel it has positive or negative associations? Discuss these at length.

From former students of this course:

"A witch is a woman who has won clear of the 'mind-bindings' of patriarchal culture, sometimes against tremendous odds. She senses the constant flow of energy moving through the universe, knows herself to be part of it, and seeks to shape it in life-affirming ways . . . A witch sees this universal energy as 'goddess'. . . She may belong to a particular tradition of the Craft or seek to find her own way, alone. She knows through experience that spiritual practices that the patriarchy labels 'super-stition' are actually techniques which connect one with the deep mind or right hemisphere of the brain and that these practices are valid—they WORK! A witch may not 'man' barricades, but she is, in the deepest sense, a spiritual and culture rebel."

"A 'witch' is a person who is at ease with nature and herself. She has an inborn strength which she draws on to help others as well as herself. She is at peace with those around her, seeking to reach others . . . She is ruled by her heart. I am a witch. This class is a formalization of what I already am."

"A witch is Me! A Witch is wise and uses her wisdom to help others. She is an herbalist, a healer, a myth teller, a diviner, a woman whole in herself, who is not afraid to say no, or even yes, when the time is right. She has an inner beauty, and love enough to spill over onto others. She is a caretaker for Mother Earth and the Universe. She is thoughtful about what she does and says, and is careful to harm none in her work. She is Goddess, Maiden, Mother, Crone, a whole woman."

"Witch is a woman who claims the mystical powers of the goddess as found within herself. She uses these powers to create life enhancing and ever deepening experiences for herself and her sisters. She understands the interrelatedness of elements in the universe and uses that understanding to make things right, i.e., harmonious, aligned, and able to express their intrinsic goodness."

And, the classic definition from W.I.T.C.H.:
". . . Witches have always been women who dared to be: groovy, courageous, aggressive, intelligent, nonconformist, explorative, curious, independent, sexually liberated, revolutionary. (This possibly explains why nine million of them have been burned.) Witches were the first Friendly Heads and Dealers, the first birth-control practitioners and abortionists, the first alchemists . . . They bowed to no man, being the living remnants of the oldest culture of all—one in which men and women were equal sharers in a truly cooperative society, before the death-dealing sexual, economic and spiritual repression of the imperialistic Phallic Society took over and began to destroy nature and human society.

W.I.T.C.H. lives and laughs in every woman. She is the free part of each of us, beneath the shy smiles, the acquiescence to absurd male domination, the make-up or flesh-suffocating clothing . . . There is no joining W.I.T.C.H. If you are a woman and dare to look within yourself, you are a Witch. You make your own rules. You are free and beautiful . . . your power comes from your own self as a woman, and it is activated by working in concert with your sisters . . . You are a Witch by saying aloud "I am a Witch" three times, and *thinking about that*. You are a Witch by being female, untamed, angry, joyous, and immortal.

And from Shekhinah:
A Witch is One who is in love with Goddess . . .

2. Do you identify with the word Witch? Do you see yourself as a witch? If so, why? If not, why not?

3. What makes a woman a witch? Does she claim the title after achieving certain levels of development? Through acceptance in a coven or other organization? Or can she simply say "I am a witch" three times, as proclaimed by the early '60s organization W.I.T.C.H.? Or is it something innate within, such as psychic sensitivity, a love for the Goddess or nature, creative or magical abilities, past-life experience?

4. What do you know of the negative associations with the word Witch? How do you feel about the fact that so many witches were persecuted and burned in medieval times? Would you like to see witches and Goddess-religion made acceptable in today's society?

5. Do you have a religious background? If so, what is it? If not, what impressions did you have of spiritual matters while growing up?

6. How does your spiritual background compare with what you know of Goddess religion?

7. Do you believe there is a conscious Being or aware Entity that creates life and the universe? One or many? Female or male? Both or neuter?

8. How does the concept of "goddess" affect you? Do you feel attracted, repelled, indifferent?

9. Who or what is the Goddess? Is She an archetype or psychological symbol? A force of nature? A force of society or human nature? A mythic symbol of existence? An actual Entity?

Reading and Other Resources

The book listings in the lessons are provided for your expansion and pleasure. Many wonderful Goddess books are being written today, and some of them are fabulous friends as well as supports for learning the Mysteries. I recommend them warmly (though I may not always agree with everything they say).

Z. Budapest, *The Holy Book of Women's Mysteries*, Vols. 1 and 2.
Christine Downing, *The Goddess.*
Robert Graves, *King Jesus, The White Goddess.*
Ken Keyes, Jr., *The Hundredth Monkey.*
Patricia Monaghan, *The Book of Goddesses and Heroines.*
Barbara Mor and Monica Sjöö, *The Great Cosmic Mother.*
Ann Wilson Schaef, *Women's Reality.*
Starhawk, *Dreaming the Dark, The Spiral Dance.*
Diane Stein, *The Kwan Yin Book of Changes, The Women's Spirituality Book.*
Merlin Stone, *Ancient Mirrors of Womanhood, When God Was A Woman.*
Barbara G. Walker, *The Women's Encyclopedia of Myths and Secrets.*

Womanspirit publication. If your local bookstores don't carry this, you can send to Womanspirit, USPS 358-450, Wolf Creek, Oregon 97497-9799. *Womanspirit* is no longer being published, but the timeless back issues are still available.
Lunar Appointment Calendar designed by Shekhinah Mountainwater. A blank moon calendar, made to be filled out yourself, which uses the Moonwheels discussed and included here. Includes instructions, articles, background information, moondates, tree moons, and other lore. Send $13 plus $2 for shipping costs to

Shekhinah Mountainwater, P.O. Box 2991, Santa Cruz, California 95063.

The Lunar Calendar, Dedicated to the Goddess in Her Many Guises, edited by Nancy Passmore. This venerable moon calendar was the first to be released at the beginning of the current Goddess movement. It is based on the Celtic tree-moons as described in *The White Goddess*, by Robert Graves. Each page shows a spiralling lunar month, which gives moon phases and patriarchal dates as well as tree lore, poetry, articles and more. Lacks room for day-to-day additions, but is excellent for reference in creating your own calendar. $15 to LUNA Press, Box 511, Kenmore Station, Boston, MA 02215.

We' Moon, an astrological moon calendar and appointment book for women. Excellent day-to-day coverage of moon phases, astrology signs, and seasonal lore in a Goddess vein. Set up like a regular engagement calendar, with spaces for each day. Uses the patriarchal months only, and does not have a circular layout. Beautiful art and articles on women's spirituality. Send $10 plus postage to Mother Tongue Ink, 37010 S.E. Snuffin Road, Estacada, Oregon 97023 (telephone: 503-630-7849).

Witch's Almanac, a venerable compilation of dates, astrology, planting lore, etc. was out of circulation for a while but is now available again. Send $4.95 plus $1 postage and handling to Pentacle Press, P.O. Box 348, Cambridge, MA 02238.

The Goddess Remembered, A Spiritual Journal, The Crossing Press, Freedom, California, 1990. This is a beautiful blank book with art and poetic quotes, suitable for use as your *Book of Shadows*.

Acknowledgments: Affectionate thanks to Jeannine Parvati for inspiring opening poem for Cycle 1. Thanks to Debra Kaufman for first alerting me to the five-element system as an alternative to gender-based descriptions of our qualities. *Shekhinah's Tarot* is sister deck to the *Book of Aradia* tarot by Jean Van Slyke and the *Daughters of the Moon* tarot by Ffiona Morgan and the D.O.M. collective. All three decks came out of their original collective project, then called the *Matriarchal Tarot*.

Note: All images in this book (except for the Hecate Wheel, p.239) were originally conceived, designed and drawn by Shekhinah. They have been redrawn for *Ariadne's Thread* by Anne Marie Arnold. The Hecate Wheel is a traditional Greek/Celtic mandala, redrawn by Shekhinah.

Mnemosyne is pronounced "nem-ah-sin-ee."

CYCLE 2
Altars

I come to the altar,
Where burns the fire divine,
And there stands my goddess,
With arms outstretched to mine,
"O come to me my dear one,
And we'll together shine,
For you are mine forever,
And I'm forever thine."

Now that you have met the Goddess, begun your magical journal, and formed an ethical approach to the Craft, you are ready to set up your altar. Altars are widely used by people of many faiths. Their primary purpose is to give honor and reverence to the Goddess, and to that which we feel is sacred—the mystery and wonder of creation, the miracle of being, the source and destiny of all things, the magic that dwells within us and within the universe.

Altars are a wonderful way to create sacred space, a special environment where we can let our minds relax and focus on the deeper and larger aspects of existence. They help us to create our own reality by imprinting the subconscious mind with the meanings of those symbolic objects we place thereon. Your altar is a place for you to be with yourself and the Goddess undisturbed, where you can meditate on your joys or sorrows and find release or affirmation from within. It is also a power spot, a place to tap into the deep self, develop your psychic abilities, perform rituals, cast spells, and strengthen your magical will. It is a place of healing, where visualizations and realizations can help you to dissolve old wounds, and it is a place of inspiration where the Muse-Goddess can enter and awaken your creativity, refresh and renew your spirit. It is a place to "charge up" your special sacred objects and tools of magic.

There are many opinions as to what is the "proper" way to arrange an altar. Each religious group usually has its own traditions and special set-ups that reflect their particular belief systems and styles. As a Goddess woman I prefer to have altars that express my love for the Goddess and woman. I also like them to be centrally focused and evocative of circular energy. There are many ways to build a circular, Goddess-centered altar. In this Cycle I will share with you some of my own approaches, but

I encourage you to be creative and discover your ideas as well.

Primitive altars were actually synonymous with the hearth. In homes dug into the earth, or built of elephant bones and hides, or grasses and tree branches, the place of fire was often at the center of the structure, with an opening above to let out the smoke. Where people gathered, where food was prepared, where light and warmth was to be found was a place understood as precious and sacred. Magic was not separated from nourishment and survival and ancient tribal people honored the connections. To them the hearth was the Mother Herself, one of the oldest sources of veneration, her life-giving fires emanating from Her life-giving belly, her sparkling waters from Her breasts and womb, Her foods from Her magnificent flesh. Thus any implements used at the hearth, like pots, vessels, utensils, were also sacred. These were the first magical tools. The Hearth/Altar Goddess has many names in many cultures: Heartha, Vesta, Demeter, Chantico, Kikimora, Poza-Mama, Uks-Akka are a few.

Later, altars were made to be representative of the Goddess, and formed in the shape of a woman. Just as we "dress up" the Solstice tree at Midwinter to express our celebratory feelings, so do we dress our magical altar goddess, perhaps adorning her with lovely draperies, flowers and leaves, or the many symbols of her gifts and powers. A cup of the priestess' menstrual blood was the first chalice, filled with the sacred liquid of life. Eventually the liquid became wine or water, but the essential meanings remain the same. Bread made from the sacred grain of the Goddess' earthen body was usually placed as an offering in honor of nature's abundance and nourishment. Sometimes this bread was braided in three strands, representing the Maiden, the Mother and the Crone. (Jewish people still use the holy braided bread, called *challah*.) The familiar wafer of Catholic and Christian ceremony—the "Body of Christ"—descends from the earlier "flesh of our Mother," as the sacramental wine descends from Her original Blood of Life.

Other objects representing the body of the Goddess are crystals, stones, potted plants, bones, shells, seeds, and so on. We can understand altar arrangements in terms of the five elements of the Witch's Star: the fire, the air, the earth, the water, and the spirit. These correspond to the Goddess as energy, electricity, volcanic flame (fire), breath, thought, speech, wind (air), river, ocean, lake, stream, spring, blood (water), flesh, soil, plant, stone (earth), psyche, soul, consciousness, design, space (spirit).

Occasionally our altars become too demanding and complicated. We find ourselves distracted by all the paraphernalia, all the "shoulds" and "shouldn'ts" of the various traditions we've explored. In these moments it is helpful to remember that a woman can be her own altar. Each of us has within us the fires of our energies, the spirit of our psychic abilities, the air of our thought and breath and the water of our emotions. If we were alone on a barren island or cast into a prison cell, we still could do magic with the sacred elements we all possess. The earth, too, makes a natural altar. With nothing more than a patch of ground to sit on, the sky above, a tree to admire, we can cast many a powerful spell. Our use of altars, artifacts and magical tools is like the part of the space ship that falls away, once the passenger section has been launched. Inspiring as they are, it's important to realize that their value is primarily symbolic.

Nevertheless, altars are fun to create and use, and they can provide many wondrous things. Nothing is quite so special as walking into a ritual space where a beautiful altar has been prepared with love and care. And in an age when our creative imaginations may have been weakened, our ability to focus undeveloped, our minds easily distracted by the many pressures of daily demands, altars can be of enormous help in honing our magical skills.

Altar Politics

In times when our religion was being attacked and overthrown, often it was our altars that were the first target for destruction. In the ancient Goddess temples, and later in the sacred groves or witches' hearths, altars were the gathering places where people came to give reverence to the Goddess and take strength for the struggles of their lives. When oppressors smashed a holy place, they were symbolically dismantling an entire reality/belief system with one violent blow. In the Burning Times all Goddess-related artifacts, sacred places, statues and altars were outlawed.

The farther we have grown from the Goddess, the more separate sacredness and magic have grown from the simple actions of living. The more male the deity, the farther away temples and altars have grown from the hearth and those things usually done by women. Nowadays our hearth is likely to be an electric stove with no sacredness attached to it, and if we attend any holy places, they are likely to be down the street or across town in a church or meeting hall. In the mainstream churches or temples, altars are often barricaded, and only certain elite attendants are permitted to go near or touch them. Altars, once places of personal power and healing, have become tools of oppression, used to hypnotize people into submission, to surrender their power to some distant deity who is too busy and "important" to concern himself with "common folk" or common things.

Sacredness, once understood as that which we cherish and hold close, has come to mean something untouchable. Sex must therefore be "dirty," the artist must be "weird" or corrupt, the earth must be raped and exploited, women the least valued members of the community, and the mundane activities of life devoid of meaning.

It is therefore not only a magical act to build once again our Goddess-centered altars, but a political act as well. In doing so we are saying that we are taking back those powers and realities that we once lost to the patriarchy. We are not "bowing down" to their gods, but worshipping (giving worth-ship) to that which is divine within us as women, and in the earth and the universe as well. In this reclaiming we are performing an act of healing, as we make physical representation of those things we hold sacred, giving a new message to the deep self that says, "She has returned, woman is worthy, and all will be well . . ."

Altars really are magical too, I have found to my delight. Objects and decorations that we place and cherish begin to absorb the energy of our thoughts and feelings. I have seen a statue come to life when the candles were lit around her, and felt that she was really looking at me, perhaps sending messages. Stones that sit at length upon the altar add greatly to the intensity of vision when pressed to the heart or held in the hand. Written spells, prayers or vows tucked beneath candles or other related objects can be wonderfully enhanced. Skeptics and cynics reading this may say "pooh" and insist that it's all in my lively imagination. Perhaps so, but what does it matter, if the magic works? Magic is after all, founded upon imagination! In fact, the two words are really the same.

At the same time I don't wish to imply that we must allow ourselves to be enslaved or controlled by magical objects. One hears tales, for example, of a ring of protection which, when lost by the wearer, made her prey to terrible dangers. We don't want to get so hooked into our symbols that we forget or lose the powers within us. As in so many things, there is a balance point, where altars can support and help us, yet leave us free as well.

Raising Power

When witches use the word power, we are not talking about power over anyone, but, as Starhawk so beautifully puts it, power from within. To be a witch is to be a woman of power, or one who uses her psychic abilities at will. Everyone possesses the potential for this, but in our society only a few have developed it. In tribal, nature-oriented societies people have always operated together psychically. Their shamans or priestesses or medicine women may be especially talented in this area, but all members of such tribes are familiar with psychic or altered states.

As our techno-industrial culture has advanced, more value has been placed on the rational conscious mind, and the powers of the deep mind have been sorely neglected. In these times of opening, some of us are re-learning the old wisdom, and all aspects of the mind are becoming available again. Psychic liberation is the ultimate revolution, for people free in their souls cannot easily be controlled. That is why the followers of the Old Religion were so systematically wiped out. They were a threat to the new patriarchal power-structure that has demanded conformity to male gods and to rationalism.

Raising power is done with breath, visualization, relaxation, desire, sound or hypnotic mantra, movement and trance. These "techniques of the sacred" can also be aligned with the five-pointed witch's star. (More to come on these in Cycle 10.) The rational mind is suspended for a time, as we enter the "other side" or alpha mind. In this state we can program our unconscious mind to produce automatic behavioral responses of our choosing. Old conditioning and disturbances can be cleared away, and new suggestions introduced. A profound communion with the forces of the universe can result, which gives healing and rejuvenation.

In traditional witchcraft this trance is used to "raise the cone of power." The cone is a funnel-shaped vortex of psychic energy. It swirls round and round the group or individual, with its base on the earth and its peak overhead. Out of this funnel we can project the energy and images we wish to send into the universe. If all goes well, they will return to us as experience or manifestation—the fruits of our spells. The cone is created simply by imagining it and wanting it to be there. (See The Rainbow Cone Meditation, page 29.)

To raise power it is necessary to surrender and let go of ordinary everyday reality. This takes trust, a safe space, and practice. You may not have a powerful experience the first time you try . . . realize that like any skill, psychic ability must be developed. In setting up and consecrating your altar, you will have an opportunity to begin. Journeying through this course will help you to gently and safely open to the concepts and images that support psychic growth. If at any time during your rituals you find yourself becoming afraid or threatened, know that you can always stop and come back. Simply tell whatever energy or entity that looms to go away, tell yourself "I am perfectly safe," ground and center yourself and open your eyes. Affirm that you are here, that all is well, that the Goddess loves you.

Altars are especially helpful in the work of raising power. A good altar can open us up almost automatically upon first viewing. The act of candle-lighting can give us a rush of inspiration. Ringing the altar bell or striking the drum can clear our minds for the work to come. Sitting and gazing quietly can fill us with peace. Looking upon the images of the Goddess, handling appropriate stones, burning incense—all these things help to put us into the desired frame of mind and mood.

Arranging Your Altar

. . . The Hallowe'en altar is darkly draped. An East Indian tapestry of the Goddess Kali in Her death aspect dances upon the wall above. From the large table, folds of blue and grey and black fall richly to the floor. One can make out winding shapes within the curves of cloth and an image of the eternal Tree of Life.

Two large orange candles glow warmly at each end of the altar's generous lap. Behind them are vases filled with brightly-colored straw flowers, dry and crisp. Dried eucalyptus branches curve gracefully, emitting their pungent, purifying scent.

Two silver chalices are placed down front, filled with sweet-smelling colored powders. Purple for power, black for banishment, red for love and pleasure, green for healing, brown for protection and grounding. A priestess lights them early, to smudge and bless the room during preparation time. Thick streams of smoke arise, sparkles and hisses dance in the shiny silver cups. The candle-lit room fills with a magical mist . . .

. . . In the summer of '90 my students and I planned a special Lammas (Habondia) ritual for the women in our community. As part of the ceremony we wanted to bring each woman up onto the altar itself for a few moments, and honor her as the Goddess. I made the platform very low and sturdy, so that women could easily step up and feel firmly supported. For this I used an old wooden and metal pallet I happened to have around. It was battered and not particularly beautiful, but wonderfully sturdy. To conceal its roughness I used a thick rainbow-striped blanket a friend once gave me years ago. It was perfect, carpeting the pallet completely, and giving the women a rainbow to stand upon!

On the back wall I hung my Indian bedspread with the Tree of Life motif. This is a large piece and so would be the first thing to catch the eye upon entering the room. Around the top and sides I hung green boughs of the local flora, including some branches of rosemary for their powers of protection and association with the Mother Goddess.

We couldn't use candles for this altar, as it would have been dangerous with women dancing about them with swirling skirts. Since the pallet was quite small, we had to keep it mostly bare. But on the floor at either side we placed large baskets of gorgeous Goddess-shaped breads that women had baked for the occasion. These were passed around the circle during the ceremony, so that everyone could celebrate the earth's gifts and partake. People also brought vases of flowers, and these I arranged behind the breads. The overall effect was quite wonder-full . . .

. . . The first time my lover and I got together, I made a special Aphrodite altar. I draped the table with an old red velvety bedspread I found, and on the back wall I hung a flower printed cloth—white with many roses. The centerpiece was my statue of Aphrodite, about two feet tall. I set her even higher by standing her on a pretty box, so one could feel her presence overlooking everything. My garden was burgeoning with roses of all colors that year, so I could be lavish. Two large vases flanked Aphrodite on either side, and smaller bouquets were set here and there. More roses were placed at the altar's base. I used large red votive candles, as well as two smaller ones. The smaller ones I blessed with love oil, but did not light until my lover was there. These we lit together and placed side by side in the center, to represent ourselves and the flame of our love. I had written my vows on some parchment and this too was handily placed in front for ceremonious reading . . .

From years of experience with set-up I have learned that an altar is really not separate from the space it is in, though we may give it a special "set-apart" significance. When I first began creating altars I usually tried to find a handy spot that wouldn't interfere with already existing arrangements in my room. My altars were adapted to the needs of the space, rather than the other way around. Later, when my priorities had shifted and I had moved a few times to new spaces, I would decide first upon the placement of the altar, then decide where everything else would go. Now I dream of designing a building with the altar setting as my starting point.

Obviously, we don't always have so much choice, and even an empty room will present some limitations as well as options. A wall with built-in cupboards, windows and doors may not be the best place to put an altar. A section of the room where there will necessarily be a lot of traffic may not work either. Altars need to be protected, as they usually have delicate things upon them, and candle flames must be reckoned with.

Often the corner of a room will prove to be the best place for an altar. Corners can provide protection, as we are less likely to move around in them; yet they are visible and can command the space impressively. I especially like corners because they have a way of focusing the energy in the same way as a pointed crystal or pyramid, sending it back out into the entire room.

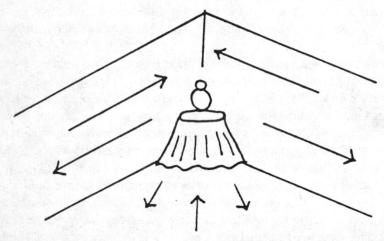

Sometimes altars work beautifully in front of a window, or beneath, provided the view outside is conducive. One student/friend of mine has a house in the mountains with a big picture window in the living room looking out on the glories of nature. She set her altar table low in front of this window, with a very grand effect. One must be careful, however, if it is a window that is frequently opened.

Some walls with built-ins work very well too. If there is room for a table, the surrounding shelves can be incorporated into the setting and used for altar storage.

Central altars are a powerful ancient tradition. A low, round table in the middle of a ritual circle gives everyone a clear view, and is particularly good for group work. A room used mainly for ritual may benefit from having an altar in the center, where participants can stand or sit facing any direction. Central altars present some problems however. They can inhibit free movement in the ritual space, especially if a priestess needs to cross and re-cross the circle during ceremony. Set-ups tend to require objects that can emanate and be seen from all sides. (A statue with a front and a back will have its back turned to half the participants.) Candles or anything with a degree of height may block eye-contact or other views of one another, which could cause some obstruction in the circle energy.

Still, for simple sit-down circles a low or even flat altar can be a fine addition. These are especially nice for small intimate circles where everyone can reach them easily and participate in their use.

Nowadays when I am about to set up an altar, I first choose its location. If I am planning to set up in a corner, I check to see what lies above, below, to either side, and at eye level. Clear and empty corners are wonderful, as they give space for draperies, hangings, tall statues, as well as underneath space for storage and secret spells. I sometimes think of the altar as a mini-universe, with the flat table surface representing the earth, the upper dimensions as the sky, and the hidden recesses beneath as the underworld. I try to leave a little clear space to either side of the altar, so that other objects and room activities won't crowd or distract.

Next, I choose the furniture. I like to use a sturdy round table with enough surface to play with, and of a height that is comfortable for both sitting and standing. I have noticed that if I can only stand at an altar I feel as though I'm doing my rituals "in passing." Sitting down implies that I am here to stay for a while, ready to really get involved. However, standing or passing the altar is wonderful for those in-between times when I'm busy with other activities, or when I wish to dance or perform a stand-up ceremony.

Round tables are not always easily come by. Sometimes I've added a flat round piece to a square table or chest. Once I have my base, I am ready to consider the draperies. If I plan to drape the back wall, I will need to do this before moving the table into place. I may also want to hang a tapestry, painting, or other image high up on the wall, so that it will overlook the altar as well as the room. Hanging plants are also an option; lighting is another factor to consider. A couple of wall-lamps might be needed and extension cords can be strung.

Next I usually drape the table itself. I select fabrics in keeping with the theme or season I wish to emphasize, for example: green for spring or summer, black for winter, red for Aphrodite or Beltane. I might pick a floral pattern for spring, or solid golds for summer. Essentially, the three traditional colors of the Goddess are Red for the Mother (Summer), White for the Maiden (Spring), and Black for the Crone (Winter). But of course such broad themes are open to much variation. I love blue and often drape my altars in this color for Fall, or to evoke a particularly mystical and watery feeling. Sometimes I will use a number of cloths, placing them here or there for accentuation.

If you have a beautiful table, you may wish to leave the legs bare by keeping draperies short or confined only to the surface. Most of the time I prefer long drapes that sweep to the floor abundantly. This has several advantages; for one thing it provides a secret and private space beneath that can have many uses. When standing back from such an altar, the effect is continuous from top to bottom. It draws people in, and gives a feeling of completeness. It looks like the altar is a Goddess, adorned and dressed. The hem of Her skirts can be a fine place to put magical objects, arranged as offerings "at Her feet."

There are many kinds of altar set-ups, but I find they tend to fall in or between two general categories: those made to be permanent or ongoing, and those set up for special occasions. In my temple at home I have a large altar that is essentially permanent, though I do occasionally clear and rearrange her, wash or shake out her coverings, and move a statue or two. On her large lap I may make more frequent changes, adding special candles for a new group of students, or placing some particular stones or flowers. I usually have my large statue of Aphrodite at the back, raised up to give Her more visibility, as well as creating more surface area and adding to the dimensions of the space. Sometimes I have a large statue of the Three Graces to one side of Aphrodite, with a plaque of the Muses on the other side for symmetry. These group pieces have many meanings to me, though the main message they convey is about women and sisters in harmony. All of these pieces are powerful and tend to dominate the altar energy and give an ongoing presence to all meetings and rituals. Sometimes I move two and just keep one out for a while. I also have a small head of a Crone that I like to put out during the darker months.

I always try to set up my altar surface so that the eye is led to a central location, and then moves naturally from this focal point. I know that many witches prefer to arrange their altars according to four directions, but I find that this can scatter the energy. Focus is essential for successful magic, and a focused altar can provide great support for this. All through this course you will hear me saying that I feel more power and magic in circles than in squares. Yet squares can work well within a larger circle frame.

In deciding what objects to place upon an altar, much depends upon the desired effect or theme. You may wish to give honor to a particular Goddess, cast a certain kind of spell, observe a seasonal rite, acknowledge a life passage: a new love, the birth of a child, and so on.

Most of my altars incorporate the five elements in some form. There are probably an infinite number of ways to represent these, and I'm sure you will learn and invent many as you go along. You will find a few examples and suggestions on page 52.

As you can see, categories tend to overlap, and some objects can evoke more than one of the five elements. While some practitioners may have more set traditions in these matters, I tend to be flexible. In general, magical symbolism depends more on personal feelings than external regulations. If an object is particularly evocative to you, it will probably make a fine altar piece.

Element	Meaning	Objects, Beings
AIR	Breath, wind, sound, speech, communication, thought, image, meaning, concept	Athame (witch's knife), bells, incense smoke, feathers, music and instruments, poetry, songs, bird images, butterflies, Fairies, Cloud and Wind Goddesses: North Wind, Iris. Stones: clear quartz, snow quartz, blue lace agate, turquoise, chrysocolla
EARTH	Body, flesh, bone, endurance, planet, substance, manifestation, results, matter, practicalities, Mother, life source	Soil, plants, coins, money, jewels, pentacle, stones, crystals, bones, food and pine cones. Earth Beings: wood nymphs, dryads, trolls, elves, trees, pine cones. Stones: smoky quartz, obsidian, onyx, moss agate, jade, green aventurine, chrysoprase. Earth Goddesses: Gaia, Demeter
FIRE	Energy, movement, will, power, passion, electricity, action, interaction, growth	Candles, incense, censers, cauldrons. Lamps and other lights, volcanic rock. Fire Beings: salamanders, fire fairies. Fire Goddesses: Lucina, Amaterasu, Chantico, Pele. Stones: carnelian, tiger eye, ruby, garnet
WATER	Emotion, passion, compassion, life-source, connection, agreement, communication, friendship, love, caring, forgiveness, flow	Chalices, cups, sea water, well water, purified or blessed water, blood or wine, flowers in water, shells, coral, seaweed, river rocks, ocean stones. Water Beings: mermaids, ondines, sea nymphs. Water Goddesses: Yemaya, Tethys, Ondine, Aphrodite, Sarasvati. Stones: opal, blue quartz, pearls
SPIRIT	Source, psyche, soul, outer space, inner space, infinity, cosmic intelligence, Deity, consciousness, psychic energy, Beingness, intention, design	Goddess images, statues, paintings, etc. Crystals and gems, smoke, prayers, chants, mantras, mandalas, feathers, music. Divination tools: tarot images, mirror, crystal ball, scrying bowl, runes, etc. Lights and crystals, sparkles. All Goddesses... Stones: clear quartz, amethyst, sodalite, luvulite (sugalite). Devas, fairies, ghosts and spirits

More About The Elements

You may have heard of the five steps or keys to magic: See, Know, Will, Dare, and Keep Silent. These correspond to the five elements of the witch's star, as spirit, mind, action, emotion, and body. *Seeing* is psychic seeing or inspired vision: telepathy, clairvoyance, clairaudience and all the varied ways we can perceive in spirit. *Knowing* is mental conceptualization, or the meaning and information we invest in our rituals and spells. To *Will* is to make things happen, and to act accordingly. *Daring* is the warrior who quells our doubts and fears and forges ahead despite the risks and opposition. *Keeping silent* protects and conserves the energy of our magic. Many spells have failed because careless magicians forgot to maintain silence. Just as a tiny seed begins its life in darkness beneath the earth's surface, or the embryo grows within the womb's protection, so does magic need its period of gestation and concealment.

All of these keys have their political side too. When our witch's eye has been opened, we *see* the truth—that magic is real, that much of the world's trouble begins with rejection of the Goddess and women, that healing and harmony will come when we learn to love and claim them again, and that once we accomplish this our future horizons will become limitless. When we *see* all of this, we *know* what is right and how to proceed, we know the Goddess, we know that we are the Goddess, we know that we are magical and beautiful and powerful, and that nothing can ever take this knowledge away. Seeing and knowing give us the *will* to do magic, to act in concert with our sisters, to demonstrate our beliefs in the choices we make, to build our altars, cast our circles and invoke our deities. Seeing, knowing, and willing give us courage and help us to *dare* to be what we are in the face of many oppressions, and to dare to do what we know is right and good.

Lastly is *silence*, not only for preserving the magic, but also for understanding the dangers involved. When we are silent it is because we remember the Burning Times, when nine million people (mostly women) were tortured and murdered for the practice of our religion. Covens had to meet in secrecy, and one slip of the tongue could mean agonizing death for oneself or beloved friends and relatives. Since that time secrecy has often been associated with the Craft. Not that I wish to promote paranoia. The world has changed since the Burning Times. We are at the threshold of a new age when many secrets are coming to light, and the powers of the individual will be more and more accepted. But great change comes slowly, and there are still many minds that are clouded with old conditioning and attitudes. It is helpful to maintain a wise discretion in magical matters. Each of us must reckon with the degree of openness or lack of it in our own social circumstances, the risks involved, or the possible benefits of shaking things up. There are times when it is appropriate and transforming to share, and times when it is best to keep silence. I look forward to a time when magic will be practiced communally by many people, and this can only happen if the information gets out. But I urge you to use good judgment in spreading the word.

Levels of initiation are another factor in deciding when to be open and when to conceal. Not everyone is ready to hear deep wisdom, and the information could be shattering, or fall on deaf ears. I think of these issues in terms of the old Bardic robes of early Celtic cultures. On one side the robe was a coat of many colors, worn by the poet/priestess when she wanted to be seen and known for what she was. On the other side it was a cloak of invisibility, and could be turned inside out and worn that way too. In our cloaks of silence we are like the ancient women-of-power who turned their robes the other way for a time. In our open demonstrations we are like them too, wearing our bright colors for all to see.

Creating a Personal Altar

Now is the time in our journey together to create and consecrate your personal Goddess altar. This altar will be just for you, and is not meant to be used or touched by anyone else. We need a power spot that is our very own, especially when we are starting out on the magical road. A private altar is like having a magic "room of one's own," a place where you can discover your own powers and energies, develop your ideas and creations, open your heart and converse freely with the Goddess. No one else is there to disturb or distract, no other energies but yours permeate; no other magic will confuse or interfere with your intentions and spells, no other theologies will rear up to do battle with your own.

Solitude is important for developing personal strengths, and magical solitude helps develop magical strengths. It helps us to become independent in many ways, firm in our knowledge of ourselves and what we can accomplish. Time spent alone at your altar will bear many fruits, not only within your own being, but in your ability to practice with others as well. The best groups are made up of strong people who know themselves and their commitments clearly.

This altar will be a support to you for the duration of this study. The magical objects will gradually absorb your unique energy and thoughtforms. They will become familiar friends, reflecting back to you clearly all that you have projected into them. You will need this kind of clarity for understanding, for discovery, for spell-casting, for rituals, for healing. After you complete the thirteen Cycles you may wish to dismantle this altar; on the other hand you may find you want to love and keep her always.

Creating your own power-spot might present some difficulties. For centuries women have been denied personal space as well as sacred space. We are expected to take care of other people's spaces and not ask for any of our own. If we are lucky, we might be able to have a share, but often there is an unspoken taboo on claiming one all for ourselves. Terms like "greedy" and "selfish" rise to the lips and mind, and we can find ourselves feeling guilty about wanting something for us. We may also be afraid to upset or offend someone in our lives who may not be comfortable with the idea that we have an altar.

Truly one little spot in the vastness of the universe is not too much to ask. While tycoons control thousands of acres and political leaders great empires, all a witch really needs is a bit of space to call her own. No one should be denied this simple and basic right—great things can come of it.

The first step in building your altar is to find an appropriate place. Find a secluded area where you are not likely to be disturbed. If you don't have a room of your own, perhaps you can curtain off a corner. If you live in a warm climate you might be able to set up outdoors or in an outbuilding. Be sure the space is safe and protected. Let it be known to those you may be living with that this will be your special, sacred place, and ask for their cooperation and support.

Altars need a degree of specialized energy in order to emanate clearly and powerfully. If you mix their energies up, your magic will also be mixed up. Make sure that anything you place on or near your altar has sacred significance for you. Garbage, or ordinary household items may not be appropriate things for an altar, unless you are using them in some ritual context. Things that are a part of ordinary consciousness can drain the magic away. Altars work best when they are beautiful and give a suggestion of extraordinary reality.

After you've decided where to place your altar, you will need a table or box or some kind of sturdy base. Please don't feel that you must go out and spend a lot of money for altar supplies. Not that I am opposed to this; if you have the resources and wish to support the magical marketplace, I am delighted. There are some wonderful craftspeople nowadays who make beautiful magical things.

But such objects are often found right under our noses. You might be amazed to discover how much magic you already have in your environment. Many things can be made by your own hands as well, and these will carry your energy and will be very special. You may also find wonders at flea markets, yard sales and second-hand shops. Often the Goddess chooses to send us what we need in the most surprising ways.

My temple altar is made of one round from a large wooden cable spool, which I found at a yard sale in my neighborhood. It was extremely heavy, so I turned it on its edge and rolled it home! Four legs had been added to it, making it just the right height for floor seating or standing before it. My tiny personal altar is made of an old wooden crate, and sits up high on a shelf over my desk. Of course both of these altars are always covered with gorgeous fabrics, so their roughness doesn't show, but their sturdiness and natural wood energy are most advantageous.

Anything that is stable and at which you can work comfortably will do just fine. It should have enough surface to accommodate a variety of candles, sacred objects, incense burners, flower vases, and statues. A low round wooden table, a coffee table, a flat rock, or tree stump can make lovely altars. Or you can have a round slab cut at a lumberyard. Place it atop any firm base you have handy; then everything can be draped. Your surface needs to be smooth and level so things will not spill or tip. Be sure to protect your altar and its surroundings from accidental fire. Keep some water on or near it, just in case. Make sure your incense burners are built to take the heat; if necessary, stand them in wooden bowls or on boards for insulation. Place adequate wax-catchers under candles and make sure all candles are firmly supported. I often put my candles in deep bowls, especially the fat ones which can melt into unexpected and messy pools. Have good ashtrays for your matches and check to be sure matches are fully extinguished after using. Be especially careful of draperies and hangings around flame; set your candles well away from anything that might catch fire. Enclosed glass candles are good, especially if you want to leave them burning unattended for a while. Of course if you want to carve messages into your candles you will need naked ones. It helps to have a good supply of well-made holders, saucers and bowls on hand.

Now you are ready to drape or decorate your altar. Use your imagination and create a setting that will inspire you. A soft velvety foundation cloth, a bower of branches and flowers or hanging plants, a painting or tapestry on the wall above— all of these are ways altars can be adorned. Since this is a new altar and represents a beginning on your spiritual path, you might want to decorate her in white for the Maiden Goddess.

Finally, you are ready to place the symbolic objects of your choosing. It is best not to clutter her with too many things. The mind moves freely through clear, open spaces that give a sense of beauty and order. Begin with an image of the Goddess. Select a special Goddess with whom you feel an affinity. Drawings, paintings, weavings, statues, cards . . . there are so many representations now available. You might find something that appeals to you in a magazine or art book . . . and there are always things out in nature. The Earth is the Goddess, and so all things of the Earth evoke Her mysteries. You could make a Goddess or woman figure out of clay, or perhaps create a corn-doll, or use branches from a tree. A simple stone might suffice as well.

For your first altar consecration add two white candles, a clear, resonant bell, some incense and your *Book of Shadows*. If any of these items are difficult to come by, please feel free to find substitutes.

Refer to the element chart on page 51 for ideas on how to represent fire, water, earth, air and spirit. Your Goddess image can represent the Spirit element. Many witches keep an "athame" or witch's blade for use in carving candles, stirring incense, and cutting spells (symbolically ending them). Some keep a wand upon the altar, used to point out the directions or trace signs in the air. Some stones provide protection, such as amethyst or a clear crystal charged for that purpose. A crystal ball can help to stabilize and concentrate the energy, and can be a terrific divining tool. Some people keep a hollow pyramid for written spells or other special objects they wish to charge up. Pyramids intensify and increase psychic energy. Bells are commonly used on altars for lifting the vibrations, clearing the air, and aiding trance.

The sound of a bell or drum can induce an alpha state and banish negative thought-forms from the aura. Anything from nature—shells, stones, herbs, flowers—all bring very good energy to an altar. It is a good idea to have living plants on or close by, as they bring life force energy to all your workings.

Choose objects that arouse your sense of specialness and inspire you with their significance. This means that they are "charged" with your energy, and will support your workings. I'm sure you have such things in your possession; most people do. If not, they will come to you, now that you have begun to be aware of the process.

Place each item with care and concentration, being aware of the dynamics of the altar space, the center and the periphery. Make the arrangement so that it is balanced, symmetrical, and pleasing to the eye. You will probably feel a natural urge to do a ceremony, once everything is set up.

Care and Feeding

Altars need a regular amount of housekeeping, just like any space. Naturally, this can be a more delicate process than, say, making your bed or clearing up dinner. If there is an ongoing spell on your altar, you may prefer having a little dust to disrupting the vibrations. The best time to clear and rearrange altars is in between such undertakings. However, a spell that has been sitting around for a long time might need a little freshening up. You can aid the cleansing process by casting a work circle around the altar before disturbing anything, asking those energies present to assist and bear with you. Snuff candles rather than blowing them out, especially if you have invested them with particular meanings or energies. State that whatever vibrations are present on the altar will remain intact until you are ready to bid them farewell.

Periodic cleansing rituals, if done with care, are wonderful for altars. Such actions as washing vessels, dusting objects, shaking out cloths, rearranging or replacing magical items renew and strengthen the power. You will need to decide just how far to go. Sometimes washing a tapestry is not the best idea, if it is extremely delicate. Some cloths I simply shake out, and this too can be a mini-ritual. I might take one out into the garden and shake it a magical number of times, visualizing a clearing of the energies, while preserving the power that may have accumulated in the fabric.

Much depends upon your own feelings in these matters. By now you are probably aware that what makes you feel the magic in something will set the standard for your choices. Sometimes a vigorous cleansing will have the desire effect, sometimes minimal, gentle handling will work better.

Storage of altar items is another factor to deal with. Witches who have practiced for a while will be heard to exclaim with astonishment at how much material has accumulated over the years, and how varied are the ways in which they need to be stored.

It's a good idea to arrange some storage space when you first begin to design your altar. If there is room beneath, and your draperies extend, this can be a perfect space to keep those things not currently in use. Not only will they be out of sight and protected, but they can continue to absorb the energies of the altar as a whole. I like to store dried herbs in pouches and baskets tucked beneath or behind my altar, so they will be nicely charged up when I am ready to use them. You can also hang some of your smaller items nearby in pretty pouches or on their own. Shelves hidden behind the wall draperies make excellent altar storage. Special baskets or boxes or treasure chests can be stashed beneath, pulled out when needed. You'll probably find yourself collecting all kinds of lovely containers: bottles for oils, carved boxes, bowls, trays, cloth wraps, dishes, baskets . . . all such items will usually come in handy at some point either as part of your altar display, or for storage. These too become charged up eventually, especially if they are reserved for your magical things. They also help to protect and contain the powers invested in your artifacts.

I have learned that taking an altar apart can be as much a ritual as putting one together. This seems especially true when dismantling a traveling altar, or one that has been set up in a public place for an event. If you are in charge of post-ritual clean-up at a public hall, this may come as a surprise. Rituals done in public may require more clean-up and set-up time than ordinary workshops or lectures.

For packing up a temporary altar I usually bring appropriate containers and wraps. Snuff burning candles and set them aside to cool first to prevent wax spills. Wrap delicate things in the same cloths used for altar display, or additional cloths brought for that purpose. Some stones and other items may have their own containers and pouches. Pack heavier items first, so as not to crush the lighter ones. Messy incense burners will need snug-fitting lids or some way of cleansing them before packing them away. It's nice to have a metal container for matches too. I usually have a large laundry-sized basket for everything, stashing it beneath the altar table for the duration of the event.

The way you care for your altar and altar things will reflect the way you feel about them. As with anything in life, the more you put into them, the more they will give back. This doesn't mean you have to get over-complicated or uptight about it all; again, it is a question of balance. At first you may need to emphasize your workings more, until they become habitual. Later you will probably find that altaring has become a natural part of the flow of your life. The most important thing to remember is to approach all such activities with a sense of sacredness and reverence. The Goddess will love you back tenfold for all that you give to Her.

Consecrating Your Altar

Now you are ready to perform a ritual of blessing and consecration. Blessing means giving and receiving good energy, filling up your altar and yourself with the love of the Goddess. Consecration means making a specific dedication in accordance with your belief and devotion. This helps to send the magic energy in the directions that benefit you, protect you, and reinforce your belief in yourself and the Goddess.

Select a time when you know you can be alone and undisturbed. If you haven't already done so, arrange the items listed on page 55. Add any special images or objects that you feel are appropriate. You might like to dress yourself for the occasion as well, put on some soft music, and place a comfortable chair or cushion.

1. Light the candles and incense.
2. Seat yourself comfortably before the altar.
3. Do some deep breathing and relax in mind and body. Spend some time gazing and taking in the beauties and energies of your altar. Look into the eyes of your Goddess image and open yourself to Her.
4. Take up your bell and ring it until you can feel the reverberations. Let the last chime fade out naturally before you set the bell down again.
5. Keeping your gaze upon the Goddess, say aloud:

> Sweet Goddess
> Creatrix of all that is
> Thou from whom I came
> And to whom I will ever return
> I call upon thee now to come and bless my altar
> And the work I do in thy name.
> Please hear my vows to use this sacred place of power
> Only for loving and holy purposes.
> So Be It.
> Blessed Be.

6. Close your eyes and cast the circle, using the Rainbow Cone Meditation. Let the swirling rainbow cone surround you *and your altar as well*. Before reciting the invocation ("I am one with thee . . .") say aloud:

> The circle is cast
> The spell is made fast
> Only the good can enter herein
> The magic is made, so let it begin.

Say the invocation, then spend a little time in silence, feeling the energies you have raised, seeing them in your mind's eye.

7. Now is the time to call in those Goddesses you would like to have appear and be with you. Use the five elements as a guide, if you like:

AIR: Aurora, Goddess of the Rosy Dawn, Iris, Messenger Goddess who brings news from the Other Side, Voc, Goddess of the Spoken Word, who helps me to

Name . . . Goddesses of Mind, where Light is born . . .

FIRE: Chantico, Goddess of the sacred Hearth, keeper of the flame, Pele, flower of the volcano, rising up from Earth's inner core, Lucina, Goddess of the Golden Sun who shines upon us all . . . Fiery and passionate ones who rule the fires within me, awakening my creativity, strengthening my will . . .

EARTH: Demeter, Mother who brings the animals and the grain, Gaiea, Mountain Mother, upon whose breasts and belly we walk in peace, Tiamat who molded us all from clay . . . Goddesses of my body, sacred flesh and bone, Thou who are the Mystery of Manifestation . . .

WATER: Oceana, swelling with the tides of compassion, Sarasvati, flowing river of inspiration, Yemaya, water goddess of the deep who brings all Life and Love . . . Keepers of emotion, the beautiful feelings that sweep through me and are my strength as well as my vulnerability . . .

SPIRIT: _____ (name yourself) and Goddess of Ten Thousand Names . . . thou who reside in the Universe as well as within me . . . I am you and you are me, and so our lives are one life for all eternity . . .

> Awake and come to me now and bless my venture
> Hear my vows of devotion and loyalty
> My pledge to be ever true
> To myself and to you . . .

8. Visualize the Goddesses you have invoked. See them forming a circle of love and protection around you and your altar, as well as within you. See and hear their blessings. Say aloud:

> I dedicate this altar to myself and thee
> I will never betray thy trust in me.

9. Spend some time communing with them, receive them and experience their presence. Open yourself and listen. They may have special messages for you.

10. When you feel complete, thank all the goddesses and bid them farewell until next you meet.

11. As you see them depart, breathe deeply for a few moments and imagine the energy you have raised being sent down through your body and into the earth. (This is called "grounding" and should always be done after energy is raised.) Open the circle with your mind's eye, but know that it will continue to energize and surround your altar at all times. Close it permanently around your altar. Say aloud:

> For the good of all
> And with harm to none

The spell is sealed
And the magic is done.

12. Ring the bell again, and snuff out the candles.

The Priestess stands at the gateway to the hidden worlds, inviting us to enter her domain. She guides us through the labyrinth of the deep mind and safely back again. She is the ancient woman's symbol of inner spiritual authority.

Suggested Project

Record the experience of creating and consecrating your altar in your *Book of Shadows*. Include a sketch or description.

Questions to Ponder

1. How did it feel when you set up your altar?
2. Did you encounter any obstacles in building or consecration?
3. How did the ceremony go?
4. Were you moved by the experience?
5. Did you go into an altered state? Describe in detail.
6. Did you receive any special visions or messages from the Goddess?

Reading and Other Resources

Z. Budapest, *The Holy Book of Women's Mysteries*.
Laurie Cabot, *The Power of the Witch*.
Normal Lorre Goodrich, *Priestess*.
Jade, *To Know*.
Ann Wilson Schaef, *Women's Reality*.
Starhawk, *The Spiral Dance, Truth or Dare*.
Diane Stein, *Casting the Circle, Stroking the Python*.
Virginia Woolf, *A Room of One's Own*.
Valerie Worth, *The Crone's Book of Words*.

Star River Productions—Ancient Goddess Replications—statuary and note cards. P.O. Box 6254, North Brunswick, NJ 08902.
Jane Iris—Goddess jewelry and statues. P.O. Box 609, DEPT. OLAM, Graton, CA 95444. Catalogue $2.
Joann Colbert—Goddess portraits, posters and cards. 4141 Ball Road #178-OA, Cypress, CA 90630. Catalogue $1.
Monica Sjöö—prints of her gorgeous goddess art. 26, Jacob's CT., St. George's Rd., Hot Wells, Bristol, England.
Max Dashu—paintings and cards of Goddesses and women of many cultures, with information included. (Max also does wonderful slide presentations, called "Suppressed Herstories.") Write *Altar Runes*, P.O. Box 3511, Oakland CA.
Morning Glory Zell—Goddess figurines c/o Church of All Worlds, P.O. Box 1542, Ukiah, CA 95482.

Moonspell (Shekhinah's offerings)—Runesets, runecards, runebooks, tarot decks, oils, powders, tapes, manuscripts, calendars, witchkits, spells and charms. Send $2 for catalogue, P.O. Box 2991, Santa Cruz, CA 95063.

Images of the Great Goddess—figurines, vases, frescoes, etc. c/o Rainbow Serpent, 11722 Crownover, Williamsport, OH 43164.

Womb Am Creations—Meditation Goddesses, pots, bowls, figures of clay. Georgia Perchild, 436 Escalona Drive, Santa Cruz, CA 95060.

Amazon Earthworks—Ritual bowls, smudge pots, cauldrons, shields. P.O. Box 684-OM, Benicia, CA 94510. Catalogue $1.

Cycle 3

The Maiden Goddess

Of the three aspects of the goddess, the maiden is the first, and represents birth, newness, beginnings, play, adventure, individuality, enchantment, risk, childhood . . . she is seen as virgin, "whole unto herself," the original meaning of virginity, which had nothing to do with chastity. The maiden in her bright aspect is associated with the spring, when new life appears on the earth, baby animals are born, and the frozen waters burst to melt and flow again. In her dark aspect She is associated with Autumn Equinox and the darkening of the year. Some of her colors are pale green, white, silver, pink, deep green blue, violet and indigo. Animals associated with her are the owl, deer, and hound. She is called Diana, Persephone, Ariadne, Artemis, Kore, Lady of the Wild Things, Athene, Nimue, Bleudowedd. She is the part of us that is ever-young, delighting in the wonder of life, the wildness of possibility. She is the raw and the untame, the material from which we can shape what is to be, the potential of youth.

It is interesting that the Maiden seems to have two main aspects: the Bright and the Dark. She is more familiar in her Bright aspect as Amazon, Warrior and Liberator (Diana, Artemis, Statue of Liberty). We are less aware of the Dark Maiden (the enchantress, mermaid, priestess) but women are definitely beginning to tune in to Her.

A group of sisters in Oregon put on a Goddess gathering one summer, featuring the topic "Is there a fourth aspect to the Goddess?" Hearing about this got me thinking that the answer might be yes, the Dark Maiden.

I first learned about this Goddess from a lover, who used to call me her "dark maiden," and point out the waning crescent in the late night sky . . . She would explain that there are two crescents and two Maidens; the Bright Maiden corresponds to the waxing crescent, curving toward the right. The Dark Maiden corresponds to the waning crescent, curving toward the left. In older mythic systems, these maidens can be seen on the labyris or double-bladed ax, once used by Amazons as a tool and weapon. Over the years I have discovered the beauty of this symbol system and its potential to give healing and empowerment to women.

We all know about the great triad: Maiden, Mother, and Crone. This three-fold archetype resonates deeply in our psyches as Beginning, Middle, and End of all things, and is likely to be with us always. Yet a fourth aspect might appear within the triad—as well as a fifth or sixth. "When the myths come alive for us they change," says Starhawk. Truly, there are no limits to the Goddess, and all things are possible.

But why the special attention to the Bright and Dark Maidens? For one thing, they make a marvelous all-female alternative to the male-opposite-female symbolism of patriarchy. The Bright Maiden who waxes, moves toward the Light and the Sun. She is the young Goddess who is growing, the Amazon, the woman who takes her powers of freedom, action, strength and independence. She is the risk-taker, the woman who dares. In other words, she is all the things our society tells us should be considered "male." Because of our loss of Her image in our psyches, women find themselves either weakened or accused of becoming "like a man," when they express Her qualities. Known to us as Diana, Artemis, Boudicea, the Amazon Warrior Woman...the Bright Maiden is more familiar to us than the Dark. She has been especially visible in the current women's movement as a symbol of our righteous anger and daring.

The Dark Maiden who wanes, moves toward the Underworld, the Crone. She is associated with aging, descent, introspection and magic. The Dark maiden is the enchantress, She Who Pulls. In Her positive attributes She represents some of the lost powers of woman. She surrenders to the flow and pulls, like the pull of the moon, the suction of the undertow. This is the magnetism of magic, our power to draw to us all that we require. Images of the Dark Maiden appear to us as Ariadne, Persephone, Queen of the Underworld, the Mermaid, Sirens, Sorceress. In the Tarot she is called Priestess, and is seen with the scroll of universal law in her hand, and a golden serpent at her feet.

In patriarchy the Bright and Dark Maidens tend to appear in negative expression, and because of this, our impression of them can become distorted. Patriarchs love to keep our Dark Maidens weak and dependent upon them, and if we decide to act out of our Bright Maiden selves, they insist that we do so "like a man." These are some of the reasons why it is so important for us to find woman-identified symbols for these parts of ourselves—Goddesses that are soft *and* strong, magical *and* free.

DARK MAIDEN		BRIGHT MAIDEN	
Afflicted	Liberated	Afflicted	Liberated
Weak	Surrendering	Hard Boiled	Strong
Flaky	Spontaneous	Superficial	In control of her life
Passive	Pulling	Hyper-rational	Organized
Victim	Supporting	Militant	Disciplined
Self-Sacrificing	Compassionate	Aloof	Independent
"Loser"	Gentle	Unemotional	Objective
Myopic	Subjective	Mechanical	Scientific
Over-reacting	Intuitive	Power-over	Power-from-within
Deluded	Imaginative	Careless	Playful
etc.	etc.	etc	etc.

The main thing to remember about the Dark Maiden is that She has the power to Respond. She is the receptive and sensitive part of us, which we need for successful magic as well as personal wholeness. She is tender and vulnerable, and it is important to nurture our liberated Bright Maiden qualities so we can protect Her. Too many women with Dark Maiden qualities become victims in our society, subject to the will of others. And too many Bright Maidens become cold and hard. Feminist spirituality teaches us that we have been programmed to act out these qualities in ways that the men have devised. Liberation lies *not in discarding* them, but in learning to reclaim them in their older, female expressions.

Inevitably, this process will lead us back to the threefold and five-fold expressions of the Goddess, because they offer flow and continuum. They teach us that any one quality when isolated at the expense of the others becomes destructive and limiting. While the Bright and Dark Maidens do pair off and become partners, companions and lovers, they can be seen within the larger contexts of Maiden, Mother, and Crone or Fire, Water, Air, Earth and Spirit (see illustration). Sometimes I picture the two Maidens as Warrior and Priestess within a cycle that includes Mother, Grandmother, and Lover. Sometimes I see them as the Fall and Spring Equinoxes, known to the ancient Greeks as the Anados (Goddess arising) and Kathados (Goddess Descending). Thus we can integrate the duality of our Bright and Dark Maidens into the three-fold, five-fold, and eight-fold (the eight holy days of the year) cycles of Life and Being.

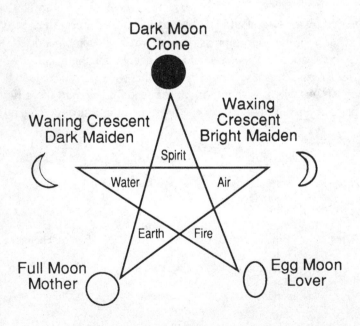

In today's society, the maiden aspect of woman is the most beloved and admired, though her powers are beset by male imagery, and considerably diluted. In patriarchy, the maiden is the princess in the fairytale, the movie star, the *Vogue* model, the Playboy bunny, and the tomboy. Commerce and industry abound for the creation and preservation of this maiden who is man's plaything and object of sexual fantasy. Women strive to be this maiden, and dread the appearance of those first wrinkles or grey hairs. The younger woman is always preferred to the elder, provided she looks and acts according to her prescribed roles. She must not be too strong or assertive, nor too powerful or independent. She is kept unimportant, decorative, weak, passive, "in her place." She is forever "Daddy's little girl," and is made to please him. Her rite of passage into adulthood is celebrated by rape or marriage to a dominant male figure. We can also see her as the "sleeping maiden," as in *The Sleeping Beauty* or the *Snow Queen*, whose passion for life has been frozen into coldness and sometimes cruelty. Often in the male psyche, the maiden becomes the "negative anima," or destructive female. Here her powers become devouring, rather than pulling, destroying rather than sharing. Such men are often trapped in relationships with people who reflect their inward negative image of woman, and act out their qualities. Much of the hatred of woman can be traced to this inner negative maiden created by the patriarchal mind. Some of her traditional names are La Belle Dame Sans Merci, the Siren, the Vagina Dentata (vagina with teeth), Lady MacBeth, Livia.

One of the most famous maiden tales is that of Kore-Persephone from the Greek tradition. In the patriarchal version she is carried off to Hades, or the Underworld, by the male god of Death. He forces her sexually and makes her his queen. Her mother Demeter, who rules all life, mourns the loss of her daughter, thereby bringing winter to the earth. This upsets the ruler of gods, Zeus, who commands Hades to release his bride. But because she has eaten six pomegranate seeds during her stay with Hades, Persephone is only granted six months upon the earth with her mother, and must spend the remaining six with her husband in the underworld. In many ways women continue to enact this myth in their lives.

This is a seasonal myth, as many are, and symbolizes the cycles from winter to spring. Demeter, the mother goddess, sends all life to sleep when her daughter is underground. Persephone represents the fate of the grain which lies in the dark all winter and will sprout and return to the light of day when spring comes. When she reunites with her mother all earth will celebrate with new leaves, flowers, animals, sunshine, and nourishment. The Myth of Kore was celebrated for many centuries in ancient Greece. The mystic connection between mother and daughter was held in great reverence by these people, despite the encroachment of masculine symbolism.

Researchers and myth-makers have found older, more female-oriented versions of this tale, where the maiden's departure is not through rape but through her own natural growth cycle, toward the differentiation of herself. She discovers her powers in the underworld and communicates with the spirits of the dead. Here we see that the profound mysteries of connection, separation, and reconnection are possible within a female framework. In my own version (*Myth of the Kore*) I envision the maiden encountering the Crone or Wisewoman aspect of herself, who teaches and initiates her into the three mysteries of eternal life, manifestation, and dissolution. She then returns to the mother, but now is equal, and a mother herself.

Hopefully, as you read this, you will begin to grasp the influence archetypal myth can have upon you. Try to see how the patriarchal version of the story has affected your view of yourself and life, and to feel how a female-oriented version can heal the maiden within yourself. Become aware of the maidens in the world around you: the young women you know, the women in media and literature, and the young woman you are and have been. Do you dance? Do you have fun? Do you take risks? Are you able to be independent, to validate yourself as a unique and special person? Can you swoon, go into trance, remember your dreams? Can you experience orgasm? Can you be vulnerable, sensitive? How often do you laugh and play? Is your body strong, able to meet the challenges and tasks set before you? Do you assert yourself, stand up for your beliefs? If so, how are you treated? See how you are rewarded for the ways in which your maiden self behaves, and if you are penalized in everyday life by yourself or others.

Other well-known maiden tales in our culture are those like *Cinderella* and *Beauty and the Beast*. In these stories there are always three sisters, two who are older, uglier, and disagreeable, and one who is young, pure, and will win the prince. This maid must undergo great self-sacrifice and suffering to reach her goal of marriage and submission. Her sisters, who seek self-gratification, will be punished with rejection and a lonely old age.

Herein we see the programming for competition and manipulation among women. All seek the prince's favor, only one will be chosen. In life we can observe the damage this value system has done to relationships among our sisters. Young women compete for the attentions of men and for the rewards of status within the system. Most women give up their friendships with other women as the world demands it of them. Mothers and daughters are also in competition with one another for the attentions of the father, and for power within the domestic sphere. The "star system" creeps in everywhere, selecting one candidate for privilege and rewards, and discarding the others. "Divide and conquer" is the pattern here, so subtly ingrained by now that we perpetuate it all by ourselves!

But, of course, times are changing, or you would not be reading these pages at this moment. Women are beginning to wake up, and the return of the true maiden in all her splendor is one of the signs. We are speaking out, stepping out, striking out on our own. We are forming alliances and loyalties to one another. We are more visible in politics, in education, in the marketplace, in sports, in theater and literature. True, the bright maiden is more apparent than the dark and both are still dreadfully male-identified.

The bright maiden can be seen among lesbians, athletic women, military women, business women, academic women, and in many professions once held to be the province of men. Her male-identification can take the form of imitation. Since men were her only role-models for power and self-fulfillment, she tends to dress, think, and act like men. In the process she may repress her sensitive dark maiden side and reject/long for sisters who display her qualities. What a grotesque imitation of feminism: women competing, posturing, star-tripping, and going to war. This is not what the goddess wants for us at all. These maidens *are* making important inroads into women's independence and power; they are trailblazers for social change. Hopefully, as they grow they will expand beyond patriarchal forms.

The dark maiden can be seen almost everywhere. Her male-identification takes the form of dependency upon him and his system. She is soft and lovely, but she cannot feel complete within herself without a man. She is often far more capable of commitment and deep connections of the heart, but she remains weak and passive most of her life. These are the severed parts of us, reflected in the current division between sisters.

To heal the bright and dark maiden self, it is essential to cultivate mythic female images of her, such as Artemis and Kore. Daddy Warbucks and Cinderella have got to go. We must envision the dark maiden as powerful, warm and deep, and the bright maiden as courageous and free. The change begins within each of us, and includes close examination of the values and symbols passed down to us as children.

Maiden Ritual

To heal and strengthen your maiden self.
To be performed at the new moon; the first appearance of the waxing crescent.

Place upon your altar a fresh white candle, budding flowers, some mugwort (Artemisia), some sprouting seeds, a ceremonial cup of fresh spring water, and images of the bright and dark maidens. If you like, you can color the ones provided in this Cycle, and use them for your workings.

As the sun sinks into the west, and the maiden crescent begins to follow her down the sky, put on some gentle, flowing music, light some candles and frankincense. Prepare a ritual bath with lavender, saffron, and laurel. (You can tie these herbs in a cheesecloth to prevent drainage problems.)

Take your time bathing. Pour the scented water gently over each part of your body, celebrating your beauty and womanhood. Imagine that with each caress of water you are washing away tiredness, stagnation and negative attitudes, bringing rejuvenation to your limbs, face, and torso. Wet your hair too, feeling all negative thoughts and memories dissolving away into the water. As you arise from your bath say to yourself, "I am Maiden, beautiful, renewed, refreshed, reborn."

Dress in something special that makes you feel young and free. Put flowers in your hair or tuck one behind your ear. Dance before your altar, imagining that all the maiden goddesses are dancing with you.

When you feel ready, seat yourself before your altar. Light the candle, saying,

> With this flame I ignite within me
> The spirit of the maiden.

Ring the bell for a while, and do some deep breathing, concentrating on the candle flame. Raise your eyes to the two maiden-goddess images and say aloud:

> I am whole unto myself
> I am the bright maiden
> Strong, invincible, and free
> I am the dark maiden
> Cloaked in veils and mystery
> I am the pulse of the sun
> And the pull of the moon
> Flowing from one to the other
> In perfect harmony
> Where I walk
> None can hinder me
> I am maiden
> Forever young and free.

Chant these words again and again as you gaze upon the images before you. Feel their meanings vibrating through every cell of your body, and out four feet in every direction, through your aura.

Take some time for silent meditation. Ask the goddess to send you strong images of powerful maiden goddesses and role models in your everyday life. See the images on the altar float toward you and enter into you, so that you and they become as one. Take up the bowl of flowers and drink deeply. Say aloud:

> Maiden goddesses, I drink of thy sweetness and strength
> And so am filled with thy spirit

Eat a sprout, saying:
> As this seed bursts with new life
> So am I filled with vitality

Breathe fully and deeply throughout the entire ritual. When you feel complete, ground the energy, ring the bell, and snuff out the candle.

This ritual should be repeated at the waning crescent moon, and thereafter as many times as you wish.

A Bright Maiden

A Dark Maiden

Suggested Projects

1. Perform the Maiden Ritual on page 69. Adapt and adjust it freely to suit your needs and circumstances. Emphasize the Bright and/or Dark Maidens, depending on how developed you feel they are in your personality, or present in your life. Do this ritual twice, at the waxing and waning crescents of the moon, and keep notes on the differences in energy, tone, and realizations that come up.

2. Research some Maiden Goddesses, strong women, and enchanting women from different times and cultures. Find out their names, stories, images, attributes, deeds, symbols, powers, animals, plants, or any other information you feel is helpful. Record your findings in your *Book of Shadows* and leave space for new information as it comes to you. Make your own stories about them, and create rituals for honoring them as well as requesting their companionship and support. Find out how they reflect and influence the cultures they come from and the histories of their peoples. Collect and make images of them in the form of drawings, sculptures, poems, songs and prayers. Some books that can help with these projects are: *The Book of Goddesses and Heroines*, by Patricia Monaghan, *The Women's Encyclopedia of Myths and Secrets*, by Barbara G. Walker, *The Witches' Goddess*, by Janet and Steward Ferrar, *The Greek Myths*, by Robert Graves, *Ancient Mirrors of Womanhood*, by Merlin Stone.

3. Explore the magical child within. Read books such as the Oz books by L. Frank Baum, the *Chronicles of Narnia*, by C. S. Lewis, the *Prydain Chronicles*, by Lloyd Alexandar, *The Dark is Rising* series, by Susan Cooper, fairy tales by E. Nesbitt and Andrew Lang, and any other fantasy material that appeals to your inner child. Create a magical play with your friends in which everyone dresses as a child in one of these stories, and interacts.

4. Imagine yourself growing up in a magic world such as Oz or Narnia. Write a story about yourself as a child in a fantasy world where there are real fairies, sorceresses, good witches, giants, dwarves, elves, treasures, quests, and wonders.

5. Have an Amazon adventure. Do something daring and risky out in the wilderness or in society. Start a business or political action group, a battered women's shelter, or stage a demonstration. Take a self-defense or weight-lifting class. Go on a wilderness retreat with a few friends and camp out for a week or more. (Be sure to learn and study survival and safety measures first—risking doesn't mean foolhardiness!) Explore and develop your woman-strength.

6. Enhance your sense of power-from-within and your identity by taking a poetic, magical name. Include in it qualities, activities, habits and connections you wish to affirm and invoke. Add any names you have been called that still hold meaning for you, as well as new names you would like to be called, so as to help integrate all that you have been and will be. For example, here is a ritual name I made up for myself and wrote out in runes on a parchment scroll:

> Shekhinah, Natasha, Ebony
> She of the Mountain Waters
> Daughter of Frances
> Granddaughter of Rebecca
> Mother of Freya and Frey
> Ondine Marina, Mermaid of the Deep
> Dweller by the Silver Lake
> Friend of the Elves and Fairies
> Companion of Cats
> Keeper of Hecate's Cave
> Maker of Magic
> Lover of the Earth and Sea
> Priestess of the Sacred Well
> Channel of the Muse
> Singer of Spells
> Weaver of Destiny . . .

Name yourself after Goddesses whose stories and qualities you identify with. Add such categories as listed above, like "Dweller by . . ." "Keeper of . . ." "Friend of . . ." and so on, including beings, landscapes and activities both mundane and magical. Include archetypal figures such as mermaids, angels, fairies, tree spirits or others that you feel an affinity with, or whose qualities you would like to develop. You can use your magical name or parts of your name at rituals, and for ceremonial purposes. Once written, have a naming ceremony alone or with your sisters, in which your name is read, acknowledged, and proclaimed. Keep this name a secret if you prefer, or use part of it as an alter ego for preserving safety in the patriarchal world.

7. Search within yourself and in myths and among symbols that you know for signs of the Bright and Dark Maidens.

Questions to Ponder

1. What Maiden stories are familiar to you from childhood?
2. Was this aspect of female personality valued in your family? If so, was value given to strength and magic, weakness and dependency, tough insensitivity?

3. What Maiden Goddesses, if any, are familiar to you? Do you feel any special affinity to one or two in particular? Dark or Bright Maidens? Combinations of the two?

4. What has your experience of the Maiden been in your life? Have you known women who exemplify Bright or Dark Maiden qualities? Do you experience the Maiden in yourself?

5. Do you feel encouraged by those around you to be independent and/or "follow your bliss" (i.e., go after your dreams)? Did you experience this in childhood?

6. Do you play? Take risks? Stand up for your rights? Feel free in your body—to dance, do athletics, defend yourself? How are you treated by those around you in regard to these behaviors?

7. Do you dream? Feel deeply? Can you surrender, be sensitive and receptive? How are you treated by those around you in regard to these?

8. What are your relationships like with other women? Do you enjoy women and like to be with them? Do you care about women? Do you experience sisterhood, trust and support with women, or competition, alienation, back-stabbing, gossip?

9. Do you have lasting friendships with women?

10. Do women come first in your life, or do men? Equally?

Reading and Other Resources

Lloyd Alexandar, *Prydain Chronicles*.
L. Frank Baum, *Oz Books*.
Susan Cooper, *The Dark is Rising* (series).
Lord Dunsany, *The King of Elfland's Daughter*.
Dione Fortune, *Moon Magic*.
Nor Hall, *Mothers and Daughters*.
Andrew Lang, *Colored Fairy Books*.
C. S. Lewis, *Chronicles of Narnia* (series of 7) and *Space Trilogy*.
William Shakespeare, *As You Like It*.
Charlene Spretnak, *Lost Goddesses of Early Greece*.
Evangeline Walton, *Song of Rhiannon* (from the *Mabinogian*, a Welsh epic).
Other fairytales: *Molly Whuppie*, *The Lute Player*.
Myth of the Kore is available from Shekhinah Mountainwater, P.O. Box 2991, Santa Cruz, CA 95063. Send $5 for script or $12 for tape.

CYCLE 4

The Mother Goddess

So sayeth the goddess:

I am Mother Goddess
Source of life and love
Breathing vision into manifestation
Bearing children of body and soul
I am the blood of life
The pulsing throb of passion
I am the full moon glowing in the sky
And the beauty of all creation
I sustain all form
With the milk of my devotion
And dissolve all woes
With the power of my love
I am the starry sky
The rolling earth
And the heaving sea
From me all doth proceed
And all shall come back to me . . .

The second or central aspect of the goddess is the Mother, source of all creation. She is represented by the full round moon and the blazing sun. Her season is when life reaches its zenith, the sun is hot, the fruit ripens upon the tree and we make ready for the harvest. The mother goddess swells with life, with babies, with green and abundant life. She is the moon swelling to fullness, the waves swelling in tidal rhythm, the lover swooning in orgasm. Her color is red, and she is full of burning desire. Her passion brings all forms into being and her love sustains them. Some of her names are Demeter, Madrone, Gaia, Aphrodite, Habundia, Kuan-Yin, Mother Nature, Oceana, Brigit, Nuit, Amaterasu, Maya, Mari, Ix-Chel, Shakti, Pele . . . her names are as endless as the infinite forms of her creation. She is Life itself, the conscious starstuff of which all is made.

The Mother Goddess is the "land of milk and honey," the endless abundant stream of nurturing that pours from her breasts, her heart, her womb, sustaining and bringing growth to all. She is the mature woman within us who takes responsibility, makes commitments, builds cultures and families. From her great loving heart flows endless compassion, as the rivers flow from the underground caves, up to the mountains, and down to the sea.

But she is not a martyr as some magical symbol systems would have us believe. She is the mother lion who gently licks and cuddles her cubs, but will also protect them with intense ferocity. She is the great ocean that gave birth to us, gentle one moment and turbulent the next. Her anger appears when she is violated, and is always for the sake of furthering life. With great tenderness her womb nurtures us, and with great convulsions we are expelled or birthed into the next life phase.

In the cycle of beginnings, middles, and ends, the mother takes the middle or central place and orders the manifest universe. She arranges every design both seen and unseen—the starry constellations, the intricate veins of a leaf, the microscopic patterns of cells. She contains all the elements of spirit, air, fire, water and earth, dancing them all continuously in and out of being. In this sense she is all three aspects of the goddess, and contains the maiden and the crone within her. That is why you will find that many cultures worshipped goddesses who had many aspects but one name, such as Hecate, Ishtar, Selene and Isis, all three-fold goddesses.

The red magic of the Mother goddess is the most acceptable of woman's powers in today's human society. Birthing, healing, nurturance, sexuality, organiza-tion, and love are necessary to everyone in order for us to exist. There are still cultures where mothers are given an important and central role within the private sphere, such as in Italian and Mexican families. The Jewish mother is well known as a strong, even heroic figure who miraculously sustains her family through troubled times. The Catholic/Christian Virgin Mary, though weakened and submissive, is adored and prayed to in many parts of the world. The Japanese Shinto religion pays homage to Amaterasu, a goddess of the sun. In India there is tremendous love for the divine mother in her aspects of Maya, Kali, Lakshmi ... And yet, when we look more closely at the manner in which the mother powers are treated, we find that there is great oppression. Mothers of the world are often denied participation outside the intimate sphere, in the community. Many have little or no life of their own, having learned to live through children, husbands, and other family members. Many women find themselves trapped in the mother role, forced to repress the Maiden and Crone aspects of their personality. Mothers' opinions are trivialized, dismissed. At social gatherings they are expected to serve and stay in the background. Mothers are often discarded, devalued and rejected if they are older, or if their bodies show the signs of having borne children. Hysterectomies, clitoridectomies, mastectomies, so commonly practiced in patriarchy, all reflect a profound rejection of the mother powers. The indiscriminate use of natural resources that is now upsetting the ecological life-stream of our mother earth also reflects this profound rejection.

The six powers I have named—birthing, healing, nurturance, sexuality, organization, and love—have all been raped or taken over by masculine systems:

Birthing: In ancient tribal cultures women were the natural midwives and welcomers of the newborn. Giving birth and "catching the baby" were celebrated with ritual and held in great reverence. A birth was an event to be acknowledged by the entire community. The mother-to-be was treated with loving care, and seen as the goddess incarnate. As the male medical profession took over, birthing became an illness, and often a disaster. Doctors would intone passages from the Bible about the necessity of mothers' suffering, as they delivered babies in unclean and violent ways. Today, most births occur in the impersonal hospital settings of modern medicine. While there has been some improvement in techniques, the doctor is still the distant and powerful controlling head of the event. The mother gives her power to him and submits to his birth ritual. The current movement back to midwifery and babies being born at home is a clear promise of great healing in this aspect of human life.

Rebirthing, a psychic breath technique, developed by Leonard Orr, is becoming a respected practice. Through simple breathing the seeker can recall and release the trauma of her own birth. It is becoming well known that most of us carry tension and psychological as well as physical blocks caused by the violent manner in which we were born.

Healing: Like birthing, healing was once the province of women. It was understood that the spirit as well as the body must be tended, and that a disturbance in one meant a disturbance in the other. Knowledge of herbs and their psychic as well as medicinal properties was central to these ancient healing practices. The sick were not left out on the streets to die if they had no money, as is often the case today. Mental illness was a community responsibility. Often healings would be done in circles of women, accompanied by chanting, dancing, burning herbs, and laying on of hands. Though shamans or medicine women provided their wisdom and love, it was understood that ultimately we heal ourselves through release from the causes of disease. The male medical profession has supplanted and, in many ways, replaced this healing tradition with its often violent and impersonal approach.

Nurturance: Nurturance, once held in the highest esteem, is now one of the lowliest tasks in the patriarchal value system. Mothers who stay home and raise children are seen as non-working, out of it, excluded from the important and meaningful tasks of living. Children are also kept separate, severed from the life and work of the community. Breastfeeding, the most natural expression of mother-love, is only just beginning to be accepted again. The mother-child bond is often broken, sometimes quite early in the child's life. In native cultures this bond was honored deeply and ritualized. It was seen as essential to the perpetuation of generations of culture. Mothers are natural teachers, and have much wisdom to share with their children. Yet often children are sent elsewhere for learning, and the mother instead teaches them the programs of patriarchy. It was the grandmothers in China who bound the feet of small girl children, the women of Africa and Egypt who perform the clitoridectomies on young girls.

Another aspect of nurturance is energy for we all need energy to live. Today's "energy crisis" shows how far we have removed ourselves from the infinite resources of nature. Every element of the Mother is teeming with energy that we could tap to benefit the entire world. The powers of fire, water, earth, air and spirit provide all that we could possibly need.

Sexuality: The mysteries of sexual fire are integral to the mother goddess and to magic. Desire in her traditions is holy, for it brings passionate union and the impetus for creativity. Witches used kundalini or sexual fire in their rituals; this was the power they raised, and it was for this that they were burned in the millions. The energy raised in the shamanistic "lunatic" sensual dance of their rituals was deliberately released for transformative purposes. Making love was also recognized as a power and a mystery . . . lovers were understood to be blessed by the goddess. The story of patriarchy is a story of sexual repression that ranges from the puritanical idea of "original sin," to modern pornography, with much rape along the way. We are all affected by the severance of sexual energy from love and ritual. Sexual union has been desacralized, except within the context of circumscribed, heterosexual marriage, and then often severed from pleasure and passion. Hence the familiar dichotomy between wives and whores: the "good" women, who nurture and are denied passion, and the "bad" women, who are permitted sensuality, but are denied the social respectability given to wives.

Organization: The goddess organizes her universes with exquisite precision. Her seasons, her cellular patterns, her cycles of time and motion, the delicate balance of fire, air, water, earth, and aether are the ultimate role models we humans have for structuring our lives and our societies. Before the rise of technology and industry, structures of society, buildings, villages, etc., were close to nature in form and type. Time was measured by the blood flow of women, the passing of the seasons, the turning of the moon. People gathered in circles, celebrated and danced in circles, made policy in circles. From the grass huts of Africa to the yurt of Tibet or the tepee of Native Americans, homes have been modeled for centuries after natural form. The farther away we have grown from the mother's ways, the more linear, alienating, and sterile have become our methods of organization. Cities and homes are built in lines and squares, people meet in rows or dance in isolated couples . . . groups are hierarchical, as are entire societies. Even families have become the microcosm of the patriarch's universe composed of God over Husband over Wife over Child over Animals over Plants.

Love: The love of the Mother goddess is like the glue of the universe . . . the sacred force that keeps all beings and things connected. It is the love that births the fierce wish for her child to be safe, to grow into beauty, and to find happiness in adulthood. It is the love between friends who enjoy and care about each other, the love between lovers that draws and binds them together in ecstatic union, the love in families and communities. It is the love of the tree for the sunlight, the wind for the mountain, the water for the moon, the animals for the earth. It is the love we have for ourselves, and it is the goddess' infinite love for herself and all she creates. Love makes us healthy and happy to be. Loving touch is good for the nervous system, and can heal many hurts. Knowing we are loved makes us strong and able to create and build together.

In patriarchy there exists a widespread love famine. Many people are lonely, work in alienating and unfeeling situations, feel disconnected, hate themselves, die alone. Sexuality is often severed from love, becoming a series of physical sensations, leaving the spirit starved. The hierarchical nature of society separates lovers, mothers and children, old people from young people, handicapped from whole, women from women . . . and so on. How many of us remember being unloved as children? While many religious teachings help to bring love into people's lives, there is so much rejection of the female mysteries that much of Her love is blocked out. It is perhaps in the aspect of love that our greatest healings are needed on this planet. In learning to love ourselves and one another and the earth we can bring about the greatest transformations of all.

To know the Mother is to know unspeakable awe. Her enormity is beyond our ability to comprehend. Much of the fear of women and mothers could be an expression of fear of this total awe. People of our world seem to be closed off to ecstatic worship, to their kinship with all beings, and to the childlike wonder at the mystery of it all. Poets, artists and visionaries remain more open, more vulnerable perhaps, so that they can bring this intensity to the rest of us.

One such work of art is the film *The Secret Life of Plants*, developed by Stevie Wonder. The film reveals that plants are extremely conscious and as capable as we are of loving and feeling and caring. From this awareness it follows that we will understand that all the universe is alive and breathing, feeling and aware. Such an understanding confronts us with the vastness of life and consciousness. Most of us have a natural barrier of resistance to this total confrontation. Perhaps we would short-circuit, so to speak, if we allowed ourselves to see and hear the thoughts, voices and feelings of so many beings, to experience the existence and consciousness of every cell, every microbe, every fiber, plant, animal, insect, bird, human, planet, star, solar system, galaxy, dimension, universe . . . Perhaps we need a taboo, to some extent, or we'd be swept away and lose our minuscule control over our tiny life-clusters.

Yet I feel mankind has gone too far with his taboo, to the point of severe repression. We need a little wonder in our lives, occasional release from daily restrictions, to plug in to the majesty and magnificence, to cut loose, swoon with ecstasy, be reminded of our infinite source . . . in other words, we need ritual. And most especially we need ritual acknowledging the female source of life. To shut this experience out entirely, is to shut out life juices that keep us vital. Man has become so shut down that he allows himself outrageous atrocities toward animals, plants, oceans, air, mother earth, women, and himself as well! His superiority complex keeps him separate from the lives he feeds upon. It seems to me to be a very great arrogance to assume that a rabbit or ant or bush has any less awareness than myself. Their awareness is of a different type, perhaps, but equally alive, aware, and capable of feeling.

The primitive consciousness addresses this issue so beautifully, teaching us that all life feeds on other life, that we too will be "eaten," that any life we take should be taken with reverence and gratitude. It is only the culture of the "superior" white male species that wages such devastating wars, that gouges great slices into the earth, our mother's living flesh, causing untold ecological upheaval. And by the same token, from men come the traditions of rape and the enslavement and abuse of women. Our bodies are like the body of the goddess . . . our breasts and bellies and thighs her wonderful curving hills and mountains. Our sensitive emotions are like her ocean waves, and her weather. Our energies, our fires and desires, are like the great fires within the earth. To slice into us is to slice into Her, and vice versa.

What is this great fear of Mother, this incredible rejection that has caused the oppression of so many of our sisters? Kim Chernin, in her book *The Obsession*, proposes that both men and women experience a period during childhood when mother is overwhelmingly powerful and huge, having over us the powers of life and death. Our mothers cuddle us and give us food and make everything okay for us when we are tiny. They can also refuse our requests, or not be there when we want them to. Thus they are the first fulfillers and the first disappointers of all our desires. Mothers become the target of all our hopes and all our rage. Kim Chernin ties this realization in with the current weight-loss movement which has advanced and grown at the same pace as the current women's liberation movement. She says that the great hills and valleys of a large woman's flesh are taboo, like the hills and valleys of earth, because they remind us of our mothers when we were small and helpless, and they so huge and powerful. Hence in our culture we witness women obsessed with making their bodies tiny and thin, who dread the protrusion of a breast, the swell of hip and thigh. Along with the sisters who are having their wombs sliced out and their breasts cut off, we are witnessing sisters who have parts of their bellies or legs sliced away, or who suffer from anorexia nervosa, a disease that makes them terrified of food, and so they literally starve themselves. In other words, the patriarchal Goddess is anorexic!

It would be easy to view the rise of patriarchy as a prolonged adolescent rebellion of the child-race of Man against his parent mother-race, Woman. In this light one can see the female movement as a great weaning, so that this child can grow up and take loving responsibility for his impact on the universe, becoming himself a mother, in love with the goddess in himself. When we reach maturity in our individual lives, we forgive our parents for the disappointments we may have known with them, pick ourselves up, and move on. We come to terms with the qualities or essences that they have passed on to us, claiming them for our own, instead of attempting to slice them away from ourselves. Eventually we find our own ways of expressing and using them, thus creating the next wave of reality and society.

Such a wave seems in evidence now. The changing times are upon us and we can see the beginnings of a new pattern: the return of midwifery and herbal skills, the emphasis on healthy, natural foods, the emergence of respect for ecology and nature, the reclamation of sexual freedom and autonomy, the reclamation of all womb-related powers, the outcry against rape and battery, the growth of community participation by mothers, the rise of alternative religious and spiritual practices . . . patriarchy is dying, and being replaced. And so I suggest that we cease complaining and beating our heads against its old crumbling walls. Even though I have just discussed its transgressions at length, I am not asking you, my dear reader, to spend your life in similar invectives. I simply want the ritual of Naming, that we may know clearly all that we wish to avoid. None knows as well as the Mother: *That which we attend shall flourish.* Once we have seen and named the demon, we must cease to give it any kind of energy, or we will be adding to its existence. What we want is to create the alternative—safeness and harmony in a loving universe.

Women's mysteries honor all three of our phases as necessary to life and wholeness. The healing of the mother aspect is a key to understanding and partici-pating in a very real way with the current revolution of consciousness. All social revolution arises out of the desire and need for human liberation. All loving mothers wish freedom and liberation for their children. And so we must find ways to receive and express the Mother without perpetuating her oppression.

How can we accomplish this healing? We must begin with ourselves. Ask yourself: Are the maiden, mother and crone aspects of yourself expressed equally? Do you feel trapped in the mother role? Do you enjoy giving mother-energy? Do you receive mother-energy? How do people in your life relate to the mother-aspect within you? Are you creative? Do you enjoy this aspect of yourself? Are you loving and emotional? Do you feel you have enough love in your life; did you as a child?

Essential to our healing process is finding affirming images of strong mother goddesses. These can be found in many places: in books, ancient tales and sculptures, modern art forms, feminist works, and most of all, your own imagination. Remember, the magical approach to medicine addresses the thought-forms in the spirit as well as the afflictions of the body, the emotions as well as the flesh. We are programmed by images, and create our reality out of this programming. We can re-create our reality with new and healing images. This is my purpose in providing you with the simple goddess images from my tarot deck. Archetype is image is myth is religion is reality.

There are countless myths of the mother goddess to be found at the root of every culture on earth. Every religion has its creation myths to describe the appearance of life and the universe. Because creation is so overwhelming and unexplainable, we find that we need a simple, childlike and poetic way of explaining it for ourselves. A creation myth is one of the first steps in building any magical system, for it gives form and name, thereby giving us a way to grasp and relate to the ineffable. Becoming adept in magic means becoming familiar and comfortable with the forces of the immanent, ineffable goddess of all creation. When we cast a spell we become Her channel, allowing Her energy to come through ourselves and become the manifestation of our desires. We therefore learn to speak the poetic language of myth when we cast our spells, to utter the names of the goddess when we wish to call her to our aid.

The best myths are the ones that come from the unconscious or deep mind, in a moment of sublime inspiration. One of the passages you will experience in becoming a practicing witch is the creation of your own mythology. It begins with a simple story of how all comes into being, and develops into a pantheon of your own special, most-beloved goddesses. Later you will find that each goddess has her own story, and that further stories come from the interaction of these goddesses. Hopefully, by the time we get to the seventh Cycle on the Muse, you will be ready to make your own creation myth.

Myths of the Mother Goddess

In an age when the female is being redeemed, many new female-centered myths are appearing, and many ancient ones are being reclaimed:

In the beginning, Eurynome, the Goddess of All Things, rose naked from Chaos, but found nothing substantial for her feet to rest upon, and therefore divided the sea from the sky, dancing lonely upon its waves. She danced towards the south, and the wind set in motion behind her seemed something new and apart with which to begin the work of creation. Wheeling about, she caught hold of this north wind, rubbed it between her hands, and behold! the great serpent Ophion. Eurynome danced to warm herself, wildly and more wildly, until Ophion, grown lustful, coiled about those divine limbs and was moved to couple with her. Now, the North Wind, who is also called Boreas, fertilizes; which is why mares often turn their hindquarters to the wind and breed foals without the aid of a stallion. So Eurynome was likewise got with child.

Next she assumed the form of a dove, brooding on the waves, and in due process of time, laid the Universal Egg. At her bidding, Ophion coiled seven times about this egg, until it hatched and split in two. Out tumbled all things that exist, her children: sun, moon, planets, stars, the earth with its mountains and rivers, its trees, herbs, and living creatures . . . (From *The Greek Myths*, volume 1, page 27, the Pelasgian Creation Myth. Collected and retold by Robert Graves.)

Who has not heard of that most ancient time when women descended from the heavens, climbing down the great rope that hung from the sky to walk upon the earth, searching for new plants and roots that they might carry back to their home in the heavens? And who has not heard that when the women arrived the men were still animals, their bodies covered with fur, walking upon their hands as well as their feet? So it was that chancing upon the rope whose end touched the brown soil, the animals jumped at it and snapped it with their sharp teeth—so that the women from heaven were forced to remain upon the earth. It was in this way that the women of heaven and the male animals of earth began to live side by side and upon their mating with each other, they brought forth the people who now live upon the Toba Lands.

Yet one woman still lives in the heavens for each day we see the fiery Akewa as She climbs from the lowest part of heaven to walk across the wide skies, bringing us Her golden light and warmth, giving us the gift of Her brilliant being—until She travels so far to the other side that She slides into the abyss at the end of the world, leaving us for the night. Just like any other woman, Akewa grows old and tired so that She walks across the heavens slowly. At that time the days are very long for Her brilliant light moves as She walks along but unlike any other woman, Akewa also grows young and in Her youth moves quickly, so that when She is young, the hours of daylight are few . . . (This story from Argentina is from *Ancient Mirrors of Womanhood*, page 80, a collection of authentic goddess myths, compiled by Merlin Stone.)

> Comes to pass
> Yea in the beginning of things
> That She, Mother Goddess
> Is a-giving
> Is a-giving
> Is a giving of birth
> Unto Her own self
> She
> She flex
> She heave
> And the mountains moan
> And moan
> And a great opening
> Opens up to the world
> And a maiden is born . . .
> from *Myth of the Kore*, by Shekhinah Mountainwater

Notice how these myths portray the goddess as Her own source. Many legends are reflections of actual historical events. We now have much evidence to show that the oldest forms are female, and that woman is the original race of humans. This evidence shows itself in many areas. Biologically, the human embryo always takes a female form first, and the male Y chromosome is a mutation of the female X chromosome. Historically, matriarchies precede patriarchies the world over, by seven to nine-thousand years. In religion, Goddesses were worshipped in every part of the world long before the appearance of gods. When gods began to appear, they did so as sons and lovers of the goddess, achieving their divinity through their connection to her. It was a far more recent development that introduced almighty father gods like Zeus and Jehovah. Another biological fact: Many species of animals reproduce parthenogenetically (without sperm). There is now documentation of human parthenogenesis, which, apparently, was the original form of reproduction. Z. Budapest, a well-known witch and priestess, claims that her own mother was born that way.

Blood is also one of the ancient powers of women and the mother goddess. The earliest rituals were based on the acknowledgment of women's sacred, life-giving blood. The onset of menses, called Menarche, was celebrated for all young women as recognition of their passage into womanhood and participation in life's mysteries. In many cultures menstrual blood mixed with water was used to fertilize the crops. The resulting vitality of the grain was a source of awe and respect for the magic of women's blood. The time of moonflow was known as a period of psychic sensitivity and visionary experience.

Nowadays moon blood is seen as a "curse." Women have been taught for 2,000 years that their moon time makes them "unclean." How many of us suffer all manner of pain and discomfort during our bleeding time? How many of us were given joyous ritual to celebrate our first flow?

As you can see, the topics and issues connected to the Mother are vast and complex. In this beginning study we can only make a start in examining them. Yet their importance is paramount and the healing work they require is essential to our lives, our politics, and our magic. "It's death not to love your mother," says Alice Walker. We all come from mothers, we all mother in some form, we all need mothering, and we all return to the Mother.

The Manifesting Pentacle

The pentacle or five-pointed star is one of the Mother Goddess' particular emblems. This figure has excellent archetypal resonance deep within the psyche, as it has been used through the ages by mystics and adepts of magic. The five points indicate the qualities that bring about manifestation, which is the Mother Goddess' province. Hence, in the Tarot, the pentacle represents the earth element: the material plane, the body, money, practical matters, survival, and so on. It is the final phase of the creative process, when image, faith, courage, desire, and action materialize into the substantial. Like the Mother Goddess, it contains all other elements within it, and in fact, is made up of them.

Other ways of expressing these points or stages are: Birth, Initiation, Consummation, Repose and Death; Spirit, Air, Fire, Earth, Water; New Moon, Waxing Moon, Full Moon, Waning Moon, Dark Moon; Aura, Mind, Action, Body, Emotion; Sight, Hearing, Touch, Taste, Smell; the five points of the human form, the five fingers of the hand.

As you become familiar with the pentacle, you will come to see how all things come into being in a developmental continuum that begins in the inner or invisible realms. This is the process of magic, which we will go into more deeply in Cycle 10, Rituals and Spells.

Ritual to Heal and Honor the Mother Self

Construct a pentacle, as pictured in this Cycle. Make it out of sturdy materials that can be cut out and colored. Color each point in accordance with its element. I suggest silver or gold for spirit, pale blue for air, red for fire, deep blue for water, and green for earth. Or make up your own color system. Write in the qualities of each point, as shown. When you are done, set it upright upon your altar, so that it is facing you.

Copy, color, and cut out the mother goddess image provided with this Cycle. Also place this upon your altar.

At the full of the moon: do this ritual by yourself out in nature. If it is safe and feasible, prepare to camp out overnight. Pack an altar bag as part of your equipment, containing: a red cloth, a red candle (with sturdy, fire resistant holder), two smaller candles, one black and one white, the pentacle you have made, the goddess image you have colored, a bell, some dried rose petals to burn, and anything else you consider essential to your mother rite. If you have children, bring pictures of them, or something they have made. Also pictures of your mother, grandmother, grandchildren, or things they have made or given to you. Bring your magical journal along to keep notes of your experience.

When you select your campsite, look for a special place for the altar. Have your campfire close enough for burning magical herbs during your ritual. Situate your bedplace so that you can see your altar when you are lying down. Lay the wood in place for your campfire. Cast a magic circle by walking clockwise 'round the site and declaring it sacred space.

Arrange your altar just before sundown, placing all the objects with care. Add a few friends from the environment—a rock or two, a pine cone or leaf. Be aware that you are in the presence of the Goddess and that you have come to honor Her. Open yourself to the beauty and power of nature. Watch and listen for Her sounds and signs. Record any significant visions or apparitions in your *Book of Shadows*. Often She will speak to us through Her wild creatures, Her plants, Her breath of wind . . .

As the full moon rises, light the red candle, saying:

Oh mother, I dedicate this altar to you.
I dedicate this day and night to you.
Come to me now and enclose me in your protection and love.

Light the white and black candles, saying:

As the maiden and the crone are contained within you
So do I light their flames also.

Light your campfire, and when it is blazing well, throw some of the rose petals into it. Take up your bell and ring it steadily, chanting:

Awaken O loving spirits of the earth
Of the sky
Of the waters
And the fire
Awaken before me, behind me,
To the left and right of me
Above and below me
And deep within me
Awaken loving spirits of the Mother
Come to me now
Surround and protect me in this space
Heal me of all hurts and wrongs
Make me at peace with all creation . . .

Ring the bell a little longer, and then listen to its reverberations fade. Replace it upon the altar and chant MAAAAAAAAAAAAAAA for as long as you like. (Ma is the universal mother call, and is a fitting replacement for the male "om" chant.)

Direct your attention to the goddess image on your altar, and meditate upon it in silence for awhile. Open yourself to any visions, realizations or messages from the goddess within and without. Mentally take her image into yourself, and say the first invocation listed with the Rainbow Cone Meditation in Cycle 1, page 29. Close your eyes and ground the energy. Snuff out the candles and prepare to sleep. Keep your journal beside you, so that you can record your dreams upon waking.

In the morning, relight your candles and burn some more rose petals. Write down your dreams and anything else you consider significant. At the altar, concentrate on the pentacle, turning each point upward in turn as you ponder the meaning and life of the five elements they represent.

For the rest, improvise. Let your imagination take over and create your own ritual. The best rituals are spontaneous, and therefore alive with immediacy. Write down your inventions, that you may use them again in the future. When you feel ready, conclude your ceremony, pack up your equipment, douse your campfire thoroughly, and open the magic circle.

The Mother Goddess births all things from out of her own substance, dancing all the elements in and out of Being. She is the Source and Center of All.

Suggested Projects

1. Perform the "Ritual to Heal and Honor the Mother Self" on page 85. If you are unable to do this ceremony out in the wild, find a reasonable substitute. The main thing is to be sure that you will be safe and undisturbed. (Some students have taken their dogs with them, or asked a friend to camp nearby and keep watch. Others have set up in their back yards or living rooms.) Give attention to any feelings or images that come up regarding the mother role in yourself, in society, in those you have mothered or who have mothered you, in the Goddess. Write about your experience in your *Book of Shadows*.

2. Research some Mother Goddesses and threefold Goddesses from different cultures. Find out their names, stories, images, attributes, deeds, powers, symbols, animals, plants, and any other material you find helpful. Record your findings in your *Book of Shadows*, and leave space to add new information as it comes to you. Make up your own stories about Mother Goddesses, and think of ways to honor them as well as ask for their support in rituals. Find out how they are an outgrowth of their respective cultures and the histories of the people who worship them. Collect and make images of them in the form of drawings, sculptures, poems, songs, and prayers. Some books that are good resources for these projects are listed in the Maiden Goddess Explorations on page 74. Make note of any seasonal information that may be helpful in planning your holidays. Give attention to which Mother Goddesses you feel drawn to, or if there are any who will become special to you.

3. Study mothers, parenting, and the qualities of the Mother Goddess as well as mother-daughter relationships, in life and literature. Describe in your *Book of Shadows* the varying approaches to nurturance and support in different cultures. Are these qualities respected and valued or exploited and denied? To what degree are addictions prevalent in these cultures, and how are they connected to the degree of nurturance? Develop some theories and approaches for reinstating a healthy respect for nurturance in our society. Create and perform rituals on such themes as healing the wounded child, replacing addiction with support, giving honor to mothers and Mother Goddesses. Books that can help: *Of Woman Born*, by Adrienne Rich, *Mothers and Daughters*, by Nor Hall, *My Mother Myself*, by Nancy Friday, *Woman and Nature, the Roaring Inside Her*, by Susan Griffin, *The Obsession* and its sequels as well as *In My Mother's House*, by Kim Chernin, *When Society Becomes an Addict*, by Ann Wilson Schaef, *Healing the Shame that Binds You*, by John Bradshaw and Uzuri Amini's chapter on rituals for healing the wounded child in *The Goddess Celebrates*, edited by Diane Stein.

4. Mother Earth is the Mother Goddess, and loving Her is a primary part of Her magic. Investigate current green politics activities and find out how you can get involved. Read James Lovelock and other works on the "Gaia Principle" that emphasizes the awareness of Mother Earth as a living organism. Create and perform rituals to help you get into communication with the Earth as a conscious Being.

5. In earth-oriented cultures, landscape is an inherent part of personality, lifestyle, and magic. Cultivating such relationships helps to keep those parts of the earth alive, and also helps keep human magic-makers alive and healthy. For example, there are desert witches, sea witches, forest witches, mountain witches. Claim and honor a particular landscape as your ally—a meadow or wooded glade, a rocky shore or mountainside, a desert oasis, canyon, or valley. Cultivate a relationship. Go and spend time there, draw pictures, write poems, study the plant and animal life there. Let your heart be your guide and choose a setting that you love and find inspiring. Discover the resident deity, make altars there, write stories, research histories. Carry images of those places in your mind's eye, meditate and recall them at your altar. Learn of their magic and the energies their stones, plants, and other materials may offer for your spells, rituals, healing and nourishment.

6. Perform a ritual to banish and heal the effects of rape in our society and/or in women you know. (This could include yourself, if you have been raped.) Gather a circle of sisters and have the woman or women in need of healing lie down in the center and relax. Ask each in turn to talk about her experience and her feelings about it. Have everyone place their hands over or on her womb and any other affected areas such as her throat and heart chakras. Imagine that you are drawing out the effects of invasion and abuse from this woman in body and spirit and sending it away forever. Replace these negative energies with positive images such as safe, happy, and healthy organs and protecting Goddesses standing guard at all entrances to the body's temple. This type of ritual can also be done symbolically, imagining a Goddess or all women in the center of the circle, being healed and made safe from rape. Replace rape with loving pleasure.

7. Research and learn about alternative approaches to birthing and midwifery. Find out if you can attend a natural childbirth, and make a record of your experiences, feelings, and realizations. Look back and try to remember your own birth, or the times you may have given birth yourself. Give attention to the feelings you had (or your mother or child had), on both spiritual and physical levels. Think about whether it felt safe, sacred, frightening, joyful, painful, pleasant, ecstatic, mundane or magical. Books that can help are: *Conscious Conception*, by Jeannine Parvati Baker, *Spiritual Midwifery*, by Ina May Gaskin, *Reclaiming Birth* by Margot Edwards and Mary Waldorf.

8. Honor and claim some animal allies. You can select animals of air, water, earth and spirit; for example: an eagle for air, a dolphin for water, a cougar for earth, a phoenix for spirit. Animals that are presently endangered are especially appropriate. Ask the Goddess as Lady of the Beasts to help you find your animal allies. Before going to sleep at night say a prayer asking for dreams that will reveal your animal allies. Meditate upon this at your altar or in ritual circles, and open yourself to information about your animals. Books that can help are *Daughter of the Runes*, by Lindsay Badenoch, *The Way of the Shaman*, by Michael Harner, *Heart of the Fire*, by Cerridwen Fallingstar, *Medicine Cards*, by Jamie Sams and David Carson. Find and create rituals to help you get in touch with your animal allies. Learn their lessons and skills and what symbolic wisdom they can teach you by their behavior and habits.

Questions to Ponder

1. What Mother Goddesses are familiar to you, if any? Do you feel a special affinity with any in particular?

2. What is your relationship like with your own mother? How are you compatible or incompatible? Are there wounds in need of healing in this relationship? How might you remedy this? Do you share with your mother about your current sexuality, spirituality, politics or any other controversial subjects?

3. If you have been a mother, what has this been like for you? Have you felt fulfilled, happy, empowered, frustrated or rejected in your mothering?

4. Have you nurtured in ways other than in the capacity of a mother? For example, teaching, sympathetic listening, nursing, giving advice, giving guidance or direction, cooking dinner, community volunteer work, helping the elderly or the homeless? How was this for you? Did you enjoy it, feel invisible or unrecognized, used or appreciated?

5. How do you feel about your body?

6. What is your experience with menstruation? Have you ever participated in a moonblood ritual? If so, describe in detail. If not, would you like to?

7. What is your experience with birthing? Can you recall your own birth? How was it? Have you ever attended or helped at a birth? Human or other? What was this like for you?

8. How do you feel about abortion? Have you ever had an abortion? If so, how was

this experience for you? If not, do you know anyone who has, and how it was for them? Do you feel a need for healing in this regard, or to make peace with the unborn child?

9. What is your understanding of the politics of rape? Have you ever been raped? If so, have you done any healing work to release this trauma? If not, how do you feel you have been protected? Have you learned martial arts, "model mugging," or other such self-defense techniques?

10. Which of the powers of the Mother Goddess appeal to you? Do you see yourself developing in any of these areas? If not, why not? If so, how will you go about it?

11. Do you see yourself as a nurturing person? Do you feel a need for nurturance?

Reading and Other Resources

Lindsay Badenoch, *Daughter of the Runes*.
Jeannine Parvati Baker, *Conscious Conception* and *Hygieia, A Woman's Herbal*.
Kim Chernin, *In My Mother's House* and *The Obsession*.
Gina Covina, editor, *The Lesbian Reader*.
Elizabeth Gould Davis, *The First Sex*.
Marilyn French, *The Women's Room*.
Nancy Friday, *My Mother, Myself*.
Ina May Gaskin, *Spiritual Midwifery*.
Susan Griffin, *Woman and Nature*.
Nor Hall, *Mothers and Daughters*.
Esther Harding, *Woman's Mysteries*.
Erich Newmann, *The Great Mother*.
Vicki Noble, *Motherpeace*.
Marge Piercy, *Woman on the Edge of Time*
Adrienne Rich, *Of Woman Born*.

Jeannine Parvati Baker teaches a magnificent correspondence course on the mother mysteries. Write her c/o Hygieia College, Box 398, Monroe, UT 84754.

CYCLE 5

The Crone Goddess

Bony Old Crone
A-sittin' alone
A-stirrin' Her pot
And makin' a moan . . .

The Crone is the third and final aspect of the three-fold goddess. She is the dark moon, the wintertime, old age and knower of mysteries. She is associated with the color black, death, and transformation. The Crone time brings the harvest of experience, when we reap the accumulated benefits of all that we have learned. We begin our crone phase with the first appearance of silver hair, and embark with her fully with the coming of menopause. The Crone is a teacher or wise one, sometimes called the "wayshower" as she shines the light of wisdom for all to see. She passes her learning on to the next generations, thereby giving roots and continuity to cultural tradition. She brings patience and seasoning to the raising of children, healing of the sick, and the deciding of community issues. Some of her names are Hecate, Cerridwen, Kali, Baba Yaga, Wind Woman, Morag, Hag o' the Mill, and Morrigan. She is associated with the cat, the snake, and psychedelic herbs.

In myth and legend the Crone is often seen with her great black cauldron, stirring up brews for magical transformation or bringing the dead back to life. She appears in many fairytales with a gift of wisdom for those who will receive with reverence.

She is the fairy godmother who has just what we need to overcome the obstacles in our paths. She is the old woman of the woods, who lives alone in a humble cottage and can teach many secrets. In Native American tradition she is Wind Woman or Medicine Woman, and heals both body and soul with her knowledge of magic and herbs. In *The Sleeping Beauty* she is the thirteenth fairy whose rejection causes Beauty's hundred years of sleep. She is as necessary and integral to our lives as the Maiden and the Mother, and her loss is bitter and crippling.

In patriarchy no aspect of woman is as denigrated as the Crone. Man fears the old woman who reminds him of death and his own mortality. Her images of wicked witch, hag, ol' bag o' bones, etc., are signs that her power is feared and repressed. Because women are mostly valued for their nurturing and child-bearing powers in this culture, they are seen as useless when they become old. Widows, no longer sanctioned by respectable marriage or mothering, are rejected in many parts of the world. In India, the tradition of "suttee" is still practiced, whereby the wife of the deceased must throw herself upon her husband's funeral pyre. Older women are often isolated and ignored, shelved in old age homes, suspected of evil doings. During the Burning Times a single older woman was automatically assumed to be wicked, and in those days accusation was synonymous with condemnation. What a terrible blight we have cast upon the world in discarding the wise women who have so much to give! Think what communities would be like with magical crones in the schools, in hospitals, in the work place, presiding at rituals, giving psychic guidance to those in need, or counsel to political leaders. It is perhaps the Crone's power that represents the greatest threat to the patriarchal system, else why would it be the most suppressed?

Fear of the dark side of the personality is a key cause of this suppression. To be depressed, to have grief over losses in one's life, to feel sad or have problems or weaknesses—these qualities are not very acceptable in patriarchy. They are seen as signs of failure. We must be forever "on top of it," smiling and happy, and most important, productive. To admit the Crone is to admit the dark side of ourselves, which is like the dark side of the moon—the Crone's moon.

The Crone's moon is hidden, and cannot be seen shining in the heavens. It is significant that astronomers and astrologers call her the New Moon, thereby effectively ignoring the presence of the Crone. I propose to return the New Moon to the Maiden goddess, which is her proper place, and reinstate the Old Moon as the Crone's. We can therefore count our moon cycles from the first appearance of the slender waxing crescent, and acknowledge the darkening end as the time of the Crone. To acknowledge this time is to allow for the natural cycles of our being as we move through the ups and downs of living. This is a far healthier way of life where each of our phases is embraced and loved, rather than the ulcer-producing or cancer-producing approach of repression and denial.

Fear of death is another primary cause of the rejection of the Crone. In older cultures, life and death were known to be an endless cycle through which we pass again and again. Death is simply a kind of birth to be midwifed as carefully and lovingly as any other. The soul must be delivered, to emerge into the next world. The realm of the dead, or the "other side" does not have to be seen as a burning hell of torment or an end to being, but a beautiful place of rest and learning, and preparation for the next life. The more loving and accepting the myths of a culture are toward death, the more respect is usually given to the crone, and to the female in general. In our culture we have gone from images of the Last Judgment, replete with sin, guilt, fear and torment, to images of nothingness and cynical rejection of any spiritual hope of immortality. In Greek mythology the land of the dead, known as Hades, is a shadow place of ghostly souls, ruled at first by Persephone, Queen of the Dead, and later by Hades, the male god who raped and supplanted her. In Egyptian mythology, death is an elaborate ritual in which the soul undergoes special rites of passage to reach the other side. She/he must meet with Ma-at, a crone, who weighs all the deeds of the life just lived. This is a far gentler and saner evaluation than the Last Judgment theory. In Sally Gearhart's *The Wanderground* (which can be seen as contemporary myth), one crone selects and prepares her own dying ritual, and is attended and supported by her community. I always hope, when it is my time to go, that someone who loves me dearly will be holding me lovingly through my final moments, just as we wish our mothers to hold us when we are born.

Currently we can see the beginnings of a healthier approach to death. Elizabeth Kübler-Ross, a pioneer in the field of work with the dying, has introduced techniques for giving support and healing to those involved. Many of her patients have reported blissful out-of-body experiences and given clear proof that death can be a beautiful experience. The hospice movement is a very hopeful sign, offering places of peace and comfort to those at death's door, where they can be with their loved ones and find the nurturance that is crucial at such a time.

But we have a long way to go. Women in our society have a deep-seated fear of aging. It is conventional to lie about one's age as we grow older, and to reveal ourselves to be past 40 is a great risk. Wealthy women spend thousands of dollars on the removal of wrinkles, face lifts, hair dyes and so on, to conceal in any way the fact that they are growing old. Older women are tormented by feelings of failure, uselessness and being left out. And they are not simply paranoid; older women do get fired from their jobs and pushed out of participation in many ways. The myth of the overbearing "mother-in-law" whose involvement is irritating and unwanted is a source of much oppression toward older women. It is true that older people can become interfering and overly controlling toward young adults who are seeking autonomy. But this phenomenon would not prevail in a world where community input by seniors was the norm and a natural channel for their powers. Those families that do retain the grandmothers and great-aunts keep them in circumscribed and servile roles. "Old" has become synonymous with "ugly," and old people are considered no longer worthy of love or sexual desire. It is time we begin to see beauty in the aging process, the wrinkles that tell the stories of our lives, the silver hair that crowns us with honor.

The association of loneliness with old age is a common one. A wise crone understands the power that can be attained in solitude. She knows that all-one-ness is the true meaning of being alone, and is actually what the word "alone" is made of. There is a point reached in solitude when we no longer feel isolated because we have found our connection to all beings in the universe. In fact, it can be lonelier among people who do not understand this principle, than off by oneself among the trees and stars. True contact with the self in the deepest sense brings contact with all existence. This can be a wondrous experience, bringing great creativity and insight. The Crone teaches us to withdraw from the world to find peace and sustenance for our return journey into the struggles of living.

As in many empowering experiences, aloneness is stigmatized in the male-centered world. We are kept in herds, identifying with those outside of ourselves, and taught to be afraid of singularity. Many social benefits, such as insurance and credit, are denied to single people, and bestowed generously upon couples and families. To be strong and self-identified is frowned upon, and feared, especially in women. Rarely do we see people eating by themselves in restaurants, or attending movies alone. Those who do so are considered odd or unfortunate, deprived of company. Most go straight from the arms of their parents to those of their husbands, never experiencing a period of autonomy that is so necessary for the development of personality. Thus they remain childlike and dependent on others for most of their lives. Nowadays, many women are being deserted by their mates because their dependency has become a burden and a bore. They find themselves devastated and ill-equipped to deal by themselves with living in the world. Men, on the other hand, are given images of solitary heroes such as Superman and Perseus, and are encouraged from childhood to develop themselves as unique and of value as "rugged individuals." Speaking out in our own behalf is not acceptable for women. If we show pride in ourselves and who we are, we are considered egotistical. If we let our needs and desires be known, we are called selfish. The Crone can be a very healing image for us, affirming noble and creative solitude and the development of our unique selves.

Solitude is one of the doorways to the deep self. It is especially useful for the cultivation of our powers of concentration. Most of us, as we begin to grow in our magical abilities, find that we seek solitude more and more, as it enables us to focus intensely on the objectives of our spells and rituals without distraction. The more conversant we become with this experience, the less the glamour and superficial trappings of society attract us, and the more depth we seek when we do re-engage.

The Crone understands the power of silence. Many spiritual journeys include a period of silence, or teach its discipline. Some adepts take permanent vows of silence, for it opens up energies on the psychic level. Silence is the fifth step of magic, necessary during the gestation or formative period of our spell's workings for preservation and protection.

It is essential that we practice silence in our meditations and rituals, for it opens the door to universal consciousness. Significantly, many people are very uncomfortable in total silence, and will continually seek to fill it up with noise and other distractions. When we can quiet our conscious minds, we can listen with the inner ear to deeper voices.

The Crone is a knower of mysteries, secrets of existence, or hidden things. She presides in the dream worlds, guiding us through the unconscious labyrinths of our deep minds. She teaches us the symbolism of our dreams and helps us to understand and shape them to our choosing.

In the darksome cave of sleep

Flowing, floating down and deep
O Wise One, I move through Thee,
Thy imagery will ever wend,
Dreaming to the dreamer send,
Surrender
I now to Thee . . .

There are alternative cultures where dreaming is highly respected, such as that of the Ohlone Indians, where dreams are followed for guidance in life decisions. In Dorothy Bryant's *The Kin of Ata Are Waiting For You*, such a culture is pictured. The protagonist, a man from the violent patriarchal world, comes to live among these simple native people who dwell close to the earth and in tune with nature. He is afflicted by horrible nightmares for many years, and it takes much healing to bring him to "nagdeo," or good dreaming. The tribe of Ata gathers every evening to listen to the dreams of selected individuals. All will have their turn to tell of their stories and visions. Each morning they pair off and perform a simple ritual of sharing dreams. Any dream that is considered an important teaching is acted upon by the entire community.

What a contrast to our society, where the term "dreamer" is derogatory, and implies one who cannot cope with reality. How many of us have had compelling and visionary dreams that we then dismissed as "mere" fantasy. In the practice of magic we learn that all reality begins in the dream or inner worlds.

As in the domains of Maiden and Mother, we are seeing the beginnings of improvement in this province of the Crone. Sigmund Freud began a process of alerting us to the significance of dreams, and Carl Jung did important work in this area. Jung did extensive research in symbolism, and while many of his interpretations are patriarchal, he has gathered information of great value. He has introduced credibility to the concept of "archetypes" or universal symbols, of which the Maiden, the Mother, and the Crone are prime examples. Jung realized that dream symbols are messages from the psyche that give insight and instruction for our lives.

Along with the dream worlds, the Crone guides us into the land of memories and the past. Some say that memory is the only treasure we can carry with us into the next world. Our memories are precious indeed, teaching us the many lessons of experience, and aiding us in making decisions for the future. As the wheel of life turns again and again, we begin to recognize what we have known before, and to plan or rearrange our responses, so as to create a different outcome. Thus the Crone becomes the Seer or prophetess, as her skill in recalling the past guides her in divining the future. Here we can see why so many myths speak of the Fates, the three crones who spin, weave, and cut the thread of our destinies. They reveal that the past, present and future exist simultaneously, for in each moment of now we are reaping the seeds planted before, and planting the seeds of what is to come.

The image of spinster is often connected to the Crone. In its derogatory aspect of "old maid" it has been used to oppress those women who chose not to marry or bear children, or those who are forced by circumstance to remain single. Again we see the prejudice that loves only the wedded and birthing aspects of woman, and despises the singular independent woman who knows her own power.

Women and Goddesses have engaged in spinning, sewing and weaving since the beginning of civilization. On a practical level they are keeping the world secure by providing the cloth that shelters us. Metaphysically, spinning and weaving keep the universe together. As the spider pulls the thread of her web from her body, so do we pull out the invisible threads of our thoughts and energies from our psychic bodies to weave the reality around us.

Thread is not only fate, but also the meanings that help us to understand and interpret the Crone's realm. Ariadne's thread which guides us through the labyrinth of this study is a thread of meaning. In addition to earth/womb and tomb the labyrinth is also the deep mind, where we can become hopelessly lost or "insane" if we do not have a thread of understanding for the visions and demons we encounter there. It is when we can name or interpret such encounters that we regain choice and can return to the light of waking consciousness.

Here is where the Dark Maiden meets and merges with the Crone, residing in the underworld, in dark places such as caves and overgrown forests. She is there to receive us in death or sleep, to guide us and give instruction. She is also seen at crossroads, places of change and choice, and therefore, death. In selecting one direction, we must forsake the others, at least for a time. Our crone selves give us the strength and wisdom to make the best choices.

In life many choices have to do with understanding the difference between good and evil. The Crone is the best of guides in such decisions, for none knows as well as she what the outcome is likely to be. In Maiden-Mother-Crone or triadic thinking we can find liberation from the old patriarchal dualism of good versus evil. For two is an opposition, an either-or set of horns upon which we are perpetually torn or crucified. Two gives us the rigid model of man versus woman that denies the possibility of homosexual or bisexual love, and keeps us all in strictly prescribed roles. It gives us the trap of life versus death that keeps us forever clinging to the one in terror of the other. It gives us the "good versus bad" women, between whom man is forever having to choose, being trapped hopelessly with the former, or damned forever with the latter. And the same applies to good and evil, for each end of a polarity must imply the other, and so we are caught forever.

.Thus appears the linear "God versus the Devil" between whom mankind perpetually dances, repressing one or the other to the point of destructive explosion. "Black" is evil and "white" is good, which accounts for the rejection of dark-skinned people.

Maiden-Mother-Crone is a three, and therefore becomes a circle, through which we can flow around and around forever, as do all the natural rhythms of the universe. The foremost interpretation of this trinity is that of Birth, Life, and Death, a perpetual cycle of experience. The colors of this threesome are White (Maiden), Red (Mother), and Black (Crone). *The Crone is the missing link*, the last element of the triad that has been lost for centuries. By returning her to the picture, we transform women from the "wife/whore" to the sister/lover/solitary we are meant to be. We move from male/female to female/androgyne/male, and accept the possibility of passionate fire passing among them in any variety. We also allow for the female qualities of the male, who is born of the female and has breasts and traces of clitoris and vagina, who can cry, swoon, have visions, and be creative. And we move from good/evil to a circle of loving/beloved/loveless. Evil is now understood as a stuck place in the flow of this cycle. Those who "do ill" or commit evil are cut off from love, or caught up in guilt caused by the old linear way of thinking. A good healer knows that dis-ease is made of stuck energy, whether it be on the psychic or physical plane, and healing comes when flow is restored.

Crones understand endings, and therefore, banishings, or spells to rid ourselves of unwanted or stuck energy. There are three steps to a banishing spell. The first is Naming or diagnosis . . . the confrontation with that which we wish to banish. This requires courage and honesty, and the willingness to understand its nature. The second step is Elimination, or the commandment to vanish. This can be done in a variety of ways. The five elements are good keys to remember in banishment, even as they are in creation. An unwanted energy can be buried or physically removed (earth), dissolved or washed away (water), burnt up (fire), blown away or mentally/verbally dismissed (air), or psychically removed (spirit). The third step in banishing is Replacement, and like the Crone, is often overlooked. Something new must be created or invoked to fill the space left by the old form, for "nature abhors a vacuum," and the old will return if we do not create the new in its stead. Thus the Crone understands that all deaths are truly births.

On the following page is a diagram of the pentacle of the Crone, the dark pentacle of banishment. In the Mother lesson we learned about the manifesting pentacle, which teaches five steps of creation: Envision, Bid Welcome, Enact, Desire, and Manifest. Each step corresponds to its element of Spirit, Air, Fire, Water, and Earth, or Psyche, Mind, Will, Emotion and Body. Just as all things transit into being from the invisible to the visible planes, so we can reverse the process and undo that which we have created. This power is as essential as the Mother power. Without it, we can become caught in our creations, many of which we may find undesirable, or no longer needed. Banishing is especially useful in making necessary changes in the world, such as the elimination of war and rape. Since the Crone is effective in banishment, we can see why she is feared.

Some witches take the dark side a step further, and perform hexes or punishing spells. I do not encourage this practice. I am a firm believer in the Law of Three, which instructs us in the karmic principle of return—all energies which we send out into the universe will rebound back upon ourselves three-fold, or at least in kind. Awakening the dark side is a great responsibility, and banishings are best when performed "with harm to none." However, we do have the right to protect ourselves from those who would harm us, and sometimes it is necessary to perform Bindings, or spells to stop someone from destructive behavior, or Healings to change their consciousness. But spells involve our own energies, and in a way we become a part of the one upon whom we are casting our magic. Interference with free will is wrong, unless in dire emergency. In most cases it is best to have the consent of all involved, and always it is best to confine our magic to only the most positive and beneficial purposes. We become what we hate, even as we become what we love, and people who spend all their energies grappling with the evils of the world may find that they eventually become the very things that they rail against. This is why it helps to keep in mind the cardinal rule, "Harm none, and do as thou wilt," especially when considering a banishing spell.

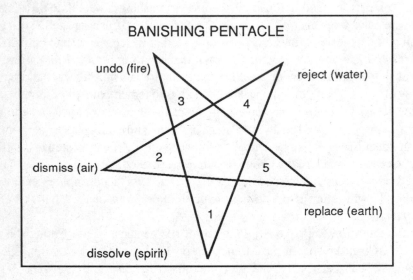

We can become Crones in our uses and understanding of the five elements of creation:

Spirit Crones are conversant on the psychic planes, easily traveling in and out of our bodies, telepathic, clairvoyant, prophetic, divining, understanding the cycle of Birth, Life, and Death and the rituals thereof, skilled in casting spells and the uses of dreams.

Air Crones have profundity of thought, quickness of tongue, are adept in poetry, myth and language, the composing of verbal spells, the eloquence of asking aid from forces and elements. The Air Crone is also a Cutting Crone, for our minds are like cutting edges that sort and separate our thoughts. Naming a thing separates it out from the rest of creation. Cutting is also criticism, pruning, saying no, discipline. When we reach the crossroads of our lives, such as the time of passing from child to adult or maiden to mother, we must cut the umbilical cord of our habits on the old path in order to be free to embark upon the new. The cutting Crone is sometimes called Atropo, the third of the three Fates in Greek mythology.

Fire Crones possess understanding of the secrets of fire and energy. They know the ways of conserving, storing and spending energy wisely, using vital forces with care and discrimination, rather than scattering them carelessly and wasting them. Fire is also kundalini, sexual fire, which a wise crone knows how to channel and direct for desired purposes. Fire is will, in which the Crone has achieved mastery. And on its simplest level, fire is our natural source of heat and light, and can be used for magic in many ways. A seasoned witch usually knows how to build and sustain fires, as well as to contain them safely, and extinguish them when necessary.

A Water Crone is no longer a slave to her emotions, nor does she repress or deny them. She is adept in her relationships with others, knowing enough detachment for an overview, and enough caring for compassion. She knows that her desires are sacred and worthy of cultivation and fulfillment. The Water Crone looks deep into her reflection in underground waters. When the water catches the light of the moon, she is there to find insight and divination.

A wise Earth Crone knows her body, knows the earth, is adept in health care for herself and others who seek her aid. She is familiar with the seasons and methods of planting and cultivation, herbology, and agriculture. And she is also wise in ways of money, seeing its connection to human love and service and precious human energy. She is sensible, practical, and dependable, keeps her promises and understands commitment, knows how to work as well as play.

Crone Tales

I strongly urge you to cultivate an interest in stories of crones, of which there are many, and also to read the works of crones, of which there are more appearing today. Tillie Olsen, Ella Young, Jane Ellen Harrison, Mellow Rye, Elsa Gidlow, and Brysis Buchanan are a small sampling of the names of sister crones whose writings we can benefit from and enjoy.

Cerridwen, one of the Welsh or Celtic goddesses, appears in her crone aspect in many tales. She is especially known for her Cauldron of Inspiration, named Aven, in which she stirs a magical brew for a year and a day. This elixir is prepared for a chosen poet, who, upon its consumption, becomes knowledgeable in many things. He will be able to understand all languages, including those of the birds and beasts, and the meaning of all existence. In one tale, the child Gwion is set to stirring the pot for Cerridwen, while she attends to other affairs. By accident a spray of juices flies out of the cauldron. One drop lands upon his thumb, which he automatically puts into his mouth to soothe. Immediately he becomes one who is enlightened and aware of the past, present and future of all things. Cerridwen knows instantly what has happened and sets out in pursuit of Gwion, much enraged, and fit to kill. Gwion flees, turning himself into a hare. She becomes a greyhound, and he dives into the water, becoming a fish; she becomes an otter. He flies up into the air and becomes a bird, and she becomes a hawk. He becomes a grain of wheat on the floor of a barn, and she becomes a black hen and swallows him. Later, back in her own form, she discovers that she is pregnant, and eventually gives birth to Gwion as her own heroic son, Taliesin. He grows up to be a great magician and bard of the land. In Celtic myth there are many such tales which indicate, in my opinion, how women were tricked into giving over their mysteries to men, thus allowing the birth of patriarchy.

In legends of the Bannock Indians of Idaho, a young girl disappears into the sky. As retold by Thelma Hatch Wyss, she meets Wind Woman, who lives with a tribe of people there. Wind Woman is a healer or Medicine Woman, and teaches Star Girl all she knows of herbs and magic. She takes her into the forest, showing her how to find and harvest the wonderful healing plants, and back at the tepee, how to prepare and use them. Later, Star Girl returns as an avatar to her own people to pass this wisdom on. (See explanation of Aradia in Teacher's Guidelines.)

Hecate is perhaps the best known of mythic Crones in our part of the world. She is said to await travelers at crossroads, and to be a guide into the underworld, or the land of the dead. She has been called the Queen of the Witches and is often invoked by members of the craft. Hecate is an important figure in the famous myth of the Kore, or Persephone. In the patriarchal version she is the one who witnesses Kore's abduction, and informs Demeter and Zeus of what has transpired. In my updated version, Hecate is the one encountered by Kore in the underworld, who teaches her the three mysteries of Immortality, Creation, and Dissolution . . .

Kore:
Aaaaaaaamaaaaa! Aaaaaamaaaaa! Aaaaamaaaaaaaa!
I am bereft, alone!
Demeter, Mother, Goddess-me
I reach out in this darkness
To find thee not. Who what am I
With thy presence gone?
O I am lost in endless longing,
invisible, unseen
To the World unknown, unheard, unfound
Undone . . .

Crone:
Not so my little one.
Fear not—you have yourself
For all and ever . . .
Let grey wisdom's arms enfold thee now,
Thou art here because thy time has come

> To learn the secrets of the soul.
> Let go of life and earthly love for now
> And I will show to thee thy greatest lover . . .

Once Persephone understands these mysteries she is transformed and is now Kore, her own adult person. She is ready to return to the upper world and the arms of Demeter, with whom she is now an equal. All life is renewed with this reunion, and spring returns to the earth. Thus we can see the importance of reinstating the Crone as the transforming principle that brings renewal and the continuance of life.

All of us are, or will be, crones one day. We can choose to work on our expectations and images of old age, and do what we can to ensure that we grow old with the grace of the goddess. We do not have to resign ourselves to ill health and loneliness, or dreary conformity, especially if we begin now to develop positive images for the future. By the same token we have the option to connect with crones living in our communities. We can reach out to them, make friends, find the love and the wonder that are there to be shared. And if we are crones, we don't have to isolate ourselves; we can reach out too!

Ideally, the crone times of our lives are the most fulfilling and powerful of all. In an enlightened society we would be consulted for our wisdom, relied upon for our psychic attunement. The appearance of silver hair would be a crown of honor instead of a sign of shame.

> To be old is to be kissed
> By the moon . . .

As we get closer to the end of our lives the veil to other worlds gets thinner; out-of-body experiences are more likely to happen. We may be able to see auras, perform telepathic communication and prophesy. Our spells will be more effective after all the years of practice. This can be a time of liberation from the pressures of ego development and responsibility associated with the Maiden and Mother stages. Instead of impoverished "shopping bag ladies" scrounging in garbage pails for a grim survival, let us have councils of beloved crones who are trusted and respected. Now, when the movement of woman is stirring on the planet, is the time to begin.

But we needn't be rigid about the appearance of our cycles. A maiden can mother, a mother can be wise, a crone can be nurtured. From a child can spring pearls of wisdom, and at that moment the crone is present. As women we can always be in touch with all our phases at any time in our lives.

Ritual to Heal and Honor the Crone Self

To be performed at midnight, at the dark of the moon.
Be sure that you are completely alone and undisturbed.

Fill your cauldron with dried sage for burning. Dress all in black, drape your altar in black, and use a black candle. Carve the Crone's pentacle into the candle.

Before the ritual, spend a few hours, and if possible a full day and night in total solitude. Eat a meal by yourself, savoring the peace and the food. Meditate upon the crone, the dark side of your nature, the sorrows and fears you have known. Keep notes in your journal, and record all significant realizations. Go out and find a crone stone for your altar.

Light your candle at midnight, and seat yourself before the altar. Light the sage and inhale some of the smoke, letting it pass over you and fill your aura. Sage is an herb of wisdom, appropriate to crone rituals. Copy and color the crone image provided with this Cycle, cut it out, and place it upon your altar. Do some deep breathing, and let yourself go into trance; close your eyes. See yourself entering a cave and descending down long, dark passages into the bowels of the earth. Let yourself see your own special Crone there, awaiting you beside her cauldron of wisdom and transformation. She helps you into the cauldron where you are bathed, healed, liberated, renewed. (Healing: Mother; Liberation: Maiden; Renewal: Crone.) She gives you three gifts: a crystal for insight, a sickle blade for cutting, and a dried snake's skin for transformation. You tuck these into your robes, saying:

> Hecate, Cerridwen, Kali, Dark Moon Woman
> Wise One who knows the secret ways
> I receive thy gifts in joy and in solemnity
> Always will I treasure these
> Always will I remember their teachings
> Many thanks. Blessed Be.

The Crone embraces you, kisses you on each of the cardinal points of your body, embraces you one more time, and sends you on your way. See yourself ascending up through the passages of the earth, out under the night sky, and back to your position before the altar.

When you open your eyes, sit in silence for a while, gazing upon the candle, the flame, the image of the crone. Take the image into yourself, become one with her. Open yourself to any insights or prayers that may come.

When you feel complete, ground the energy and snuff out the candle.

Binding and Banishing Spell

When we Bind and Banish, we are saying "No" to those behaviors and phenomena that we wish to rid ourselves of, whether they be within ourselves, in our circumstances, or emanating from others. We can do this "with harm to none," as opposed to the concept of hexing, which is not always harmless. This is a Crone function, one of the many lost aspects of ourselves and the Goddess that we need to reclaim.

This spell came to me when I was asked to help create some ritual for our Native American sisters and brothers at Big Mountain. It is made to put an end to the negative energies that threaten them, and therefore threaten us all. It can also be adapted or rewritten to apply to anything you may wish to banish or bind. The rite can be done either alone or with a group.

On light-weight cardboard, draw and write images and names of the evil you wish to bind. For example, a broken tepee, to represent the uprooting of people from their hearths, an image of the Earth with a crying face, an image of a man with a cross x-ing out his heart to show a closing of the heart, words like Greed, Scarcity, Separation, Irresponsibility, Disrespect, and so on. Crumple this cardboard up into a loose ball.

Wind black yarn around the image twenty-one times, chanting as you bind, once for each line of the chant:

> With the thread of the crimes
> of your own design
> I bind your evil
> Three times seven times
> I bind you from Behind
> I bind you from Before
> That you'll hurt my people
> Never ever more
> I bind you from the Left
> I bind you from the Right
> I bind you by Day
> And I bind you by Night
> I bind you from Below
> I bind you from Above
> That you may ever know
> The laws of Life and Love
> I bind you with your own
> Good conscience Within
> And so let this magic
> Unfold
> And spin . . .

Tie off the ends of the yarn with three sturdy knots to seal the spell. Next burn up the wrapped image in a good, crackling, need-fire. [From the Old Saxon, nied-fyre, that is, a ritual fire produced in the ancient way by rubbing two sticks together, considered particularly effective in extreme times. If you find it impossible to kindle your fire this way, you can simply rub two sticks together as symbolic gesture.] Chant until it is thoroughly burned:

> Goddesses of darkest night
> Send our troubles all to flight
> Burn them in thy sacred fires
> And replace them with our hearts' desires!

Once all negative energy has been removed, do a positive visualization to replace it. For example, an image of people dancing in rainbows.

Be sure to cast a strongly protective circle around all participants before you begin.

Lady With the Lamp

On the path of evolution
Comes a lady with her light
Trudging up the hill around her
Come the people in the night
As she climbs her lamp grows brighter
'Til the people turn and sigh
"Turn down, turn down your lamp, dear lady,
We can't take it; it hurts our eyes!"

But the lady never falters
For the people cannot know
She follows her inner lantern
Must not lose its golden glow
"Come with me," she calls so softly,
"Don't fear the light; 'twill strengthen you,
"Always I must stumble slowly
"Towards my inner light, like you . . ."

"So we all will climb the mountain
Into day and into night
Ever reaching, ever growing
Ever on through dark and light,
Some of you will pass me quickly
Some of you will throw a stone,
Some of you will climb beside me,
Sometimes I must climb alone . . ."

"Some of you will reach out to me
Asking for a helping hand,
If you fall and if you stumble,
I will help you, if I can,
But if you cry to turn my light down,
This, my loves, I cannot do,
Turn down, turn down my lamp; no never!
Though my love for you is true . . ."

On the path of evolution
Comes a lady with her light
Trudging up the hill around her
Come the people in the night,
As she climbs her lamp grows brighter
'til the people reach and cry,
"Shine on, shine on your lamp, dear lady,
We can make it, by and by . . ."

A song written for the Hermit card in the traditional Tarot,
transformed to "The Crone" in Shekhinah's and the Matriarchal Tarot.

This is the Spirit Crone, which replaces the Hermit in older decks. She is the Teacher, the Wise One who knows the secrets of Life and Death, third aspect of woman and the triple Goddess. She shines the Light of Understanding into the sacred Darkness of our Mysteries.

Suggested Projects

1. Perform and record the Ritual to Heal and Honor the Crone Self on page 104. In preparation, see if you can find actual artifacts to represent the gifts She will give you on your journey: a crystal for insight, a snake skin for transformation, and a crescent blade for cutting. Or find three things you would like to have as gifts from the Crone and substitute them. Bless them before the ceremony and keep them on your Crone altar. You might want to tape the journey-part of this ritual ahead of time and play it back for yourself while in trance. When you come back to this world, hold and meditate upon each of the three gifts for a time, and visualize ways in which you will use them in the future.

2. Research and write about Crone Goddesses, as suggested for the Maiden and Mother Goddesses in Cycles 3 and 4.

3. Study crones and crone qualities in life and literature, as suggested for the Maiden and Mother Cycles.

4. Create a dream journal for yourself and keep it beside your bed when you are sleeping. Record your dreams as soon as you awaken, even if it's the middle of the night. Many dreams are fleeting, and will be forgotten quickly if they are not captured in that sleepy-waking state. Watch for patterns in your dreams—symbols and situations that reappear. Get to know your own dream language. Before falling asleep ask the Goddess to send you strong and helpful dreams. Read up on dream work and dream therapy, and techniques for affecting destiny through conscious dreaming. Some books that can help are: *Dreams and Dream Groups: Messages from the Interior*, by Renée Neu (The Crossing Press), *Waking Dreams*, by Mary Watkins, *Dream Work*, by Jeremy Taylor, and *Dream Weaving: A Journal for Dreamers*, by Mary Sojourner.

5. Do some exercises to help you recall your past lives. (An excellent book that can help with this is *Mother Wit*, by Diane Mariechild.) Record your findings in your *Book of Shadows*. Make note of past-life experiences that may still influence you today, what they have taught you, what strengths you have gained or obstacles overcome.

6. Make friends with a crone or do something special for one that you know.

7. If you are a crone, have a Croning! This is a ritual to celebrate your cronehood.

Much like a birthday, a Croning is designed to honor and delight the crone who is being celebrated. Tell your friends and loved ones all the fantasies you have ever had and ask them to do some of them for you. Have a massage, for example, be taken out to a lavish dinner, be showered with gifts and attentions, have poems read to you and written for you, songs sung to you, attention given to whatever stories you wish to tell or thoughts you wish to share. Ask all your friends to help you heal yourself, to cast off old wounds and fears, and to replace them with affirmation and love. Ask everyone to tell you all the good things they see in you, and how much they love you. Have them support you in facing old age and death and any fears you may have about these inevitabilities. Ask them to help you look back on your past and forward to your future. Menopause is a good time to have such a ritual. If you are past menopause, have one anyway!

8. Put on a crone-oriented event such as a Goddess workshop on the Crone. Invite crones to speak, teach or lead, or discuss in panel format issues of importance to Crones.

9. Start a "Crone Counsel" in your community, for people to come to for advice, healing, mediation, knowledge, information, help with decisions.

10. Do some "crone magic." Banish or bind the patriarchy or other social ills such as rape, power-over, war, oppression, poverty, child abuse, rejection of crones, fear of old age, fear of death. See the "Banishing and Binding Spell" on page 105 for guidelines on this.

11. Make a detailed picture of your ideal old age, and cast a spell to make it happen. Do the same with images of your death and life on the "other side." Plan your next life and how you would like things to be next time around. Write up all of these in your *Book of Shadows* for future reference, rituals and spells.

Questions to Ponder

1. How do you respond to the image of hag or crone? Are you attracted? Repelled?

2. What Crone Goddesses are familiar to you? Are there any that you identify with or feel close to?

3. Do you consider yourself a crone? If so, how do you feel about this? If not, do you look forward to old age?

4. Do you know any crones, personally? Are they strong, healthy, happy and

fulfilled? Are they good role models for your own cronehood?

5. How much solitude do you have in your life? Do you enjoy being alone?

6. Do you usually sleep well? Do you dream? Do you remember your dreams?

7. What are the ethics of binding, banishing, and hexing, in your opinion?

8. What is your definition of evil? What do you think is the best way to deal with evil?

9. How do you feel about death? About silence? About darkness?

10. Are you aware of being affected by the energy of the dark moon or Crone's moon?

11. Do you believe in a hereafter? In life after death? In reincarnation? In spiritual immortality?

Reading and Other Resources

Mary Daly, *Gyn/Ecology*.
Sally Gearhart, *The Wanderground*.
Timothy Leary, Ralph Metzner, Richard Alpert, *The Psychedelic Experience*.
Raymond A Moody, *Life After Life*.
Shekhinah Mountainwater, *Myth of the Kore*.
Tillie Olsen, *Tell Me A Riddle*.
Valerie Worth, *The Crone's Book of Words*.
Thelma Hatch Wyss, *Star Girl*.

Broomstick, A crone journal. San Francisco Women's Center, 3543 18th Street, San Francisco, CA 94110.
The Kelpie's Pearls, children's fantasy.

INTERLUDE

This marks the end of Gathering, the First Passage of *Ariadne's Thread*. You have learned a little about the background of Goddess-awareness, developed some ethical concepts, built your altar, and spent some time with the Three Aspects.

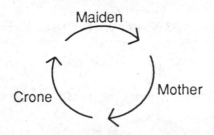

Let us pause a moment, before moving on to the Passage of Spinning, and consider these three archetypes as a continuum.

Wholeness in Goddess thealogy and magic can be understood as loving interconnections among the Maiden, the Mother and the Crone. Wholeness in Goddess sociology can be defined as happy interaction among women of all these age groups. And wholeness in Goddess psychology can be understood as harmony and flow among the three aspects within us. Patriarchy has served its interests by dividing these, and forcing them into separate worlds. As a result we often find ourselves torn apart both inwardly and outwardly. On a social level we can see that women of different ages are segregated from one another. Cosmologically we tend to see Birth and Death in severed opposition, rather than as a continuing movement of Birth, Life, Death, Rebirth. And, we find that within ourselves we have either lost touch with or been wounded in one or more of the three aspects.

Over the years of working with women on these issues, I have noticed some fairly consistent patterns. While not true in every case, I have found that the Maiden material can be the most difficult to deal with, while the Mother Cycle closely follows in its degree of intense confrontation. The Crone, on the other hand, often comes as a welcome relief. Women say that this is their favorite of the three, that they love the Crone and are happy to make Her their own. I think there are profound reasons for this, the main ones being that society has co-opted and distorted the first two archetypes to its own ends, while the third has simply been repressed. Not that this is any less damaging in the long run, but it has had the saving virtue of leaving the Crone relatively intact. In Her hidden underground role, we can discover Her in Her pure and original form. The Maiden and the Mother, I'm afraid, have come in for much more distortion, because patriarchy must have these parts of woman in order to survive.

I feel, therefore, that we have a right to be gentle with ourselves about these things, and realize that ultimately we are not to blame. So please, don't beat yourselves up, dear sisters, if you discover, for example, that your Bright Maiden has been weakened, or you have been trapped in the Mother role, or your Crone is nigh invisible. Once we become conscious of these problems, we are in a position to begin the healing. In any case, we can always use them for magic, and this too will help to heal us.

Another point to consider is that we do have our innate personalities, and even in a healthy, natural state some qualities will tend to be more pronounced than others. The Goddess has not stamped us out on a conveyor belt, and the variations are beautiful—something to be celebrated. There will always be Amazons, Mothers, Priestesses, Lovers, Teachers, Leaders, and so on. In working to heal and understand ourselves, we can also look at these qualities in terms of a five-fold system, as shown in the little star chart on page 66 in the Maiden Cycle. By calling them Daughter, Lover, Mother, Sister and Grandmother, we can create a useful grid for making peace with the many qualities and gifts a woman can have. Thus we move from the Three to the Five, and can see both cycles as interconnected symbols of manifestation. When we understand their turnings, we can begin to spin a woman-loving world into being.

The essential thing to remember is that all three aspects are powerful and beautiful and necessary in their original forms, and freedom lies in having choice to be or not to be any and all of them at will. In addition, now that you know the threefold Goddess, you can continue to get acquainted with Her magic, and the many ways She can support you in your rituals and spells.

And so, congratulations! You have bravely faced the first Mysteries, and made your way through this part of the labyrinth. If you like, you can light a candle of thanksgiving on your altar, and give praises to Ariadne, Themis, Mnemosyne, and Idea—and any other Goddesses you wish—for helping you thus far.

Now, if you are ready my sister, take up once again the ball of Ariadne's thread, and set it to rolling into the next passageway . . .

> O red and rosy mother
> O black and velvet crone
> O silver crescent maiden
> In thee my soul is one . . .

SECOND PASSAGE

SPINNING

CYCLE 6
Luna

"The witch is the product of the love between the earth and the moon."
                                                            —*Mar-Garet Andreas*

Since the beginning of civilization, and before, the moon and her energies have been associated with woman. The moon is mysterious, for she appears and disappears, as if by magic. She is the maiden, the mother, and the crone, as she cycles through crescent, full, and waning phases. She pulls the tides of the earth and the blood tides within us. She teaches us the phases of our own personalities, as we cycle from inward-turning aloneness to outward-moving accessibility. The moon is the Sun of Night, the eye of the goddess that opens and shuts throughout the month. She is one of our most visible signs of the passage of time, and one of the best guides for keeping our calendars. Her energies are deep, moving into psychic and unconscious realms.

Luna, Selene, Shing-Moo, Fleachta of Meath, Brizo, Brigit, Mona, Arma, Aphrodite, Hecate, Eurynome, Doris, Lucretia, and Diana are some of the many names given to the goddess of the moon. In many cultures moon and goddess were synonymous, representing the feminine principle, the source of life, woman, instinct, and the great round of birth, life, and death. The attitude of a culture toward the moon is usually an indicator of that culture's attitude toward women. In patriarchy we have moved from a lunar approach to a solar approach to reality. Time, once measured by moon cycles, is now measured by the path of the earth around the sun. The moon, representing the unconscious, Eros (or Aphrodite), the intuitive mind, emotional and psychic energies, has taken a back seat to the sun, which has come to represent the everyday, rational thought, the practical world, and the male logos. A cosmology has resulted that places sun and moon as opposites, and male and female gods as opposite, mutually completing the universe. Since the male is seen as dominant, the sun has gradually ascended to power, and the moon has been placed in the background.

This symbolic set-up results in the subjection of women, and of the female energies in general, including those present in men. Both women and men in patriarchy have learned to cultivate the "solar" qualities and to repress those associated with the moon. Thus much of our healing lies in the cultivation and acceptance of these dark "feminine" forces. The call to attend to these qualities in ourselves and the universe is one of the most essential messages of the current feminism. In many ways we have come to know this through our reflections on the Crone and the Dark Maiden. The more we have suppressed these aspects of ourselves, the more dangerous and troublesome they have become. Patriarchy is actually built on this suppression, naming the "male" solar forces as good, and the "female" lunar forces as evil. The result becomes the projection of the "shadow," or destructive expressions of the psyche. Much suffering is caused by this artificial division in our personalities, for the depths of the psyche are the source of passion and dreams and forces of life that are essential to our well-being.

As discussed earlier, it is my theory that this polarization of male and female forces has led to the dilemma we find ourselves in today—a universe composed of opposing energies, one of which must dominate and conquer the other. Oppositions are linear, leading to either/or thinking. Thus the first hierarchy—male over female. From this follow all other oppositions and hierarchies of our society, such as race, class, us versus them, god versus the devil, and so on. For a man the healing comes in embracing and accepting both ends of this opposition and learning to move through them cyclically. This is his union or immortality—the perfection of self. Hence the myriad fairytale endings where prince and princess or god and goddess—the symbols of these inner opposites—unite.

For a whole society, however, I feel it is necessary to go a step further. Magic, when it is truly powerful, grows out of a deep connection to the feminine principle, not as one end of a pole with maleness on the other end, but as all-encompassing, self-creating woman/goddess birthing all that is (see the Great Round illustration). For women are not part male; we do not have a Y chromosome, and we are the older race. Herein lies the difference between women's mysteries and all other mystery systems. In this approach the sun, the earth, and the moon are seen as inclusive and female. Now the solar energies belong to the maiden, particularly the Amazon. Active energies are as female as receptive energies. This is the ancient archetype that precedes all male/female archetypes, and it is against the background of this understanding that we will consider the forces of the moon in this study. For as women, we can only truly liberate ourselves when we no longer have to be defined in terms of the male *in any way*. Let me reiterate: this is not a rejection of men. All life is sacred; the goddess loves all her children. But women and the world are starving and dying for the loss of our particular mysteries. We are the roots of humanity and affirming this is an essential reclamation. When Women's Mysteries are celebrated widely again it will be a great healing for the planet and everyone on it.

In learning to view ourselves in this autonomous way, it is very helpful to learn about the sun's female mythology. It was a great surprise to me to find that there are many sun goddesses, some still worshipped today! Amaterasu of Japan is honored by followers of the Shinto religion, for example. At certain times they set up mirrors to catch her reflection, as part of their ritual of sun worship. In one legend it is said that she retreated into a cave at wintertime, and was enticed out by one of her

THE GREAT ROUND, FEMALE PSYCHE GROUND OF BEING

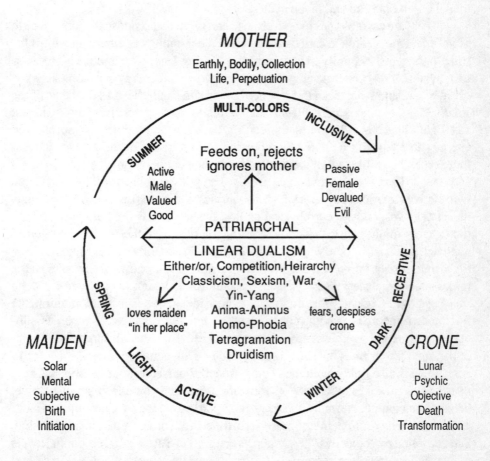

MOTHER
Earthly, Bodily, Collection
Life, Perpetuation

MULTI-COLORS

INCLUSIVE

SUMMER

Feeds on, rejects
ignores mother

Active
Male
Valued
Good

Passive
Female
Devalued
Evil

PATRIARCHAL

LINEAR DUALISM
Either/or, Competition, Heirarchy
Classicism, Sexism, War
Yin-Yang
Anima-Animus
Homo-Phobia
Tetragramation
Druidism

loves maiden
"in her place"

fears, despises
crone

RECEPTIVE

SPRING

DARK

LIGHT

MAIDEN
Solar
Mental
Subjective
Birth
Initiation

ACTIVE

WINTER

CRONE
Lunar
Psychic
Objective
Death
Transformation

119

priestesses dancing before the open cave mouth with a mirror. When Amaterasu caught sight of her own reflection, she was so dazzled that she forgot to hide, and so brought the return of spring.

Actually, if you think about it, the sun and moon both have their tides or phases. The sun has both a shorter and a longer cycle—the daily round and the yearly. She has times when she is closer to us and times when she is father away, just as the moon does, and thus creates our seasons. She has her hidden periods of night and her accessible periods of day. And so a complete consciousness of time and energy cycles must include awareness and appreciation for the sun and the moon, as well as the earth and stars. Stonehenge and other circles of standing stones in Europe have been found to work with both sun and moon cycles.

There are cosmologies in both science and myth that propose the moon's birth as an emergence from the earth, and the earth's beginnings as emergence from the sun. This suggests a family triad of mothers, moving from grandmother, to mother, to daughter, and is concordant with the intimate triad of energy pulsating between earth, moon, and woman. In this cosmology the sun can be seen as the heart of the solar system, around which all her planet-children revolve, receiving nourishment and light. The moon becomes the earth's daughter/sister, bringing specialized energies that have been altered by reflection from the sun. Each has its place and function in the whole, not in opposition but mutual cooperation.

Mello Rye, a well known shaman crone and priestess who has combined Celtic with Native American consciousness, also proposes such a cosmology. In her view, the earth corresponds to our physical bodies, the sun to our fires or spirit, and the moon to our minds. This is a very interesting alternative to the "logos versus eros" approach to sun and moon, which divides the mind in half. Giving our minds entirely to the moon opens up a realm of wonderful possibilities, for now we can unite all the layers of consciousness, sub-consciousness, intuition, dreams, alpha, beta and delta minds, etc. We might say that the crescent or maiden moon is instinct/intuition, the full mother moon is waking consciousness, and the dark crone moon is sub-consciousness and psychic states. We can freely move or cycle through these layers of the mind as our lives unfold, all equally valued, all equally female.

Luna is also linked with the feeling aspect of ourselves, our emotions. These rise and fall in waves much like other natural tides, and come from an instinctive, unconscious source. The more polarized, male and "solar" we have become, the more "science" oriented. Unfeeling approaches to the cosmos predominate in our thinking. Science, ruled by "objective" perception, is our god. The deeper and emotional levels of perception are often repressed. The intelligent aliveness of the universe and everything in it is relegated to the world of non-sense. Because of this we often become alienated from the light of the everyday world, ruled by sterile objectivity. When we begin to discover the moon we find a world we have longed for, that validates many parts of ourselves that we may have been afraid or ashamed of. In quantum physics it has been found that there really is no such thing as objectivity, because any observed phenomenon is always affected by the observer, even a mechanical one. Subjective reality is no longer at odds with objective reality. All the stuff of matter is alive and feeling and intelligent.

In her wonderful book *Woman's Mysteries*, Esther Harding points out that we are sorely lacking in emotional education. We are not taught how to deal with our feelings, particularly the more intense ones that emerge with birth, death, passion, and separation. While ancient cultures developed ritual for this purpose, our own teaches repression and avoidance of most deep-feeling states. We therefore never know the release or epiphany that ancient rituals afforded our wise predecessors. Instead, we become intellectual robots, brilliantly computing data for the production line, and never feeling or experiencing our deeper selves. Typically, in modern society, the results are cancer, heart attacks, high blood pressure, and so on.

People who could be called "lunar" are deep-thinking, vulnerable, emotional, passionate, sensitive, psychic, highly intuitive, sensual, dreamy, passive, soft, instinctual, spontaneous, wild . . . all qualities associated with the female, all repressed to some degree in patriarchy. To the extent that a culture is in touch with the moon it will generally be supportive toward these qualities. In our culture "male" qualities, often called "solar," are considered desirable: aggressiveness, action, courage, effort, competition, pushiness, conquest, heroism, mastery, physical strength, pragmatism, materialism, and so on. We are a society with its psyche severed neatly down the middle. Men and women take up their positions on either side of this split, with occasional cross-overs like macho women and wimpy men. Everyone suffers because only union can bring wholeness and peace. Men are taught to be tough, "go-get-'em," and make it to the "top." Women either support them on their way up, or climb on the "go-get-'em" bandwagon themselves. Those who remain on the lunar side are victims of the brutish solar house, closeted, afraid to risk, obedient or underground, tending to be powerless in the everyday world.

Harding validates the cyclic nature of our personalities. She suggests that we attune ourselves to our tides or inner seasons of light, full, and dark, and learn to organize our lives accordingly. Nor Hall in her book *The Moon and the Virgin*, also goes into this subject in depth, describing the female personality in relation to the phases of the moon. Both Hall and Harding are Jungians and therefore somewhat limited by their male/female perspective, but their research into the dark side of self is invaluable.

The dark moon of the self is a period of withdrawal from the everyday world. It offers an opportunity to commune with ourselves and tap the creative potential therein. To return to this way of life necessitates leaving the "rat race" approach, and validating slowness, inwardness, and being here now.

In "primitive" cultures women withdrew from society during the time of their blood flow. This was the origin of the concept of "taboo," which meant something set apart because it was numinous and sacred. Later it came to mean something dangerous or accursed. Menstruation is a vulnerable and very psychic period for us, and much power can be regained by honoring it. Before industry and electricity, women would usually bleed in unison at the dark of the moon. Withdrawal was a ritual—a communal event among sisters, when they would bleed into the earth, catch their blood for the ceremonies, exchange mysteries and mutual support.

The concept of Lunaception, as developed by Louise Lacey, stems from the discovery that light affects our fertility cycles directly. It was found that when women slept in total darkness, having a soft light only three nights of the month, they could control their ovulation and bleeding time. Apparently, when we had natural moonlight and no interfering artificial light, the time of full moon was the time of ovulation, and the time of dark moon was blood-time.

Because of the periodicity of women's blood, the earliest calendars were kept by observing its ebb and flow. Animal horns found in Paleolithic digs had moons carved into them in series from crescent to full to dark. These rhythms were our first method of measuring, which led to myriad sciences we benefit from today. Thus true magic and true science are one. Moonflow is the root of every cultural advance.

"She who bleeds, yet does not die..."

Because women could grow thriving crops by fertilizing them with their blood, birth children and measure time, they were most awesome in the eyes of men. This was especially so before the discovery of the sperm's role in procreation. Men can only bleed by piercing the body, or by other violent means.

The vulva was a source of reverence in such cultures, and many statues and drawings have been found showing goddesses with sacred genitalia prominently shown. All ritual was born of worship of this holy source of life and knowledge. The skirted altar was the lap of the Mother, the bowl of wine or blood her all-giving womb and vulva, the cup of milk her sustaining breast, the wafer or bread her nourishing grain grown from her earthen body.

As men became jealous of such awesome power they gradually denigrated the blood and bodies of women. In the process, they developed their own blood rituals of imitation: circumcision, sub-incision (slicing the penis lengthwise to give it a bloody, vaginal appearance), crucifixion, and surgery. Women were excluded from rituals and denied access to the mysteries they had invented. Myths of the accursedness of women's bodies and blood became men's weapon of conquest.

Today we are faced with the overwhelming task of healing the great damage done to women and society. Much of the terrible suffering our sisters experience at moonflow can be traced to the psychic injuries inflicted by these phallo-centric attitudes.

Blood is more than fertilizing; it is also vibrant with psychic energy. Nothing seals a spell as bindingly as blood. It is healing and affirming to keep track of your bloodflow in relation to the phases of the moon. As the moons go by, you should begin to see a pattern. Some women bleed at the full moon, some at the new; find out your own cycles. You will also become sensitized to your fertile or ovulating times, your ups and downs in emotion and energy throughout the month.

The moon affects the fertility of women and all other life on earth as well. Farmers have been planting by the moon as long as we can remember. In the dark unknown womb of night comes new life, lit by the germinating, fertilizing light of the moon. Her special, deflected light sends ultra-violet rays that have been found to influence the growth of plants. It has been said that parthenogenesis is accomplished by exposing our bare bellies and genitals to the light of the full moon. Many animal species mate according to the cycles of the moon. Full moon time is known as an intensely fertile time. This is the instinctive energy of Aphrodite, honored in the past with love ritual by many nature-oriented people.

Today full moon time is often crazy-time. Crimes are committed, "lunatic" states are expressed. In the patriarchal Tarot the Moon card is said to mean insanity or mental instability. What was once honored with sacred love ritual has become explosive or destructive energy.

On the Line of Dualistic Patriarchal Values
(see p. 121)

SOLAR	LUNAR
Good	Evil
Light	Dark
Male	Female
Sterile	Fertile
Clean	Dirty
Sacred	Profane
Reason	Madness
Life	Death
Control	Chaos
Hard	Soft
Aggressive	Passive
Productive	Lazy
Neat	Messy
Smooth	Hairy
Angular	Undulant
Left Brain	Right brain
Efficient	Artistic
Objective	Subjective
Above (Higher)	Below (Lower)

This list on the previous page is a small sampling of the belief system we are dealing with in present society. The split begins as a thought form, and can be traced to simple symbolic structures. (For example, the yin/yang symbol of the Orient, the sun/moon dichotomy of the alchemists, the anima/animus theory of the Jungians, the god/goddess universe of the Druids, and the tetragrammaton of magicians.) In all of these systems there is an attempt to honor and give equality to both ends of the polarity, but do not be deceived. While pretending to create a world supportive of the female, they are still perpetuating the dichotomy, and thus the role stereotypes that oppress us all. This, I'm afraid, is the fatal flaw of even more advanced movements such as Neo-Paganism, modern Witchcraft and the New Age spiritualities. Liberation can only come by returning to the Great Round, as shown in the diagram on page 119.

Studies of the Druid faith of Celtic countries reveal that their rituals concerned women's bodies and were synchronous with sexual and seasonal tides, as well as the tides of ocean and earth. They knew of ley lines or magnetic flows within the earth itself, and built their henges and monuments along them. Community ritual was timed with the alignment of all these magnetic and tidal forces, as well as inward ones of mythic inspiration. These practices reveal much wisdom and some adherence to the principles of female energy. However, as Druidism comes to us in a male/female dichotomous form, we can only conclude that corrupting influences had already taken hold.

Moon Magic

The energy of Diana Moon arouses us to ecstasy, to inspired states of intoxication, vision and passion. She is the wild and freedom-loving huntress of the forest of night, pictured with animal companions that represent her instinctive forces. She takes us out of our everyday selves, inspiring us with creative purpose. Luna pulls on all the elements within and around us, both physically and psychically. Our mother earth actually bulges out into space when Luna pulls on her water and substance. The air and other atmospheric vapors are also pulled cyclically by the moon. These are the tides of blood, water, thought, emotion, sexuality, and the psyche. They have their peaks and valleys, and magic has much to do with attuning ourselves to their rhythms.

We talked about the power of pull in the Maiden Cycle, in relation to the dark side. "Push" or assertiveness is a solar, active energy, necessary for getting things done in the everyday, waking world. "Pull" is the magnetic energy of magic, for it is with pulling energy that we draw to us that which we desire. This most ancient and hidden power of woman must be recovered if we are to know ourselves in fullness. Receptiveness and pull are intimately connected. To receive is to swoon is to orgasm is to surrender, as the moon surrenders and reflects the light of the sun. Pull is the realm of enchantment that draws us to seek and wonder at its magic.

Much of the women's movement is about "push," or the recovery of influence in the everyday world. This is important, for being trapped in the receptive is a severe limitation that has made us victims. But we must not make the mistake of discarding the powers of pull.

> Moon goddess pull
> Moon goddess pull
> Pull away to freedom
> Pull away to freedom
> Pull away
> Pull away . . .

Many women cannot swoon or surrender or feel deep emotions, or have orgasms. They are blocked by fear, by social disapproval, by the desire to avoid victim patterns. The receptive woman is often scorned in feminist circles, almost as much as she is among patriarchal men. The receptive man is anathema to the macho, dominant male. As women we are somewhat more fortunate than men in this regard. Many of us have had the freedom to develop our psychic and emotional aspects and in these areas are much freer and healthier than most men. Because we have cultural roots in a long standing tradition, we can feel that the moon is truly ours.

Surrender is essential to trance states, and trance is a basic ingredient of all magic. You cannot go into trance without relaxing and letting go. It is in trance that we program the deep mind with images and affirmations. This is the stuff that spells are made of. The moon illuminates this inner mind, sometimes called the realm of Faery. This is the fantasy land of our imagination, the dream world, lit by Luna's soft and silvery light. This light stimulates the imagic plane. Image-making is magic making is imagination is fantasy that becomes reality.

Witches learn to cast their spells according to the phases of the moon. Luna fertilizes the psyche, opening connections with the subconscious and alpha mind, and thus adds juice to the casting. A witch knows she is not omnipotent in and of herself; she knows that greater effectiveness lies in aligning herself with the forces of nature, thus becoming a channel or conductor of energy.

The new or maiden moon is a time of beginning. Just as plant seeds are put into the earth at new moon, so thought seeds can be introduced into the psyche for the casting of spells. New moon is birth time, planning time. Luna stimulates the imagination, bringing up fresh new images, ideas, revelations, insights. At the new crescent you might ask for aid at the beginning of a project, for a fresh approach.

The full or mother moon is ecstatic, celebratory, overflowing. It is harvest energy, abundance, the manifestation of what was planted at maiden time. This is a time to make love, or give special acknowledgment to the love goddesses. Full moon is a good time for community ritual, for sharing magic with others, for orgiastic celebration, sensual delights, and nourishment.

The dark crone moon is a time of endings. Banishings are best done at the dark moon. Withdrawal is the essence of this time along with incubation, transformation, divination, prophesy. Witches go deep within at the dark moon, to find thought forms that may be causing illness or difficulty. They ask for release and dissolve the unwanted images, to be replaced with positive ones at the next new moon. This is also a good time for dealing with old business, matters of the past, tying up dangling threads.

Remember that in this system the new moon is the first slender crescent, and it is by her that we count the beginning of the cycle. The dark moon belongs to the Crone.

Moon Time

It is a fact that there are thirteen lunar cycles every third solar year. This is where the power and magic of the number thirteen originates. Patriarchal months number twelve, so that they can be easily ordered into four seasons and a polarized view of time. "Thirteen is bad luck," is a slogan of patriarchy. (Covens traditionally number 13.) Being an odd number, it is more random, not so easy to control. It is also more cyclical and dynamic, for you cannot build it into a square without sacrificing one moon. The thirteenth moon in patriarchal time is called the "blue moon," and you can find her as an "extra" full moon if you study a conventional calendar.

Learning to keep time by the moon is one of the basic building blocks of the craft. There are many moon calendars from many parts of the world. I have chosen to work with the Celtic tree calendar for a number of reasons. It is relatively accessible for one thing. Its European origins give it resonance in this place and time, and its connection with Celtic magic is very attractive to me. The tree lore is magically useful, too. Each moon is linked to a particular tree that serves a seasonal as well as magical purpose. There is also language connected with each cycle, for the first letters of the tree names are an alphabet.

There are thirteen consonants in the alphabet, each of which goes with its month and tree. There are also five vowels, which are applied to five solar holy days. We can see how the ancient Celts linked their mysteries with language in a very graphic way, for to them poetry and myth were essential ingredients of magic, and trees were seen as the Goddess' thoughts. From this base grew the bardic tradition, which later deteriorated into the troubadours of medieval courts. If you listen to the folk music from that part of the world (the British Isles) you may notice the incredibly haunting melodies and mystical lyrics of love and the supernatural. There is much goddess energy in this culture, even today. We will go into the poetry and language aspect of magic in our Cycle on the Muse. For the present, let us concentrate on the matter at hand—that of seizing the time.

Julius Caesar officially abolished lunar time reckoning in the year 45 B.C., introducing his Julian Calendar, which was later transformed into our current

Gregorian Calendar. In the Fifth Century A.D. the Council of Constantinople officially declared the cyclic view of the universe as heresy! Governing powers usually have a hand in the development of calendars, particularly when conquering new territory. Our own 12 month calendar is noticeably male, with its months named after Roman emperors or gods, and numbered in linear fashion. This is one of the most effective ways of ordering society, and controlling people's lives. Our familiar 40-hour work week and nine-to-five workdays have become the hallmark of our lifestyles and the way we value our use of time. Day is good, and should be filled with productivity and action; night is for sleeping only.

> Early to bed, early to rise
> Makes a man healthy, wealthy and wise

Months are rows of squares on our calendars, having little relation to the moon. A return to the goddess is a return to cyclic rhythms of time and the great harmonies of the universe. This is revolutionary in every sense of the word.

This moon calendar is provided so that you can reflect on some of the significances given to moon cycles in a magical, female-oriented tradition. It is not complete, however, without the solar holy days or stations of the year, which we will discuss in Cycle 8. As you develop sensitivity to the moon's cycles and changes, you will find your power and magic growing rhythmically and naturally through time.

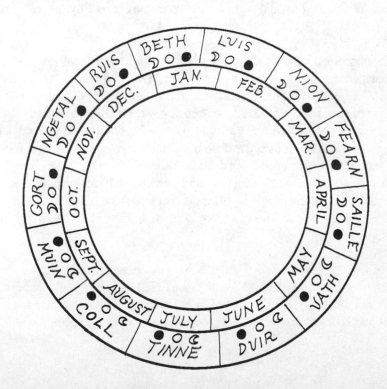

Birch Moon Beth B

The Birch is the tree of inception or beginnings. She is self-propagating, and so is an excellent symbol for the goddess as Her own source. Her branches are considered to be protective and can be used for dispelling evil influences. When a lover offers a branch it means, "You may begin." With the Beth or Birch moon the wheel of the lunar year rebirths and we can plant our seeds or plans for the coming cycle.

Rowan Moon Luis L   (Also known as Quickbeam or Mountain Ash)

With the Rowan Moon, life forces quicken and take hold. Seeds are forming beneath the wintry earth. The red Rowan berries are said to give the sustenance of nine meals, and to heal the hurts of the wounded. Rowan wands were once used to detect the presence of metal and spirits can be summoned over fires made of her wood. She is known for her oracular powers, and thickets of Rowan have been found in abundance near the sites of standing stone circle.

Ash Moon Nion N

> "I am the Ash, I am Nion
> A life and water tree . . ."
> —Anna Michaud

The watery Ash moon is a time of rains and floods. The wood of the Ash tree is said to give protection from drowning. Yygdrasill, the Scandinavian mythic Tree of Life, was a great Ash tree, beneath which the goddess as the fates or Norns gave prophesy and justice. She is used to conjure rain and "court the flash of lightning."

Alder Moon Fearn F or V

The Alder is deemed a most sacred tree, connected with the powers of fire and the ability to withstand the corrosive effects of water. Her wood is used in the making of charcoal. When cut she bleeds a red sap much like human blood. Legend has it that a cruel man once cut down a great Alder tree that was inhabited by a tree spirit. She screamed and bled as she fell, and a terrible curse fell upon the man. He was haunted by the hag Famine, and was forced to devour greater and greater amounts of food with no satisfaction. Finally he turned and devoured himself. This is a clear symbol of the patriarch's abuse of his goddess-source and eventual self-destruction. The Alder Moon heralds the coming of Spring when the maiden goddess is reborn. The waters of winter recede as the energies of fire swell.

Willow Moon Saille S

The graceful Willow is a most magical tree, long associated with muses, witches and goddesses of the dark underworld. Willow is called Helice in Greek, and gives her name to Mount Helicon where the nine Muses dwell. Thus she is particularly akin to the moon and states of divine madness, ecstasy, and psychic intensity.

Hawthorne Uath H

Hawthorne or May is a cleansing moon, a time of chastity and purification. Our sister ancestors would clean out the temples at this time and abstain from sexual contact in preparation for the orgiastic rites of Summer. In Ireland, Hawthorne grew over sacred wells and it was considered most unlucky to cut them down. Though Graves tells of all the negative associations with this tree, mostly in regard to "enforced chastity," I propose that earlier symbolism associated the Hawthorne with Lesbian love. The flower is said to have a strong female scent . . . perhaps a more ancient chastity had to do with women's abstention from sex with men during the Hawthorne Moon?

Oak Moon Duir D

This is the seventh moon, central to the number 13, with six on either side. The Oak is the sturdiest tree, and forms the pivotal power of the year. Duir means door—the sacred dolmen opening ruled by Cardea, goddess of the hinge, who looks both forward and back in time. Thus we can approach this moon time as an opportunity to assess our progress at mid-point of the cycle and plan out our intentions for the six remaining moons. The Oak is the Queen of Trees, whose roots grow as deeply into the earth as her branches reach overhead, symbolizing equal power in conscious daily life and the subterranean worlds of magic. Her wood burns hot and slow and is best for sustained fires.

Holly Moon Tinne T

> "The holly and the ivy,
> When they are full grown
> Of all the trees that grow in the wood
> The holly bears the crown."
> —Traditional

With the Holly moon the year begins to wane once more. Holly means "holy," and is said to be a tree of protection and defense. Native Americans believe that the thorns of holly leaves repel evil spirits, and plant Her around their homes. Holly is always green and flowers anew at this time, making her a good symbol of sustained life in the face of the waning sun.

Hazel Moon Coll C

Over the Well of Connla the Poet grew the magical Hazel tree, whose nuts contained all wisdom. As these fell into the water, they were fed upon by the great Salmon who lived there, and was consulted for insight and prophecy. The year becomes wise as she grows in experience and cycles toward her darkening time. Hazel is the moon of wisdom, numbered nine and sacred to the Muse.

Vine Moon Muin M

"Wine is the true drink of poets," says Robert Graves, who found out that its original purpose was holy. The transformed grape induces altered states that give birth to poetic revelation and divine ecstasy. Today we know wine as a social ritual, and have almost lost its ancient uses. Muin is the vintage moon, a time of joy, exhilaration, and wrath. It is also the second harvest moon, containing the Autumn Equinox, often called the Witches' Thanksgiving.

Ivy Moon Gort G

"I die where I cling," is the message of the Scorpionic ivy. She represents fidelity, friendship, and attachment. Gort is a darkening moon, approaching the high holy day of Hallowe'en, when the death of the year is honored. Winter preparations are in progress; the goddess turns within.

Reed Moon Ngetal Ng

This is the twelfth moon, the number of established power, preceding the death moon numbered 13. Reeds have musical connections in their use as wind instruments. As scepters, they are symbols of command.

Elder Moon Ruis R

The Elder tree grows beside water and keeps its fruit well into December. It has been considered unlucky by those who fear witches, who were said to use its branches for their magic flying brooms. The flowers and inner bark are purifiers and are used for therapeutic purposes; also the flower is useful in love and friendship spells. The Elder moon helps us to accept and understand the Crone aspect, as we meditate on the necessity of endings in order to have new beginnings.

Moon Tales

The Magic Flute is a patriarchal rendition of the opposing forces of good and evil, represented by the Sun King and the Queen of Night. Night is Dark is Death is Scary is Female. Day is Bright is Right is Reason is Male. The Queen's daughter falls in love with the Sun Prince. The Sun eventually wins the battle over possession of the princess, and this is seen as a "happy" ending. The Queen of Night fades out in despair, having lost her daughter to the forces of patriarchy or the "real world," or Hades—however one looks at it.

The old English folk tale *The Buried Moon* tells how the moon goddess decides to come to earth one night. But when she gets here, she is seized by demonic beings who bury her under a heavy stone. The people are increasingly distressed as she ceases to appear in the night sky. One crazed man remembers her silver light shining in the woods, and tells the local wise woman. This crone instructs the community to search for certain signs and they will find her. Sure enough, they find the stone deep in the forest and roll it back to let the Moon Goddess spring back up into the sky in all Her splendor.

Like so many an innocent folk tale, this legend has deeper layers of meaning that are not so innocent. The moon as the power of night is overwhelmed by the fear of people who attempt to bury her "beneath a stone." But her light is essential, and they must eventually seek her out and return her to her proper place in the psyche. The wise woman, or crone, is her own dark side, through whom her rebirth can be discovered. This legend can also be interpreted as a description of the natural lunar cycle, and the yearly as well, for Luna is closer to us in Winter, and farther from us in Summer. In addition, I like to think of this tale as a symbol of the suppression of female forces in patriarchy, and their subsequent rebirth that we are witnessing now.

The moon pulls the deep tides of our bodies, minds and spirits. She is ever changing yet ever remaining, the reflection of our womanly essence and powers, reminder of the quickening, waxing and waning of all things.

Suggested Projects

1. Research a Moon Goddess that you feel drawn to. Discover Her names, stories, attributes, deeds, plants and creatures that are sacred to Her. Make your own Moon Goddess myth and write it in your *Book of Shadows*. Draw upon the imagery of Maiden Moon, Mother Moon, and Crone Moon. Some books that are helpful for these projects are: *Lost Goddesses of Early Greece*, by Charlene Spretnak, *Moon Magic*, by Dione Fortune, *The Book of Goddesses and Heroines*, by Patricia Monaghan.

2. Research and learn about the scientific lore of the Moon: her seasonal and monthly patterns, the directions she moves in, the energy she emanates, her eclipses and pulls upon the earth, her ties of blood and water, her relationship to the sun. Discover theories about her origins and speculate on how she came into being. A book that can help you get started is *Moon Moon*, by Ann Kent Rush.

3. Perform a moon ritual. Select a warm full-moon night when you can be naked in her light. Take a "moonbath" and feel her energy washing and entering you. Do a rite of "drawing down the moon." Do this by standing in Her light with feet and hands spread apart. Raise your hands in a cup-like position in order to receive Her energy. Breathe deeply and send a grounding cord down from the base of your spine into the earth. With your breath and your imagination, pull moon energy into yourself with your in-breaths. See yourself filling up with silver, so that silver light glows in all your cells and radiates out into your aura. Make wishes on the Moon, and give a moon-offering such as pouring some of your moonblood into the earth. Do a moondance. When you feel complete, breathe the energy into the earth, ground and center yourself again, and say thank-you and farewell until next time. Record the experience in your *Book of Shadows*, and make note of your wishes. Keep track of them later, when they come true.

4. Make a moonwheel as shown on page 127, with the 13 tree months. Keep in mind the calendar project coming up in Cycle 8, in case you will wish to put these wheels together. Make it large enough to accommodate tree or leaf drawings, Goddess-lore, magic, seasonal information, plant lore, moonphases, and anything else you might wish to add later. Set your wheel up with a marker, so you can turn it as the moon turns and keep track of her movements in the sky.

5. Save some of your moonblood in a bottle in the refrigerator, and use it to water a special plant. Keep notes over a few moons and watch the effects your blood has on

the plant.

6. Do a ritual alone or with your sisters to heal and reclaim the powers of your moonblood. Begin by writing or sharing blood stories, such as first menstruation, how it feels to bleed, whether or not it is pleasant or painful, and why, how you have been treated by friends, lovers or family when your bloods arrive or the subject comes up. Use the Beltane ritual on page 171 in Cycle 8 for ritual guidelines. Bring some of your saved moonblood and make blood drawings, write promises to love yourself, to love women, to honor women's bleeding. Sign these in moonblood. Have the ritual when you are bleeding and bring sheets of paper or cloth or cardboard to sit on and make "blood prints." Use these for divination, and see if you can interpret them like ink blots.

7. If you have not already done so, use the Moon Code on page 35 to keep track of your cycles in your daily moon calendar. Add your own images to the Code as needed. Keep watch over the moons and notice at what phases your blood comes, when you ovulate, and if you are more or less psychic or emotional at certain moontimes. Be aware of Maiden Moon, Mother Moon, and Crone Moon, and how these affect your energy, emotions, and activities.

Questions to Ponder

1. How important has the moon been to you in your life over the long term? Were you tuned in to Her energy as a child? Did you hear stories about Her? Do you feel close to Her now?

2. What faces or figures can you find in the face of the moon? Have you ever "swooned into the moon?" Taken a moon bath? Slept in moonlight?

3. Do you notice any emotional or psychic effects in yourself at different moon-phases? Do you bleed at a particular moonphase?

4. Do you still bleed? Regularly or not? How do you feel about your moonblood? Are your moonflow periods pleasant, painful, both? Do you notice any changes since embarking on this study?

5. What are the connections between women's pain at moonflow and the ills of patriarchal society?

6. Do you experience the moon as female? The sun? How do you respond to the cosmology of Sun/Earth/Moon as Grandmother/Mother/Daughter?

7. Do you see reality in dualistic terms (i.e., male/female, solar/lunar, life/death, good/evil, and so on), or cyclic terms, or both? None of the above?

8. Do you feel you have been conditioned to accept a view of solar qualities as male?

9. Can you imagine yourself as solar, fiery, assertive, independent and strong in a female image? What Goddesses come to mind as symbols of this?

Reading and Other Resources

Dion Fortune, *Moon Magic.*
Robert Graves, *The White Goddess.*
Nor Hall, *The Moon and the Virgin.*
Esther Harding, *Woman's Mysteries.*
Louise Lacey, *Lunaception.*
Ann Kent Rush, *Moon Moon*
Diane Stein, *Casting the Circle.* See for moon rituals.

The Lunar Calendar, Nancy Passmore. I use this beautiful calendar and recommend it highly. Based on the tree calendar shown here and Robert Graves's invaluable contributions. Luna Press, Box 511, Kenmore Station, Boston, MA 02215.

The poem fragments below and on page 125 are excerpted from *The Buried Moon*, an epic ritual piece by Shekhinah. They are available on the tape *Songs and Chants of the Goddess.*

She shine silvery
Silvery up
Silvery up to the darking sky
She silver fly
She silver fly . . .

CYCLE 7

The Muse

This, the seventh Cycle, is a fitting place to meet the Muse. Seven is the central number in the cycle of thirteen, and is a pivotal position in the sacred year of thirteen moons, ruled by the Oak Tree in the Celtic Calendar. As the Oak is the center of the year, so the Muse is the core of magic.

The Muse is our universal symbol for creative inspiration. Whenever we receive an idea, a vision, a new poem or song, an invention or ritual, She is present.

The Goddess as Muse has been a long-standing tradition, both before and during patriarchy. In Wales she was called Cerridwen or Caridwen; in Ireland Brigid; at Delos in Greece, Brizo; at Parnassus, the Nine-fold Mountain Mother. During the Bronze Age and earlier the Goddess was worshipped from Palestine to Ireland as the Triple Moon Goddess, sometimes called Leucothea or the White Goddess. Her role as Muse, with the ability to inspire all acts of creativity or generation, was adored. In Greek culture she survived as the Nine Muses, placed under the tutelage of their sun god, Apollo, though her powers were much weakened by then.

> "...In Greece there were nine: Kleio, she who tells stories; Euterpe, she who pleases well; Thaleia, she who blooms; Melpomene, she who remembers; Terpsichore, she who loves to dance; Erate, she who is erotic; Polymnia, she who invents; Ouramia, she who dwells in the heavens; Kalliope, she who loves to sing."
>
> From *Dreaming*, by Nett Hart and Lee Lanning

In Wales the Muse also became nine-fold, emerging in miraculous birth from the sacred waters of Cerridwen's Cauldron of Inspiration. This very cauldron later became the famous Holy Grail of Christianity.

Before the severance of creative acts into separate parts, the making of art, poems, babies, metal crafts, food, calendars, science, magic and ritual were all seen as essentially the same, and all inspired miraculously by the Goddess herself. As patriarchy relegated her to ever more obscure corners of social function, the Muse became devoted primarily to artistic expression.

It is no coincidence that the artist today suffers terribly from isolation from her/his community, not to mention the total repression of creativity in most people! The tradition of poetic suffering is inherent in a society that suppresses or exploits the powers of the Muse. We have so lost touch with Her principles and traditions that we have nigh forgotten how to describe Her.

Society tempts the artist in many ways, with glamour, power, money and acclaim. Should she turn toward these glitters, she will lose the Muse, and her art will be reduced to entertainment, sales production, and support of male values. The muse has been put in chains, made to serve the principles of Apollo, god of intellectual, rational thought. Art forms that come out of this tradition support authoritarian governments and deny individual freedom. True muse-inspired art can never do this, for it is born of magic invocation that springs from deep within the soul.

People who opt for Apollo's way may think they are fulfilled, but even among these the star system prevails, singling out a few for recognition and leaving the many by the wayside. For the most part, creative expression is not owned by the common folk, but is relegated to those "stars" who appear on distant stages or in slick packages. Behind the scenes are the business interests that manipulate and control the entire phenomenon. In a twisted sort of way everyone still worships the Muse, often paying substantial sums of money to attend their stars. Even in the women's movement the stage has become the new altar. Reverence and respect are given to these few stars, while the goddess is often still denied.

Robert Graves tells us in his book, *The White Goddess*, that the origin of all poetry was magical invocation of the goddess. Its utterance was ritual, its purpose both practical and spiritual, its language entwined with myth and nature. As a poet, he gives full allegiance to this tradition, saying that a true poem must express Her, and the more excellently she is portrayed, the better the poem. To be a poet requires full time serve to the Muse who, he believes, gives joyous creativity as well as great suffering. The modern poet must be willing to risk the latter for the sake of knowing the glories of the former.

Graves's view of the poet's role is profound but painful. He equates the sacrifice with that of the sacred kings who died each year for the Goddess, which he reminds us, is the Perennial Theme of all true poetry. This is, so to speak, a kind of poet's religion. Graves discovered a mythos that is female and nature-oriented. It has a definite moral code, exacting discipline, and roots in a genuine and incredibly old white-skinned European folk tradition. As such it is extremely valuable to present-day magic makers, though its more violent attributes are subject to careful scrutiny.

Of all the five races on earth, the white race is the most alienated from its cultural roots. Perhaps it is poetic justice, since white peoples have been perpetrators of oppression upon all others. White women and their Goddesses were the first to be conquered, then recruited as the helpmates of the conquerors in their ensuing exploits. They are therefore the last to recall and uncover their lost Muses.

Sisters reading this who may be of any of the five Black, Brown, Red, Yellow or White Tribes, please bear with me. My intention is not to perpetuate racism, but to heal. The patriarch has cut us apart and nothing serves his interests so well as to keep us that way. But the wound reveals the cure, and sometimes the process of examination can be painful. In my ideal vision I see us all as a Great Rainbow Tribe of five colors, equally loved by the Goddess, equally deserving of our magic and our muses. This is not to say that I seek a "melting pot" of assimilated cultures where individual identities become blurred. What I imagine is that each tribe retains its special traditions and memories, while all five maintain mutual acceptance and understanding.

But this cannot be done until all the holes in the tapestry are mended. As a white-skinned priestess I cannot be fully healed until I can reclaim my white-skinned roots. I take instruction from my sisters of other cultures, who have reclaimed their shamans, medicine women, healers, gurus, brujas, gypsy fortune-tellers. I see their magnificent legends and histories being revived today, bringing a return of racial pride and identity that is strengthening and healing. There is a saying, "A nation without a dream will die." But no matter how much I adore and absorb the beauties of my sister tribes, a part of me is still dying inside. I look around me and see that the magic of my own roots is still suppressed, the most suppressed of all. Sibyls and witches are despised, myths considered nonsensical, folk traditions superstition. In lieu of these I am told to worship the almighty dollar and the latest football hero. I see the spiritual starvation of my young white sisters and brothers, which drives them to the feet of the gurus and teachers of other nations. There is much spiritual sustenance and inspiration to be found there, but it can never be complete.

And yet the wisdom of our past is available to us today to guide us in healing the split with the Goddess-as-Muse. What we have rejected as "primitive" is actually an essential, visceral understanding of the darker side of existence—the spirit realm, the mysteries of birth, love and death. In fairytales, in mythology, in folksongs and folklore, in the inspirations of muse-possessed women such as Sappho and Isadora Duncan, we can find the balm our spirits so sorely need. There is still great creative energy in the standing stones of Ireland and Wales, in the ancient spiral caves and mounds of England. The legends of Greece and the British Isles are a compelling and haunting legacy. (See book list at the end of this Cycle.) Many fairytales and myths give wise explanations of deep psychological problems in simple, symbolic lan-guage. (Carl Jung has written much on this subject.) In folksongs we can find amazing knowledge, from herbal lore to historical events, to human understanding, not to mention the great range of poetic and musical qualities.

The Goddess comes in all colors. I realize that every nation has lost Her to one extent or another, and none of us are exempt from the process of healing and reclaiming. We are all sisters under the skin, and patriarchy has infected all female origins. So let us validate the search of every woman for her cultural roots, even as we extend our hands in mutuality. Let us dust off the statues of the muses of all nations and learn to love our own as well as those of one another.

It is ironic that the most central aspect of magical knowledge is also the most difficult to describe. The Muse's inspirations are manifested in a mysterious, ecstatic impulse of truth and wonder that cannot be explained in linear prose. All my development as a writer and teacher of magic is actually a web of bridges between this infinite creative principle and you, the receiver. Yet the impulse itself is beyond philosophical verbiage, beyond technical explanations of so-called "impressive expertise." I have only added on these layers in order to reach you. Take them away and you will find a simple primordial figure of a woman with her mouth wide open, pouring forth songs that come from . . . does anyone really know where?

> My voice is a bird
> In my throat
> That longs to fly
> Into Some One's
> Willing ear . . .

How can I say what cannot be said? It is the dilemma of finding the way to bridge the gap between rational, linear reality and that other realm for which we do not yet have a complete language. The closest we can come is through poetry.

> Gently truth will touch you when she comes
> No loud fanfare blares her forth
> But in the deepest space of silence
> Angels' silver calls embrace the earth . . .

The Muse Goddess and Her Elements

> Who has seen the wind?
> Neither you nor I,
> But when the trees bow down their leaves
> The wind is passing by . . .
> —traditional

In Celtic myth there are many tales of harps awakened to song by a mystical wind, or inhabited by the singing spirit of a woman. One folk ballad called *Binnorie*, tells of two sisters who are both wooed by a young knight. He must wed the eldest, but he secretly loves the younger woman. The older sister, filled with jealousy, pushes her sister into the sea. A harper happens by, and makes a harp of her breastbone and strings it with her golden hair.

> A harp he made of her white breastbone
> Whose sound would melt a heart of stone
>
> The strings he framed of her golden hair
> And lo! Of itself it played an air . . .

The spirit of the drowned woman has taken up residence in the harp, and sings the truth of her murder. Though this tale is told in a patriarchal setting, the presence of the goddess can be felt in spine-chilling beauty. This is the test of a poem or any art form; if the Muse is present you will feel her, and be enchanted.

> *A riddle:*
> Discover what it is.
> The strong creature from before the Flood
> Without flesh, without bone,
> Without vein, without blood,
> Without head, without feet . . .
> In field, in forest . . .
> Without hand, without foot.
> It is also as wide
> As the surface of the earth,
> And it was not born,
> Nor was it seen . . .
> *Answer: The Wind*
> (From the *Book of Taliesin*,
> translated from the Welsh by Lady Charlotte Guest)

In Irish myth there is a legend that the wind sang through the ribs of a whale's skeleton on the shore one day. And this was the breath of the Goddess vibrating the bones, making the first music that ever there was . . .

> Air witch
> Throat full of song
> Spinning sweet spells . . .

Breath, or wind, is synonymous with inspiration and magic in mythologies the world over. In pagan Ireland, the four cardinal winds were held to bring the qualities attributed to their directions: The West Wind brought food and clothing; the North Wind death and resurrection; the South Wind fruit, honey, and music; the East Wind brought gold and endless riches. (It is interesting to compare these with the magical uses of the directions, as found in European witch traditions, and Native American traditions.) In the Judaic Genesis story, god breathed life into Adam. In Christian mysticism, the Dove breathed god's seed into the womb of Mary. In Greek myth, the Goddess Eurynome was impregnated by a fertilizing wind. The yogis teach us the great importance of developing and appreciating our breathing.

In India, the Hindus believe in Voc or Vac, Goddess of the spoken word. From her we get such words as voice, vocal, invoke, invocation. Her mouth is the birthplace of sound and meaning, equated with the transforming cauldron, the ever-giving vulva, the all-quenching cup, the mystery-giving cave. This powerful female image is one of the few we can discover that affirms the muse-abilities of women.

> Though they are only breath
> Words that I command
> Are immortal
> —*Sappho*

Speech is a truly wondrous thing. It begins in the mind with images created by the I-magi-nation, is carried through the lungs on the wind of our breathing and out of our mouths as articulated sound. The process of creation has begun, as shown by the five-pointed witches' star, beginning with vision or image, gaining the density of air (thought and speech), water (desire and courage), and fire (will and action) on its way to becoming reality. Our foremothers understood this as the Power of Naming, and gave it deep respect. They knew that to name a person or thing is to control it, for it then must behave according to the nature of that name. This is why many deities had secret names, known only to those who upheld their rituals. There are many legends wherein the enemies of certain tribes would defeat them by discovering their gods' secret names and speaking them aloud in spell-battles. Individuals had secret names as well, given them at birth, and perhaps known only to those closest by blood or ritual. To give one's name away was to give one's soul away.

Today feminists are discovering the power of naming. By applying it to the sources of their oppression, such as "sexism," "rape," "power-over," or "phallocentric," they are taking important steps toward liberation. It is very difficult to extricate oneself from a situation that one cannot describe or understand. To name is to identify. When witches banish, they know that the first step is naming the demon or that which is to be eliminated. The same principle applies in creating new and positive spells.

Some political feminists take a critical position, however, in relation to followers of the Muse-Goddess. Though it has dawned on them that language and naming have power and provide a key to their liberation, they have not yet made the leap into non-linear language realities, finding them "unreal," or "escapist." They are still thinking linearly, and are therefore still of the reality they profess to resist. The only way to truly change the world is to cease to operate in a patriarchal belief framework, and leap into a whole new way of thinking. Or, as my friend Liberté is fond of saying, "Take a one-hundred-eighty-degree turn in consciousness."

Nowadays the spoken word receives little reverence, while authority is given willingly to the written or recorded word. People are careless with their speech, telling half-truths or making promises they don't keep. Social pressures tempt us to lie continually, often threatening our survival if we do not comply. Truthfulness, our birthright, has become clouded in word games. One cannot be a successful spell-maker this way. A good witch knows the impact of language, and uses it with care.

This is where honor comes in. As a cooking pot, Cerridwen's cauldron was said to refuse sustenance to liars. It was decorated with a rim of pearls a long-time symbol of truth. To depart from truth was to depart from the Muse's favors. To be muse-possessed is to be truth-possessed.

In magical terms, this means that your word cannot be powerful if you do not say what you mean, and live up to what you say. Every time you back down from your verbal commitments you are creating a haziness, a shakiness in your language, for your speech no longer conveys the truth of what is actually occurring. Moreover, the unconscious mind, being incapable of deception, wants to believe what your spoken words are saying. This principle is at the base of all affirmations and spells. Truth is rich with aliveness, with nowness, beauty, and realness. It gives potency to magical language. Clouded truth confuses the spell, and can be detrimental to your magic, if not downright dangerous.

> ". . . Beauty is truth, truth beauty, that is all
> Ye know on earth, and all ye need to know."
> —*John Keats*

In addition to the element of air, the Muse has been represented by the other four elements as well. In Irish mythology, the goddess Brigid was adored as the giver of flame—the hearth flame that provides sustenance, the flame of passion in love and battle, and the "supersensual" flame of poetry.

> Fire witch
> Breath to the flame
> Kindles passion . . .

Hers was also the flame that tempered the metals of the smithcrafts, which were given by her earthen body.

The Muse has a watery tradition as Aphrodite, goddess of Love, who was born of sea foam. Sappho and her sisters at Lesbos worshipped Aphrodite as the source of beauty, passion, and poetic inspiration. The Welsh Aphrodite was more earthy. Named Olwen, she presided over the wild apple tree. Its fruit was said to give poetic immortality.

Many poets have been inspired by Mother Nature, who can be seen as the Muse in her earth aspect. A poem that describes the beauties and wisdom of nature is also an invocation of the goddess.

> Earth witch
> Ear to the ground
> Listening to Her heartbeat . . .

The Five-Fold and Three-Fold Muse

One can view the Muse in terms of the five elements, and also in terms of the three aspects of maiden, mother, and crone. As Maiden-Muse, she is the untame and wild quality of artistic inspiration, that risks social disapproval and will flee at the loss of spontaneity. She is the art of revolution, the songs that change the world, the paintings that open the eyes of the people. She is also biting satire that crumbles our illusions with wit and laughter.

As Mother-Muse she is Beauty, the Passionate One and Lover. Many poets fall in love with a human representative of the muse, and receive their creative inspiration through their passions. The lives of artists are often the tales of their loves, of the ecstasies and agonies of the heart that so deeply affect their work and insights. The Mother-Muse is a healing force, bringing union through uplifting experiences.

The Crone is the dark side of the Muse, and the most difficult to accept. For in this aspect she is most exacting, demanding faithful adherence to her standards and allegiance to her truths. Deny her this and lose her. This is her implacable law. We can also see her dark side in the frustration and isolation of most creative people. Often even those who are successful are known to have self-destructive habits such as alcoholism, drug addiction, or egomania. This could be seen as the Muse's dark revenge for attempting to exploit or mis-use her powers.

Graves makes much of the Muse's dark side, accepting it as a kind of poet's crucifixion. As stated before, this too is a part of the violence in our culture that must be re-examined. It is my theory that these cultures of bloody sacrifice to the Goddess were not the true matriarchies of even earlier times. We know, as described in the Moon Cycle, that men invented blood sacrifice in attempt to imitate the moonblood rituals of women. And yet there is a symbolic truth in what Graves points out. For a man to be possessed by the Muse he must be able to surrender to the female energy in himself and in the universe. He cannot express Her magnificence by controlling or manipulating Her, but by letting Her come through him. This can be a painful struggle for those who are trained to the typical power-over machismo of patriarchy.

It is also true that a choice to live by muse principles often entails sacrifice for any artist, male or female, in today's world. Temptations to sell out, write lies, live lies—all must be forsaken for Her. One cannot live in a way that defies her part of the time and expect her to appear in one's spare time. In my own experience I have had to come to terms with this Crone side of the muse, though I spent some years in resisting and attempting to avoid her. The fact is that to embrace the Goddess herself, not only as muse, but in all her aspects, is to swim upstream. Allegiance to her is necessarily allegiance to truth, beauty, and a completely different social order than the one we observe today. Any attempt to deceive her or divert her energy into the system will result in her departure. This will show itself in the style of life one finds oneself living, the manner in which one spends one's time, and the quality of one's work. I reached the crossroads and made my choice, and put up with the inconveniences. For though the poet must accept the dark aspect of the Muse, her rewards are the magnificence of her artistic expressions and their ability to travel beyond, into the hearts and minds of others.

Would she manifest this way in a woman-centered culture? Perhaps her ruthlessness is due to the male setting she finds herself in today, that attempts to co-opt and dilute her powers (i.e., Hollywood, modern TV commercials, etc.). And perhaps it is the harsh side of nature that we all must come to terms with— the devouring insects, overwhelming storms, earthquakes or volcanoes . . . She is a life force and as such is both magnificent and dangerous. We must address her with respect and reverence. This does not mean that she is unjustly cruel, however; only male-centered gods seem to promote detached, insane violence. The goddess never destroys except for the purpose of furthering life and love, and keeping the natural order.

Magical Poetry

image . . . imagine . . . imagination . . . magic

The best spells are inspired by the muse. They are created in that mysterious, ecstatic impulse of truth and wonder that is ultimately inexplicable. Like all good art, they are born of urgent necessity. A witch learns to cultivate language that conjures vivid images and evokes strong feelings. This is not the intellectual language of textbooks or pedantic speech. Poetic language is non-linear, mythic, and spontaneous.

> Once upon a midnight time
> Moon goddess come
> Moon goddess come
> Come silvery
> Come silvery down
> To the darking sky . . .

Magic poetry does not necessarily follow the rules of punctuation, tense, spelling, use of pronouns, etc., to be found in linear prose. This depends on the needs of the poem. Because of its rigid structure, prose may prove inadequate to the task of true expression, for it can easily be used to deceive or distort the truth. Poetry, by its very nature, can never be guilty of this for the true life it describes takes it beyond grammar.

We might say that muse poetry is the language of the right brain or dream world. Starhawk suggests that it is a bridge between left and right brain consciousness, joining image and emotion with reason and understanding. As such it is especially useful in creating successful spells and rituals.

Earth, sea, wind and fire
Bring to us what we desire . . .

Magical poetry works best when there is rhythm, rhyme, and repetition. Rhythm is hypnotic and relaxes the conscious mind, opening up the doors to the deep mind and trance states. Rhyme also helps through the repetition of similar sounds. Repetition brings things into being. If you place two mirrors facing one another and stand between them so that you are reflected in both, you will see your image go on to infinity. Repetition of verses works on this principle, creating infinite reverberations into the cosmos and psyche. These vibrations create reflections of themselves, and continue to echo long after the witch has worked her spell. This is the purpose of mantra, or chanted poetry. In the womb a child is made from the dividing of one cell into two, two into four, and so on, until a whole body is formed. Mantra effects the cells, the mind, and the emotions in this manner. It causes the aura to vibrate at certain rates, accompanied by appropriate images. The more relaxes and focused the mind, the more certain the programming of the deep mind.

Don't be afraid of monotony or prolonged repetition of one simple image or phrase. A single note can contain the music of the spheres. The greatest things are the simplest. We are so distracted by dazzling displays of complex technical variations, that we can forget the underlying simple themes of timeless truth. The more you repeat your invocations, the more effective they will be, and the deeper you will go into altered states of consciousness.

The Perennial Theme of Muse Poetry

In the traditions described by Robert Graves in his book, *The White Goddess*, all poetry and myth tells a perennial tale of the goddess. Graves says that the basic story is of a battle between two male gods, one who represents the waxing year or forces of life, and one who represents the waning year, or forces of death. They fight for the love of the goddess who is their mother, lover, and destroyer. The waning god wins, and the cycle of life and death begins again. In ancient Welsh and druidic traditions this tale was told in the thirteen chapters or months of the sacred year, and acknowledged with full-moon ritual at each of its stations. Simultaneously, a five-fold version was told in pace with the solar year, with five holy days to represent them. The thirteen lunar chapters were assigned tree-letters. These were the consonants. The five solar stations (falling on the equinoxes and solstices, and one extra Day) had the vowels a, o, u, e, and i. These were also linked to particular trees. Thus we see how myth, poetry, magic, tree-lore, time, language, ritual, and the cycles of life (maiden, mother, and crone) are inextricably bound up in one another.

There are many examples of muse poetry to be found, particularly in the ballads of British poets.

I met a Lady in the meads
Full beautiful, a fairy's child
Her hair was long, her foot was light
And her eyes were wild—

. . . She took me to her elfin grot
And there she wept and sighed full sore,
And there I shut her wild wild eyes
With kisses four—

And there she lulled me asleep
And there I dream'd Ah Woe betide!
The latest dream I ever dreamt
On the cold hill side.

I saw pale Kings, and Princes too
pale warriors death pale were they all
Who cried La belle dame sans merci
Thee hath in thrall.

I saw their starv'd lips in the gloom
With horrid warning gaped wide,
And I awoke, and found me here
On the cold hill's side . . .

—From *La Belle Dame Sans Merci*
By John Keats

In keeping with the perennial theme, the goddess appears here in a form that is at once enchanting and dangerous. She is beautiful, irresistible, and deadly. The combination is compelling, haunting, spell-binding.

The Theme has many versions. In some the goddess finds her lover torn in pieces, and weeps over him. Her tears mend him and bring his resurrection (Ishtar and Tammuz). In some the dying god is a king, and his adversary a dark son (Arthur and Gwydion). In some he is immaculately born, as in the Christ tale, dies a sacrificial death, and is later resurrected. Jesus' story was the last in a long line of such myths, and turned the tide because of its omission of the female deity for whom the earlier kings had died. Graves believes that the man Jesus did this deliberately, knowing full well that he was reprogramming the mass unconscious, by using an old ritual custom in a new male context.

The Essene Gospel quotes Jesus as saying, "I have come to undo the work of the female." He proclaimed that none would have to die after him, for he was symbolically accomplishing this feat for all time. This must have been a great relief to the men of that era, and probably had much to do with the growing acceptance of Christianity. Obviously, this myth could never have had such impact if the preceding rituals of the dying kings had not been long established.

Here again we must scrutinize our muse-traditions with care. While honoring the beauty and power of these stories, and acknowledging their extensive influence on our culture, as feminist witches we must look deeper. Could the Goddess truly sanction such cruelty? Why must time be represented by male gods? Why must the dark and light seasons be symbolized so violently? Where are the female myths that describe our life and time cycles? We know that female cultures preceded male cultures, and yet a purely female Theme of poetry cannot be found in traditional literature.

I was unable to develop a purely female mythos until I had accepted the possibility of lesbian love. That is because passionate love is so deeply bound up with any mythic view of the universe. The Perennial Theme as told by Graves is intensely heterosexual. The Goddess' power of life and death comes through the passionate love felt for her by the gods. It wasn't until I experienced passion as the expression of Aphrodite, Goddess of Love, that I could move into the realm of poetry as purely female.

Re-Writing The Perennial Theme For Women

I found my first clue in the Greek myth of Kore/Persephone. This myth was enacted with elaborate, seasonal ritual for 2,000 years at ancient Eleusis. In the patriarchal version, the maiden Kore is born of the Mother Goddess Demeter. Kore is raped by Hades, god of the dead, and carried off to the underworld to be his queen. Hecate witnesses and reports this occurrence, and Demeter mourns bitterly, bringing winter to the earth. Zeus, the primary male deity, orders Kore's release. But she has eaten six pomegranate seeds with Hades, and so must return to him for six months of each year. Her resurrection each spring and subsequent reunion with her Mother are the cause of great rejoicing.

> All golden now she springs to the earth
> And alights to turn the brown grasses green
> Her mother's tears mix with her own
> And fall to make the green more green . . .

Despite the rape and violence, this is a compelling tale. All three aspects of the Goddess are present. The mysteries of birth, adolescence, death, separation and resurrection are described in a poetic, female context. The only flaws are the power-over dominance of Zeus and Hades, and the subservience of the goddesses.

Once realizing this, it was a simple matter to rewrite the myth of Kore. In my new version she still sojourns in the underworld, but now it is the Crone she encounters there. Her lessons are of the life, death, and immortality of her Self, not as wife but as autonomous woman.

> *Crone (to Kore):*
> You have your self
> For all and ever . . .
>
> . . . Beyond time
> Beyond space
> Beyond infinity
> The essence of thy being persists
> Loving so to be
> Through all sufferings
> All joys
> Through countless seasons and designs
> Countless bodies old and young
> She is with you
> Dancing love's divine dance
> Mirroring self in each beloved's soul
> Returning ever and again to center
> The quivering flower's core
> The Kore—
> You!

And so our new Perennial Theme of poetry is now totally female. It can also be applied to the stations of the year, or holy days, as I will describe in the next Cycle.

You may question the wisdom of this change and wonder how the male fits into such a cosmology. First of all, we must realize how destructive male supremacy has been, and that its inception is bound up with the loss of women's mysteries. A healing of our psyches can only be complete when the female myths are told once more. This does not mean male myths and male/female myths should not *also* be told. In the universe of our loving Mother, there is room and love for everyone!

Secondly, men are part female. They are the younger race and also come from the goddess. They have breasts, and their genitals are formed from the female vulva. It is a known medical fact that occasional male babies are born with milk in their breasts. As explicated by Carl Jung, men have within their psyches the anima or the female aspect of the male self. Many men are troubled by a negative anima and find themselves in trouble with women as a result (see Maiden Cycle). Much of Carl Jung's work has to do with the healing of man's relationship with his female side. Men need positive experiences of the goddess desperately.

We also need new myths to celebrate and explain the appearance of the male race, as an offspring of the older race of woman. My friend and former student Oceana has come up with a beautiful tale:

> Generations of wimmin passed, all learning and teaching, all caring for one another.
> One day, a womon, who was fast approaching the moment of giving birth to her first
> child, was squatting on the warm earth. Wimmin were in a close circle around her,
> chanting and singing softly. The air was still in this moment of high noon; only the
> wimmin's voices were heard, rising together, to help the babe emerge.
>
> Pushing, struggling, yearning to be born, the baby finally was received into
> the arms of the joyous and astonished mother; for the child was formed of a body
> different than her own.
>
> "Diosa Madre," whispered the wimmin.
>
> "Mother Goddess! We give thanks to you, for this precious new being, so
> special and different, so unique in his form!"
>
> And it was thus the first manchild was born into this world.
>
> —from a *Creation Myth* by Oceana Kolours

In addition to my work with the myth of the Kore, I have also played with the
familiar Greek myth of Phaeton in an attempt to explore some poetic ways of
describing the appearance of patriarchy. In the traditional version, Phaeton is the son
of Apollo, who daily drives the chariot of the sun across the sky. Phaeton, who is only
half immortal, becomes jealous of his father, and demands permission to take over
his duties and partake of his glory. Apollo consents, and Phaeton drives the chariot,
only to lose control and plunge to his death.

In my version, Phaeton is really immortal, born of the Mother Goddess who has
made all things. But he does not realize his immortality, fearing that death will put
an end to him for all time. He goes to his mother and demands to drive the sun-horses
across the sky. She consents, and he takes the reins:

> . . . So Phaeton took his Mother's reins
> And drove the horses forth,
> What mortal plays with such a toy?
> Or lives to know such heavenly joy—
> And brings dawn to the earth?
>
> Up in the sky he burned and soared
> 'Til he felt nigh to a swoon
> The folk below rose for the day,
> The beauty took his breath away,
> And now it was high noon . . .
>
> . . . Faster and faster the chariot flew
> But he heeded not his pace,
> "Farewell to death," he cried, and swore

That he would ride forever more,
And take his Mother's place . . .

The horses now were streaming fire
The earth was streaked with red . . .

. . . He never heard his Mother's cry
As to his death he sped,
Nor heard his tortured people sigh
As he hurled like lightning, through the sky
And fell to earth, now dead.

Well, Phaeton got up from the ground
And laughed up to the sky,
"I know you, Goddesses, one and all,
"And why I had to take this fall,
"And I'll see you bye and bye . . ."

Thus we have a myth that combines the dying-and-reviving-god of the old Perennial Theme with a new approach that gives an interpretation of the causes of patriarchy. My theory is that man lost contact with his female roots when he became jealous of woman's powers. He separated himself from her, in an attempt to claim his own identity, much as a growing child turns from the parents he must outgrow. But in the process, he lost the sense of connection and power that is so necessary to his well being, attempting to retrieve it by imitation and control. He is now on the threshold of maturity, as his past mistakes are catching up with him, threatening destruction of our world.

Myths are the seed-images from which we create our reality. It is through the powers of the Muse that we experience the planting and eventual flowering of these myth-seeds. A song is heard, a poem read, a dance observed . . . and Her message is carried. We have seen many flowers, both magnificent and grotesque. It is up to us to select the seeds that will result in goodness and beauty, and to create the channels or media for this to happen. How are we to accomplish this? The current hierarchical star system has proven itself to be far from satisfactory.

We know from studies of druidism that the bardic tradition was upheld, and that bards were priests as well as poets, musicians as well as politicians. Merlin, for example, was not just one person, but a title for a succession of venerable poets who assisted the rulers of their day. Many of them played the harp and were known for their great musical skill. There are many legends of bards such as Gwydion and Taliesin, who performed amazing magical feats along with their poetry, such as producing a flock of doves with the right incantation, or answering the wind riddle by conjuring up a real wind. These bards were representatives of the goddess, and were consulted by the political leaders in all weighty matters. There were bardic colleges where candidates studied extensively before they were deemed worthy of the position. They learned about the meanings of trees, and their uses, the layers of symbolism in the tree letters, the many epic poems that had to be memorized, and secrets we have all but lost today. This was the root of the troubadour tradition, which was actually a deterioration as Christianity supplanted the goddess.

Though this bardic system was hierarchical and already corrupt as far as our purposes are concerned, we can learn much from the lore and mysteries it contains.

> In the dark and hidden times
> The poet was the priest
> At the right hand of the king
> He sat at every feast
> Then
>   came
>   down
>   the
> Patriarchal beast
> And the Magic of the muse
> All but ceased . . .

Perhaps the most important lesson is the incredible reverence given the Muse, not only as inspirer but as a primary social force. If we can take this understanding and extract it from its patriarchal setting, we can then go a step further, and re-set it into a new crown, so to speak. Or better still, discard the crown image altogether, and place the jewel into a necklace of women.

> In the dark and hidden cave
> The sibyl moaned so sweet
> The oracle she gave
> The people's needs to meet
> Then
>   came
>   down
>   the
> Patriarchal priest
> And he cast the Goddess down
> To his feet . . .

Even earlier than the bardic tradition is that of the sibyls, priestesses who gave ecstatic utterance and were consulted for wisdom. Though scholarship has uncovered only a god-oriented priestesshood of sibyls (such as the Temple of Apollo at Delphi), we can surmise that they went back much further in time. Apollo's temple was originally built to honor Gaia, the ancient Earth Mother of matriarchal Greece. Evidently, a much older, female-centered religion was supplanted. The sibyls would surely have served the goddess, and thus present a viable role model of female muse-powers.

We can only guess at the forms of such culture among women. I have a vision of sisters sitting around a mellow evening fire, their children about them, some snoozing, some listening. And songs are sung, chanted, shared. When a new song comes the goddess is thanked for blessing that woman with inspiration. Each song is a miracle, a child of the soul. The women love and respect the power of poetry, the ecstasy of musical tones vibrating through their beings. They talk about the songs, and the process of creating them. They love to listen to one another's separate single voices, and they love singing together. No one is left out or slighted. Some pieces are developed and used with ritual at their holy festivals. Out of this shared joy and reverence develop all the ensuing forms of a culture—the architecture and sculptures, theater pieces, dances, stories, philosophies, scientific inventions, and so on.

As we wish it, so may it be!

Invocation

O Muse, you are to us Mother, Sister, Lover, Daughter, and Grandmother:

As Mother you give us your forms
Of dance, and music and theater,
Of sculpted and painted beauty
Of spells of magical ritual,
Of poetry and woven words . . .

As Sister you stay faithfully by us
Through all the changes of our lives
Playing joyfully, bringing laughter
And leaping to the eyes and ears
And hearts of those who see and hear . . .

As Lover you inspire us with your ecstasy
Fill us with your beauty
Your passion of truth and wonder
Taking us beyond ourselves
Into universal love . . .

As Daughter you make us mothers
As we birth your creations through us . . .
As Grandmother you inspire the arts of revolution
And teach us your secrets and responsibilities
Warning us of the world's misuse
Of your sacred powers . . .

We dedicate ourselves to Thee
O Great One
Inspirer of our sound and song
Dreamer of the dancing forms
That come through us
Lifter of limbs
Teacher of all mystery
O Flame of poetry
We pledge our vows to Thee
To be ever true to Thee
To live our lives that you may flow
To honor Thee wherever you may appear
To respect you as an instrument of social change
And the enlightenment of all people
To assist thee with love
In blending back together
The shattered fragments
Of our women's culture . . .
To stand and defend thee

Whenever glamour or exploitation
Are imposed on thee
To celebrate your appearance in all sisters
To celebrate the artist alone
And artists together
And clarify our desires in this regard . . .
To give and receive attention
Without jealousy
Without competition
With love and appreciation . . .
To use the media responsively
Responsible to thy laws
And the needs of the people . . .
To partake of thy glory
And share it with our sisters . . .
To support those who channel thee
And speak for their value to community . . .
To cherish thine appearance
Be it public or in private
To see and receive thee as Healer
Of ourselves and all the world.

SEVENTEEN OF SPIRIT

MUSE

The Muse pours her healing waters of inspiration and mythopoetic consciousness. She renews our spirits with faith in the integrity of the universe and gives us her wellspring of hope and creativity.

Suggested Projects

1. Creation myths are the foundation stone of any cosmology. While the ancient myths have developed through time, history, and collective psychic process, they nevertheless can begin in the inspired imagination of individuals. For women to receive our own myths is to retrieve important magical and psychological material. Write a creation myth that expresses your vision of how the Goddess may have come into being, and how She might have created the universe and all that's in it. Include the appearance of women, of men, of animals and plants, of male domination as well as its future resolution. Draw upon classic archetypes of manifestation, such as dancing, singing, birthing, molding, breathing, thinking, loving or weaving the world into being.

2. "Ritual is the enactment of myth," says Joseph Campbell. Get a group together and make a ritual with your myth for its structure. Come dressed as the Goddesses and other characters in the story. If you feel awkward about performing, do it privately just for the Goddess, yourselves and each other; just for the sheer joy of it. You can have copies made for everyone, and the myth can be read aloud, round robin style. Play some background music and bring sound effects such as drums and bells. Make an offering to the Muse before you begin and thank Her when it is over. If you feel the urge, get up and move or dance or do pantomime to the words in the story. Or, try learning the story ahead of time and improvising the enactment. Write up the experience in your *Book of Shadows* and save for future repetitions.

3. Make a visual representation of your myth, such as a painting, collage, or sculpture. (There are some wonderful new sculpting materials now, such as Fimo and Sculpy that you can mold and then bake in a home oven.) Include images of the Goddess or Goddesses in your story, the beings or things they create, and symbols of their powers. When it is completed, charge and bless your work. Keep it as a sacred artifact for your altars and rituals.

4. Make yourself a ritual outfit with robe, magical jewelry, a wearable pouch for your small valuables and ritual supplies, a headpiece such as a crescent crown or mask or beads, soft slippers. Add bells, embroidery, feathers, fabric painting, appliques, secret pockets and the like. Incorporate images of the Goddess and women, such as moons, pentacles, spirals, snakes, leaves, vines, flowers or runes.

5. Make a collection of women's new creation myths, poetry and art. Bind it in a special book with magical coverings and decorations. Use this book to read aloud at

ceremonies.

6. If you feel any difficulty or blockage in creating any of the above projects, try lighting a special candle to the Muse Goddess and ask for Her help. Write out the Invocation at the end of the Cycle by hand, or a similar one of your own design, and sign it ceremoniously. Place it on your altar as an offering to Her. Spend some time relaxing and open yourself to Her messages and images.

Questions to Ponder

1. What does the Muse mean to you? How does She manifest in your life?

2. Do you consider yourself artistic in any way? Make a list of all the creative things you do, even mundane things like doodling, making up jokes, home decorating, and so on. Validate your creativity.

3. Have you been encouraged in your creativity? Blocked in your creativity? Write about past experiences in this regard. If you feel encouraged, how will you fulfill this part of yourself? If you feel blocked, what can you do to remedy this?

4. Do you think artistic creativity is important? Should artists be supported in society?

5. Compare the old patriarchal Perennial Theme with the new ones offered here. What do you like in each? What would you change? How do they make you feel?

6. Are you familiar with the traditions of the dying-and-reviving gods?

7. Can you see how the myth of Christ can be an outgrowth of these? Write about this at length in your *Book of Shadows*. How do these stories connect with the seasons and the passages of life and death?

8. How could the Persephone/Kore myth make a valid replacement to the dying-and-reviving god traditions, and how would you incorporate Women's Mysteries?

9. Why is the usual version of Persephone/Kore patriarchal? How would you go about changing this aspect of the story?

10. Do you identify with the Muse as an image of creative inspiration? Any other Goddesses or images?

Reading and Other Resources

Mary Barnard, editor of *Sappho.*
Marion Zimmer Bradley, *The Mists of Avalon.*
Isadora Duncan, *My Life.*
James Frazer, *The Golden Bough.*
Judy Grahn, *The Highest Apple.*
Robert Graves, *King Jesus and The White Goddess, The Greek Myths* and *On Poetry.*
Carl Jung, *Man and His Symbols,* and *Memories, Dreams, and Reflections.*
Ann McCaffrey, *Dragon Singer.*
May Sarton, *Mrs. Stephens Hears the Mermaids Singing.*
Charles Squire, *Celtic Myth and Legend.*
Evangeline Walton, *The Mabinogian.*
The Dead Sea Scrolls.

CYCLE 8

The Goddess Year

In the mythology of Japanese Shintoism, the Sun is a goddess named Amaterasu. She created winter when she grew upset one day and hid herself in a dark cave. Her priestesses sang and danced outside the cave entrance to entice her out again. When she peeked through a crack in the closed cave mouth, they held up mirrors to catch her light. Amaterasu was so dazzled by her own reflection that she forgot to hide, and emerged to bring once more the season of light and abundant life.

I have been a Lunar creature most of my life, loving the dark and winter seasons, the silvery light of the moon and dreamy states of poetic musing. The sun seemed so male to me, given to male gods like Apollo of the Greeks and Ra of the Egyptians. I experienced the light of the sun shining on a world of crass materialism, violence and competition. The nine-to-five workday of this solar reality appeared oppressive and boring. Like Amaterasu, I preferred to hide in my cave during the day, and come out and shine at night with Luna.

The moon has long been given to women, and the sun to men. It was an extensive journey for me, through many mystical studies, music, poetry, magic, goddess lore and feminism before I could begin to reclaim the sun. It was upon reading *The First Sex* by Elizabeth Gould Davis that I began to consciously remythologize those parts of being that I had been taught were male. The sun is Fire in every sense of the word, and I needed to experience fire as female.

Discovering sun goddesses was a wonderful liberation. As a woman I could exult in my reflection in all aspects of the universe. Though I will always be a predominately watery and psychic personality, the fiery element does not have to represent a contradiction. It can be understood as a complementary energy that adds stimulus and health to experience. I can be free to cultivate it, both in myself and in relation to others.

Now I experience the Sun as the oldest Goddess in our planetary system—the Star Mother of us all. She contains within her the forces we have come to know as male, even as the race of woman once contained the male. Out of Her were birthed her planet children who continue to dance around her in space, receiving the nourishment of her heat, light, and magnetism. She is the throbbing heart center, radiating a love so powerful we can barely begin to perceive it. To look upon Her is overwhelming to our sight, for her brightness can literally destroy our eyes. She shines on all creatures equally, and is a great role model of unconditional love, collective consciousness and the essential oneness that underlies the myriad varieties of being.

Queen of Light
Fiery One
I entice you from your cave of darkness
Sweep through me once again
Dazzle my sight
With your brilliance
You cannot resist me
For I dance before the doorway
Of your mouth
Open—mouth open—I sing
Sing and sway
To call you back again . . .

The mirror turns
Returns reflecting you
In me and me in you
And so we weave
This shining web
Of one another . . .

Behold! She comes
In all Her splendor
Golden Goddess of the day
Wheeling, spinning back to us
Returning, come what may

O miracle—Her dress is flame
Her blazing arms reach out
To span the sky
She hides no more!
She comes to see me dance . . .

Pulsating blinding torch of life
You touch my body, touch the Earth
Embrace my sisters every one
That we may bloom and flower
And claim again the Sun . . .

Sola births our years, one every twelve or thirteen moons. To understand Her Sacred Year is to feel the endless swirl of the planets and stars. Imagine yourself upon a carousel that passes through the seasons. Perhaps your journey would begin at Winter Solstice, and you would see the sparkle and darkness of winter cold and snow. As the carousel spins slowly, the landscape is transformed, gradually changing to the delicate greens and golds of spring. You smell blossoms and hear the call of birdlife. You spin on, and watch the colors deepen, becoming bright and rich with summer heat. Abundant life throbs everywhere. And then as winter returns, the flames of transforming death light up the landscape. Perhaps you would begin to feel Her dance . . . a sense of Beingness, a consciousness that is dancing through Birth and Life and Death, around and around, again and again.

> And She will bring the buds in the spring
> And laugh among the flowers
> In summer's heat Her kisses are sweet
> She loves in leafy bowers
> She cuts the cane and gathers the grain
> When autumn leaves surround Her
> Her bones grow old and wintry cold
> She wraps Her cloak around Her . . .
> —*Traditional*

In mythopoetic terms, the year has a life span like any other living creature on earth. She has infancy, maidenhood, adulthood, and motherhood, cronehood, death and rebirth. Or, in other words, she is born, bleeds, makes love, gives birth, gives milk or food, ceases to bleed, dies, and is reborn. The life and death of the year has been enacted in mythologies for many ages. The different stages have been deified, personalized, filled with emotional portent, and often seen as adversaries or lovers. Ritual holy days are observed around the world that connect with the affirming of life in the dark, the praising of the harvest, the mysteries of growth, sensuality, and death. The metaphors we are offered that symbolize these cycles affect our view and expectations of time.

Today's patriarchal year is a very peculiar part male, part nil entity. He has a well-celebrated birth near the Winter Solstice (December 25), at which time some loving connections are made amongst earthlings, much money passes hands, and some suffer from loneliness and alienation. In spring this year-god dies a horrible death upon a cross, and is shortly thereafter resurrected and ascends to heaven. In summer he seems to have disappeared entirely, perhaps replaced by a football hero or two. In autumn his old enemy, the hag or wicked witch gets some press, though of a limited sort, and everyone begins to prepare for the agonies and ecstasies of his up-and-coming birth. What sort of view of reality does this impart? Can you celebrate each seasonal passage with meaning and joy? Do you feel yourself, as a woman, reflected in *any* of these celebrations? Do you get a message that there is something sacred, something magnificent going on that you are a part of, in harmony with? Is it any wonder that so many people have lost their rituals altogether and view time as an empty mechanism without purpose or meaning?

We need a communal, mythopoetic view of life and time, for "a nation without a dream will perish." Rob a people of its culture, its visions, its mysteries, and that people must die out. I propose that the ancient life-affirming mythic rituals of goddess-loving cultures was supplanted by the violent, hierarchical rituals of men and their gods. Though they have been observed for many centuries, they have gradually led to a state of spiritual impoverishment. Lacking the color, magnificence and community spirit of the feminine principle, they have withered, for the people have turned away in search of sustenance. The result is a culture almost entirely lacking in ritual practices of any sort.

Because we are so starved for the goddess and her images, and because we urgently need to re-align our Mysteries with our holy days, I have found it necessary to develop a female myth of the year. I believe that every time we invoke Her, sing of Her, dance to Her, make festivals for Her, act out Her stories, we are fostering life and nourishing our own survival. Patriarchy is on the road to self-destruction. Our only hope, if we are not to die with it, is to create the alternative reality. This is especially true on the psychic plane, for that is where all reality begins.

> 'Cause the battle rages
> On the psychic planes
> And all the people
> Playin' all their gains
> Gotta git to the frontier
> Where the new way reigns . . .
> (To be sung to the tune of "Bury Me Not On the Lone Prairie")

Therefore, in this writing, we will consider a poetic myth of the year that is entirely female. Our year goddess is three-fold, five-fold, and eight-fold. (She is also thirteen-fold in her lunar cycles.) Each of her names represents a stage of her life cycle. As Kore she is the maiden born in the spring, the appearance of new young life upon the earth. As Diana she is the Virgin who bleeds yet does not die. As Aphrodite she is the Lover who is initiated into the mysteries of passion. As Habundia she is the Mother, birthing abundant life, dancing all forms into being. As Persephone she is the Descending Maiden who moves toward the dark, the underworld, and her own separate self. As Hecate she is the Wise Crone of winter who knows the mysteries of birth and death. As Lucina she rebirths herself in the form of a shining star. Thus the infant year begins again, a new self, a new journey. As Aradia she is teacher and learner in the underworld as seeds take root and prepare for spring.

In composing the year story, I have drawn upon the eight-fold pagan year currently observed by many goddess-oriented groups. In this time scheme, the holy days fall upon the solstices, the equinoxes, and the four intermediate or "cross-quarter" days. I have applied this sequence to the Greek myth of Persephone/Kore. Though this myth came to me in patriarchal form, I have "re-membered" it in female terms.

There are two births in this year, as each maiden becomes first a mother, then a crone. She who is born at the spring, conceives her child in summer and rebirths her spirit at midwinter, will now become a mother at the next spring, and her mother will become a crone. Thus the cycles actually overlap endlessly.

The early Celts celebrated a five-fold year, which included the equinoxes, the solstices, and one extra day for the birth of the Divine Child. Each of these holy days was assigned a vowel from the Celtic tree alphabet. A was for Ailm, the Silver Fir tree. This is the birth tree, known as balsam fir in North America, and can be traced through the ages as the original Christmas tree. Her day is Winter Solstice, the birthday of the year. O was for Onn, the furze or gorse, burned upon the hilltops to commemorate her day, the Spring Equinox, celebrated as the maiden's youth and growth. U was for Ura, the Heather tree, named after the Gallic Heather Goddess, Uroica. She is a tree of fullness, ripeness and passion, and her day is, of course, the Summer Solstice. E was for Eadha, the Aspen tree, whose day is the Autumn Equinox. This is the tree of the year's aging. Her leaves tremble constantly, and her divinatory meaning is loss of hope. And the fifth tree is I, for Idho the Yew Tree. She is the tree of death and stands beside the Ailm of birth. Her day is immediately before Winter Solstice, known as the extra day and sacred to Hecate.

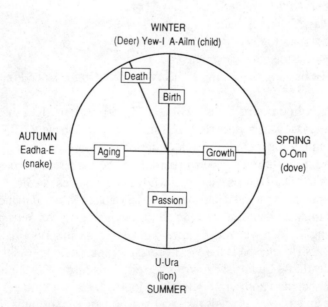

We can also envision a three-fold year, based upon the Maiden-Mother-Crone symbolism so basic to our feminist thealogy. This can be useful in taking us out of the four-season concept, which tends to set up a duality between life and death.

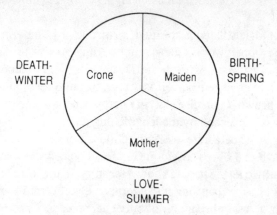

Rituals for the Eight-Fold Year

What follows is a suggested female alternative for community celebrations of the mysteries. These holiday festivals are offered as practices for your enchantment and delight. They are not meant to be rigid dogma. Your own sense of the magic is the main thing. We have seen the results of religions that are institutionalized. Their rituals become empty and boring. A healthy balance between tradition and invention is usually best.

These rituals are adaptable to a variety of situations. You may wish to do one solo and speak all the parts yourself. Some groups prefer a leader or guide to memorize the steps of the ritual and keep the energy flowing. This usually works better in groups of people who have not worked magic together more than a time or two. Older groups whose members know each other well may prefer to share the responsibilities and take turns priestessing various aspects. My experience is that the more people know one another, the less leadership is required, and vice versa. It is best to discuss these issues ahead of time, and form agreements so there will not be any confusion when the time comes.

In planning your holy days, start with some reflection on the meaning of the season. Research the rituals of other witches and friends. Then go within and "research" yourself. Find your own impressions. How does the coming of winter or spring affect you emotionally? What political or social significance are you aware of? What memories are brought up? What goddesses, elements, types of spells come to mind? What needs do you have, such as for healing or support? All of these are good themes for holiday celebrations.

Lucina
(Winter Solstice)

. . . And She births the spirit within us, bringing light and hope to us all . . .

This is the time of the Maiden's spiritual birth. Having undergone death and separation from the upper world, she has met with the Crone and learned the mysteries of Immortality, Manifestation, and Dissolution. She welcomes the spirit of the child within her, even as she herself is reborn through recognition of her own immortality. In the heavens a precise shift of energy is occurring. The longest night or time of darkness is succeeded by the lengthening days.

At Winter Solstice I celebrate the divine childself or infant year with a story of the moon giving birth to a star. The Moon Goddess decides she wants a child, and sends a legend to earth to let the people know. Her story, in the form of a wind, enters the poets of the world, who then sing it to everyone else. At mid-winter the people watch the full moon, as a shining star births out of her and dances across the sky. The star becomes the animals of the seasons— a dove, a lion, a snake, a deer, and finally a golden child who flies down to earth to teach us of love and the nature of things. (See the five-fold year, page 162.)

In this holy day I have kept many traditional practices that seem to me universal and of value to the health of our psyches. The major difference is that the Divine Child is female. In celebrating her we can celebrate and heal all the experiences of our own childhoods. As women we are in dire need of a metaphor of the yearly birth of our Selves.

This is a wonderful story to act out with children. The Solstice time is especially for them, for they represent the child in all of us, the Younger Self, that is forever innocent and new, spontaneous, trusting and full of wonder. Decorating a life symbol, such as a tree, is entirely appropriate, being a very old pagan practice from long before the birth of Christ. And the exchanging of gifts is as old as our race—a natural gesture of love and appreciation for those special people in our lives. This is the longest night, a dark time in which to invoke the light. We hold to those we love and build great fires to invite the light and love of the sun's return.

Gather indoors, where it is cozy. A space with a fireplace is preferable. Decorate the altar with evergreens and sparkly things. The altar, in fact, can be the fireplace or the solstice tree. Have lots of candles. Cook magical and festive foods. Lots of hot and steamy dishes are good for the cold season. Have gifts for each participating child on or at the foot of the altar. Wear deeply warm and richly colored clothing—reds, blacks and royal blue, etc. Wear crystals and stars and silvery sounding bells.

Join hands and form a circle. One person stays out and turns all the lights off, then begins lighting candles in the dark.

All chant as the light increases: Lucina, Amaterasu, Sola, Akewa, Inanna (and other light goddesses you might know).

Invocation spoken by priestess:

> The Divine Year has died and is now reborn
> Miraculously the Golden Star Child returns
> To embrace us all with Her innocence and love

Each child is led to the center of the circle. All radiate love to her for a moment or two, and shower praises, hugs, and kisses. Each child is presented with a gift.

Pass the rattle around the circle and tell your own stories of the solstice. Share memories, feelings, legends, experiences.

Caroling: Sing to your heart's content.

Give thanks, ground the energy, open the circle.

Feast and make merry!

Aradia
(Candlemas)

. . . Igniting a blaze in the darkness, to kindle the coming spring . . .

Candlemas is a traditional time to take vows or acknowledge the work of a priestess. Many new witches receive their initiation into a circle or coven at this time. As a long-time priestess, I like to renew my vows at this time. This is also a good time for learning, or remembering what we have learned. As the goddess is being initiated beneath the wintry earth, so do we again review the mysteries and their lessons. I have dedicated this holy day to Aradia, the Avatar Goddess whose spirit incarnates as Teacher to bring us the wisdom and lore of the Craft. Purification is another prevalent theme at this time, a kind of early "spring cleaning." Many people light candles and great fires to welcome and call back the forces of light.

Each member prepares her written vows a few days ahead, to be read and signed at the ritual, which is performed at night, indoors. Decorate the altar in white, with many white candles. Wear white clothing. Cook white foods, such as moon cakes, fish, bread, mushrooms, white sage tea, etc. Prepare a bowl of "charged" or holy water, taken from a pure natural source, for anointing. If you plan to sign any written vows, save some of your moonblood ahead of time. (Consecrated red wine or juice can be substituted for blood.) Also gather commemorative emblems, such as herbal wreathes or crystal pendants and the like, to be gifted to new initiates.

Cast the circle, raise the cone, chant Aradia, Sophia, Cerridwen, and other goddesses of wisdom.

Invocation (spoken aloud by a priestess):
> O Goddess, we are your priestesses
> We dedicate ourselves to you forever
> Our minds hold images of thee
> Our lips speak thy names
> Our eyes behold thee in every living thing
> Our hearts are filled with love of thee
> Our arms embrace you in our sisters
> Our loins delight in your holy pleasures
> Our feet walk forever in thy ways
> We gather in this magic circle to welcome and honor you
> And to call back your ever-returning light . . .

Candle-lighting ceremony: A priestess lights the first candle on the altar, using it to light all succeeding candles. All chant Maaaaaa as light increases. Let your voices swell as the light grows.

Planting psychic seeds for the year: A priestess takes up the bowl of consecrated water, saying:

> Tonight we nurture our souls with spells for the year to come
> Let each sister charge this water with her hopes and plans.
> (She places the bowl in the center of the circle, and begins with her
> own visualization, i.e., "I envision my healing, my body strong and
> free," or "I envision my fulfillment," etc.)

Go around the circle, each sister placing her vision into the bowl. Then one woman takes the bowl and dips her finger into the water and anoints her neighbor on the brow. Draw a pentacle or a crescent or something magical on her forehead, saying:

> May you dwell ever with the goddess
> May the goddess dwell ever with you
> May the dream seeds you have planted
> Take root, and flower, and come true . . .

She then hands the bowl on to the woman she has just anointed, who then turns and blesses the next woman in the same manner. All perform the same ceremony until the circle is completed. The first woman returns the bowl to the altar.

Honoring new witches: Each one is presented with an emblem to commemorate their entrance into the craft. Each one is kissed and embraced by a priestess, who welcomes them saying:

The goddess takes you into herself
As you take the goddess into yourself
So be it
All: So be it
Priestess: Blessed be
All: Blessed be

Reading of vows: New witches read their vows to the goddess, themselves, and their sisters. All listen, affirm, and bless each reading. Vows are signed in blood or consecrated wine.

Previously initiated priestesses or witches read their old or revised vows with the others affirming and blessing them.

Affirmation, chanted by all:
As I love the goddess, so I love myself
As I love myself, so I love the goddess
As I love the goddess, so I love my sisters
As I love my sisters, so I love the goddess
As I love the goddess, so I love the earth
As I love the earth, so I love the goddess
As I love the goddess, so I love myself,
As I love myself, so I love the goddess, etc.
(Make up your own words).

Sharing of wisdoms: The rattle is passed to those who have teachings or insights to share like a new healing technique, an herbal spell, or a teaching dream.

A priestess chants, affirming the mysteries:
Behold the all-wise goddess
As she resides in the Underworld
Great is the miracle of the truths she has learned
For she has separated from her Mother
And confronted her immortal Self
And she has created life and form
With the power of her own mind and desires
And with her simple love
She has dissolved all undesired pain
Soon she will rise up once again
And with her will come the spring
Soon she will be reunited with the Mother
And we will welcome her with joy . . .
So be it!
All: So be it!

Priestess: Blessed be
All: Blessed be
Concluding chant:
    Aradia, Sophia, Athene, Tara, Dann
    (and any other Goddesses of Wisdom).

Ground and center, open the circle, share food and socialize.

Kore
(Spring Equinox)

. . . The year is a dancing woman, who is born at the coming of spring . . .

At Spring Equinox I usually do a retelling of the entire Myth of the Kore. The spirit of the Maiden is now embodied. This is the time when she is reborn from the dark in a physical birth, as opposed to her spiritual birth at Winter Solstice. The Mother conceived nine months earlier at the Summer Solstice, and now gives birth to Spring. For she is the Earth, birthing the appearance of new life. The animals, plants and elements birth with her, and young life flourishes everywhere. Resurrection and reunion are the underlying themes of this holy day, as the maiden reunites with the mother, whom she becomes.

In the Western world our most familiar holiday at this season is Easter. The dying and resurrected deity must suffer when he bleeds, and is never permitted to reincarnate physically. He must remain forever disembodied, taking up residence in Heaven or the spirit realm. And yet the basic themes of death and resurrection can be felt at Easter. The games played with female fertility symbols such as eggs, rabbits and baskets all echo an earlier pagan mystery. In fact, doesn't the name Easter sound suspiciously like Ishtar? Regardless of the metaphors used, this is a powerful time, and people of all beliefs can feel it. The day and night are of equal length, beginning the next wave of magnetic energy that will peak at Beltane. The coming of spring is always a magical time, as the air sweetens and grows warm, buds and flowers open, and babies are born.

One of the main political purposes of this ritual is the creating and mending of bonds among women. The mother/daughter bond, held to be of value in goddess-worshiping societies, is never mentioned in modern spring celebrations. Concurrently, we observe a widespread severance between the generations of women. In patriarchal custom it is more suitable or convenient for women to bond to men and to leave their female bonds behind, or at low priority. The loss of camaraderie, sisterhood, love, affection, friendship, and support has been disastrous to women. Out of the bonds of women grow life, creativity, social conscience, tradition and roots. When the ancients danced and sang at the reunion of Demeter and Persephone, they demonstrated a profound understanding of this principle.

The telling of the year story can be done in many ways. Someone can read it aloud, or each can take a segment of the story round-robin style, or theater can be made of it. It can be powerful to include group chanting of all the names of the goddesses who appear in the tale.

Hold this ritual outdoors in the afternoon, in a quiet spring meadow. The ground area should be flat and safe for dancing. Prepare ahead of time: spring foods, salads with flowers (such as nasturtiums) and greens, colored eggs and other egg dishes, fruits of the season, also grain foods that honor Kore as the fate of the grain or Corn Maiden. Cakes, breads, legumes—all are appropriate. Make garlands of leaves and flowers for all to wear. Dress in delicate costumes—filmy floating faery clothes in spring colors like pale green, rose, yellow, and violet—or go in splendid nakedness with a flower in your navel. Have some sweet fruit wine on the altar.

Set up the altar to one side of the circle area, preferably facing east. Decorate with flowers and green leaves and grasses from the surrounding area. Eggs, buds, umbilical cords and other birth symbols are good for spring. Have yellow and pale green candles. Prepare some dried herbs in a cauldron to be burned during the ritual: lavender, dried rose petals, thyme, etc. Place a ball of yarn, long enough to weave 'round all the women.

Entrance into the circle: Create a birth canal with everyone's bodies. Each woman is birthed through everyone else into the circle. All chant:

> From woman you were born into the world
> From women you are born into this circle

Cast the circle, raise the cone, chant the names of Maiden Goddesses: Kore, Diana, Persephone, Psyche, Sappho, Tenuviel, and any others you may know.

A priestess lights the candles and burns the herbs, saying:
> We gather in this circle to welcome the Maiden
> The old Mother Goddess shape-shifts once again
> And brings to us a young and laughing daughter
> She returns once more from the darkness,
> And her sweetness makes us melt with joy
> She comes, with fragile buds and green
> She comes in beauty, dancing, singing
> With fragrant blossoms in her hair
> That which was separated has been reunited
> That which died is now reborn . . .
> *All:*
> That which was separated has been reunited
> That which died is now reborn
> So be it, Blessed be.

All join hands and close eyes. Let voices arise from around the circle, giving thanks for the spring and the return of life, and for any other blessings in your lives. Make wishes and support one another's visualizations.

Healing ceremony: Each woman takes the center position and lies down. All gather 'round to heal her with sound and visualization and the laying on of hands. Chant the woman's name, place healing green or other colors into her chakras and aura. Let her speak briefly of her healing needs. At completion, several women help her up as though she is a newborn baby. Do this with all women who desire healing.

Libation: A priestess passes the wine bowl, saying:

> Drink of this sweetness,
> Let the life forces sweep through your veins
> Juice of the goddess from the body of the goddess . . .

She then passes a loaf of bread, breaking off the first piece to feed to her neighbor, saying:

> Eat of Her body, the blessed sustenance of grain
> Be strong and grow as Persephone has grown up from the Earth

Let the wine and bread be passed 'round the circle. Each woman feeds or offers to the next. The last woman returns them to the altar.

Affirming the mother/daughter bond and connections between women: One priestess takes up the ball of yarn and winds a strand around her neighbor, saying:

> We are daughters of our mothers
> We are mothers of our daughters
> We are sisters, we are lovers
> We are friends and good grandmothers
> We are women like a river
> Flowing on forever and ever . . .

All continue this chant, repeating it again and again, as the yarn is handed 'round and entwined around each woman. When the last woman is woven in, she ties the end to the beginning of the strand, sealing the web. Let the chant wind down to a natural conclusion. The first woman then untwines the yarn, still tied at the ends, and rolls it up into a ball, to replace upon the altar. One priestess will take this yarn home and save it until Autumn Equinox, when it will be cut to symbolize the separation of Demeter and Persephone. Each woman can keep her piece, to be retied next spring.

The telling of the tale: To be done in a previously chosen manner by one or more participants.

End with a circle dance, such as the hora, singing:

> We are the flow, we are the ebb
> We are the weavers, we are the web
>
> We are the weave, we are the web
> We are the spiders, we are the thread
>
> We are the spiders, we are the thread
> We are the witches, back from the dead
>
> We are the witches back from the dead
> We are the flow, we are the ebb, etc., etc.

Ground and center, open the circle, feast and make merry!

Diana
(Beltane)

. . . In spring She comes to power, when the red of Her moonbloods come . . .

This day celebrates the bleeding and flowering of the Maiden, the menarche of the year. Kore becomes Diana, or comes of age and is now her virgin self.

To truly appreciate this holy day, try to go back to the time when women's blood was adored and used for its potent life-sustaining qualities. When a woman began to bleed she was honored and declared of value and importance to the tribe. Special rituals of initiation were performed—private ones for the women only, and public ones with the entire community. The blood of a woman meant blessings from the goddess and the assurance of life's continuation. It was considered a great gift. Like the fruit and flowers of plants, the woman bleeding was the woman flowering. Blood was publicly displayed, used for anointing, and ritually poured into the earth to aid the growth of the crops.

May Day is the familiar holiday that falls near Beltane, celebrated with the Maypole dance. The phallic emphasis is obvious here. It is another example of the lack of female symbolism in patriarchal rituals. Meanwhile, our once glorified blood and genitals have become a source of secret shame and suffering. This holy day has special significance as a political tool to reclaim and heal our blood powers.

Like all the mysteries of the flesh, blood power is psychic as well as biological. It adds intensity and life force to spells, promises, and bonds. Beltane season is a good time to save our blood and anoint ourselves or one another during the ceremonies. The violent sacrifices of people and animals were done for this purpose, for people knew there was power in the blood. But the blood of woman is peaceful, and can be as highly charged by her ecstatic dance as that of an animal who has died violently. (See discussion on blood in Luna.)

In preparation for Beltane, think about your own experience with moonflow. Has it been painful? What significance can you find in this for yourself, knowing the honor our blood was once given? Do some planning with your moon calendar, so you can catch and save your moonblood in time for the ritual. The best method I have found is to wear a diaphragm during moonflow. The bowl shape and rubbery material work well as a receiver of fluid. Put your blood into a special bottle and store in the refrigerator. Cold keeps blood from coagulating.(If you are concerned about AIDS and prefer not to use blood, red wine or juice can be substituted.Or if for some reason you don't get a chance to catch your moonflow, use wine or juice.) Place some in a closed container upon your altar a week or so ahead of time, to charge it up.

This ritual can also be performed outdoors, perhaps in a grove in the woods. Remember that outdoor ritual spaces need to be private and good for dancing freely. Also be sure about fire safety if you plan to build a fire. If these factors are a problem it would be better to have your ritual where it is safe and you will not be interrupted.

Adorn the altar in red: red flowers, red draperies, red candles. Make garlands of leaves and red flowers for each woman to wear. Wear red clothing, body paint, jewelry, etc. Prepare red foods: rhubarb, beets, radishes, apples, red beans, carrots, red potatoes, berries, strawberries, red wine, red cabbage, fruit juices, etc. I have had great success with a sauté of mixed vegetables that included finely cut beet slices. The color from the beets made everything a deep wine red!

Mix everyone's blood in a ritual bowl and place upon the altar.

Begin with a procession into the ritual area, wearing garlands, ringing bells, singing as you come. Two priestesses remain at the site and form a doorway for all to enter through into the circle. Chant:

> Blessed be the Maiden within me
> For she bringeth courage and freedom
> Blessed be the Mother within me
> For she bringeth love and life
> Blessed be the Crone within me
> For she bringeth wisdom and understanding . . .

All are blessed at the entrance with a kiss from each priestess and words of welcome. All take their seats in the circle.

Close your eyes, breathe, center, raise the cone with the chanting of maiden goddesses' names: Diana, Kore, Artemis, Persephone, Iris, Ngame, and others.

Invocation—Priestess lights the candles on the altar, saying:

> All around us the Good Earth is blooming
> Diana has adorned her hair with fragrant flowers

The Maiden comes into her own Self
True self
Wild self
Free self
Behold the Maiden who has grown to this splendor
Behold the Maiden who brings us the promise
Of life and love and laughter . . .

All: Hail Diana!

Blood ceremony—A priestess takes up the bowl of blood and holds it aloft, saying:

This is the blood that promises life
The essence of She Who Bleeds Yet Does Not Die
Blessed is the blood of woman

All: Blessed is the blood of woman
Priestess: There's power in the blood of woman
All: There's power in the blood of woman
Priestess: There's life in the blood of woman
All: There's life in the blood of woman
There's love, there's magic, etc.
(Chant can be improvised, added to, and so on.
Other voices can take the lead.)

During the chanting the priestess goes around anointing each woman in the circle by painting a moon or pentacle (be creative) upon their brows.
Chant evolves into affirmations spoken around the circle:

We are women reclaiming that which was taken from us.
We are women reclaiming our blood and its powers.
No more will they have us believe it ugly or shameful,
Or unclean . . .
Praise the goddess in us that bleeds
Praise the goddess in us that gives life
Praise the goddess in us that loves
(Continue, add more, improvise . . .)

Priestess returns bowl to altar and resumes her seat during the above.

All chant: As a babe in blood I am born

As a maid with blood I flow
As woman in blood I birth
And from blood the milk doth go
With age comes the ending of blood
And the shadow of death I know . . .

Telling of blood stories: The women pass the rattle and share their experiences with blood: what their first flow was like, whether it was celebrated or kept hidden, whether it was painful or whether it still is, etc.

Priestess: Behold the Maiden now comes into full bloom
She is Virgin, Whole Unto Herself
We are Virgin, Whole Unto Ourselves
The Maiden bleeds but does not die
The Maiden flowers and will bear fruit
Behold the free wild and strong woman
Who belongs to no one
Behold the bright maiden
Warrior Woman, Amazon Woman
Risk-taking woman, Free-spirit woman
Let her strength be our strength
All: Let her strength be our strength
(Her power be our power, her beauty be our beauty, etc.)

Amazing feats: The rattle is passed to those who have strengths and successes to share. Some may have had a liberating or joyful experience in life, some may have skills to show, or something they have created, some may have accomplished political work, etc. All members support and celebrate with praise and cheers and blessings.

Close with the following chant, rise and sway, holding one another around the circle:

I am whole unto myself
Centered in the Kore of me
I shall give and shall receive
Goddess goddess loves me

Ground and center, open the circle, feast and celebrate!

Aphrodite
(Summer Solstice)

. . . And She dances and spins toward summer,
to the beat of Her passion's drum . . .

This holy day honors the mysteries and passions of Aphrodite, Goddess of Love. The goddess has been born and grown to womanhood, and now encounters her Divine Lover. She undergoes the death and rebirth of self that occurs when merging with another. She is impregnated or made fertile with future creations, be they flesh or spirit, human or divine, political, practical, artistic or social. This fertilization can be seen as self-made, community-made, or mutually created by the Lovers. Her lover can be a woman, a man, herself, her work or the Goddess. Loving couples or groups may wish to have special blessings today. This is a time of ecstasy and surrender.

Even as the sexual tides of our bodies rise and fall, so do the larger life tides of magnetic energy caused by the interplay of darkness and light. Aligning ourselves with energy waves—sexual, lunar, earthly, solar, magnetic, and so on—this is what ritual is all about. Many cultures and mythologies acknowledge the magnetic pull and reversals of these energy waves. They become personalized deities, and often are seen as lovers. It is now known that plants are literally excited by the presence of lovers in their vicinity, and this stimulates their growth. Rituals of an orgiastic nature were widespread in the ancient world, practiced for their ability to fertilize or amplify this process in nature.

Since this is the twentieth century and we are a product of our times, I have not designed a ritual that includes open lovemaking. Many people are not ready for this, and no one should have to feel pressured into it, though this is a matter of discretion within individual groups. The most important thing is to acknowledge and affirm Aphrodite in our lives.

As the heterosexual model of sexual love and reproduction became dominant, the divine lovers, male and female, ascended in mythology and religion. In the druidic faith the goddess received her divine consort at certain times of the year. Consecrated priests and priestesses made love in the plowed furrows of the fields as a ritual sacrament to the furthering of life. Many ancient royal marriages were consummated publicly so that the word could go out that life was assured symbolically through the mystery of their union. Among the Celts a poet often achieved his greatness through his passion for the Muse-goddess in the form of a human woman.

Now that we know about parthenogenesis, we can envision a universe of more variation. The ecstatic waves of passion can in themselves be understood as a mysterious and miraculous life force. These waves are kundalini or shakti in motion. They are aroused through chemical and spiritual magnetism between beings. When flowing powerfully they result in a union of forces that gives birth to something or someone new. Aphrodite is a mythopoetic name for this primordial, natural process.

She appears between women, men, men and women, old and young, rich and poor alike. Aphrodite is one of the most potent forces in our lives. Passionate love between people engenders great creations, ideas, revolutions, babies, poems, and causes.

It now makes sense in our enlightened century to re-mythologize the passionate magnetic climaxes of the year, so that any arrangement of gender is possible and sacred. Since the mysteries of women loving women have been buried so long, and the practice of women's mysteries along with it, I have chosen to create a ritual that celebrates these in particular, for it is here that the need is greatest. My theory is that in reinstating these practice we will restore balance and health to the planet.

Whatever your sexual preference, loving women is crucial to magic and to liberation. There are many ways to love a woman, not just sexual. We can share passion through mental exchange, through working together, changing the world together, doing magic, being sisters. We must work to undo the programming that has made us adversaries, and find all that is lovable in women. Friendships between women, women in business together, in partnerships, and the myriad forms of human sharing . . . all are ways of loving one another. Seeing the goddess in women, the beauty, wisdom, goodness and strength, is another way. To pursue this love to an ultimate expression of sexual passion is an option open to those who choose it, and can be seen as valid by those who do not.

This ritual, therefore, is for women of any sexual preference, but who all support woman love, practice it in some form, or wish to do so.

Sexual passion is a wild force of nature that has its own rhythms and laws. Attempts to cage Aphrodite or pin down the magical ecstasies of lovers will only result in Her departure. Therefore in this ritual we also celebrate the free wild spirit of Aphrodite, or woman's ability to bask in Her fires, yet keep her virginity or selfhood.

Come together outdoors, preferably by the ocean, Aphrodite's legendary birthplace. Festoon the altar with roses of every shade. Burn rose incense, anoint yourselves with rose scent. Have a bowl of consecrated rosewater on the altar. Bring red candles for passion, in red glass to keep out the wind, and garlands of roses for all to wear. Wear the clothes that make you feel the most beautiful. (Also place a bowl of red wine with roses and strawberries floating therein.)

Make a firepit in the center of the ritual circle area by scooping out the sand and ringing it with rocks. Mix dried rose branches in with the firewood.

Prepare sensuous foods: avocados, mushrooms, rose ice cream, melted cheese dishes, mangoes, whipped cream on fruit, red wine, rich sauces, etc.

Join hands, cast the circle, chant love goddesses' names: Aphrodite, Isis, Astarte, Inanna, and others.

The Priestess lights the altar candles, saying:

> With this flame we ignite the spirit of Aphrodite
> Goddess of passion and love

Great is the magic of Aphrodite
Who brings us joy and ecstasy
Great is the mystery of Aphrodite
Who brings us union, separation, and reunion
Great is the love of Aphrodite
Who brings inspiration to all the world . . .
Hail Aphrodite!
All: Hail Aphrodite!

Each woman lights a branch of rosewood at the altar and uses it to light the fire in the center of the circle. Chant simultaneously:

In the forest on my knees
Breaking brittle bones of trees
O Mother
I feel thee
Raising up the breath of fire
Thy wondrous gift of true desire
Surrender, I now to thee . . .

One priestess opens the circle and leads the group dancing to the water's edge. One priestess remains behind to tend the fires. Each woman is ritually undressed and bathed in the ocean. All proclaim her beauty and sacred womanhood. She is dressed and crowned with a garland of roses. The first woman to be bathed returns to the circle and trades places with the one who remained, so that she may also be ritually bathed. All then return to the circle and take their seats.

Priestess reads aloud a sacred pact to Aphrodite:

Aphrodite
Magnificent Goddess
Life force
Sacred passion
Burning desire
Sensual ecstasy
Mother of pleasure
We choose to live our lives that we may know thee
To welcome thine embrace
And cherish all true lovers
Through all time
To honor the depth of feeling
You awaken in us
And always to keep our hearts open

To you and to them
To give and receive of thy pleasures
That are forever at one with thee
And magic
And ritual
And love
To honor thy presence in other lovers
Whether thou appearest in one
Between two
Among three or more
Be they old, young, rich, poor, male, female
Black, brown, yellow, white, or red
We will stand by thee
And their right to know thee.
We promise never to use thy divine energy
To control or exploit another
And to protect ourselves from those who would so use us
To say no to sexual advances
When thou art not present

And sweet goddess
We also make this promise
To ourselves and thee
That we remain ourselves
Whole-unto-ourselves
As we dance and merge through thee
And re-emerge again . . .
And seek to comprehend the thorns
That grow among thy roses
For thou art a wild bird
O Great One,
That must fly to be free . . .

So be it
All: So be it
Priestess: Blessed be
All: Blessed be

Blessing of lovers: The rattle is passed around the circle and lovers come forward to be blessed, or individuals send blessings to lovers not present. Priestess anoints the cardinal points of their bodies with the rose water, saying:

> May Aphrodite bless you always with her love
> Your lips that kiss in sweetness
> Your heart that beats with desire
> Your breasts that give life and beauty
> Your womb and yoni that give so much pleasure
> Your feet that walk in Her ways . . .

Lovers kiss one another at each of these places of the body, then return to their places.

Healing of lovers: Those desiring special healings of problems or barriers between lovers, or obstructions to love in the world now ask for healing and blessing from the circle. All support, affirm, and call upon the goddess to help them.

Libation: Priestess takes up the bowl of red wine with strawberries and roses floating in it, saying:

> Drink of the wine of holy pleasure
> Eat of the fruit of holy pleasure

She takes up one strawberry and feeds it to the next woman in the circle, then hands her the bowl to drink. Each one does the same in turn for her neighbor till all have eaten and drunk. The bowl is returned to the altar.

All rise and dance around the fire, singing:

> We will rise with the fires of freedom
> Truth is the fire that will burn our chains
> We can stop the fires of destruction
> Healing is the fire running through our veins . . .
> (This chant is from Starhawk's coven.
> Music is included in her book *Dreaming the Dark*.)

When energy dies down, ground the energy and open the circle. Feast and make merry. Lovers who wish to can depart for their rites of ecstasy.

Habondia
(Lammas)

. . . Tis then She becomes so fertile, with the Life that is to come
And She flows with the Love that feeds us, 'til the Harvest Time is done . . .

The goddess is ripe and swelling with life. The earth puts forth her bounty. First fruits are weighing down the branches of the trees. Farms and gardens yield their summer harvests. This is a time to give thanks to the goddess for her many blessings and celebrate the gifts life brings. We also celebrate the heat of the waxing sun as we approach her sign, Leo. Sunny weather brings us out of doors, into the light of everyday. We are seen, known in our communities, coming together for projects of work and play. Since patriarchy has designated the sun as male, we note an increase of aggression and competition at this time. During the in-between-times when sacred kings were sacrificed to the goddess, the symbol of male surrender to the female principle was considered important to the survival of all. In modern times it is appropriate to represent this surrender more gently, but represent it we must, as we seek the softening, nourishing influence of female energy to temper and enhance the boldness of the male energies.

In this day and age there are truly many things to be thankful for. As women many of us have incredible numbers of choices: We can marry or not, have children or not, seek careers, live alone or not, develop our potentials. In this age of information and growth, many more of us have access to choices that were not always available in the past. We are continually exposed to streams of knowledge coming to us through media, through literature, art, and word-of-mouth. This indeed is a kind of abundance that we sometimes overlook.

In realizing our abundance, we must also come to terms with the different levels of privilege that still exist in the world. Not everyone has as much freedom. Those of who live in the U.S. often have great material privilege as well. Habondia's day is a good time to reflect on issues or privilege and class: to send energy and support to those who have less than we, to give thanks and appreciation for that which we do have, to invoke increase with our magic as needed for ourselves and others, to pray for the end of hunger and homelessness in the world and the dissolving of all such inequities. Issues of class have been known to divide sisters, and are a great handicap in building a cohesive movement for change. Let Lammas be a time for communication on these issues, for weeding out our hatred toward those who have (for all should have, and having does not make us bad), or our contempt for those who have not (for many are lacking and this in no way means we are inferior or unimportant.) Privileged sisters can teach us their strength, their willingness to deserve, to take good care of themselves. Women of less privilege can teach us their openness, their ability to care and be loyal, to survive in adversity, to act in community. Together we can step off the patriarchal staircase of hierarchy and power-over, and end the severance of these aspects of our natures that keep us alienated and afraid of each other. Economic class issues are pivotal in any realistic attempt toward world change. Failure to address these will lead to a dead end and no change at all.

Other themes that are appropriate on this summer holyday are animal spirits and the playfulness of the child-self. This ritual includes a ceremony to honor our totem animal guides and our kinship with all the creatures of nature. I suggest that games be played after the circle is opened to let the child self come out in free expression.

Hold this ritual at dawn, out of doors in a grassy meadow, with a good view of the eastern horizon where the sun will rise. Prepare the altar the day before. Decorate with fruits and vegetables of the harvest, an image of the goddess as the abundant all-giving One, and musical instruments to be played as the sun rises (drums, bells, flutes, etc.). Make a firepit in the center of the ritual circle area and pre-lay the firewood, ready for lighting. Also set up next to the firepit a vessel of water and a vessel of soft earth. Each woman cuts a length of branch to represent the male energy in her life. Place a basket with a good supply of dried sage.

Make summer foods: fruit and vegetable salads, flower salads. Fruit can be sliced and laid out on platters in beautiful mandala patterns; also vegetables can be prepared this way. It would be helpful to have a house near the meadow for storage and safekeeping of pre-made dishes. If you are out in the wilderness, prepare the foods after the ritual.

Camp out for the night, so that all will be together to greet and "sing in" the dawn. As the sky lightens, all take a ritual bath in a lake or stream nearby (if this is feasible). Dress in light summer clothing: rainbow colors, lots of body paint, nudity, bells on wrists and ankles, etc.

All assemble and sit in circle, as the first bright edge of the solar disk appears. Have instruments in your laps, ready to use. All hold hands. A priestess lights the altar candles, another lights the fire. All watch and listen in perfect silence to the symphony of dawn. When Sola is one-third risen all raise their voices and sing Her names: Amaterasu, Lucina, Inanna, Sola, Akewa . . . letting your voices swell and grow as the light grows, adding drum beats, bells and other sounds as desired.

When the sun is completely risen, the priestess speaks:

> Hail goddess of the sun
> Hail Mother who loves us with all-pervading heat
> Hail Habondia who pours her cornucopia upon the earth
> Hail Gaia, Earth Mother, who births all creatures

She takes up the bowl of sliced fruits, saying:

> This is the body that promises sustenance
> The sacred flesh of our Mother
> Eat and be filled, my sisters

She turns to the first woman in the circle and feeds her from the bowl. This woman then takes the bowl and turns to feed the next woman, and so on until all in the circle have been fed. The last woman returns the bowl to the altar.

A priestess says this spell for abundance:

> O Habondia, great is thy bounty

Endless are the streams of thine abundance
We call upon you now to nourish us
And those around the world who are in need
Teach us to receive and know that we deserve
Teach us to give and share the overflow . . .

Women call out from around the circle their requests and visions of abundance;
"I see myself with showers of money pouring down upon me," "I see my friend with
a happy home," "I see a hungry child eating her fill," "I see . . . etc." All affirm and
support each vision: "So be it. Blessed be. That which we have seen and said shall
come to be. As we wish it, so shall it be . . . etc."

All sing:

We are the daughters of the moon
We are the sisters of the sun
We are the mothers of the earth
We are women, we are one
(Repeat to taste.)

The rattle is passed to each woman who wishes to share her stories of male
experience within herself or in life, whether positive or negative. Be free to share any
and all oppressions that need to be purged and healed.

A priestess takes up her branch and holds it up to the sky, saying:

Once the goddess birthed only Her Self
And that which we have come to know as male
Was contained within Her
Then it came to pass that the male grew separate
And came forth as Her Divine Son and Lover
All was well while He loved Her
But then He changed, and the world changed with Him
Turning away from the Mother in jealousy and fear
Forgetting his source and sustenance
His eyes turned only upward as He forgot
Or raped the earth from which He came
Causing Himself and many sisters much suffering.
Now is the time for Him to grow up
And take his place in the natural order
And so on this day we seek to heal the split between male
    and female
To bring us back into harmony and peace once more . . .

She plunges the branch into the fire, the water, and the earth. Each woman in turn does the same with her branch, taking time to speak of any men in her life, or of aspects of her own nature that may be male identified. Each sends healing, enlightenment, etc. Finally all take the branches once more and burn them completely in the fire, chanting and dancing around the circle together:

> Let the patriarch be no more
> Let the sons and lovers return
> Let all men know true magic
> Let both women and men be mothers
> And in the fires of passion burn . . .
> (Repeat until all branches have burned up)

A priestess takes up the basket of dried sage, saying:

> I greet my totem animal spirit guide, the cat
> (Or snake, or whatever creature she feels is her ally)
> And make this offering
> Let our sister and brother creatures be honored always . . .

She throws some of the sage into the fire and passes the basket on to the next woman. Each woman does the same for her totem animal, until the circle is completed.

All howl, yip, squeal, chirp, meow, etc., beating drums and ringing bells . . .

Celebration of choices: A priestess begins with phrases such as, "I celebrate the freedom in my life," or "I celebrate my children," "I celebrate my lovers," "I celebrate my solitude," "I celebrate my independence," etc. Women take up the chant, calling out their celebrations until all have given thanks.

> *Priestess:* Praises and thanks to the goddess
> For all she has given
> *All:* Praises and thanks to the goddess
> For all she has given
> *Priestess:* Praises and thanks be to women
> For all they have given
> *All:* Praises and thanks be to women
> For all they have given
> Praises be to the earth, children, old ones, etc.

A moment of silence and meditation.

All rise and put their arms 'round one another in the circle, swaying and singing together:

Mother goddess keep me whole
Let thy beauty fill my soul
Maiden goddess keep me whole
Let thy power fill my soul
Crone goddess keep me whole
Let thy wisdom fill my soul . . .
(Repeat and flow with it, let voices fly and soar,
sing it in a round, enjoy . . .)

Priestess: Let the circle be opened
And the feasting begin!

Persephone
(Autumn Equinox)

. . . And She dances and spins toward darkness all dressed in autumn fire
To descend to the time of shadow, and rest from the world's desire . . .

The Year Goddess approaches her Crone time now, as the nights begin to lengthen
and the days to shorten once more. We feel her bite, the crispness of the air, the
brightness of the moon. Pomegranates and nuts ripen. Storehouses are stocked with
the harvest. Demeter yields Her daughter to the underworld. Kore descends to
become Persephone, to confront the inevitability of death, change, and separation.
This is a time of both mourning and joy, as we face the darkness and look back over
the year we have just lived. For many witches this begins the most powerful time of
the year—the dark time when the sun's light recedes to give more focus to the moon
and the deep self of the female principle. As Kore must separate from the world and
her Mother for a time, so must each of us undergo this mystery in our lives. Rituals
of grieving are appropriate now, as well as acknowledging the rebirth and joy to
follow.

The separation between mother and daughter, and that between lovers, is a
dominant theme of this time. We are in deep need of rituals that help us through these
transitions. Many daughters never achieve a full sense of self, remaining dependent
and frustrated all of their lives. Many mothers never fully let go of their children. Thus
both are caught and cannot grow to their reunion as equal adults. Most lovers rarely
undergo a closing ceremony when their passions end. Often splits continue to cause
anger and hurt for many years. Because of the fear of death and endings, grief is
frequently suppressed, and so continues to drain and sicken us indefinitely. "The way
out is the way through." We cannot reach rebirth if we cannot allow for death. Thus
we know neither life nor death, but a kind of stasis that is void of movement or

meaning. We fear the deep emotions that arise at such times, following the dictates of social propriety, and burying our grief with shame. (There are many cultures that provide mourners at death, or support the open expression of grief.)

Hold indoors. If you do not have an indoor sacred space, consecrate a living room and make an altar. Clear the center of the floor for the circle. Decorate the altar with autumnal plants: seeds, grains, nuts, pomegranates, etc. Drape with a dark color, such as blue or grey, and place an image of the Crone, a skull or bones, dried autumn leaves, autumn-colored candles. Wear autumn colors: rusts, browns, greys and dark blues. Make crowns of autumn leaves for all to wear. Prepare a sumptuous feast, for this is a harvest time. Place the ball of yarn used last Spring Equinox, and beside it a cutting tool, such as an athame or scissors. Prepare some separated pomegranate seeds in a dish.

Cast the circle, breathe, chant Persephone, raise the cone.

One by one the lights are all extinguished, and the circle sits in dark and silence for awhile.

A priestess chants:

> The old year wanes
> The moon swells to power
> The sun shrinks, to be reborn
> Maiden and Mother fly apart
> The Crone comes in to Her own
>
> We celebrate the darkening of the year
> With songs of death
> Come moon, give us your kiss
> Come Old One
> Give us your wisdom . . .

Another priestess begins a group relay chant:

> We can see in the dark
> *All:* We can see in the dark
> *Priestess:* We can feel in the dark
> *All:* We can feel in the dark
> *Priestess:* We can live in the dark
> *All:* We can live in the dark
> *Priestess:* We can touch in the dark
> *All:* We can touch in the dark
> *Priestess:* We can change in the dark
> We can know in the dark, dream, love, make love, be born, die, etc.

Let the chant build and subside, improvise, breathe deeply . . .

Ritual of mourning: A priestess cries: Alas for those who have left us and departed in death . . . aiieeeeeeee!!!

All cry and wail and moan, calling out the names of beloved ones who have died, or from whom they have been separated: mothers, children, lovers, friends, etc. Let the wailing build to a crescendo and wane naturally to its conclusion.

Priestess now lights the altar candles saying:

> As the light dies, so is the light reborn
> As life ends, so is it begun
> As the grain is cut down, so is the new seed planted

She takes up the dish of pomegranate seeds and feeds one seed to the first woman, saying:

> That which has died shall be reborn
> That which was separated shall be reunited
> Eat my sister of the seeds of death and renewal

The first woman eats the seed, then takes the dish and does the same for the next woman, and so on around the circle. The last one replaces the dish upon the altar.

Ceremony of bonding and separation: A priestess take up the ball of yarn and asks for the goddess' five-fold blessing:

> Maidens, Mothers and Crones
> We call for your blessings and support
> Give us strength for the time of separation
> Wholeness within ourselves
> Deep love for ourselves
> And wisdom from the underworld.
> Bless this yarn, symbol of our eternal connection.
>
> Bless it with your holy spirit
> Give us vision and dreams
> (She holds the yarn up and all place their visions
> within for the coming winter.)
> *All:* So be it!
> Bless it with your holy air
> And give us understanding
> And Naming power
> (She passes it through incense smoke.)
> *All:* So be it!

Bless it with your holy fire,
And give us the power
Of Will and Action
(She passes it over candle flame.)
All: So be it!
Bless it with your holy water
Give us Love
And infinite Compassion
(She sprinkles it with consecrated water.)
All: So be it!
Bless it with your holy earth
And give us harmony within our bodies
And with all nature
(She touches it to the earth.)
All: So be it!

Next she unwinds the yarn, which is still tied at the ends from last spring, and twines it around all members of the circle. Then she takes her athame or scissors and makes the first cut, saying:

Great is the wisdom of the goddess
For she gives us our time of rest
And separation from the world's desires
That we may be refreshed and renewed once more
For all forms must die to be reborn
Now let the cutting crone fulfill her purpose.

She hands the knife on, and all take turns cutting the yarn where it connects between each woman. Priestess turns to the first woman again and takes the severed strand, winding it gently around her wrist and tying it with a loose bow. All chant:

May the circle never be broken
May the earth always be whole
May the rattle ever be shaken
May the goddess live in our souls.

All continue the chant as each woman winds the strands of yarn around her neighbor's wrist. All wear their yarn until they get home that night, and then save it upon their altars until the following spring.

The rattle is passed and women share their grief at death or separation, their strengths and recoveries. Members affirm, support, and bless each sharing.

All join hands and close their eyes, visualizing a safe and cozy winter for all present, for the end of violence, war, rape, etc. upon the planet.

Closing chant: Maaaaaaaaaa . . .

Open the circle, share food and good will.

Hecate
(Hallowe'en)

. . . Now Her hair is touched with silver, winter's wisdom claims Her soul . . .

Hecate's day is widely considered the most powerful time of the year. The Crone indeed has come into her own as we observe the onset of wintry weather. Of all the matriarchal holy days, Hallomas has survived into the twentieth century the most intact. Though the Crone is denigrated as the "wicked witch" and the presence of death is treated as a joke, we can see an underlying magic being celebrated. The "trick-or-treating" of the children is a throwback to a more ancient observance of the cycles of life, for children represent future rebirth and universal hope for renewal. The powers of the dark feminine principle come to the fore and can be tapped for profound effects.

Until Spring Equinox Persephone will reside with Hecate in the underworld, learning the mysteries and powers of the deep self. She experiences her solo magic, her eternal soul, her abilities to create and uncreate, or heal. This is a good time for divination, communicating with the dead, strong dream teachings, and banishments of all kinds. The veil between the worlds of life and death is thin, and the powers of the dark are available to us. Some consider Hallomas the New Year, the end and beginning of the goddess' cycle. In olden times witches would hold their greatest gatherings to honor Hecate, sometimes called "the Queen of the Witches."

Hold indoors at midnight. Create a large encircled pentacle on the floor, big enough to contain all coveners. (Yarn pinned to a carpet can work, or masking tape on a wooden floor.) Decorate the altar in black with images of the Crone. Have black candles and banishing incense. Wear black robes and paint a black pentacle on your brow. Prepare a cauldron with dried herbs (sage, rosemary, the dried crowns of the last ritual, etc.). Prepare triangular pieces of parchment, one for each member to write her banishings down. Place a crystal ball at the altar's center, and have a tarot deck handy. Also place images of old people, grandmothers, mothers and other relatives, or those departed. Have both pomegranate wine and fruit.

Cook magic foods: (one of my students once made a rainbow cone cake!) hot apple pie, steaming vegetable or meat loaves with surprise gifts cooked inside, vegetable pies with sour cream, pasties, seed cake for the winter journey, etc. Bring all your mojo to be re-charged on the altar, your crystals and wands, herb pouches, tarot decks, etc.

Priestess lights the altar candles, saying:

> Welcome wise ones, we call you to our circle

Join hands, cast the circle, chant Hecate, Cerridwen, Kali, Baba Yaga, and others. Raise the cone.

Summoning the Crones: A Priestess chants:

> Now is the time of mystery upon us
> Now come the Crones of ancient times
> *All:* Welcome!
> *Priestess:* The Spirit Crones with their power to dream
> *All:* Welcome!
> *Priestess:* The Air Crones with their power to cut and name
> *All:* Welcome!
> *Priestess:* The Fire Crones with their cauldrons of transformation
> *All:* Welcome!
> *Priestess:* The Water Crones with their powers of divination
> *All:* Welcome!
> *Priestess:* The Earth Crones with their knowledge of Nature's ways
> *All:* Welcome!

The priestess moves to each arm of the star as she calls on the crones of each element. (The spirit arm points north and toward the altar.)

A priestess now takes up the bowl of pomegranate wine, saying:

> Drink o my sisters
> The blood of the fruit
> Of death and rebirth

She passes the bowl to the first woman, who drinks and passes it on.

> *Priestess:* Now it comes to pass
> That Kore is become Persephone
> She resides in the underworld with Hecate
> And learns the mysteries of life and death
> *All:* Even as we
> *Priestess:* Blessed is the Goddess who lives and dies forever
> *All:* Even as we
> *Priestess:* Blessed is the Goddess who creates all things
> *All:* Even as we
> *Priestess:* Blessed is the Goddess
> Who takes all back into Herself in death

All: Even as we
Priestess: Blessed is the Goddess
Who renews and rebirths all that has died
All: Even as we
Blessed be . . .

Song:
O mistress of the night
The shining stars of thee
The endless deep of all thy mystery
I lose myself in thee
I find myself in thee . . .
(To the tune of Lady Mother of all)

Herstorical healing:

Priestess: O my sisters
Let us remember
The Burning Times
The centuries of persecution
Let us remember the rape and oppression of woman
Priestess chants or sings: Nine million witches were burned
All: Never again!
Priestess: Nine million witches were burned
All: Never again!
(Women sing out or call out, improvise)
Six million Jews were killed
Never again!
One thousand at Jonestown did die
Never again!
How many black people were slaves?
Never again!
How many martyrs been slain?
Never again!
How many sisters were raped?
Never again . . . (expand to taste, repeat, etc.)
Nine million witches were burned
Never again!

Priestess: We are the witches of centuries
Once men came in jealousy and violence
To destroy the goddess' ways

But She rises again and again
We are reborn forever
Song:
O you can't kill the spirit
She's like a mountain
Old and strong
She goes on and on (repeat, let it swell and fall)

Banishing Ceremony: A priestess takes the leaves of parchment and passes them 'round the circle.

Priestess: We call upon the spirit world
To aid us now in banishment
Let all unwanted matters
Be dissolved away.

Women write in silence upon their parchments all unwanted phenomena, crumple them up and drop them one by one into the cauldron. As each woman goes to the center she says aloud (if she so chooses) that which she is banishing: "I banish rape," "fear," "poverty,"—powerlessness, loneliness, alienation, power-over, shock treatments, war, etc. Don't be afraid to be personal. This is a great time to rid ourselves of old patterns that we no longer need. "I banish my unawareness, my jealousy, my class prejudices, my fear to be myself, my fear to show anger, my fear of success . . ."

When all have dropped their parchments into the cauldron, a priestess lights them and stirs up the flames. All chant until the parchments are thoroughly burned:

Goddesses of darkest night
Send our troubles all to flight
Burn them in thy sacred fires
And replace them with our hearts' desires!

Repeat and let the chant rise to a peak of intensity. Don't be shy about shouting and letting your emotions out. Hecate will hear you now. (The next day, one or two priestesses can take the ashes and wash them out to sea or downstream or into a lake. It is best to let the ashes go, turn your back and walk away without looking back.) When the fire has died down, all join hands or put their arms around each other and sing:

In the darksome cave of sleep
Flowing, floating down and deep
O Wise One, I move through thee

Thy imagery will ever wend
Dreaming to the dreamer send
Surrender, I now to thee . . .

Dream Ceremony: The rattle is passed and each sister relates a dream or vision she has had that feels significant and instructive. She may receive interpretive feedback and support from the group as desired.

Priestess: Goddess grant us all good dreaming.
Nagdeo!
All: Nagdeo!
Priestess: Let us celebrate the crones of ancient times
The crones we have known
The crones of present time
The crones of the future
And our own crone-selves

Women call out the names of crones: grandmothers, mothers, aunts, themselves, crones of the past, etc. Let the names be repeated and sung by the group. Good wishes and blessings are sent to all crones of the earth.

Visualization: All speak their visions of fulfillment in old age: "I see myself healthy when I am a crone." "I see myself loved when I am a crone." "I see myself loving, in abundance, creative, surrounded by beauty, etc." Voices randomly call from around the circle. All respond, "So be it!" to each vision. Then chant together three times:

As we weave it
So doth it be!

Divination: Priestess takes her tarot cards and calls upon Hecate to help bring insight and visions for the coming year. She mixes the cards and spreads them out in the center of the circle. Each woman chooses a card. Chosen cards are laid out in a small circle within the circle. All women lend their insight and support to the interpretations.

Priestess: Many thanks o Wise Ones
For assisting us with magic,
Love, and inspiration.

All join hands and close eyes, hum, ground the energy.
Open the circle, feast and make merry . . .

Seasonal Magick

The year is a dancing woman
Who is born at the coming of spring
The year is a dancing woman
Of Her birth and death we sing . . .
In spring She comes to power
When the red of Her moonbloods come
And She dances and spins towards summer
To the beat of Her passion's drum
'Tis then She becomes so fertile
With the Life that is to come
And She flows with the Love that feeds us
'Til the Harvest Time is done
Then dances and spins towards darkness
All dressed in autumn fire
To descend to the time of shadow
And rest from the world's desire
Now Her hair is touched with silver
Winter's wisdom claims her soul
And She births the spirit within us
Bringing light and hope to us all
Igniting a blaze in the darkness
To kindle the coming spring
Then dreams 'til Her resurrection
And Her story again begins . . .
The year is a dancing woman
Who is born at the coming of spring
The year is a dancing woman
Of Her birth and death we sing . . .

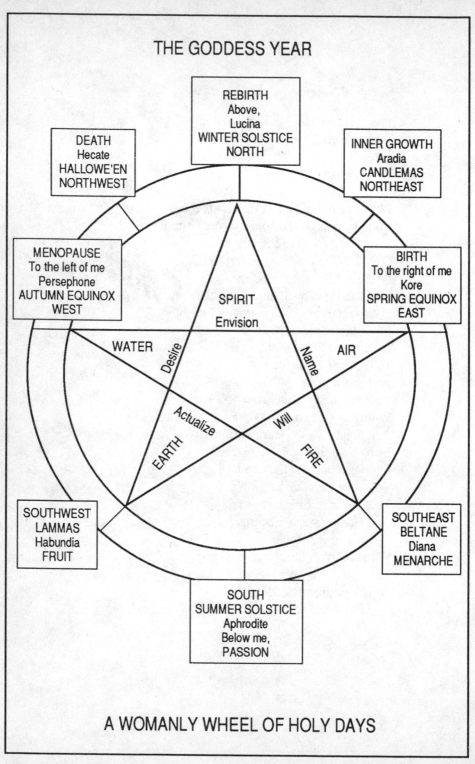

THE GODDESS YEAR

REBIRTH
Above,
Lucina
WINTER SOLSTICE
NORTH

DEATH
Hecate
HALLOWE'EN
NORTHWEST

INNER GROWTH
Aradia
CANDLEMAS
NORTHEAST

MENOPAUSE
To the left of me
Persephone
AUTUMN EQUINOX
WEST

BIRTH
To the right of me
Kore
SPRING EQUINOX
EAST

SPIRIT
Envision

WATER   Desire   Name   AIR

Actualize   Will

EARTH   FIRE

SOUTHWEST
LAMMAS
Habundia
FRUIT

SOUTHEAST
BELTANE
Diana
MENARCHE

SOUTH
SUMMER SOLSTICE
Aphrodite
Below me,
PASSION

A WOMANLY WHEEL OF HOLY DAYS

Suggested Projects

1. Study and collect seasonal myths of different times and cultures. See how they relate and compare to holiday practices that are familiar today. Look for their differences as well as their common threads. Note the deities involved, their relationships and gender. Note the positions of Goddesses in these stories, and their degree of influence.

2. Study the holiday practices of a variety of cultures. Look for evidence of Goddess worship in these traditions. (For example, egg-painting at Eastertime or calling on the spirits of the dead in late fall.) Glean out Goddess-oriented traditions that appeal to you and make a record of these for use in your own celebrations.

3. Make your own myth of the Goddess Year. Use ideas offered here or in other traditions ancient or current. Take into account the universal passages of Birth, Growth, Death and Rebirth, or Maiden, Mother, and Crone.

4. Make eight subsidiary myths for each of the holy days, focusing on the mood, landscape and themes of each. For example, write a story of childbirth for Spring Equinox, a story of a woman's first bloods (or the Goddess' first bloods) for April 30th, a goddess love story for Summer Solstice, and so on. Use these stories as thematic material for enactment, reading aloud, costumes, altar designs, food and any other elements of your ceremonies.

5. Make a "feminary" or scrapbook or ritual record-book of your holy day practices, myths, food recipes, costumes, prayers, songs, and any other relevant lore. Add photos of the actual events, memorabilia, reminiscences. Keep and use for future holy days. Leave space and pages to add material that accumulates over the years.

6. Examine and discuss or write down your feelings and experiences regarding the holidays. Give thought to the roles women and men have played at holiday celebrations you remember. Make note of the emotional climate at family gatherings, among friends, or other groups. Analyze these in the light of information you now have of Goddess-oriented celebrations and feminist awareness. Sort out what you want to retain for future holidays and what you wish to discard.

7. Select a ritual from this Cycle, preferably one that falls on or near the time of this project. Perform it with a few women or adapt it for doing alone. Write it up in your *Book of Shadows* and preserve for future use.

8. Make a sunwheel to fit with your moonwheel. Add colors that suggest the seasons, images of Goddesses, names for the holy days, thematic material, dates and other lore. Complete your calendar with other wheels for patriarchal months, days, and zodiac signs as shown below. Bless your calendar wheel and keep it at your altar, turning it as the seasons turn. Suggested colors for the seasons: Kore-to-Diana, Green. Diana-to-Aphrodite, Red. Aphrodite-to-Habondia, Rainbows. Habundia to Persephone, Blue. Persephone to Hecate, Purple. Hecate-to-Lucina, Grey. Lucina-to-Aradia, Silver. Aradia-to-Kore, Pale Green.

To Make A Goddess Clock

To make a perennial Goddess calendar wheel, cut out 5 rounds of flexible white cardboard—the bigger you make them, the more information you can include. Find the centers. I used dinner plates and platters to get my rounds, and cut out paper patterns which I could fold in quarters to get the centers. Place the thinner paper circles over the cardboard ones, and poke a tiny center-hole mark onto the cardboard with a pin. Then with a pencil and ruler you can mark off your dividing wedges or lines.

1. One circle for the solar year and seasons has 8 segments. Fill in the 8 holy days of the equinoxes, solstices, and cross-quarter days with their goddesses, themes, etc. This wheel can be colored to match the seasons. See color suggestions above in Suggested Project 8.

2. One extra big circle for the thirteen moons, with her phases around the rim. Fill in tree names, drawings of leaves, goddesses, magic lore, and any other materials related to moontime. Our foremothers measured time by the moon and their own blood cycles, so it is appropriate that this be the most prominent wheel in the calendar. There are thirteen lunations every third year, and twelve lunations the other two years in between. A thirteen-spaced wheel can work for both types of cycles simply by skipping Ruis (the Elder Moon) every twelve-moon year.

3. One circle for the signs of the zodiac.

4. One circle for the patriarchal months, in case you want to keep track of where the rest of the world is.

5. And one giant circle of days; 366 lines so as to include February 29 for leap year. If space is limited, you can skip every other day, using 1, 3, 5, etc. This wheel is optional and you may prefer to rely on a more detailed calendar for your day-to-day entries. (See illustration on bottom of page 199.) Each round fits into the next larger one so that all nest together nicely. Pin them at their centers to a piece of wood, the wall, a table, or whatever is convenient. Make a marker to show where "now" is, turn

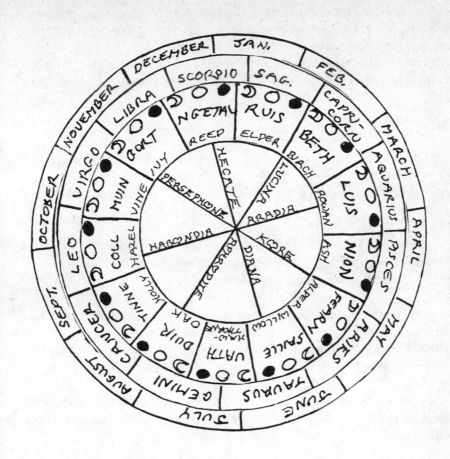

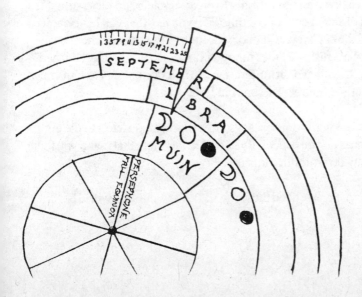

all wheels so that day, month, moon, zodiac sign and season all line up at the marker. This is a perpetual calendar and can be used every year. It doesn't have to be perfectly accurate, as each wheel can be adjusted individually.

Note: The wheels 1, 2, 3, and 4 drawn here actually do fit together in case you'd like to copy them and make a tiny version of this calendar.

Questions to Ponder

1. Do you have special feelings around the holidays? Any special memories?

2. Have you celebrated holidays in recent years? If so, how? Do you feel disenchanted with most holidays?

3. What sort of reality do you feel is generated by standard holiday practices? Is it possible, within that context, to find meaning and joy in these traditions? Can you feel yourself, as a woman, reflected positively in any of these celebrations?

4. What sort of reality do you feel is generated by the new goddess-oriented practices? Can you feel yourself affirmed as a woman? Are you attracted to the new approaches to holy days? Do you see yourself adopting any of them and keeping them in your life?

5. Do you experience a sense of sacredness, of something miraculous going on, when the holidays come around? Do you think holy days are important? If so, why? If not, why not?

6. Now that you have been given an opportunity to create circular, goddess-oriented calendars, do you have a different concept of time? Do you feel that you have choice regarding the passage of time? Can you spend your time as you choose more easily now? Do you feel more or less rushed? Does time go in a straight line and feel limited? Or does it go on and on, 'round and around forever? How does your view of time affect your feelings about the future? The present? The past?

7. How do you feel about linking Women's Mysteries (birth, blood, etc.) to the eight solar holy days? Which ones do you especially like? Are there any that make you feel uncomfortable? If so, why do you think this is?

8. Suppose women everywhere practiced these rituals. What would the world be like?

Reading and Other Resources

Z. Budapest, *The Grandmother of Time* and *The Holy Book of Women's Mysteries*, Vols. 1 and 2.

Pauline Campanelli, *The Wheel of the Year*.

Carol Orlock, *The Goddess Letters* (the myth of Demeter and Persephone retold).

Starhawk, *Dreaming the Dark* and *The Spiral Dance*.

Diane Stein, *Casting the Circle*.

Marion Weinstein, *Earth Magic*.

Valerie Worth, *The Crone's Book of Words*.

The Beltane Papers. Octava has wonderful recipes for the holidays. P.O. Box 8, Clear Lake, WA 98235.

The song "Seasonal Magick" is available on tapes: *Witch-A-Way* ($13) and *Songs and Chants of the Goddess*, Vol. II ($10) from Shekhinah Mountainwater. The melodies for the chants "We are the Flow, We are the Ebb," "I Am Whole Unto Myself," "Blessed Be the Maiden Within Me," "Mother Goddess Keep Me Whole," "O Mistress of the Night" and "In the Darksome Cave of Sleep" are all on my tape *Songs and Chants of the Goddess*. I have a tape available with a telling of the Winter Solstice Legend, and two beautiful Solstice carols made for community singing ($10 plus $2 postage). The chant "As I Love Myself . . ." included in the Aradia ritual is on Vol. II of *Songs and Chants of the Goddess*. The chant "As a babe in blood I am born . . ." (The Five Blood Mysteries) is on the tape *Witch-A-Way*. The chant "Nine Million Witches" is on Vol. I.

INTERLUDE

. . . spinning, spinning, ends, beginnings . . .

And so we come to the end of the Second Passage, named "Spinning" for the turning of three major wheels of Goddess reality: the wheel of the moon's turning through the year, the wheel of the earth's turnings around the sun, and the wheel of Women's Mysteries. The hub at their converging centers is the Goddess-Muse, She who inspires our endless re-telling and re-living of the tale of Birthing, Living, Dying, and Return. All three spin in unison, and are concentric with the initial wheels of Maiden/Mother/Crone and Spirit/Air/Fire/Earth/Water.

You now have at your fingertips the means to spin with Goddess reality through time, through the elements and seasons, and through the mystical transformations of your beautiful womanself. Even if you decide to end or pause in your journey here, you have the means to live a Goddess-oriented way of life. I hope you will always spin with these magical wheels, my sister, and that with each turning you will grow and learn about them ever more deeply.

You rest now in the quiet depths of Ariadne's cave. Here is a moment to reflect and light a candle for thanksgiving, and for courage to face what is to come. Behind you lie the many chambers and corridors you have visited, and the wisdom you have found. Ahead of you the passage takes a turn to the left, and slants gently downward into darkness. Deeper and deeper the journey goes. Will you take up the gleaming silver ball of thread once more, and set it to rolling down this next incline? Only you can decide.

The Goddesses are still here with you, ready to assist, encouraging you to go on. "Would you like to learn to read the runes or tarot cards?" whispers Mnemosyne, enticing. "Or to cast spells and make things happen?" She flows across the cavern like water, and waves a near-transparent hand as if to conjure.

Themis is more substantial, like the earth. "Now that you have gathered the information of Goddess ways and begun to spin with them on the wheel of life, you come to the next level of your powers, that of weaving the web of your own destiny." She strokes your brow, brushing back a stray wisp of hair. "Are you ready for the mysteries of Aphrodite, Goddess of Passionate Love? Or my own mysteries of community?"

Idea skips playfully over to the arched opening, exclaiming with delight. "Look! There's a lamp here in this niche!" She turns and lifts the small brass lantern she has found. It magically glows at her touch, sending a beam of pure gold down the waiting passageway. You gasp to see that it is lined, walls and ceiling, with sparkling crystals of every hue. How can you resist? The silver ball of thread lies gleaming in your hand . . .

THIRD PASSAGE

WEAVING

CYCLE 9

Divination

Ishtar speaks:
To give omens do I arise
Do I arise in perfectness
—Quoted by Nor Hall, in
The Moon and the Virgin

An old woman walks up a winding mountain path. Luna washes the trees and rocks with her silver magic. The woman is bent, and wrapped in black. She mutters under her breath a prayer or mantra as she climbs. The way opens before her and reveals a small silver pool nested in the earth. Crouching before it, the woman sways and sings, calling upon the spirits to aid her in her seeing. As her trance deepens, she begins to see forms taking shape in the moonlit water. A woman holding a child... a king being crowned ... a queen on her deathbed ...the rise and fall of a nation...

A merchant of ancient patriarchal Greece, who seeks an oracle, enters the great temple of Apollo at Delphi. The priest leads him down a staircase into the cavernous earth below. There he sees a woman, known as the sibyl, seated upon a tripod which rests over a great hole in the cavern floor. Gaseous fumes rise up and surround her; as she breathes them into herself she goes into trance, and begins to babble incoherently. A group of priests gather nearby, recording their impressions on tablets they hold . . .

A gypsy encampment can be seen, silhouetted in the twilit countryside. Firelight flickers on the hulking sides of the circled wagons. A stranger comes from the village and knocks on one caravan door. An old woman opens, admitting her into her tiny home on wheels. Tucked into the far end is a table where she motions the stranger to seat herself. Taking the chair opposite, she pulls a deck of cards from somewhere amidst the folds of her voluminous skirts. She begins to pull out cards and lay them on the table. "I see that you are in search of spiritual love," she says. The woman nods, amazed at her perception . . .

Though divination once held an established and respected position in many societies, it has fallen into disrepute, along with many goddess traditions. And yet, like Her, it has never really left us. Gypsies are still consulted at fairs, brujas and shamans still searched out in their hidden caves. Mediums and psychics can still be found in this day of rationality and technology. Though the Bible has done much to hush up the discoveries of astrologers and the wisdom of tarot cards, these divination systems are being revived today. In fact, laws against divinatory practices that have been on the books for ages are now being overturned. For example, in August of 1985 the *San Francisco Chronicle* announced that the California Supreme Court ruled that "Fortune-tellers who charge for their psychic services cannot be banned from operating in a city . . ." This is a major breakthrough for modern-day magic makers.

In the study of ancient societies we find an endless array of divination techniques. Sibyls in their caves babbled in trance in the temples of the goddess or gods of their day. Pythias were priestesses who danced and struggled with pythons; their movements were then interpreted. In Sumeria a priestess would allow a certain snake to bite her. Its venom would put her in an inspired trance. In Rome priests would gain knowledge of the future by examining the entrails of slaughtered birds. Celtic peoples divined from the flight formations of birds, or by scrying in the waters of sacred pools that caught the light of the moon. Many native people found answers by throwing bones or seeds and examining their patterns. In many cases these oracles held very powerful positions. They were consulted by leaders and kings and their prophecies were followed and acted upon. Often war or peace would be made on the basis of a "seeing."

Through the ages there have been famous prophets and seers. Nostradamus, who lived in France in the sixteenth century, predicted many things that came true. People today still believe that his warnings of world devastation in 1999 should be heeded. Mother Shipton, a famous witch of fifteenth-century England, made many prophecies, both political and personal, that came true. Edgar Cayce, the "sleeping prophet" of our own century, diagnosed illnesses while in trance. He predicted earthquake disaster in California. I remember when one of his earthquake dates came up. When the big one didn't happen, I thought we must be preventing it with our positive thoughts!

What is divination? Why do humans persist in the pursuit of prophetic knowledge? Perhaps we would rather not know what is going to happen! And then there is the question of free will. Are we able to create the destinies of our choosing?

Witches have always had some way to tell what is hidden, or what will occur. They take the sensible "an ounce of prevention is worth a pound of cure" approach. Events are the reflection of consciousness, which exists in and of itself. Apparently there is an accumulative effect; the future "jells up" after a while, or as we witches might say, "the wheel has turned." There may be aspects of the future that we still have time to change, that the precognitive seer can spot for us. However, it is still difficult to determine which foreseeable events will happen no matter what we do to try to prevent them, and which can actually be avoided.

Aeschylus, for example, was told that he would die from a severe blow on his head. On the appointed day he went to the desert, to a completely empty spot, to avoid the disaster. A passing bird of prey dropped a turtle on him from the sky, cracking his skull and fulfilling the prophecy!

In the story of the Sleeping Beauty, the thirteenth fairy predicts that the princess will prick her finger on a spindle at the age of 16, and die. The twelfth fairy softens the blow by changing Beauty's death to 100 years of sleep. The king spends the next years ridding the kingdom of all spinning wheels in an effort to prevent the fulfillment of this prophecy. But when the fatal day arrives, Beauty stumbles across an old woman in a tower, spinning, of course.

A disaster signal is a warning that consciousness has been creating a certain combination of energies that are building up toward an explosion or cataclysm. The antidote is to *change consciousness* rapidly enough so as to alter the thoughtforms that are building toward danger. This can be done with ritual, solo or collectively, as appropriate. In a cohesive magical community, divination would be an accepted method of prevention therapy. Those with the "sight" would read the future occasionally to see what was forthcoming. If foretold events are found to be desirable, the community would celebrate and affirm them; if not, a banishing or transforming ritual would be enacted. Thus we would take conscious responsibility for what we now do haphazardly—create our collective reality.

Today the question as to whether or not foretold disasters will occur is crucial. Native Americans have predicted total destruction by war, earthquakes, etc. So have Cayce and Nostradamus. World leaders are stockpiling weapons of war at this very moment, enough to destroy our precious world many times over. And yet, like Cayce's earthquakes, we can prevent these things with our positive and loving thoughts and actions. After the October 17, 1989 earthquake that powerfully rocked my home in Santa Cruz, there were hundreds of little quakes. All those little quakes felt like a good thing, for the earth settled a bit more each time, making a larger upset less likely. This same principle can be applied sociologically and psychologically. It translates into small-scale confrontations, such as admitting one's sexual preference, or pointing out oppressive situations firmly, but lovingly. Though these are risky and take courage to do (as they can create minor "earthquakes"), they can, in the long run, prevent large-scale hostilities such as mass slaughter and war, or destruction on a more personal scale.

In my opinion, Goddess-consciousness is the all-important antidote to preventing predicted disasters. Loving Her as the earth will prevent earthquakes. Loving Her as spirit will prevent denial of spirit. Loving Her as ourselves will prevent oppression of ourselves. Loving Her as children will prevent the abuse of children. Loving Her as magic will prevent the misuse of power. Loving her as community will prevent the fragmenting of human social responsibility.

How does divination work? When a seer probes or scries into what is hidden, she is tuning into the deep mind. The everyday rational mind is suspended for a time so that the timeless "other side" may come into view. This ability had been called the sixth sense by many, and is the same faculty with which we cast spells, perform banishments, read into the subconscious, or make miracles. Our minds have been compared to an iceberg, the conscious rational part being that which is visible above the surface of the sea. The larger and deeper aspects are vast beyond our intellectual awareness. Interestingly, the patriarchal approach is to suppress the deep mind and dwell exclusively in the rational, using the evidence of the remaining five senses.

Actually, all divination systems perform the same function. They provide a point of focus to help us relax, concentrate and made contact with that other mind. In this "shadow realm," past, present and future are simultaneous, and it is possible to see any aspect. It is only the conscious waking mind that needs the linearity of progressing "nows"; a brilliantly clever illusion we create, that we may have a ground for experiencing.

The farther back we go in social histories, the more we find traditions and conventions that accept and converse with the sixth sense. Ancient religions always included it, whether in the elaborate ceremonies of the Egyptians and Sumerians, or the simple earthy dances of the Native Americans. In many ways, the forces that destroyed these traditions can be described as those of the rational mind and the insistence on the evidence of the physical senses. This retreat from the non-rational is typical of a mentality that fears the goddess powers. It reached its zenith in the nineteenth century, when fashionable philosophers declared that the earth is a mechanism, that life has no particular meaning, and that the universe has no soul. The physical world became mythologized as male, with male images to represent its various functions. The aspects of the deep mind—telepathy, precognition, visualization, dreams, trance—were relegated to the world of the female and labelled frightening, evil, or at best, absurd.

While women have been punished and despised for possessing such powers, we have managed to develop and practice them behind the scenes. As witches we have a great heritage in the uses of the deep mind. But we have been horribly persecuted, and have much healing to do. We must transcend all the negative conditioning of our culture before we can allow ourselves to freely express through our deep selves.

The most important aspect of this healing rests in our attitude. We need to acknowledge first of all that we have these powers, and secondly, that it is okay to have them. In addition, we need to develop firm ethics, promising ourselves never to use these abilities to violate or exploit anyone. Then we need a never-ending vigilance toward the input from the world around us. Images of satanic evil, destructive psychic cults, fear of the animal passions, ugly witches, wicked crones, are some to watch for. All must be carefully screened out from what we know is precious and good within us. Next, we need to find reinforcement from positive sources, and there are more and more of these all the time. Physics, therapy, parapsychology, mysticism, new age ministries and sciences, new healing techniques are blooming with the discoveries of the things the witches knew before the beginning of recorded history. Finally, we need to begin practicing our own forms of divination, for nothing teaches appreciation and acceptance like simple experience.

The Goddess As Fate

Women were the first diviners and goddesses among the first symbols of destiny. The Moirae of Greek mythology were a famous triad of crones who were said to spin, weave, and cut the thread of fate. The spinning wheel has many layers of meaning as the wheel of time and fortunes, of birth and life and death, of the passing of the seasons, of the cycling of all things, and the creation of form (thread) from chaos (rough wool). It is empowering for women to recall such archetypes of our abilities to weave our destinies. Interestingly, the goddess of fate has survived into patriarchy as Lady Luck, often invoked when the Wheel of Fortune is spun at carnivals and gambling houses. What a far cry from Her former awe-inspiring position!

> She weave
> She spin
> She gather, she
> The morning
> Noon
> And night of me
> Budding spring
> And swelling summer
> Chilling winter
> Weaveth she
> Up and outer
> Down and inner
> Weave and gather
> Silent spinner
> Spider woman
> Spinning three
> Timeless times
> Of destiny . . .

In Norse mythology there was also a triadic crone-goddess symbol for fate—the Norns. They were said to be found under the great Tree of Life or Yggdrasil, where they would be consulted for answers to all questions. The Graeae or Grey women, also of Greek culture, appear in the saga of Perseus and the Medusa. They are shown sharing a disembodied eye, which they take turns looking through in order to "see." In the patriarchal version of the tale, Perseus steals this eye and uses it to ferret out the Medusa for slaying. Robert Graves has (in my opinion) a better interpretation, saying that the eye represents poetic insight, which is the lesson Perseus has come to seek at the feet of the Wise Ones.

Hecate in her Crone aspect is also associated with fate and divination. She is seen at crossroads, or places of choice and change when the wheel of destiny is turning. Another Greek goddess, Tyche, was said to turn the entire wheel of the universe and stars. Glinda, the Good Sorceress of the Land of Oz, was a wonderful goddess in disguise. She had a magic book in which all things that ever happened were automatically written as soon as they occurred. This is a great symbol of the deep mind, which *does* record all events!

Goddesses of fate can be found in every culture. Some of their other names are the Morrigan, the Zorya, the triple Guinevere or Brigit, the Horae, the Muses, the Gorgons, the Fairies, Fortuna, and triple Aphrodite. In many cases they were triadic, representing Maiden, Mother and Crone, or past, present and future. In most cases she was a weaver; in fact the word destiny comes from the Latin *destino*, meaning that which is woven.

In the tarot, the Wheel of Fortune card is said to rule the entire deck. In my own version, which I have named Moirae, I have chosen to represent the three as Maiden, Mother and Crone. Thus they represent the beginning, middle and end of fortunes. The card still bears the same essential meanings as the old tarot version—a turn of circumstance, an act of goddess, etc. But now we can envision this process with relation to our ancient female archetypes.

The goddess divines the future, and at the same time, she creates it. She is our symbol of insight and also of our responsibility for the destinies we create, both individually and collectively. Herein lies the delicate balance between self-fulfilling prophecies, predestination, and full conscious choice. While some futures have progressed too far to be avoided, this does not mean we need to firmly expect negative circumstances. If in scrying we find a misfortune, we may still have time to change that vibration by substituting a positive image or action. On the other hand, some futures are inevitable, and we are far wiser to accept and prepare for these than to avoid them or pretend they are not there. The more consciously we create now, the more control we have over what will take place later.

This does not mean we are omnipotent in all things, however. There are millions and millions of consciousnesses creating in concert. Each of us is like a little rower, rowing the boat of our own consciousness into the eddies and streams of all others. We can "make waves" and wakes, influence or respond to the flow. This is why societies cannot be free until enough of its individual members take responsibility and power to become a strong enough wave of change. "There are no individual solutions," teach the feminists. People who live in isolated privilege, meeting only their own needs, are living in towers of self-deception that must eventually come tumbling down. We are an interacting whole and will only know true healing when we begin to create true community. This is the meaning of the tarot card called The Tower, or Lightening.

You may have noticed that certain circumstances and types of people appear in your life again and again. This is one of the messages of the Wheel of Fate. We send ourselves karmic lessons as many times as needed until we learn them well. Each time they come 'round we are a little better prepared than the last time, for we have accumulated a little more information and consciousness with which to deal with them. As we adapt our thoughts and behavior, we change our destiny, and eventually no longer need to observe the same phenomena, unless we choose to. Those at less conscious levels feel themselves to be subjected to circumstance and to have little or no choice in its shaping. For them this will be true until they decide to step in and take a hand in the wheel's turning. This is the tradition of "witch," the root of which is to bend or shape reality. From the Fool to the Crone in the tarot, we can see the two extremes of dealing with fate, from unconscious innocence to responsible knowing.

The Tarot

Tarot is a divination tool, based on the synchronous fall of the cards to reflect both apparent and hidden elements of the moment. Its archetypal symbol system is rooted deep in Western culture, and there are many theories regarding its origins. Archetypes are the seeds of myth and it is out of mythology that we build our realities.

Legend has it that a person imprisoned with a deck of tarot cards, if given enough time, without contact or any kind with the outside world can, by studying the cards, learn all knowledge there is to know, create the situation needed for his liberation, and any other desired reality.

Fantastic as this may sound, I believe that it is true. Tarot cards are like keys to the doors of the unconscious mind, where all of these abilities are stored. We cannot fathom the depth and power of this unknown part of ourselves. That is why study of the cards is endless, and brings endless possibilities.

In the thirty or so odd years that I have worked with and explored the tarot, I have to say that the process has worked profound transformations upon me. I began with songs, as music was my primary focus. I was enchanted by the tarot, its mystery and color, and the images that compelled me in ways I barely understood. I had been writing songs based on myths for several years, and tarot seemed like a natural subject for me.

The first tarot song I wrote was Blue Lady, about the High Priestess card, included at the end of this Cycle. I had just experienced a kind of death and severe trauma, and was in a state of despair. It seemed that there was no reality that mattered, no god, nothing beyond the body but whiteness and spiritual stasis. The Priestess brought me out of it; she gave me hope again.

In my song-vision, the Priestess became my redeemer. She returned to me the power of naming myself, or of having an identity, of orienting myself in time and space, and the desire to keep peopling my existence with images, relationships, experience. In other words, she brought me back from despair and into being again. She helped me to face and defy the Cruel King, who was my adversary, the voice of self-hate and social indifference. She gave me the strength to keep creating alternatives despite his presence, so that he gradually faded away. I know that he is still out there, and that his voice is very loud in the lives of many people in the world, that I alone could never totally conquer him. But at least for now in a corner of the universe, one woman has a magic garden, and that is enough to keep me going.

All of this the image of the Priestess was able to evoke in me. This is pretty amazing, when you think about it! And then, when we realize that each and every card in the tarot has such potential wrapped up within it somehow . . . it is stupefying. Wise indeed were the makers of these cards.

The origins of tarot are as mysterious as the cards themselves. Manly P. Hall conjectures that they are the descendent of certain mystical tablets of ancient Egypt. Waite and Case suggest that they were consciously and deliberately made by a specific group of wise men. Z. Budapest insists that women made the cards to protect our mysteries from patriarchal annihilation—a very enticing myth to the twentieth-century witch. My theory is that the tarot is folklore, like myths, legends, fairytales and folksongs. Some of the purest and deepest wisdoms are stored in this repository of culture, made by the "folk," and indeed, who are they but ourselves?

Much of what we now consider folklore is descended from mystery teachings, myths and religious beliefs from forgotten cultures. From gods of mythology to princesses of fairy tales is a far smaller leap than some might suspect. Most of the great religious treatises, such as the Koran and the Bible, have been written and rewritten many times. I suppose some dusty scholar-types would pooh-pooh my equation of the tarot with such respectable works, but I think careful study would prove me correct. The tarot is overflowing with profound religious thought, universal archetypes and symbols of human experience. Use of the cards can open up the deep mind and help us tap into our powers. This is potent stuff that can harm or heal, like magic itself, and must be used with love and care.

When I do tarot readings for people, I try to be very sensitive to questions of free will and choices in creating futures. I feel it is unethical to consistently say that a particular future is inescapable. I prefer to address the fact of the seeker's own power and choices or options she might have in affecting her destiny. In my circular layout it is easy to get into a flow of time, sensing how this moment is leading to the next and is a result of what came before. We are always reaping the seeds we planted, and planting the next crop with every step we take; past, present and future are simultaneous. We are dealing with tendencies, orbits and momentum of events, not necessarily hard and fast futures. Sometimes, however, the future does "jell" and a sensitive reader can spot these approaching ridges of energy. When I see one I try to be absolutely honest and trust my inner voice. If it is a positive future I celebrate and affirm this. If it looks heavy or painful, I try to encourage the seeker to look for positive elements elsewhere in the reading, or qualities and resources within her personality with which to deal with the inevitable. I try to help her see what patterns have led up to the difficulty and what she can do about moving beyond it into a more positive approach. Sometimes I see social issues at work, or larger forces that have swept the seeker along.

I have found that the most important element for success in any reading is trusting that "still small voice" within. This means not being rigid about previously learned meanings of cards, but always being open to the truth of the moment. I also find it valuable to invite the seeker to participate fully in selecting the cards as well as interpreting them.

Shekhinah's Tarot

Since traditional tarot decks express a male-dominant social mythos, I felt it would be healing and transforming to develop a female-centered deck. I began in a collective of women, helping to create the Matriarchal Tarot, later to become the Book of Aradia Tarot. During the seven years of work with my partners I developed my own deck on the side, calling it Shekhinah's Tarot. This deck is unique in many aspects, but also contains many of the same elements as the collective decks.

In traditional tarot decks there are five suits or sections. The largest, called the Major Arcana (greater mysteries), usually contain 22 cards. These depict various psychic and spiritual themes. The four remaining suits, called the Minor Arcana (lesser mysteries) are Wands, Cups, Pentacles, and Swords. They are considered the representation of various everyday life situations.

In Shekhinah's Tarot there are also five suits, called Spirit, Blades, Flames, Cups, and Pentacles. The idea of "greater" and "lesser" mysteries has been modified. While there are still a larger number of cards in the Spirit suit (21), the five suits are seen as a continuum of energy, as previously discussed in relation to the pentagram or Witch's Star. (See Cycle 4, *The Mother Goddess*.) The court cards of the old tarot (usually called Kings, Queens, Knights and Pages) have been replaced by Maiden, Mother and Crone goddesses. There are 13 cards in each of these suits, as opposed to 14 in traditional tarot Minor Arcana suits.

The Spirit suit expresses the spiritual journey of the Self or s/he who seeks reflection in the tarot. It shows the mysteries of birth, death, transformation, love, power and all underlying themes of experience on the wheel of existence. The Blades express the thought plane, or mental activities. This includes the rational mind, as well as intuitive levels, and various aspects of communication. The Flames express action and interaction, the range of behavioral patterns and the human will. The Cups deal with emotions, relationships, and subconscious levels. The Pentacles are about the earthly plane, practical matters, money and manifestation. The five suits are seen as equally mysterious and "ordinary." They can be purely themselves, or can overlap to encompass one another.

The following is a brief explanation of each of the Spirit cards. For the most part they correspond to the Major Arcana in traditional decks, with some variation.

0. *Self* (Replaces the Fool) This is the zero position, the potential within the cosmic egg of being. Here the seeker begins her journey with confrontation, her own divinity revealed in the mirror of the cosmos. Denotes innocence, foolishness, purity

of spirit.

1. *Witch* (replaces the Magician). Everywoman (or man) creates her destiny, using the powers within herself. The spiral above her head is her auric or psychic abilities, the cauldron is the cup that holds the waters of her emotions and the deep self, the spoon and flames represent her will in action, and the pentacle is her alignment to earth, the final manifestation of her spell. Magic is being done, creative powers are at work.

2. *Priestess* (replaces Hierophant and the High Priestess). As the Witch looks without to affect circumstance, so the Priestess looks within to affect the soul. Her magic is ritual, the wisdom of the ancients, prophecy and divination. She sits at the threshold of the deep self, ready to guide us through the labyrinth, revealing all that has been concealed. She is the ultimate spiritual authority—the channel, shaman, sibyl, road woman, healer that resides within us all.

3. *Maya* (replaces the Empress and Emperor). The Great Mother Goddess dances thunder with her feet, birthing the universe in all its myriad forms. Her child is herself repeated, the world, and all of us. This card reflects the mothering principle, that which nurtures, creates, builds, and takes responsibility. Harmony with her is abundance and joy, alienation from her is spiritual as well as physical poverty.

4. *Frey* (replaces positive aspects of Devil card). After birthing Herself for eons, the Goddess now brings forth a new form, her Divine Son and Lover. He is a sensuous, loving man, in harmony with the female forces in himself, a good role-model for the New Age male. Capable of nurturance, creativity and sensitivity, he is usually supportive of women's ways. He can also be the Trickster God or the Horned One of the witches. Adverse positions can indicate patriarchal influences or under-mining of the female.

5. *Aphrodite* (replaces the Lovers). The sacred flame of passionate love arises, bringing with Her all the joys and risks, the challenges and choices that must be made. Aphrodite is the majesty and ecstasy we all seek in merging with another, no matter if they be rich or poor, male or female, old or young. She is also the lesson of self's return to self, thus the thorns that always accompany Her exquisite roses.

6. *Boadicea* (replaces the Chariot). A Celtic warrior queen who led her people (the Iceni) of ancient Britain against the conquering Romans. This is my image for the Chariot of older decks, which tells of the triumph of will as the seeker takes the reins of her life and moves into the world. If she is centered and strong all will go well; if not, there may be difficulties.

7. *Power* (replaces Strength). In taming the forces within, the seeker achieves the true power of gentleness and strength of character. This can bring to her all that she may desire, for the universe smiles on those who have reached inner harmony. Should the kundalini-lion overwhelm her or be suppressed, a power-struggle may ensue.

8. *Oppression* (replaces negative aspects of Devil card). Here is the evil of the world depicted as heavy stones that crush the witch beneath them. This was one of

the ways our magical predecessors were destroyed. The stones represent negativity, machismo, power-over, cruelty, stagnation, entrapment. They also show attitude—the thoughtforms that sometimes perpetuate our oppression. All of us are capable of being the oppressed or the oppressor; no doubt each of us has been both in our time. Liberation is always possible; begin with a search of your beliefs.

9. *Crone* (replaces the Hermit). The seeker comes to Wisdom—the deep knowing aspect of self that is aware of all great truths. She may emerge from within, or appear as a teacher, a spiritual guide, a wise woman or man. The Crone understands the power of solitude, the magic of dreams, the uses of memory, the knowledge of the past.

10. *Moirae* (replaces the Wheel of Fortune). The wheel of karma turns and circumstances shift into a new cycle of beginnings or endings. The Moirae are the Fates of Greek mythology—three goddesses who spin the thread of time, weave the web of life, and cut the thread of destiny. This is a Maiden-Mother-Crone triad, and so we arrive at the beginning on a higher octave of the spiral, as ten is made of one and zero, and a new universe is created.

11. *Athene* (replaces Justice). Here is the balancer of fate, She who deals in matters of conscience. She serves the cause of natural justice, forever adjusting destiny through moral decision, understanding of fair play, and protection of the sacred mysteries. Her labyrs shows that she is the Guardian at the Threshold of self, the Amazon defender of all that is true and precious within us.

12. *Hanging One* (replaces the Hanged Man). The ego surrenders, letting go of personal control, to let a deeper force have its way with her. Sometimes this takes the form of a sacrifice; one thing must be released that the better may take its place. Sometimes it takes the form of martyrdom, as the changer rubs up against the resistance of social status quo. And sometimes it is a joyful game, like that of a child who hangs innocently upside down from the limb of a tree (as shown in this deck) seeing her laughing reflection in the cosmos. The more freely we can let go, the easier the experience will be.

13. *Transformation* (replaces Death). The husk falls away, the serpent sheds her skin, the Phoenix flies up once more from her flaming egg. Death in the new age is shown as rebirth, for this is the truth of all our changes. Not necessarily a physical death, this card is about the deaths we live as we go through the transformations of the self.

14. *Temperance*. The soul reaches for perfection, tempering herself in the fire, the water, the spirit, the air, and the earth. She tests her flexibility, develops clarity, reaches for more discipline and the skills of combination and artistic expression.

15. *Luna* (replaces the Moon). The seeker is pulled by the powers of the moon that magnetically draw up the hidden forces of the deep mind. Luna is the Eye of Night, She who sees in the dark. She has long been the symbol of the feminine, the receptive, the sensitive, dreamy and poetic side of human nature. Disturbed moon energy can be craziness or insanity; harmonious moon energy is ecstasy.

16. *Lightening* (replaces the Tower). The Goddess' wrath can be felt; it is a flash of energy that destroys those structures based on illusion or attachment to false power or permanence. Flow with it and the light will bring joyous liberation and awakening; resist and there may be some pain involved. In her journey to individuation the self encounters one more cataclysm as the last veils are stripped away.

17. *Muse.* Now the Goddess pours her healing waters of inspiration and meditation, taking the seeker onward into peace and understanding. She heals us through poetic insight, trance journeying, celestial music and universal realization.

18. *Amaterasu* (replaces The Sun). The radiant heart of our solar system, this star-goddess is our own grandmother who birthed the earth that births us. Amaterasu is her name in the Japanese Shinto faith, still active today. She pours forth fiery love, bringing rejuvenation, health, expansion, abundance, and playful, childlike energy.

19. *Celebration* (replaces the Last Judgment). Having reached full awakening, the seeker now connects with all other beings of the universe. She may find herself in a circle of sisters performing community ritual, converting to a new religion, or evaluating her progress thus far. She dances in the arms of the goddess, knowing she is forever loved, forever divine.

20. *Nut* (replaces the World). And now we come back to zero, and the seeker/ goddess begins again. She has journeyed through all the stages of the tarot or life experience, and knows herself to be whole-unto-herself forever; she is a microcosm of the macrocosm, the infinite egg hatching out new existences. This is the completion of the Spirit suit, the completion of the seeker's present cycle, and the cycle of time, called by some the Sacred Year.

TAROT WHEEL

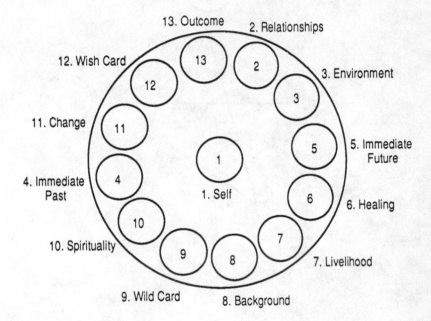

This is the layout I use with my own deck. If you have a deck, or would like to get one, you are invited to try it! Mix the cards thoroughly, center yourself, and choose one card for each position on the wheel. Remember to trust your inner voice. Sometimes it helps to have a specific question before you begin; this gives the reading a focus or direction.

PENTAGRAM TAROT LAYOUT

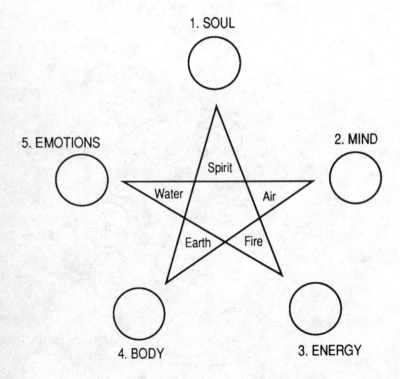

Here are two more tarot layouts you can try. The same principles apply as with the tarot wheel.

ONDINE'S TREE OF LIFE LAYOUT

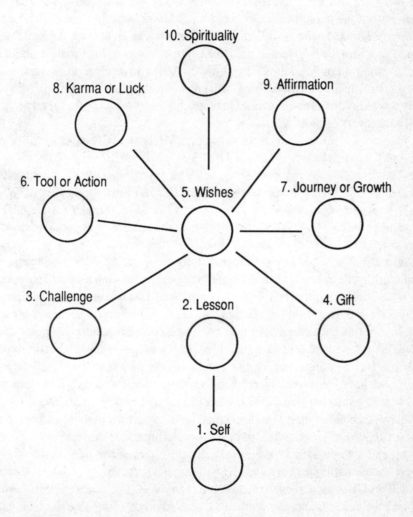

10. Spirituality

8. Karma or Luck

9. Affirmation

6. Tool or Action

5. Wishes

7. Journey or Growth

3. Challenge

2. Lesson

4. Gift

1. Self

Runes

Runes are magical letters, and served as alphabets as well as divinatory tools in a number of ancient cultures. The runes we see most widely in use today come from the Celtic and Teutonic tribes of old Northern Europe. While most sources usually credit the Norse god Odin with their invention, earlier information reveals that they were actually created by women. Carved into chips of wood or bone, these angular letters would be cast upon a cloth or rug upon the ground, much like tarot cards are used today, and then psychically read or interpreted by women seers of old. In the spring of 1990 I had the good fortune to meet with Monica Sjöö (co-author with Barbara Mor of the magnificent *Great Cosmic Mother*, and illustrator of the cover of *Ariadne's Thread*), who is well known for her work as an artist and researcher of Goddess lore. Monica is Swedish, and so has good access to information about the old runes. She told me that the original myth of their invention gives them to the Goddesses of Fate in that part of the world, known as the Norns. This coincides well with what we know of such Goddesses in other cultures, who were frequently writers as well as weavers of destiny.

The Norns were usually pictured as Maiden, Mother and Crone, or Past, Present, and Future. Their names were Wyrd (or Urd), Verthandi, and Skadi, or Fate, Life, and Death. The first Norn, Wyrd, once stood alone as the original deity, encompassing the qualities of all three. Her name, cognate with Urth, Earth, Mother Earth, Wurd, Werd, Wierd, and Word, shows that the ancients linked their understanding of fate with language and writing. The Norns, said to be the writers of the book of destiny, were also referred to as "die Schreiberinnen," or "the women who write."

Since the time of women's runic traditions, these symbols have been cast into near oblivion by the forces of male domination. Medieval church authorities declared them evil, of course, outlawed them, and pronounced their own mundane alphabet as the only legitimate one, thus helping to create widespread illiteracy all over Europe. In our times the runes have been making a comeback, but mostly in a male-oriented context, with male gods as their inventors, and male occultists as the experts on their use and meanings. Surviving traditions of the past few centuries, however, obscure, generally seem to agree on male-oriented interpretations for the letters.

I first began to explore the runes in a casual sort of way in 1986 and 1987. I didn't know then about their female origins, but I felt drawn to them and could tell that they had power. At that time I was also discovering and learning about the magic of stones, and it was a natural pastime to paint the old runes on these earthy friends that were accumulating in my home, and try them out for readings. I made a few sets for myself and friends, and even made some pretty velvet pouches to store them in. But when I wanted to embroider women's names in runes upon these bags, I ran into problems. There was a little information on using the runes to spell out words in the books I found, but not enough to really write with them completely. I could tell that there were holes in the knowledge available to us about the runes, and it also became clear that much of what I could find was under a veil of patriarchal bias.

And then a student and friend of mine, Kris Aaron, suggested that I create a woman-identified rune system. "You'd be the perfect person to do it!" she exclaimed, in reference to the fact that I had already done similar work on the tarot. At first I didn't think I had the time, plus I felt a peculiar reluctance to tamper with these venerable letters.

Then on Summer Solstice of '87, the goddess-lightning struck. I fell into a state of enchantment and, in a single day, the symbols for my Womanrunes were born. I realized that if I had already had the good sense to rework the tarot in a womanly vein, why be so shy about reworking the runes? Suddenly I was liberated, and the new symbols poured out beneath my pen. Like the priestesses of old, I opened myself, and the Goddess sent me Her magic.

I had long known that many tarot systems include alphabet letters with their major arcana, and had often thought it would make sense to give some witchy letters to Shekhinah's Tarot. And so, when I made these runes, I arranged them so as to coincide with my cards. Eventually, when I am ready to release my deck for publication, Womanrunes will be included with the designs. While there are 73 cards in my tarot deck, there are only 35 runes (plus one blank one called The Mystery Rune) in my magical alphabet. The first 21 are aligned with the Spirit cards, while the remaining 14 are aligned with various cards throughout the deck. Each of the rune symbols is also aligned with one or two of the sounds we make when we speak, so that they can be used for magical writing in addition to their divinatory uses.

While my runes are comparatively young and have much room for further development, I am amazed at how well they work, and how easily women have learned to use them. Runes have the ability to be remarkably simple, and yet continue to reveal layers upon layers of deeper meaning. Because of this they make an ideal introduction to the world of divination. For those of you reading this who are just beginning, I warmly recommend that you give Womanrunes a try. For a starter set, I suggest you draw the symbols shown on page 220 on blank index cards that have been cut in half. Include the number and meaning of each rune, so that you will immediately receive a combined set of information whenever you look at it:

7.

POWER

14.

TEMPERANCE

24.

PROSPERITY

WOMANRUNE NAMES AND PRONUNCIATIONS

0. The Circle, Rune of Self
   i as in high

1. The Witch's Hat, Rune of Magick
   w as in women

2. The Crescent Moon,
   Rune of Divination
   l as in love

3. The Yoni, Rune of Making
   m as in mother

4. The Flame, Rune of Fire
   r as in roar

5. The Heart, Rune of Love
   ah as in far

6. The Labyris, Rune of Will
   b as in beauty, p as in purple

7. The Dancing Woman, Rune of Power
   oo as in book

8. The Box, Rune of Limitation
   ng as in wing

9. The Dark Moon, Rune of Wisdom
   j as in jade, ch as in chime

10. The Wheel, Rune of Fate
    i as in it

11. The Pendulum, Rune of Karma
    a as in cat

12. The Reflection, Rune of Surrender
    u as in up, the bending vowel

13. The Flying Woman,
    Rune of Transformation
    n as in now

14. The Bowl, Rune of Temperance
    e as in wet

15. The Whole Moon, Rune of Psyche
    ee as in lean

16. The Lightning, Rune of Awakening
    ss as in summer, zz as in zoo

17. The Moon and Star, Rune of Faith
    oo as in moon

WOMANRUNE NAMES AND PRONUNCIATIONS

18. The Sun, Rune of Healing
    aw as in Your

19. The Dancing Women,
    Rune of Celebration
    y as in yes

20. The Great Wheel, Rune of Infinity
    oh as in zone

21. The Egg, Rune of Naming
    h as in heather

22. The Sisters, Rune of Friendship
    g as in good, k as in kiss or crest

23. The Seed, Rune of Waiting
    sh as in shor, zh as in measure

24. The Tree, Rune of Prosperity
    d as in door, t as in touch

25. The Crowned, Rune of Unconditional Love
    ow as in how

26. The Winged, Rune of Freedom
    th as in thick, th as in the

27. The Bowl of Reflection, Rune of Solitude
    ea as in bear

28. The Tool, Rune of Labor
    ff as in fine, vv as in vine

29. The Moonboat, Rune of Journeys
    French "r"

30. The Pentacle, Rune of Protection
    a as in same

31. The Two Triangles, Rune of Focus
    German/Welsh gutteral - "ckh"

32. The Two Circles, Rune of Merging
    African "click"

33. The Bowl of Dancing Women, Rune of Honor
    e as in her

34. The Hearth, Rune of Nurturance
    French nasal

35. The Mystery Rune

You can leave the backs of the cards blank, or decorate them with a simple design that looks the same from all sides. This way, when the cards are face down, they will all look alike, and you won't be able to tell whether they are reversed or upright, or what images they conceal, until you turn them over. When I create runecards I sometimes like to draw The Wheel, or my Rune of Fate, on the backs:

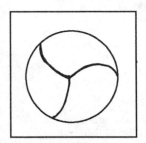

Once you have made your cards, wrap them in a suitable cloth or pouch, and bless them as you would any other magical tool. Keep them on or near your altar when not in use. When you wish to use them for divination, take them out and shuffle them for a while, as you center yourself and focus on your question. When you feel ready, pull one or two cards out of the deck and see what they have to tell.

Runes and the Chakras

Chakras are centers of consciousness, said to be astrally located at seven points along our spines. The word "chakra" means wheel in Sanskrit, and most of the information we have about them comes from Hindu and Yogic traditions of India. These wheels are said to spin at varying rates, depending on their function. Each corresponds to an aspect of our lives and beings. The First, or Root, Chakra located at the base of the spine, connects us to the earth, the physical plane, practical matters and therefore Grounding. In my Womanrune system I chose The Seed, Rune of Waiting, to represent the Root Chakra. The Second, or Belly, Chakra is located behind the womb and takes in all the sexual and creative energies related to the womb and yoni. In Womanrunes my symbol for this chakra is The Yoni, Rune of Making. The Third, or Stomach, Chakra is located at the solar plexus and relates to functions of survival, stamina, power and influence. The Womanrune symbol for this chakra is The Dancing Woman, Rune of Power. The Fourth, or Heart, Chakra connects with all the functions of the heart—love, emotions, passion, and compassion. Its Womanrune symbol is The Heart, rune of Love. The Fifth, or Throat, Chakra is connected to speech, thought, communication, truth, and trust. I've chosen The Egg, Rune of

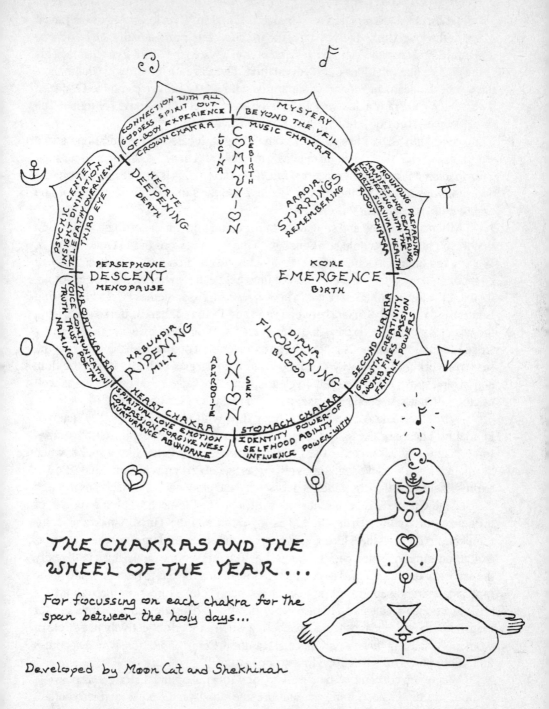

THE CHAKRAS AND THE
WHEEL OF THE YEAR...

For focussing on each chakra for the
span between the holy days...

Developed by Moon Cat and Shekhinah

223

Naming, for this chakra. The Sixth Chakra is the Third Eye, located near the pineal gland at the level of the brow. This is the psychic center of telepathy, clairvoyance and intuition. I gave the Moonboat, Rune of Journeys, to the Third Eye Chakra. This is the chakra that functions during divination. The Seventh, or Crown, Chakra is at the top of the head, and connects our spirits with all the universe and the Goddess. The Crown Chakra is a doorway and can be an exit out of the body. I assigned The Great Wheel, Rune of Infinity, to the Crown Chakra.

An eighth chakra has recently come to light, located in the aura, one arm's length above the head. I call this the Music Chakra. (Diane Stein refers to it as the Transpersonal Point in her book *Stroking the Python*.) This is a more esoteric chakra and functions mostly on the spiritual level. I use the familiar musical symbol, the eighth note, to represent this chakra.

Mooncat, a friend and student of mine, came up with the brilliant realization that the eight chakras could be aligned with the eight seasons of the Goddess Year. We worked on this together and came up with the chart on page 223. A chakra can be meditated upon for the entire span of time between two holy days. For example, focus can be given to the Root Chakra between Aradia (Candlemas) and Kore (Spring Equinox), to the Belly Chakra between Kore and Diana (Beltane), and so on, around the wheel, as shown. You can adopt this practice if you wish, by using the Rainbow Cone Meditation on page 29, spending an extra amount of time with the chakra of the season. Working in this way can help align the energies of body, mind emotion, action, and spirit. It can also help to clear up any blockages or disturbances, as well as strengthen and deepen abilities connected to each of the chakras.

When the chakras are awakened, they flow with an energy known as shakti or kundalini. These are also names of the Goddess as the stuff of manifestation, or life-force. Kundalini is said to rest at the base of the spine, coiled like a snake, when dormant. This is what we sometimes refer to as Snake Power. When our Snake Power expresses through the Root Chakra, it is earthy and practical; when it comes through the Second Chakra it is sexual. It comes through the Stomach Chakra as power or influence, through the Heart Chakra as love, through the Throat Chakra as communication, through the Third Eye as psychic abilities, and through the Crown as exaltation and connection with all things. Each chakra sets the mode, but it is all really the same kundalini energy. To reclaim the flow of this force is to reclaim some of the most ancient and suppressed powers of woman. Total expression through all the chakras at once creates a state of ecstasy or bliss. This state can be harnessed for magical purposes, and is especially effective when aligned collectively in a circle of women. Because of this, I developed the Rainbow Cone Meditation, which becomes incredibly powerful when done in a group setting.

When you concentrate on a chakra, sit with your spine as straight as possible without straining. Close your eyes and breathe slowly and deeply, and let yourself relax completely. Mentally focus on each chakra in turn, beginning with the Root Chakra, and working your way up. Always send a grounding cord down into the earth from the base of your spine as you begin in this chakra. Breathe into each chakra and send colors, runes, or any other appropriate images into that part of yourself. If you feel there are blockages or disturbances there, make a picture of them (i.e., a murky cloud or slimy mass) and dissolve it away with your imagination. You can also use dissolving images such as water, white light, or any other color or image that you find appropriate. Always replace what you have removed with positive images that represent smooth and happy functioning. For instance, runes make very good chakra meditations, as do Goddesses, animals, plants, stones, or other familiar symbols. If you work this way through the seasons, you can align yourself inwardly and outwardly with all the cycles of nature. Choose a time each day, or each week or each moon to focus on the chakra of the season. Change to the next chakra when the next holy day arrives, and so continue on around the wheel.

Chakra work can be very powerful, and can get out of control if you aren't careful. If you feel yourself slipping out of your body, or going into a state that doesn't feel comfortable or safe, stop immediately. Bring the energy down and send it into the earth, speed up your breathing and bring yourself back to everyday consciousness. Tell yourself that you are in control and perfectly safe, that there is no need to go any farther until you are ready. Always remember to ground both at the beginning and end of all such meditations.

Astrology

Let me preface this section by saying that I am not an astrologer, in that I do not know how to calculate charts. But over the years I have collected intuitive and experiential data about the signs, have read much interpretive material, and learned some things from the connections between tarot and astrology. Tarot is my special channel for divination, and yet there is a place where all the forms interconnect. In tarot there is an order to things in terms of the five elements of fire, water, air, earth and spirit (Wands, Cups, Blades, Pentacles, Aether). In astrology there is also an elemental system of fire, air, earth and water. The twelve zodiacal signs are each assigned one of these, so that there are three water signs, three fire signs, etc. The qualities given to the elements seem to cross over easily into tarot symbolism: Fire people are volatile, temperamental, aggressive; water people are sensitive, emotional, passive; earth people are solid, stable, stubborn; air people are fragile, intelligent, and spacy, etc.

I have found these qualities to manifest in myself and people I know. Taureans really are stubborn sometimes (earth), Scorpios mysterious and deep (water), Aries impulsive and powerful (fire), Leos show-offish attention-getters (fire), Virgos highly organized and sometimes picky (earth), and so on. It is amazing to think that those qualities coincide with the positions of the stars and planets!

And yet, this is the essence of astrology, and what makes it such a powerful tool.

The planets and stars are truly connected to our inmost selves. Witches have always known that all the universe is interconnected. The same patterns can be read in the iris of one person's eye and in the remotest wheeling of the heavens. The ancients who first divined the qualities of the heavenly bodies were incredible seers indeed. They must have felt themselves a part of the great dance. Like cells and nuclei, the stars and planets spin, and their energies intermingle, setting up patterns, tendencies, qualities. And we and our tiny lives are a part of this dance; we are not alone!

Do constellations really have personalities? Can one truly say that a certain cluster of stars gives off a particular vibration, that, when zapping a person at birth, makes her behave a certain way? Who is to decide what these vibrations are like, and what are their effects?

There are many skeptics who pose such questions regarding astrology. They also point out: The stars have shifted their positions radically since astrology was invented, so that the calculations can't even be considered accurate. The behavior of people could be the result of programming. Perhaps if we are told repeatedly that we are a Libra, we will automatically become like a Libra.

Where does this leave us? My answer is that it doesn't matter. Astrology is simply another reality grid, a system that arouses the deep mind of the seer. I believe that many astrologers are truly psychic, and the chart is their means of tuning in to their own channel. This would explain why many astrologers seem to disagree about certain qualities of signs. And yet, if one astrologer is accurate for one seeker, then that is really all that matters. And if astrology is built up from the accumulated accurate data of many psychics, then there must be some truth in it after all.

We must remember that all divination systems are simply doorways to the deep mind—that part of us that exists in knowing. There are psychics who use crystal balls, tea leaves, or pendulums. Others can just look at you and tell you what they see! Any system can be accurate and inaccurate, depending on the sensitivity and integrity of the seer, and the receptivity of the seeker.

As in so many ancient abilities, astrology was first invented by women. Historians say that the practice began in Chaldea, where priestesses were in charge of watching the heavens and planning the agricultural cycles. In truth, the zodiac is an alternate seasonal myth, using various animals and symbols to represent the same stages of life and death we have discussed in terms of Maiden, Mother and Crone. This myth has passed through many cultures and changes through history. It has fallen into disrepute and risen to respectability. We are, therefore, dealing with a hybrid, which can cause confusion.

The present zodiac is male-dominated in its symbolism, and so as feminists and witches we must remember to look at it askance at times. The sun, seen as male, is born at the Vernal Equinox in the sign of Aries, the Ram. Christians connect this symbol with the Lamb of God, and therefore, Christ. At the Summer Solstice he becomes a grown man, in the sign of Cancer the Crab. At Autumn Equinox he is the bearded sage, in the sign of Libra, the Scales. It is said that the scales of the year tip toward winter at this stage of the journey. In Capricorn he is said to die and be reborn as the Christos, or Logos.

Sometimes I feel caught in a kind of schizophrenia between the patriarchal zodiac and the moon-oriented calendar of trees. To complicate matters further, we live daily by the patriarchal months, which usually begin somewhere in the middle of corresponding astrological signs. On top of all of this we have the solar holy days, also in two sets—the patriarchal holidays (Christmas, Easter, etc.) and the pagan holidays (Candlemas, Lammas, etc.). Frankly, time in today's world is a confusing mess! It is no wonder we feel fragmented and powerless.

Our foremothers did things far more simply. Essentially, they lived by the moon, and the natural rhythms of their own bodies. I have often thought how healing it would be to unify the stellar, solar and lunar time cycles. The moon would be our monthly guide, aligned with those segments of the heavens through which she passes, giving us thirteen zodiacal signs. All dates could line up, so that a lunar cycle would correspond with an astrology cycle. There are theories regarding a lost thirteenth sign called Arachne, the Spider Woman. A book by John Vogt called *Arachne Rising* gives some very interesting data on this.

This is an era of myriad systems and information overflowing from a million sources. In so many ways we of this century must learn to adapt and screen a complex range of material. It can get overwhelming at times, and when I encounter this, I usually endeavor to simplify. For me the basic Maiden/Mother/Crone paradigm is the bottom line, the form I can always return to and rely on. On the other hand, the vast body of knowledge and choices available to us now are wonderful. It gives us endless room for variety, and means that people must ultimately choose what works for them in the most individual and personal ways. This is an automatic preventative to conformity and oppressive monoliths of belief and institution.

For the present, I still find that I tune into astrology frequently in my life, even though I sometimes question its precepts. The sign Scorpio, under which I am born, seems to apply to me in so many ways; the connections are inescapable.

Geraldine Thorsten, author of *God Herself*, offers a breakdown of astrology by its twelve signs, giving female mythology and history of each. Ms. Thorsten points out that every sign has female origins in myth and history. She gives names of the Goddess to go with each sign, and background on that particular goddess and her culture. The book is lightweight and easy to read, and it is wonderfully healing to see each sign of the zodiac as a goddess. There is also a personal rundown on each sign, giving some remarkably accurate insights into human behavior.

Essentially, the zodiac is made up of a belt of stars which circle the earth's elliptical yearly path around the sun. "Ages" are decided by the point where the elliptical path coincides with the Vernal Equinox or Kore's day in our Goddess calendar. This solar birth backs up one whole sign every 2,160 years, or in astrology jargon, she "regresses." We therefore name our ages by the zodiacal position of Kore's day. When she rose in Taurus we had the Taurean Age, in Aries we had the

Aryan Age, in Pisces we had the Piscean Age, and now we are moving into the Age of Aquarius, the Water Bearer. Former ages have been characterized by male-dominant myths and social systems. The Aquarian Age promises to be a return to the primacy (not dominance) of the female, the Goddess' rebirth and the ascent of women in society. It is true that we have seen the Water Bearer pictured as male, for the most part. The creators of the tarot, however, must have known better, for they have given the sign of Aquarius to the Star card, which shows the Goddess pouring Her healing waters upon the earth and into the rivers. As the Sun rises in this new sign for the next 2,000 years, her female identity will emerge more and more in myth and legend.

In calculating an individual astrological chart, the aspects are decided by positions of sun, moon and planets as seen from the earth, against the backdrop of the zodiacal belt of stars. The birth sign is decided by the sun's position on the yearly path at the time of the seeker's birth. The rising sign is decided by the sun's position on the daily path. The moon sign is decided by the moon's position on the monthly path. I like to think of these three as Maiden, Mother, and Crone, respectively. It is also helpful to know what phase of the Moon one is born under—full, crescent, dark, etc. It is said that we are most psychic at the moon-phase under which we are born.

All these aspects form a complex dance, unique to every individual. Planets are affected by the signs they are in, and vice versa. Planets also dance with one another, forming squares, trines, oppositions, etc. This is why newspaper forecasts are simplistic at best, and should not be taken too seriously.

Astrologers also place importance on the twelve houses. My favorite astrology book is on this subject, called *The Book of Houses*, by Robert Cole. Robert compares the progression we make through the houses to the natural harvest cycle of living plants. He shows how we each have our seasons, our times of planting, growth, pollination, fruit, and so on. Using the simple charts in the back of his book, we can calculate our house positions and plan our growth cycles more consciously than we might otherwise be inclined to do. This seasonal concept is in complete harmony with our Goddess year, on an individualized scale. For example, in my yearly myth, the Goddess encounters passionate union at the Summer Solstice. In Robert's house pattern the seventh house, which can be seen as "summer," is about relationships and their fertilizing effect. He calls this the House of Pollination. Each person will find that her particular "springs," "summers," etc., probably differ from those of the world as a whole, depending on when her rising sign begins. This is a practical approach to astrology, which enables us to plan our lives, and to understand the ups and downs we go through in the course of a year.

The following is one person's very minimal run-down of the qualities of the zodiacal signs. Though they may prove useful to you in figuring out some things about yourself and those in your life, I am offering them mainly to whet your appetite, in hopes that you will pursue astrology more deeply on your own.

The Signs

Aries

Aries rules the head and is considered an intellectual, yet fiery sign. Aries people are often brilliant, sometimes to the point of genius. They are great starters or initiators of projects, but not always as good at sustaining and completing, often relying on more earthy, stable people to take over, while they move on to further adventures. They are know to be impulsive, rebellious, aggressive and active.

Taurus

Taureans are earthy people and are considered sturdy, practical and grounded. They are known to be persistent and capable, tending toward stubbornness and materialism. Taurus can however see the "spirit of the matter," in the sense that money is a reflection of loving abundance, or that practical matters can serve less visible needs. They can be most generous and loyal, providing a steadying influence to more airy and watery and fiery types.

Gemini

Gemini is a mutable air sign, ruled by Mercury, planet of movement and communication. Gemini people are head-trippers, overflowing with playful ideas and speedy thoughts. They can see many sides of a question and provide a variety of points of view. However, this ability can take the negative form of con-artist in its detrimental aspects.

Cancer

Cancer is a watery and nurturing sign, loving and emotional. In my tarot deck I have given this sign to the Mother of Water who enfolds us in Her all-encompassing love. Cancerians are protective and tender-hearted, easily concerned with the troubles of others, sometimes to the point of over-identification. They make great parents and often keep warm hearths.

Leo

Leo people are great performers and usually take the center of attention. All children are ruled by this fixed fiery sign, as they require the center for their very survival. Fixed fire is deep and steady warmth and makes Leos loyal and devoted in relationships and projects. Negative ego problems can make them obnoxiously show-offish, or repressed and shy; healthy egos make them good leaders and creative artists.

Virgo

Virgos are organizers of environments, information, etc. They can be extremely analytical and make good critics. A Virgo keeps an efficient house or office, but can be picky to the point of irritation in their zeal to be perfect. Virgos often understand the value of loving service.

Libra
Libra is the sign of balance and diplomacy and grace. Librans always try to see the other person's point of view, hence are sometimes called the peacemakers. In detriment this can make them seem somewhat indecisive or two-faced, as they find themselves caught between opposing issues.

Scorpio
Scorpio is the deepest and most passionate of signs, connecting with mysticism, sexuality and the secrets of life and death. It is symbolized by four emblems: the scorpion, serpent, eagle and phoenix, each representing a stage of transformation from the depths to the heights of consciousness. Scorpio people are intense and powerful, but can be overly temperamental and volatile if they have not tamed their egos.

Sagittarius
Sagittarius people are free-spirited, impulsive and wise. They make great travelers on the inner and outer planes as free-wheeling gypsies or adventurous thinkers. They do not like to be tied down and sometimes are considered irresponsible by more committed friends, but they always bring a fresh and exciting air to whatever they do.

Capricorn
Capricorns are ambitious, far-seeing and great at organizing groups. They make good politicians and leaders, combining high ideals with step-by-step practicality. Like the mountain goat which symbolizes them, they will achieve great heights because of their ability to climb precarious places with care.

Aquarius
Aquarius is often called the sign of universal brotherhood (sisterhood?). Its native can be quite detached and are capable of an overview that gives them a valuable understanding of social trends. Watery types may find them a bit dry and unemotional, but they are loyal to the truths they see.

Pisces
Pisces is a mutable watery sign, and very emotional and mystical. Pisceans are extremely sensitive and receptive, and make passionate lovers and parents. They are so sympathetic to others that they sometimes become victimized, and have to be careful to define their boundaries and protect themselves.

Some General Qualities of the Planets
    Sun—fiery, expansive
    Moon—watery, emotional
    Earth—fixed, motherly
    Mercury—quick, communicative
    Mars—fiery, aggressive
    Venus—benevolent, loving
    Saturn—structured, limiting
    Uranus—erratic, eccentric
    Neptune—deep, mystical
    Pluto—revolutionary, transforming
    Jupiter—generous, fortunate

Pendulums

Pendulums are one of the simplest and most direct forms of divination. They work with auric vibrations, or the energy field that surrounds the person who holds the pendulum. This type of divining is used with hazel rods for finding water, and other wooden rods for finding a variety of substances. It is often called "dowsing." The seeker holds the pendulum slightly away from her body, letting it dangle freely, and asks a question that has a "yes" or "no" answer. The pendulum will begin to spin in one direction or the other; in most cases clockwise for "yes," and counterclockwise for "no." The process is extremely delicate and requires great sensitivity for success. One must resist all temptation to direct the pendulum, and hold one's hand steady throughout.

It is easy to make a pendulum out of string and an object with sufficient weight to carry its own momentum. Raw crystals make good pendulums; so do clay beads and stones. It is best to use natural substances, as they respond more readily to auric vibrations. Place it on your altar for a new days to soak up your psychic energy. It will need to be "tuned," which means finding the correct spot on the string from which to dangle it, and seeing what your "yes" and "no" directions are.

To find the right spot or anchor point along your string, grasp it at the base where it connects to your stone or crystal, and work your thumb and forefinger slowly upward, letting it swing freely as you go. At some point the pendulum will begin to swing briskly; stop at that point. This is your spot, which can be marked with a knot.

To find your "yes" and "no" directions, ask a question that you already know the answer to. For example, "Am I swinging a pendulum right now?" It will spin one way or the other; this is your "yes" direction, and so the opposite direction will be for "no." I have added a third possibility ... if the pendulum simply moves back and forth without going into "orbit" this could be a "maybe" or "undecided" answer.

Now you are ready to do some serious divining. It helps to bless your pendulum and dedicate it to your purpose, asking the goddess to guide you in its use. Before beginning, center yourself and do some deep breathing, as you would for any magical activity. The more trance-like your mood, the better. When you ask a question, hold your pendulum firmly and *don't move your hand, even slightly*. Store it on or near your altar when not in use, preferably in a protecting pouch.

Palmistry

Sheilah Kemp is a sister/friend of mine of several years' time. She is a talented psychic in the areas of tarot, astrology, and palm-reading, but palmistry, she says, is by far her favorite medium. Sheilah has studied goddess-lore with me, and is a devoted lover of female spirituality. I interviewed her on palmistry for this lesson, thinking it would be a valuable addition.

I was impressed by Sheilah's loving and wholistic approach to palm-reading, which I have seldom encountered in standard palmistry texts or at typical booths at fairs and such. When I asked her why this is her favorite medium, she said because of the closeness involved, the touch that is required, and the connections between hands and heart.

Palmistry is peripheral in my range of experience with divination, and so this section will be brief; it is just a glimpse of an ancient art. In going through all the books I could find on the subject, it became clear to me that no amount of reading can match up to plain old experience. For example, a text will say that a particular mound on the hand will be relevant to a particular subject, such as imagination. Then it will go on to say if this mound is well-developed it means such-and-such, underdeveloped means something else. Obviously, one must have observed many hands before one has a clear means of making such comparisons! The same principle applies to tarot, astrology, crystal-gazing, and all divination methods; accumulated experience is the ultimate teacher. Another important factor is intuition. I have found that no meanings or traditions are rigidly true. They can shift or modify, depending upon the moment. (Not that I want to discourage you; we all have to begin somewhere!)

It is fascinating, however, to realize that the hand is a hologram of the whole person, just as a tarot layout or an astrology chart can be. When I asked Sheilah why she thinks palm-reading works, she said that the hand is extraordinarily sensitive, having more nerve-endings than any other part of the body, and that there are direct connections through the nervous system from the hands to the brain. There are also some central arteries that connect the hands and heart. Our hands express our thoughts and feelings in so many ways, and part of the art of reading them is noticing the unique gestures of each person.

There are many charlatans among the divining professions, and palmistry is no exception. In choosing someone to read us, we must be careful, just as we would in selecting a doctor or healer. I asked Sheilah if she felt that the existence of fakes hurt her professionally. She said yes, on the one hand, it can turn some people away and

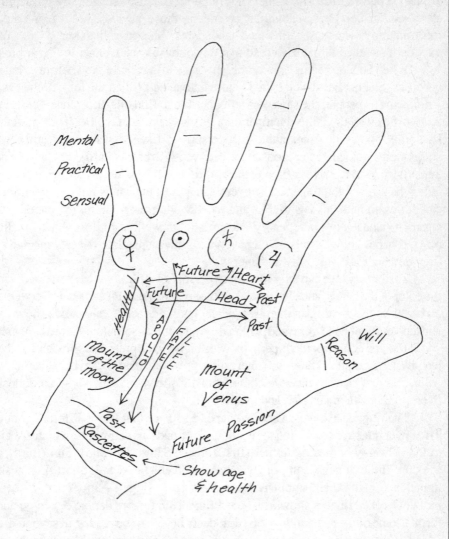

Grille - Instability
Square - Protection
Circle - Good on ☉
Troubled Elsewhere
Fork - Divided Ability
Tassles - Scattered Energy
Chains - Difficulties

Islands - Illness
Double - Intensifies
Cross - Good on ♃
Troubled Elsewhere
Star - Troubled Elsewhere
Spot - Shock; Trauma
Triangle - Good Energy

arouse skepticism, but on the other hand, it helps, because her sincerity and accuracy stand out in comparison. Sheilah is one of those psychics who can pinpoint information down to specific facts and dates. She says that her clients often experience healing through her readings, no doubt as a result of her loving approach.

When Sheilah begins her reading, she takes in the whole hand before going into specifics. She notices which hand is more active, and which the less. In the case of ambidextrous people, she says, it is still possible to find this difference. She checks both hands for flexibility, temperature, sensitivity, and color. The amount of flexibility shows how adaptable the person is; fixedness shows a stiffness or stubbornness of character, looseness can show irresponsibility or carelessness. Sensitivity to touch shows how capable the person is of deep feelings, especially along the sides of the fingers. The overall shapes of the hands fall into a number of categories, though this is variable, and most hands are a mixture. In general, large, squarish hands show practicality and artistic as well as philosophical qualities, pointed hands show idealism and psychic abilities, spatulate (flat—especially the fingers) hands show activity and energy.

Sheilah says she can tell a lot about a person's health as well as personality from the color of the hands, and also from the color of the lines. (Please read all statements on health in this writing as interesting data, not hard facts.) Pale hands show stress and tension, a subdued, reserved personality, sometimes selfishness. Red hands show a volatile and robust person, perhaps with high blood pressure. Pinkish hands are healthy, and balanced energy. (Interestingly, we all tend to have the same color palms, no matter what race we come from!) Yellowish hands show an unhealthy liver, poor health in general, and irritability.

The fingers also have varying shapes and sizes that show different qualities. Their meanings are connected to the mounds or pads at their bases, which are given to the heavenly bodies of Jupiter (first finger), Saturn (second), Sun (third), and Mercury (little finger). Long fingers show an interest in detail. Short fingers show impatience with detail, impulsiveness. Very short fingers—low energy—can be brutal. Crooked fingers show irresponsibility. Thin fingers denote delicacy, and so forth. (Some of these meanings are from dusty books, to be read with several grains of salt.) On the previous page you will find a sketch of a hand with some of the more commonly accepted names of the lines and areas. What follows is a list of brief meanings of these.

Life Line: Deals with life experience, vitality, energy.

Head Line: Mental matters, intellect, memory.

Heart Line: Emotional matters, love, conditions of the heart, physical matters connected to the heart.

Fate Line: Livelihood, finances, economics, career, life-style.

Apollo Line: Social status, enhances positive aspects of Fate Line when present.

Health Line: Also called Line of Mercury—health matters, when present; shows good health when not present.

Mount of Jupiter (base of first finger): Ambition, social status, ideals.

Mount of Saturn: When present, shows reserve and caution, love of solitude. Usually partakes of neighboring mounds.

Mount of Apollo: Achievement, artistic interests.

Mount of the Moon: Imagination, intuition, creative ability, motivation.

Mount of Venus: Love, sympathy, vitality, passion.

Mount of Mercury: Amount of humor, cheerfulness, hope.

Plain of Mars: Divided into Upper and Lower sections; Lower Mars shows willingness to fight and struggle, Upper Mars shows ability to endure.

Generally speaking, clear, strong lines are favorable; wavy, chained, or broken lines show interferences and problems. Also in general, Mounts take on qualities of areas and lines they are developed toward, become exaggerated or increased in their innate qualities when large, and decreased or detrimented when underdeveloped.

Blue Lady

You stand alone inside the door
Your light is gone, your god denied
Cry, "Come to me, o Blue Lady,
Guide me to the other side . . ."

Don't fear the dark lady,
She'll bring you to yourself . . .

For yonder stands the cruel king
All circled 'round with burning flame
Sings: "There is no hope, there is no god,
No up or down; you have no name . . ."

Now cry the dark lady
She'll bring you to yourself . . .

She comes to you, she takes your hand
She leads you to the temple green,
Do you know her now, as she knows you
And all your daemons yet unseen?

Don't fear the dark lady
She'll bring you to yourself . . .

For silver moons adorn her brow
And golden snakes adorn her feet
The veil she lifts—you reach her now
You meet her eyes, so wise and deep . . .

Don't fear the dark lady
She'll bring you to yourself . . .

thru Shekhinah
written for the Priestess card in the tarot

CRONE OF WATER

HECATE

Hecate, traditional Goddess of Fate, is shown here in her Crone aspect. She is said to preside at crossroads or places of choice and change, and is ready to offer us guidance through all transitions. Sometimes called Queen of Witches, she is often invoked and consulted for prophecy.

Suggested Projects

1. Do a tarot reading for yourself, a friend, or a group. (If you need to purchase a deck, see list at the end of this Cycle for suggestions.) You can use any of the layouts provided here, or one offered with other decks. Write up an account of the process in your *Book of Shadows*, including the questions you asked, the cards you drew, and the interpretations you made. Feel free to refer to meanings included here, or with other decks, but also try to discover your own.

2. Have an astrology chart done, and try interpreting it for yourself. You can begin with the interpretations included here, as well as further studies in some of the books listed at the end of this Cycle. Write your findings in your *Book of Shadows*, then see if they are borne out in your life over the next few moons. Continue to record your impressions during this time.

3. Make yourself a runeset with Womanrunes, as outlined here. Do a simple runing (rune reading) as suggested, or a more complex one, using a tarot layout. Describe your experience in your *Book of Shadows*.

4. Here is a list of other forms of divination used throughout the world. Choose a few that interest you and study them more deeply. Use them for divining alone, or with a friend or group. In your *Book of Shadows* write about what attracted you to the forms you chose. Describe your experiences in detail.

Aura Readings, Foot Readings (!), Eye Readings, Moonlit water, Moonlit mirrors, Crystal balls, Trance dancing, Crystal meditations, Throwing seeds, stones, oracle bones, I-Ching readings with coins or yarrow sticks, Cloud formations, Bird flights, Weather changes, changes in nature, Synchronous events, Prayers wheels, Prophetic dreams, Flashes of insight, intuitions, Appearance of animals, insects, etc., Animal sounds, Dice, Dominoes, Playing cards, Tea leaves, Apparitions: spirits, beings with messages, Numerology, Other (add your own).

5. Copy and cut out the Hecate Wheel on page 241, and mount it on sturdy cardboard. Color it with rainbows, or colors of your choice. Pin it at the center to a sturdy base, such as a piece of wood, so that it can spin. This is a prayer wheel, and when set in motion, it can help to put you in a trance state. Try using it for divination, or simply keep it on your altar and see how it affects you. (One student of mine had an extremely powerful visionary experience after coloring this wheel. Remember to ground, center and protect.)

HECATE WHEEL

Questions to Ponder

1. Do you consider yourself talented in the art of divination?

2. What experiences of divination can you recall in your life?

3. Do you feel safe and comfortable with it? Uncomfortable? If so, why?

4. Have you ever noticed "signs" in your life or environment that held divinatory significance? (Think back, write these up.)

5. Have you ever had a prophetic dream? (If so, describe in as great a detail as you can recall.)

6. Do you find that you are more psychic at certain times, such as during moonflow, or at special times of the moon or year?

7. Have you ever noticed the recurrence of karmic circumstances in your life? Have you been able to learn from these and respond to them with better choices when they come up again?

8. Do you feel comfortable with the newer female divination tools, or do you prefer more traditional ones? Is there a particular form of divination that you especially like to use?

9. Can you see yourself becoming a psychic reader, perhaps pursuing this as a profession?

Reading and Other Resources

General Psychic Studies:
E. A. Wallis Budge, *Egyptian Magic.*
Justine Glass, *They Foretold the Future.*
Nor Hall, *The Moon and the Virgin.*
Esther Harding, *Woman's Mysteries.*
Carl Jung, *Memories, Dreams and Reflections.*
Par Lagervist, *The Sybil.*
Diane Stein, *Stroking the Python.*
Barbara G. Walker, *The Women's Dictionary of Symbols and Sacred Objects* and *The Women's Encyclopedia of Myth and Secrets.*

I-Ching:
Diane Stein, *The Kwan Yin Book of Changes*.
Barbara Walker, *The I Ching of the Goddess*.
Wilhelm and Baynes, *The I Ching* or *Book of Changes*

Tarot:
Paul Case, *The Tarot*.
Sally Gearhart and Susan Rennie, *A Feminist Tarot*.
Ffiona Morgan, *Daughters of the Moon Tarot*.
Shekhinah Mountainwater, *Shekhinah's Tarot* (forthcoming).
Vicki Noble, *Motherpeace*.
Billie Potts, *A New Women's Tarot*.
Ivan Rakoczi, *The Painted Caravan*.
Jean Van Slyke, *Book of Aradia Tarot*

Tarot Decks:
Ffiona Morgan, *Daughters of the Moon* deck.
Vicki Noble and Karen Vogel, *Motherpeace* deck.
Billie Potts, *A New Woman's Tarot*.
Jean Van Slyke, *Book of Aradia* deck (in process).
E. A. Waite, *Rider* pack (traditional deck).

Runes:
If you would like to know more about these symbols I now have a small book available called *Womanrunes*. I also offer runesets of hand-painted gemstones or river rocks, and information on these is included with the book. (If you decide to order a runeset from me, please be prepared to wait a considerable amount of time.) Eventually, I will be releasing a lengthier work on Womanrunes, as I learn more about their meanings, myths, numerology, elemental associations, tree-moons, Goddesses, writing uses, signing uses, and whatever else the Goddess may send. The runes have a way of revealing themselves through use, and I encourage women to write to me and share their discoveries. Hopefully, the next book will contain a more collective understanding of the symbols. For *Womanrunes*, send $5 to Shekhinah Mountainwater, P.O. Box 2991, Santa Cruz, CA 95063.

Also see:
Lindsay Badenoch, *Daughter of the Runes*.
Ralph Blum, *The Book of Runes*.
Eric Thorrsen, *Runelore*.
Tony Willis, *Runic Workbook*.

Astrology:
Robert Cole, *The Book of Houses*.
Ronald C. Davison, *Astrology*.
Geraldine Thorsten, *God Herself*.
John Vogt, *Arachne Rising*.

My friend Sandra Pastorius, an excellent feminist astrologer, offers basic computer print-out charts for $13. Send to her at Laughing Giraffe, P.O. Box 2344, Santa Cruz, CA 95063. Be sure to include the date, time and location of your birth.

Palmistry:
William G. Benham, *Laws of Scientific Hand Reading*.
Dean Bryden, *Palmistry for Pleasure*.
Cheiro, *Cheiro's Book of Fate and Fortune*.
Walter B. Gibson and Litzka R. Gibson, *The Complete Illustrated Book of the Psychic Sciences*.

Pendulums:
You Are a Rainbow, University of the Trees, P.O. Box 644, Boulder Creek, CA 95006.

CYCLE 10

Rituals and Spells

The Rites of Kore

The woods are soft and fresh with spring. Gentle drops of sunlight kiss the new-grown green. The earth is springy underfoot, welcoming. Mother Nature stretches vast and thick, throbbing with birth, with re-connection. And the women come. We come with tents and pots and plans. We come with blankets and bells and magic. We come to sleep and wake and sing, we come to adore, to bless and receive blessing.

We sit on the earth and circle to speak and listen. "We need a ritual space." "And sleeping places." "And a fire . . ." Together we build. First a trip down into the dark belly of the woods to the magic clearing below. We tie bells and ribbons to the branches as we go, to mark the way, and sing a blessing song:

> Oh thank you Mother for this beauty
> Thanks to you for being so near
> Oh thank you for the green and golden
> Thanks to you for being here . . .
>
> Oh thank you Mother for this beauty
> Thank you for the gold and green
> For sending us your Maiden daughter
> For birthing the unseen and seen . . .

We find the altar place—two tall thin trees with a great many-terraced stump at their feet. We hang the mystic veil between them and place our sacred things . . . Mara brings a great round candle of gleaming yellow-gold, like the sun; Selene brings a crystal moon. Yoko's candle is silver, to everyone's amazement. Ariel places her tarot deck for later. Yemanja has her big beautiful conch shell. She blows a deep and solemn note before placing it lovingly on the altar. The twins, Ivy and Madrone, bring armfuls of flowers and little Ngame places all the bells. They chime and twinkle in the waning sun, echoing their sisters on the branches above. The whispering leaves and soft voices of women mingle with the ringing sounds.

We stand back together, arms 'round each other, and contemplate our handiwork. "It's beautiful." "It makes me want to start right away," Ngame squirms impatiently. "We have," laughs Yemanja, and everyone laughs and nods. Someone starts a chant to bless the altar:

> Come goddesses of fire and water
> Goddesses of earth and air
> Give your blessings to this altar
> Give a listen to our prayers . . .

We wind our ways, still singing, back up the path to fire and food. Sasha is stirring up her famous gypsy stew in the cauldron. The smells reach out enticingly; everyone is hungry. We find our bowls and cups and gather 'round. First a thank you song for the cook:

> Great are the life forms that let us eat them
> Some day our bodies too will be food
> Great is the goddess who makes things so yummy
> Great is the woman who cooks it so good!
> Yay Sasha! Yay Sasha!

Sasha beams. For a moment there are only birdsounds. We are swept up in good feelings and the sacredness of the moment. And then we are spooning the delicious steaming chunks of sensuous stew into our bowls . . .

The young moon sails across the sky and the distant "hoo-hoo" of an owl comes moaning through the trees. Tonight we will sleep in a dream wheel in the temple space below. Flashlights and lanterns bob through the dark like fireflies as women wind their way back down the bell-rung path. We set our bedding in a circle, heads at the periphery, feet to the center. Mara lights the silver candle on the altar and asks the goddess to bless our dreams. The murmur of sleepy conversation dies down bit by bit, finally replaced by crickets and stars . . .

We awaken with the dawn. Lucina is dancing playfully and low, her golden arms come slanting through the dappling leaves, fingers tugging at our eyelids. The air breathes on our faces, wafting sweet piney smells and morning birdcalls.

> O sisters wake up, wake up
> Night has emptied her cup

sings Ngame who is seven, and always the first one up. Women wake up slowly, stretching and blinking, sitting up amidst the bedding. We tell each other our dreams. "I dreamed that a woman came to the ritual, and she was pregnant." "I dreamed that my friend, who died, came back to life." "I dreamed that my sister came." "I dreamed that we were priestesses in an ancient temple cave . . ." Our dreams weave a tapestry of symbols and reality. We share and lend counsel, find the connections . . .

The ritual time approaches. We robe ourselves for the ceremony, painting each other's brows with blue crescent moons, twining leaves and flowers in our hair. Everyone looks so beautiful, transformed into magnificent beings of fantasy. Ngame dresses as the young child Kore who will be born, Selene as the Maiden who will grow. Yemanja will dance the Mother and Mara the Crone, and Ariel the swift-footed Diana . . . everyone else will be Hours or Seasons, except for Sasha in her many-colored robe, who will be the Muse. We practice the chanting as we dress:

Kooooraaaaaay . . . Maaaaaaaaaa . . . Hecaaataaaay . . .

We try to contain our excitement. Miraculously we are ready when the first sounds of voices come from above; our friends have arrived on the land and are approaching! Ivy and Madrone run half-flying to greet them and form a procession down to the temple. Everyone takes their places 'round the circle with Yoko and Willow standing, hands upraised to make a living gateway. Selene is poised beside the altar, ready to light the candles and perform the invocation.

Our friends are closer now; we hear them singing and see them appear one by one upon the path. Like us they have bedecked themselves in garlands and flowing robes. The air is electric and we are filled with wonder. As they file in slow procession through the trees we feel transported to another time. How often through the eons have we stood like this with our sisters, to come and praise the Goddess and welcome the Kore . . .

Sasha starts beating on her drum, a slow, steady rhythm. One by one the women pass beneath Yoko and Willow's upraised arms. They exchange kisses and blessings:

From woman you were born into this world
From women you are born into this circle

Gradually the circle is formed by the bodies of women. As the last one takes her place the drumming ceases. Yemanja raises her conch shell and blows a long and vibrant note. We all join hands, gazing upon one another with reverence. The robes, the flowers, the colors and shining faces make us into a vision of beauty. The energy throbs and we sense the majesty of this moment.

Someone starts the Ma, low and steady at first. Our voices blend and swell, gradually rising to a crescendo of sounding power. We close our eyes and pour ourselves out, playing now with harmonies and chords, flying into a oneness of vibrating tones. The energy pulses, undulates, thrilling our bodies and spirits, filling the forest with magic.

Now the sounds wane and gradually die, until we are left standing in a silence that is loud with intensity. We open our eyes again and gaze into one another's eyes, feeling the love and divinity in every woman. "You are goddess." "Hail to thee sweet goddess." "Blessed be my sister," and other acknowledgments are murmured 'round the circle as eyes meet and hearts connect. And we sink to the earth, taking seats and readying ourselves for the play. Selene turns to the altar and lights a match.

> "With this flame we ignite the spirit of the Maiden.
> Welcome Persephone!"

Everyone stares into the tiny flame, investing it with Maiden visions, and crying out "Welcome Persephone!" It seems that even the birds have become hushed with expectancy.

One and two at a time the women rise to make their offerings to the goddess. "I bring buds of birth for the Maiden." We twine the delicate baby flowers in our hair. "We bring sprouts for new life." Everyone eats the tiny sweet sprouts. "I bring a red candle for the flame of love between the Mother and the Daughter." She lights it from the flames of the gold and silver candles. "I bring a shell from Mother Sea." Elf brings a poem and Peny a dance. Willow has a chant to teach us all. When the circle of offerings is complete the drum's heartbeat stirs again, slow and deep.

Yemanja and Ngame move to the center before the altar. Ngame crouches, Yemanja stands and closes her eyes, listening to the drum . . . her body starts to undulate and sway. Sasha begins to speak the sacred words:

> Comes to pass
> Yea
> In the beginning of things
> That She Mother Goddess
> Is a giving . . .
> Of birth unto Her own cellf—

The drumming gathers, throbs, Yemanja moves more fully now, her pelvis swimming, heaving, her face suffused with ecstasy. Ngame comes forward to be "born" through Yemanja's wide open legs:

> ". . . and a Maiden is born!"

The two women, Maiden and Mother hold one another tenderly as everyone chants:

> KOOORAAAAAAAAY . . .

Like a musical tapestry the story weaves. The Maiden grows and dances to meet her lover Diana in the forest. Out of their swooning embrace Kore sinks to the earth and down, down to the dark realm of the Crone. The women's voices twine among the drumbeats, chanting, droning the holy names:

DIANAAAAAAA . . . HECAATAAAAAY . . .

The modes of love and death unite as Sasha's voice soars, spilling poetry like jewels into the air:

> "When She touches me
> Sweet-honey-lightning
> Sets my limbs a-quiver . . ."

and

> "I am the petals of the trembling rose
> Awaiting the kiss
> Of thy breath . . ."

The Hours and Seasons whirl around the periphery of the circle, spinning out the dizzying dance of life and love and death. Everyone is draped in black, moaning and wailing the griefs of separation . . . we all join with our screams for the pain we have known. It is as though we are dying together, knowing that we will be reborn, that spring will always come again.

> "Let grey Wisdom's arms enfold thee now
> Thou art here because thy time has come
> To learn the secrets of the soul
> Let go of life and earthly love for now
> And I will show to thee thy greatest lover . . ."

Mara as the Crone is majestic and mysterious in her grey hooded cloak. She sways and spins around the Kore, wipes away her tears and fears, enfolding her in velvet grey, leading her around and down, around and down the spiral dance of trance-formation . . . and we are crying out the great Crone names:

CERRIDWEN
KALI
ARACHNE
BABA YAGA
WISE WOMAN
HECATE

Entranced, we watch as Kore learns the mysteries of immortality, manifestation and dissolution. We learn them with her once again, celebrate with her the initiations. The Hours crown her with a garland of many-colored feathers to show the freedom of her eternal spirit, hang a gleaming crystal at her throat for her new-found powers of creativity, a belt of fragrant herbs at her hips for healing. And we sing with her the joy of knowing truth once more, invoking goddesses of wisdom:

> AAAAARAAAAADIAAAAA
> SOOOPHIAAAAAA
> AATHEEENAAAAA . . .

The drumbeat swells to the full once more and Kore is alone in the center of the circle, swaying, heaving and rising up, birthing herself into the upper world. Sasha sings:

> "She
> Laughing Maiden
> Is a-rising
> Song a-singing
> Up a-flying . . ."

Mother, Lover and Grandmother are there to welcome her, joining with the Hours and Seasons to circle dance and chant the name of her transformed self:

> PERSEPHONE! PERSEPHONE!

. . . and all our voices soar together through the trees to touch the sky in jubilation. A jay bird in a nearby tree joins in with raucous tones, feeling the change of energy. Our song is spiced with laughter.

Now the drum slows to the throbbing rhythm of birth and Persephone is in the center, moving, swaying, undulating as her Mother did for her. Mara casts off her grey crone robes and crawls to roll out from between Persephone's widespread legs. Demeter is there to midwife and catch the baby, and the three women hold and rock one another as the story begins again:

> "Comes to pass
> Yea
> In the beginning of things
> That She Mother Goddess
> Is a giving
> Is a-giving
> Is a giving of birth

Unto her own self she
Flex
She heave
And the mountains moan
And a great opening
Opens
Up to the world
And a Maiden is born . . .

As the last KORAAAAAAY swells, we all dance together, helping those who are seated to their feet. The dancers throw leaves and petals up into the air, showering us all with their fragrance. We dance and hug and laugh and cry, feeling the love and the joy of spring and the beauty of life's mysteries.

Spells are directed at circumstance; rituals are directed to the soul. In many ways they are the same, and employ the same basic techniques. Both can be done solo or with others. Both have an orderly progression of events. Both work by trance, visualization, mantra, desire, belief, movement, breath focus, and ecstasy. Both are enhanced or hindered by surrounding forces of nature, temperament and circumstance. Both can employ various symbolic tools and power objects, or be done simply with one's own body, mind and spirit. In fact, the line between them is somewhat arbitrary, as it is between matter and spirit, or the sacred and the mundane. In the tarot these two qualities are represented by the Witch (or the Magician in older decks) and the Priestess. If you examine these cards together you will see that they are similar.

Traditional tarot draws a heavier line between the sacred and the mundane than do present-day feminists of the craft. Esther Harding calls the goddess "the connecting principle." The goddess teaches us that all things in the universe interact and are related. The public and the private, the individual and society, the weather and the crops . . . all are interconnected and not split as we have been taught. This same awareness can be applied to magical systems and the tarot. To convey this interconnectedness, I changed the concepts of Major and Minor Arcana as seen in the traditional decks, naming my suits after the elements—Earth, Water, Fire, Air and Spirit. This approach can be applied to rituals and spells, as it can to the Witch and Priestess cards. A Priestess *is* a Witch, and vice versa.

Starhawk defines magic as that which changes consciousness. This is a profound thought, for any effect can be seen as a change, and we know that all reality begins in consciousness. Magic can also be defined as a spiritual science which is directed at shaping reality, or making things happen. And we can see it as a religious form, a way of worshipping the divine source of existence through enchantment.

The best spells and rituals are exactly this—enchanting. One feels swept up in a kind of heightened sensibility, inspired, exalted. Emotions flow freely, the spirit soars, the body moves seemingly of itself. Revelations come to mind, poetry to the lips. Energy is released and spins out into the universe where it gathers momentum and gradually evolves into happenings and things.

Here we can see the link between theater and magic. We know from high school history books that all theater began as ritual. The first plays were poetic mimes of the goddess and her many stories. The first poems were prayers in her honor. The essential themes of drama are still Hers: birth, love, beauty, death, separation, rebirth. But ancient rituals were more than play-acting. The enactment of birth was an echo of nature's awakening at spring. The growth of food was at once a dance and a reality. The harvest celebrated was actual nourishment. The passion of the goddess for life and the passion between human lovers was literally portrayed.

Good spells and rituals have a theatrical touch. The participants place the flowers with care, light the candles with meaningful attention, time each chant and prayer to flow. The ritual or spell begins, the power builds, peaks, dies down, and ends. Once the energy is begun and the circle cast, everything that happens becomes significant. There is meaning in everything, whether it was planned or not; even mishaps have messages. The participants become sensitized to details and nuances. The more elegantly, carefully and attentively done, the more powerful the results.

Timing is an important aspect of all ceremonies. Events should flow effortlessly, as a tree grows, "without haste and without rest." The best metaphor I can think of for a well-timed ritual is an orchestrated concert of music. Music flows like the psyche, and is a perfect model for ritual form. Different movements begin and end with grace, new movements take up the energy and carry it on. A priestess learns to sensitize herself to these peaks and valleys of energy, to know when it is the right moment to begin or end something.

Because all that happens takes on meaning in a ritual, and because flow and timing are so important, all earth-plane or practical matters are best attended to well ahead of time. Place the matches, ready for striking, with an ashtray handy. Arrange any props, power objects and offerings for convenient access. Nothing breaks trance so easily as the little distractions caused by lack of preparation. My best rituals have been well planned and carefully prepared for, and also had room for the unexpected. There is a delicate balance between this kind of order and spontaneity. Too much order is boring and static. With too much spontaneity focus is lost and the intensity dies. We prepare for everything, but in the end, open ourselves to the moment.

Nine Powers of Magic

> Make for yourself a power spot
> Bring you a spoon and a cooking pot
> Bring air
> Bring fire

Bring water
Bring earth
And you a new universe will birth . . .

Focus

The power spot could be interpreted as the spirit element. Though this can be symbolized by a physical spot in a room or on the earth, a power spot is really a focus. Focus creates concentration, which creates all that comes to be. It's like frozen orange juice, so to speak. A focus can be on any topic, with any motive. It can be represented in many ways, but you can't do magic without it. Once you have it, energy begins to gather or converge around it. Altars are one of our most familiar tools for helping to create focus. Goals can have the same effect, as can dreams or visions. Anything that holds the attention in a one-pointed and intense way is a focus.

If you think of spell-casting as a planting cycle, focus is the seed. The plant needs nourishment and love (water), encouragement (air), weeding and various other activities (fire), until it finally gives fruit or flowers (earth). A gardener waters her plant again and again, again and again until it grows to fullness. Spells often need the same type of repetition in order to come to be. A lot depends on the surrounding aspects; plant in loose or clay-filled soil and this will affect your odds of success. Plant in a windstorm and you will need to build a shelter. The more optimum your surrounding circumstances, the more likely you will have success. This is why a witch looks to the seasons, the moon phases, the astrology aspects, the social climate, her own moods and inclinations, what has come before and what is happening at the moment. As her experience accumulates, so does her skill.

But focus is step one. You can't create anything without it. I have one friend who comes to me year in and year out, always with the same dilemma—what to do with her life. But when I try to pin her down to a goal or focus, she wavers. It is too much responsibility perhaps, or she fears success, or she has been trained to believe that she will fail, or that she does not deserve to have a dream come true. The less focus one claims for oneself, the more one is ruled by those of others. We might even be able to make a case for focus being a class problem. In the win/lose set-up of patriarchy, those who are successful develop some sort of focus, those who are termed "losers" tend to be swayed by the focus of others. We could take this a step further and see it as a male/female problem. Men are encouraged to set goals for themselves, concentrate on them, achieve. Women are trained to be "dumb blondes," to have relatively little focus, to serve the focus or goals of others.

Focus brings power to spells, and group rituals as well. A good group pays attention to everything that is happening, supports each moment of the magic whether it is coming through a priestess, another member, through everyone at once, or from the universe surrounding them. Random focus will create random energy and the magic will dissipate or scatter. Some people will resent being asked to remain focused on the same thing as everyone else. They feel that their free will is being denied. This is a sad loss for everyone, including themselves, because the very freedom they seek lies in the ability to create what they choose. Creating requires the willingness to discipline oneself in order to have this point of concentration.

In patriarchy group focus is achieved most often through coercion, manipulation or strong leadership. People will listen with hushed attention by the thousands to one person singing or talking, if that person has been deemed worthy or advertised sufficiently. Yet they will not notice the chirping of a bird outside their window, or the amazing stories pouring from the lips of small children. Thus focus has been bound up with authoritarian structures. It is no wonder that people rebel and grow restless when they are asked to pay attention.

But going to the other extreme is just as entrapping. This need for disciplined focus is an issue for many teachers of the craft. We do not wish to be authoritarian, nor offend anyone's free will, yet we know that it is a basic ingredient for successful magic. This topic has much to do with issues of power and group dynamics, and I will discuss them further in Cycle 13.

When we talk about magical focus, we do not mean the hard-driving linear sort such as is required to solve a math equation. We are in a dreamy, floating, relaxed state. Magical focus is comfortable, flowing, effortless. It is a "letting" rather than a "putting" of the image we choose to work with. This allows for sudden inspirations, often the best magical source.

Trance

This altered state engages the psychic energies. Trance awakens the deep mind, which is slow, nonrational, dreamy, ecstatic, revelatory. In trance we can deprogram and program ourselves, and behave differently, with different reflexes. The famous fire-walking shamans of Hawaii, who walk barefoot on blazing heat without being burned, demonstrate the capabilities of trance. This deep mind controls us in many ways, for it is the part of us that takes on automatic programming belief/response mechanisms. Even our autonomic sensory responses, such as hunger and pain, have been attributed to unconscious programming. Witches seek to make contact with the deep mind, to learn how to use and direct it at will.

Trance is achieved by relaxing, breathing deeply, casting off anxiety, making monotonous droning sounds, moving in a simple circle dance (or simply weaving the upper torso), and visualization. When you are in trance you should feel a kind of dreamy floating sensation, pleasant and completely relaxed. A kind of electricity runs through the body with a sense of vibrating and expanding out beyond the body. You might even fall asleep for awhile, which is okay. Sometimes we can do an amazing amount of work in a trance-induced sleep. You should feel totally safe and open, able to surrender completely to whatever is happening, confident that all will be well. This is why covens are built on "perfect love and perfect trust." Trance opens one to the core, like making love or giving birth. It requires the utmost vulnerability. It is better to trance by yourself than in the company of people you do not feel safe with; it is better indoors than out if the only outside space you can find may be intruded upon.

To enter a trance state, relaxation is essential. In our world of daily tensions this may be difficult and can require repeated practice. A commonly used technique is to lie flat (or sit up; straight spine is best). Starting with the toes, clench and release each part of the body. Stubborn areas may need repeated work. Many people find it helpful to have a guide to take them through the areas of the body. Some used taped recordings of someone giving suggestions and guidance. You can record your own relaxing guidance tapes and play them back for yourself.

Slowing down is another important aspect of trance. The brainwaves of the alpha mind are longer than those of the beta or waking consciousness. This means putting aside your worries for a while, letting go of those fast-moving activities, and most important, breathing slowly and deeply.

Breath

We have talked about breath in previous Cycles, particular in Cycle 7, The Muse. For many of us deep breathing is another natural ability that we have forgotten. When we are tense or upset, we breath shallowly. Deep breathing from the diaphragm is natural; watch a child or an animal breathing and you will see full, rhythmic breaths. Breath brings nourishment to every cell of the body, and energy to the aura. A slow, even and deep rhythmic breath is one of the main ingredients of sustained trance. The yogis say that we control everything with our breath. Rebirthers have discovered astonishing healing techniques through breath. Much of our power is reduced through inhibited or shallow breathing.

The cells of our brain and body carry memories or sensory impressions of all past experiences, both pleasant and painful. When we breathe deeply we stir up those memories, giving ourselves an opportunity to erase old recordings and replace them with new ones. Thus we can affect our destinies with simple breathing!

Here is a good exercise to strengthen breathing and breathing awareness:

> *Take long and rhythmic breaths and chant:*
> I am the breather (*visualize yourself breathing*)
> Breathing in (*breathe in*)
> And breathing out (*breathe out*)
> *Repeat the above four or five times. Then change to:*
> I am she who watches the breather (*visualize yourself observing*
>   *yourself*)
> Breathing in (*breathe in*)
> And breathing out (*breathe out*)
> *After several repeats, change to:*
> I am the breath (*visualize yourself as the breath*)
> Being breathed in (*breathe in*)
> And being breathed out (*breathe out*)—developed by Andraliria

Sound

Sound vibrations, when they are soothing and peaceful, can help to induce trance. You can hum your own sounds, drum them, or play them on a droning instrument such as a dulcimer or harmonium. Or simple repetitious chants can be sung:

> Maiden mother crone in me
> All three in harmony . . .

The simpler and more repetitious the chant the better it is. A good trance can last for hours, supported by the same simple chant, and never be boring. People get bored because they are trained to expect something different, a variation. Sameness, we are told, is uninteresting. But it is possible to pass beyond the "boredom barrier" so to speak, where the simplest things become the most fascinating of all. The greatest experiences are based on the most simple factors. We must cast aside our technological programming that directs us to look for dazzling displays to hold our attention.

Droning music can be found in cultures the world over. In India there are the sitar and sarod, with their intricate rhythms and modes. From Spain comes the passionate flamenco. Our own Appalachian folk music, played on banjo and dulcimer, is full of droning sounds. Irish and Scottish folk music often is built on beautiful droning modes. The effect is enchanting and hypnotic. Coupled with poetic lyrics, this music can touch the soul. There is an ancient and universal wisdom here, coming from the grass roots, from "ordinary" people.

Eastern mystics have brought us the Aum chant, which is having immeasurable effect on consciousness. I remember being amazed at the power of this chant when I first learned it. Whenever I was in a circle, holding hands with other people, closing my eyes and droning the Aum, I would notice a strong tingling vibration moving through me at the end. Later I changed over to the Ma chant, when I had discovered the goddess. Ma is the universal mother cry and an appropriate female alternative to the Aum. Recently I have heard that the Ma chant is used everywhere! There are many goddess names that make wonderful chants, such as Amaterasu, Aradia, Diana. When one chants such names of power, one is invoking the forces that deity represents. Add this to the effects of trance, breath and sound vibration and you have a very potent spell.

Visualization

The making of concrete images is essential to magic. Most of us lose this natural ability as we grow older, because the culture provides us with so many prefabricated ones. We are bombarded by media, architecture, advertising, education, and especially TV. And yet as children we usually make images as a natural part of fantasizing. Often it is necessary to work consciously to reclaim and rebuild this ability. Children are often discouraged and told not to "make believe." Gradually they desert this aspect of themselves, thus leaving the creation of reality-making images in the hands of others.

I have found that many of my students come to me with a weakness in this area. Often when we do our meditations and the spell-throwing begins I hear abstract wishes, such as "let peace come to so-and-so," or "let my friend be healed." These are worthy and beautiful sentiments, but they are too abstract to work magically. It is necessary to create a simple visual representation of the end in mind. For example, peace and healing could be represented by an image of the person surrounded in a glowing aura of green light.

Symbols are potent thought-forms that provide impetus for deep-mind programming and universal response. The more inspiring and layered with meaning, the more impact they have. We need to rediscover the simple childlike ability to create images that symbolize feelings and events. Sometimes we can evoke an image of the event itself. For example, Mary Lou wants a car, and visualizes herself driving one. Some wishes are more complex and involve a variety of feelings and states of being. For example, Aradia wants to see harmony between friends who have been quarreling. She creates an image of them in a fond embrace, with golden cords of love connecting their heart chakras. Our magic grows more potent as our images become clear and strong. Adding the support of group focus can be very powerful indeed.

Belief

This is also a basic ingredient for success in magical workings. As we have said, doubt eats away at your spell. There can be many kinds of doubt: self-doubt, doubt in the realness of magic, doubt about the goddess, doubt about good or evil, doubt about the validity of getting what we want, doubt because social tradition does not necessarily support what we are doing, etc. There are so many forces assailing our psyches, attempting to sway our beliefs. We need to realize that we are human and subject to some extent to such influences. Therefore we need to strengthen our belief or faith in what we are doing. Blind faith is not enough. We need validation, experiences and events to help make it real.

Studying goddess traditions is so helpful in this regard. We *do* have a tradition; this is the irony of it. And it is so ancient, far more ancient than the one we are struggling with! The more we learn about it, the firmer our faith will be. Learning to see the goddess in all things is part of it too. See Her when you slice an apple across, sit under a tree, or watch a moonrise. See Her when you perform simple tasks, such as sweeping, and recall the symbolism of brooms. A goddess view of cooking turns the pot into a cauldron of transformation . . . gardening into godhood, singing into sorcery.

Changing belief programming is not an overnight proposition. We are usually dealing with years and years of repetition and acceptance. Banishings are wonderful for erasing old programs. Remember to replace what you have banished with the new reality you have chosen. A simple rebirthing exercise for reprogramming is to breathe out the negative image of that which you wish to eliminate, and breathe in the new positive image into your aura and cells. Evelyn Eaton (a powerful shaman sister who has passed over) says that the psychic babble is continuous, and we must "keep our rainbow 'round our shoulders."

Experience and practice are most effective in affirming belief/reality. Connecting with other people who are involved in alternatives, reading material on the subject, looking at art, joining in with other practitioners to do rituals and spells, spending time practicing by oneself and communing in nature . . . all these help to reinforce belief. The more community and tradition we build, the stronger our faith or "knowing" will be. These are the "taproots" of magic, which give it stability and lastingness.

Devotion

The path of the Goddess is a path of the heart. Unlike the detached meditations of the East, or the sedate Sunday prayer meetings of the church, pagan ceremony is passionate. The more deeply we feel about the goddess when we pray to her, the more moved we are by the liturgy, the more powerful the experience. The more intensely we desire the fulfillment of our spell, the more life-force there is behind the casting, and the more likelihood of success.

There is a place of truth and love that reaches the heart. People have come through many religious paths to this same center. Their sincerity and dedication shine out, whatever the metaphors or teachings may be. In this sense any religion or psychic practice can be valid when the seeker comes "in good faith." The irony of this is that the potency of devotion is real, yet the metaphors it supports may be questionable. As they say, "The road to hell is paved with good intentions." Atrocities have been committed in the names of many gods and goddesses because of the unquestioning devotion of their worshippers. We need to be passionate about the goddess, but we also need to be discriminating about the forms and metaphors that are used. If there is violence, hierarchy, manipulation, oppression or harm, no amount of devotion will make it right.

This is the dilemma we face with the rise of patriarchal religions today. Many people are running back to the fold because of the terrible crises of our time, and because they know of no alternatives. Their devotion may be real and their hearts sincere and their intentions the best. We must respect this and understand that many are finding strength and healing from the traditional faiths they embrace. They are also finding tradition and community, and these factors are real and necessary. They bring roots and stability to any belief system.

In the end devotion is a supremely personal matter, found by each of us in our own hearts. There is no doubt that it gives potency and effectiveness to any undertaking or religious pursuit. A religious movement can sweep across nations and change societies like nothing else can when that gut-level, passionate devotion is aroused in the people.

I therefore encourage you to get as emotional as you like in your ceremonies. It may take practice to allow yourself to open up. Many people are shy in our culture, having been taught all kinds of restraints. It takes years of covening, sometimes, to reach the kind of free expression one reads about in books about "primitive" ritual. The ancients were wiser than we know in their unrestrained demonstrations of appreciation for their deities.

Movement

I see movement as a fiery aspect of rituals and spells. It brings energy and actualization to any undertaking. It can take the form of dance, swaying, weaving, walking to different parts of the circle, raising one's arms in the air, etc. Or it can be actions that help to realize a spell.

Pagan rituals often include wild free-form dancing. A powerful cone can be raised as each body radiates energy and each mind shapes it.

My favorite way to move during magic-making is in a moon-wise weaving motion. (This is done simply by sitting straight and swaying in a circle with the upper torso.) I call it "stirring up the cauldron" because I feel the motion sending all my aura energies swirling into orbit. Circular and spiral movements are especially effective, as they create a continuum and are in harmony with universal movements.

Formalized movement can be used to physicalize metaphors and beliefs. The most complete meditations include the body, mind and spirit. When my children were small they trance-danced instinctively to my music. We found out later that this was an ancient ritual form. When you back up your symbols with your body you are saying, "I am becoming that which I express . . ."

Here is a simple movement ritual that can be used as a meditation for magic:

Say aloud—

Earth witch	*Crouch on the earth*
Ear to the ground	*Put your ear to the ground*
Listening to	*Listen to the sounds of the earth*
Her heartbeat	*Feel them*
Water witch	*Rise to sitting position*
Arms in the stream	*Make undulating, watery movements*
Reflecting on reflection	*with arms and torso*
	Feel watery
Fire witch	*Rise to the knees with the same*
Breath to the flame	*undulating energy, only faster,*
Kindles passion	*with arms upraised*
	Feel fiery

Air witch	*Keep flowing upward to your feet*
Throat full of song	*Move gently*
Spinning sweet spells	*Feel airy and floating*
Spirit witch	*Leap and reach, move out, dance freely*
Embracing stars	*Reach upward*
Imagining her magic	*"Touch" the stars*
Earth witch	*Gradually flow back down to earth*
Ear to the ground	*Crouch and press your ear to the*
Listening to Her heartbeat	*ground once more*

Affirmation

To affirm is to make firm. To speak aloud one's vision is to add the impetus of breath and sound. Finding words to express these visions helps give them focus through the power of naming. Names bring form where there was chaos, understanding where there was confusion. Whether alone or in groups, affirmations give a lot of power to spells or rituals. Phrases such as "so be it," "so mote it be," "together we can do anything," "all that we have seen and said shall come to be," and so forth, are powerful affirmations. Here are a few more:

> As we weave it so doth it be.

> By all the powers of earth and sea
> As I will so mote it be.

> We are women reclaiming our powers
> We are women rebirthing ourselves

> I deserve love
> I deserve happiness
> I deserve abundance
> I deserve, etc.

> I am an endless source of all that I choose to create

Writing down affirmations is very effective. Affirming one another's visions during group ritual is another way to intensify the energy. Often we need this reflection and support. A simple "So be it, blessed be" is commonly used in most witches' ceremonies to affirm and bless all undertakings. It is best to invent your own affirmations, as your own language and symbol system will resonate best in your own psyche.

Words of Power

May the circle never be broken
May the earth always be whole
May the rattle ever be shaken
May the goddess live in my soul*
*From *Circle of Hecate*

I shall live
I shall be free
Goddess goddess
I am thee . . .

Mother Goddess, keep me whole
Let thy beauty fill my soul
Maiden Goddess, keep me whole
Let thy power fill my soul
Crone Goddess, keep me whole
Let thy wisdom fill my soul . . .

Blessed be the Maiden within me
For she bringeth courage and freedom
Blessed be the Mother within me
For she bringeth love and life
Blessed be the Crone within me
For she bringeth wisdom
and understanding . . .

We are the flow, we are the ebb
We are the weavers, we are the web . . .

I am whole unto myself
Centered in the Kore of me
I shall give and shall receive
Goddess goddess loves me . . .

Let my magic be.

Let all illness
Be cast from me
Cleansed of all impurity
Free from all wrongs
I may have done
'Til goodness
And love
And I
Are one . . .

Goddess Names:
Hecate
Tiamat
Astarte
Asherah
Kore
Selene
Sybele
Diana
Aphrodite
Themis
Psyche
Cerridwen
Hathor
Isis
Bast
Persephone
Rhiannon
Arianrhod
Ariadne
Aradia
Demeter
Shekhinah
Melissande
Ea
Gaia
Kwan Yin
Tanath
Chantico
Athene
Nut
Amaterasu
Brigit
Nimue
Anu
Mari
Maya
Queen of Heaven
Ix Chel
Oceana
Habundia
Fortuna
Afrekete
Nu Kwa
Kali
Lakshmi
Sarasvati
Durga
Yemanja
Oshun
Mbaba-Mwana-Waresa

IMAGES OF POWER

 flame   life, energy

 attraction

 rose   love, beauty

 egg   birth potential
cosmos

 moon   maiden goddess
suggestion
subconscious

 tree   life

 heart   love

 square   stability
protection

 cauldron transformation

 eye   wisdom, vision

 rainbow happiness
fulfillment
perfection

 woman

 sun   happiness
optimism
radiance
healing

 spiral   infinity

 water   emotions
subconscious
flow, agreement
cleansing, baptism

 cornucopia
abundance, wealth

 pentagram

magic, goddess
protection
earth element

Affirmations are one aspect of the poetic language of spells. You can do them in and of themselves or blend them in with descriptions and requests, such as:

> Earth, sea, wind and fire
> Bring to me what I desire

> The circle is cast
> The spell is made fast
> Only the good can enter herein
> The magic is made, so let it begin

Colors

There are many color systems that assign a variety of moods and meanings to colors. This can be applied to candle magic, to drawings of power images, clothing, altar draperies, etc. Below is a suggested list of colors and their meanings. Use it if it works for you; if not make you your own color system.

Green	Healing, abundance
Brown	Grounding, stability
Deep Pink	Optimism
Blue	Peace, protection, water
White	Spirit, purity
Yellow	Expansion, success
Orange	Energy, affection
Red	Love, passion, anger, blood, womb
Grey	Wisdom, union of opposites
Black	Banishment, binding, death, mystery
Purple	Power, psychic power
Silver	Moon, enchantment
Gold	Wealth, power, venerability, sun energy

Elements

Many witches use the elements of fire, water, earth, and air as a basis for magic. These are represented by wands, cups, pentacles and swords, as in the tarot. Esoteric traditions say that wands are to summon spirits, cups are to hold power, pentacles (or platters) are to give offerings, and swords are to cut spells. These concepts are powerful and beautiful and I encourage you to try them at your own altar. I am not a strict traditionalist myself, and often find that I work magic in a more improvisational style. Yet no matter how varied my spells and ceremonies may be, I find that the old elements are always there in some form, because everything is made of them.

When dealing with elements I do prefer to think of them in five, however, rather than four. As I have said, odd numbers are more cyclical, even numbers more static and linear. Many witches cast the circle in "four quarters" designating one element to each of the directions, north, west, south and east. I have an ingrained resistance to all four-square structures, as I feel they are signs of a dualistic reality system. I would rather think of time in terms of 13 moons rather than 12 months, seasons in terms of Maiden, Mother and Crone (Spring, Summer and Winter) rather than four, gender in terms of Female, Male and Androgyne instead of Male and Female (or Female as root form, the center out of which the Male is born). I would rather cast a circle with a five-pointed star on the ground than the four directions. In ancient Rome odd numbers were sacred to the Goddess, and Her holy days were planned to be held on odd-numbered dates. Even-numbered dates were used for Her consort's celebrations. It seems clear to me that even numbers, four-square structures and gender polarities are all signs of patriarchal ascendance. I can't help feeling that a religious group that boasts of its liberating ideas is contradicting itself when it perpetuates non-cyclical grids or structures. (See chart on dualism and the Great Round in the Luna Cycle, page 119).

The Five Senses

In studying techniques of theater I learned the importance of the five senses for evoking strong emotion. The Stanislavsky method teaches "sense memory," a technique in which one recalls the sensory aspects of an experience. By concentrating carefully on what one has seen, tasted, touched, smelled and heard, one can call up powerful feelings and express them through the role one is playing.

For instance, we would do an exercise pretending to eat an apple. First we held it in our hands, feeling its texture and weight, seeing its shape and color. Then we brought it close to our noses, smelling its fragrance. Finally we sank our teeth into its flesh, tasting its sweetness and juice. This kind of work deepens the creative ability and can be invaluable to magic-makers.

One day I was talking about image-making to a former student. She wondered how a blind person, who had never experienced seeing in this life, could make images. That was when I realized that images are not necessarily confined to the visual, but also include the other senses.

For example, I have had great success doing weather work using the senses. In a meditation circle for rain-making I asked each member to describe the rain—how it looks, tastes, sounds, smells, feels. After such workings rain would always come within a few days!

The senses can be correlated with the five elements of the witch's star. I have correlated seeing with spirit, hearing with air, touching with fire, smelling with water, and tasting with earth. You can use this system when casting your pentagram circle and meditating on the object of your spells.

The Directions

Most magical systems include some concept of the directions or dimensions of space. Native Americans talk about four directions, attributing animal symbolism to each. Witches talk about the same four and designate Earth to the north, Air to the east, Fire to the south, and Water to the west. Paul Case, in his book *The Tarot*, describes the occultists' Cube of Space, a representation of all known directions, with various tarot cards and Hebrew letters associated with each plane and corner.

Why be concerned with the directions? I asked my tarot deck about this, and got the Four of Pentacles, "Security." I take this to mean that describing and defining the directions gives us a point of focus, some form of stability in an otherwise random universe. We operate in a multi-dimensional space and need to be sensitive and aware of its nuances. A case in point: While driving, I was once hit by another car from behind when not paying attention to that direction. Becoming conscious of the directions gives us control. Creating symbols for these gives us choice.

However, I feel I must question the concept of four directions or a "cube" or space. I would much prefer to operate in cycles or spheres. A four-directional universe sets up oppositions, whereas a three- or five- or seven-directional universe would be more flowing. There are many trends appearing in the world today that seem to back up this concept. Quantum physics is taking us from linear to clustered forms, architecture from square to round buildings, social changes from meeting in status-defined rows to non-hierarchical circles. Philosophy and science are discovering the connections between things such as time and space, now often called the "time/space continuum." It seems important to apply this expansion to magical systems as well.

Of course we do need linear structures and even numbers for continuity, grounding, and stability. This is one of the messages of the tarot cards numbered four, such as the Emperor. In *Shekhinah's Tarot* these powers were given back to the Mother Goddess in keeping with her sustaining and nurturing qualities. I have developed a seven-direction concept which can allow for the four and the three to co-exist.

North   South   East   West   Above   Below   Within

These words can be chanted and visualized as an effective means of casting the circle. Another way of conceptualizing this is: Above, Below, Before, Behind, To the Left, To the Right, and Within. These words allow us to bring more layers of symbolism into the process. Before and Behind are not only space, they are also time—Future and Past. To the Left and Right are the Present, and they are also Creating/Giving (Right) and Dissolving/Receiving. Above is Goddess and Infinity, Below is the path or premise, the foundation on which we rest, and our connection to the Earth. Within is the Self. The Self encompasses past, present and future. The result is a sphere. Perhaps this will be the accepted way of casting circles in the future.

> *Free Ticket to Heaven*
> Let the path be clear before me
> Let all go as I will
> And the past be clean behind me
> Let all go as I will
> And the ones I love beside me
> Let all go as I will
> And the Goddess light above me
> Let all go as I will
> And the solid earth beneath me
> Let all go as I will
> And my own true self within me
> Let all go as I will . . .
> (This chant has a melody, which you may
> be able to "hear" if you listen deeply.)

Visualizing the Pentagram for five directions is perhaps more radical, placing an odd-numbered figure on the ground. With the altar as guide to the five elements, one can bypass North, East, South and West. This works well for people who may have difficulty telling the directions. You can still add Above, Below and Within. I usually set it up this way:

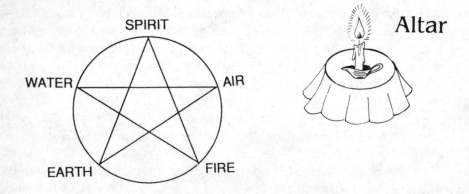

264

There are varying attitudes among magic-makers regarding the need for protection from the presence of destructive or hostile forces. Some are so frightened, they hesitate to practice. Others feel that any attention paid to such possibilities creates them, and therefore it is best to erase all such thoughts from the mind. I am into sensible prevention myself, with a minimum amount of attention. Those that are frightened make victims of themselves by not risking at all, therefore denying their power. Those who choose to ignore all evil, I feel, are naive and have probably led comparatively sheltered lives. When we open up the psychic powers we must realize that there are risks involved, as with the use of any force. It is also true that attention creates, and so we must find a healthy middle ground where we can create freely but safely.

There are beings on all planes, as well as forces, and some of them are not always nice. As women who have been trained to be nice and open to everyone, we may need to develop some Amazon energy. Just as women are learning aikido and karate and other earth-plane self-defense techniques, we also need psychic-plane techniques. This does not mean we need to become belligerent or start seeing threats at every turn. Knowing where that line is requires delicate balance and understanding. It is the same line as that between binding and hexing. Those who have been victims tend to be weak in self-protection. Often when they realize this they go to the other extreme and become violent in their attempt to compensate. This unfortunately serves to create more violence, and so the vicious cycle continues 'round the world.

True strength resides in firm but gentle guardianship. A good mother knows the difference between loving discipline and revenge. Here is a good image of protection: Place a pentagram around oneself and the environment, with a mighty Amazon goddess posted at each point, facing outward toward the world. Each has a shield with the snake-haired Medusa's face, and a labyrs at her side. These weapons are there for use in need, and stand as a warning to those who would violate. But they will be used only to protect and otherwise not at all.

Athene is a traditional image of balanced protection, and she can be found in most tarot decks under the name of Justice. In her ancient representation she had the Medusa on her breast to show protection of the mysteries. She also represents karmic protection, or the principle of return: "That which we send out will come back around."

In a natural state most of us are equipped with an instinct for self-preservation. But in patriarchy many women have lost this and become prey to the predators. We are taught that men and institutions will protect us, and that we must be open and kindly to all who come our way. The guardian in us can get blocked and often turns inward and destructive. (Starhawk calls this the Self-Hater; for more information see "The Witch's Star," listed at the end of this Cycle.) Because of this conditioning we may have to work to build up what should have been instinctive behavior. As in all healing, it begins inwardly, with an attitude of self worth. We are precious, we are wonderful, we are sacred, we deserve to be. We therefore have a natural right to protect ourselves from any destruction.

A simple self-protection is done by imagining a sphere of light around oneself and declaring that only good energies can exit or enter. Many magicians suggest white light. Another method is to imagine being within a many-faceted sphere of mirrors. The mirrors face outward. Each surface deflects any negative thought-forms which may be directed at it, bouncing them back to the sender. They must then take responsibility for their own creations. Some witches suggest we wrap ourselves in rainbows or place ourselves in a rainbow bubble or sphere. Starhawk places a sphere of porous energy so that only good can get through.

There are also many herbs that are considered protecting, such as rosemary and sandlewood. Often when I am preparing to enter a situation that may be risky or difficult I pluck a sprig of rosemary and put it in my pocket. Witches traditionally have rosemary growing by their doors. It can also be placed over doors and windows, as can pentagrams. And then there is the old reliable burning of sage, which is said to cleanse, purify and protect. Bell-ringing is an ancient tradition for protection that is very effective. But in the end inner attitude is the most important. If you believe that you are precious and well-defended, the odds are better that you will be. If you create safe and loving energy, it will come back to you in kind.

Protecting Magic

Salt—Witches have used salt for protection for many ages. Throw some over your left shoulder, wear some in a pouch, sprinkle it everywhere in your space, pour a circle of salt for rituals.

Garlic—Another ancient protection; often a clove or two are placed in an amulet pouch. Garlic also can be hung in bunches around the house.

Incantations—Invoke the names of protective deities such as Demeter, Ceres, Isis. Or create affirming chants, such as: "I am perfectly safe," and repeat them with visualization.

Stones—Certain stones have protective qualities, such as amethysts. Crystals can be invested with protecting energy and worn or kept nearby.

Candle-Lighting—Blue and white candles are used for protection. These can be anointed with rosemary or sandlewood oil, or rolled in protecting herbs.

Mother Goddesses—Protection is a motherly act in that it preserves and nurtures; therefore any Mother Goddess can be called upon in this regard. Imagine a circle of mothers surrounding you, or see yourself cradled in Her arms.

Sigils—These are drawn symbols, used to represent many things. A pentagram is a commonly used protecting sigil. A simple circle can also be used, or a square. Write your name in runes in the center along with the name of a protecting deity. Fold up the paper and place it under a stone on your altar. Create a number of sigils and fold them up; tuck them into secret places around the house. Draw them with visible or invisible ink over doors and windows. Carve them on lintels and doorposts.

Talismans—These are symbolic objects, usually worn or carried on the person—special jewelry, pentacles, ankhs, the Eye of Maat, etc. You can create your own talismans using objects that represent protection to you.

Oils and Incenses—Anoint yourself with protecting oils like rosemary and sandlewood. Burn these incenses; also sage, laurel and myrrh.

Spell For Grounding

Ingredients: Pentacle, as shown here; a few sage seeds; a piece of sage root; a large stone; two brown candles; protection oil; sage and rosemary for burning; journal; pen; parchment.

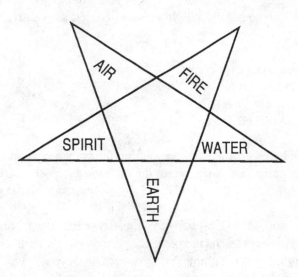

Grounding is an essential tool for survival and magic. Many of us have lost this ability, due to patriarchal conditioning. Our lifestyles tend to take us away from the earth and our connections to nature, leaving us psychically uprooted from our Mother-source. In a natural state, our auras are connected to the Earth's aura at all times, so that there is a natural flow between us and we can be continually replenished by Her vast energies. If you find that you tend to be ungrounded most of the time, you need to do spells occasionally, and also to incorporate these techniques on a regular basis, until they become habitual.

The first step to any grounding is to *slow down*. So, set aside a special day for yourself, when you can be completely alone and quiet. In preparation for your Grounding Day (!), prepare a pot or a spot in your garden for planting your sage seeds. Keep the seeds on your altar in the meantime, to charge them up.

Set up your altar the night before, so that you will see it first thing upon waking. Place your large rock beneath your altar, affirming its stabilizing energy as you do so. Stand the pentacle at the center, with its earth arm pointing downward. Prepare a cauldron with the sage and rosemary, ready for burning. Anoint the two brown candles with protection oil and arrange them on either side of the pentacle. Place all spell ingredients aesthetically and symmetrically.

Before going to sleep, anoint yourself with some of the oil. Take your dream journal and pen to bed with you. As you are awaiting sleep, ask the Goddess to send you a healing dream to help give insight on what you need for grounding, and what might be preventing this. Sleep as late as you like.

When you awaken, lie around in bed for awhile and enjoy. Write down any dreams or insights you may have had. Move to the altar only when you feel completely rested. Take your journal and pen with you. Anoint yourself once more, placing a protective bubble of golden light around yourself as you do so. Light the candles, saying:

> As these flames burn
> So grounding returns
> When they are gone
> This spell will be done.

Next light the herbs in your cauldron, letting the smoke surround and purify your aura. On the parchment write your dream messages—the obstacles and solutions to your grounding needs. Refold it and place it beneath the large stone under your altar.

Take the sage root and hold it as you meditate. Relax and center, breathe deeply for a while, letting your eyes rest on the pentacle, particularly the earth arm, sensing its downward energy. Keep breathing deeply as you close your eyes, letting the pentacle appear in your mind's eye. See it grow and expand until you are at its center, with the earth arm beneath you, pointing downward. Now see the pentacle change into the roots and branches of a tree, with yourself as the trunk. See the roots connecting you with our Mother, growing down and down into the center of the earth. Chant:

> The roots of me go down and down
> O Mother Earth in Thee I ground

Repeat this chant again and again, visualizing its meanings. Keep chanting as you take the sage root and arrange it in such a way that you can carry or wear it for some time. Then take your seeds and plant them as previously arranged. Chant the above chant throughout.

Return to your altar and sit in silence for a while, continuing to breathe and visualize your roots connecting to the earth's center. When you feel complete, snuff out the candles. Repeat this spell every now and then, until the candles are burned down. If you still need to repeat it, you can replace the candles, but be sure to light the new ones from the old flames.

Spend the day peacefully, doing simple things that allow you to move slowly. In general it is a good idea to give yourself one day a week like this, especially when you are learning to work magic. As you return to your regular routine keep the sage with you. Visit your sage plant from time to time, watering with chanting as well as liquid. As she matures, you can use her leaves for future grounding spells, and wear them in a pouch as well. Whenever you tend her, affirm your roots and centeredness; talk to her and thank her for being your ally. Repeat the chant when you feel the need.

Ritual For Lovers

To be done in a safe, secluded place, at the full of the moon.

Before sundown create a love bower. The bed is your altar. Dress it with clean, sweet-smelling pillows and coverings, scented with rose. Adorn it with red roses for passion, and laurel for purity and protection. Hang an image of Aphrodite. Place red candles and rose incense, ready for lighting. Place a bowl of red wine at the foot of the bed.

As the full moon ascends, draw a ritual bath and scatter petals of roses on the water, also add a few drops of rose oil. If possible, let the water catch the light of the full moon.

Put on some gentle and passionate music. Approach the altar bed together. Light the candles and incense, saying:

> We ignite the spirit of Aphrodite.
> Hail to thee, Goddess of Love!

Undress one another slowly, by the candlelight and moonlight. Enter the bath and bathe each other in turn. As you wash each part of your lover's body, proclaim its beauty and sacredness.

> Blessed be thy hair that caresses my face
> Blessed be thine eyes that look upon me with love
> Blessed be thine ears that hear my words of love

Blessed be thy lips that kiss, thy mouth that speaks to me of love
Blessed be thine arms that embrace me in love
Blessed be thy heart that throbs in the heat of love
Blessed be thy hands that touch me
Blessed be thy breast that contains all sweetness
Blessed be thy belly that holds the womb of life (for a woman)
Blessed be thy back that gladly bears love's burdens
Blessed be thy genitals that are the gateway to mystery and ecstasy
Blessed be thy legs that carry thee to me
Blessed be thy feet that take thee on love's journey . . .

Kiss and wash each place as you name it.
As you emerge from the water, chant together:

We are love rebirthing.

Dry each other gently and place flowing robes upon each other. Anoint one another's brows with rose oil, saying:

Aphrodite bless you

Walk hand-in-hand to the altar bed and kneel before it. Raise up the bowl of wine toward Aphrodite, saying:

Hail, Goddess of Love, who brought us together
We thank thee for thy wondrous gift of true desire
Bless our union tonight
Give us openness that we may flow into one another
Strength to return to our separate selves
And flexibility to dance and merge and re-emerge again . . .
May our love never be bound, but fly in freedom
May our hearts never be cold, but overflowing
With the heat of Thy love . . .
So be it!
Blessed Be!

Offer each other the wine. Rise and embrace. Disrobe one another slowly. Take hands and move to the bed.

The rest is beyond words.

Banishing Spell

No energy can ever be eliminated, only transformed. A banishing is actually a recycling of energy, much as storm clouds become rain. A banishing spell can be homeopathic, in that it brings out the symptoms by conjuring sympathetic pictures. Problems you are attempting to eliminate may erupt after a spell-casting; this can be seen as a healing crisis. Don't give up, keep repeating the spell.

Nature will always seek to fill a vacuum. Whenever banishing, always replace.

Ingredients: dried sage for burning; a cauldron; a clear, resonant bell; journal and pen; parchment; one black candle; one white candle; protection oil; banishing pentacle (See Crone Cycle).

To be performed at the dark of the moon, at night. (Midnight is best.) Make sure that you will be absolutely alone and undisturbed during this ritual.

Make a large pentacle on the floor in front of your altar, with the spirit arm pointing toward it. Place your cauldron in the center of the star, and place the sage, ready for burning.

Naming the Demon: In your journal make a list of all the attributes and behavior that you wish to banish. Make an anagram or name by taking letters or syllables from your list. It should be something pronounceable so that you can speak it aloud in the ceremony. Write this name on your parchment and place it on the altar.

Drape the altar in black. Carve a banishing pentacle on the black candle and a manifesting pentacle on the white candle. Anoint them both with protection oil. Arrange the ingredients of the spell in pleasing, symmetrical design. Place the banishing pentacle so that it faces you.

Light the black candle, saying:

> Around and down and back behind
> The spell of banishing now unwind

Light the white candle, saying:

> Around above and forward forth
> Fire and water, air and earth
> The spell of change now come to birth
> Come Cerridwen
> Come Kali
> Come Hecate
> Aid me in my workings

Visualize the crones gathering 'round. Sit quietly with your spine straight. Relax and breathe deeply for a while, letting your gaze rest on the banishing pentacle.

Take up your parchment with your Demon's name written thereon. Open your journal to the place where you have listed the Demon's attributes and behavior. Say aloud:

> I am here to banish Demon (name).
> She (name attributes).
> She (name behaviors).

Arise and take your bell and parchment with you. Move to the center of the star and light the sage in your cauldron. Ring the bell constantly throughout the next part of the spell. Say aloud:

> Begone Demon_____
> Begone from Above me
> Begone from Below me
> Begone from Before me
> Begone from Behind me
> Begone from the Left of me
> Begone from the Right of me
> Begone from Within me

Crumple up the parchment and drop it into the burning sage. (Keep ringing the bell.) Walk to the Spirit arm of the star, saying:

> Begone Demon _____
> Begone from my Spirit
> (*Close your eyes and visualize the negative energy*
> *dissolving from your aura.*)

Still ringing the bell, walk to the Air arm, saying:

> Begone from my thoughts
> (*Verbally dismiss your demon.*
> *Visualize your mind being emptied of its presence.*)

Walk to the Fire arm, saying:

> Begone from my Actions
> (*Yell and scream, stamp your feet, let it all hang out.*
> *Take time to think about your own actions and how*
> *you may have helped to create the unwanted situation.*)

Move to the Water arm, saying:

Begone from my Desires
(*Examine your feelings and weed out any hidden
attraction you may have had for your Demon.
Let your desire for liberation take over.*)

Move to the Earth arm, saying:

Begone from my body and my environment
(*Hug yourself and move your hands through your aura,
cleansing and clearing it. Send white light through your
hands and out into the room, through the walls and on to
surround and permeate the entire building.*)

Return to the center and let the sage smoke surround you. Say

So Be It
So It Be
Be It So

Return to the altar, and be seated. Replace the bell. Stare into the white candle flame for a while, visualizing the positive situation you wish for. Say:

When the dark candle's gone
This banishing's done
As the white candle burns
So_____returns.
So be it!
Blessed be!

Meditate until you feel complete. Snuff out the candles. Repeat this spell as often as you wish.

Remember, silence is the fifth rule of magic. Tell no one of your spells until they have come to fruition.

Spell to Strengthen the Witch Within

This is a time of the rebirth of the root cultures of many peoples. Ancient wisdoms that were lost or obscured by the power shifts of history are now coming to light through many channels. Native people are discovering their rituals, their myths, their shamans. Scientists are discovering the cyclical behavior of nature, the consciousness of matter and the connectedness of all things. Psychologists are discovering rites of passage in the human psyche, dream power, archetypes and the importance of ritual. Even the advances of technology are adding to this wave of discovery in many ways, such as through media and communication.

The image of the witch is at the root of our own cultural past. To embrace and affirm this aspect of ourselves is to tap the power of tradition, longevity and cellular memory. Though there is bound to be some resistance in these transitory times, I believe that the wave of change is on our side. We are moving into a wonderful renaissance that will effect the entire planet. The crises we see around us in the world are the result of a need to change our perception of reality, for reality has already skipped ahead of us. Once we understand, harmony sets in.

In preparing for your spell, first do some serious thinking about just what the image of the witch means to you. Make a list of all her qualities, her powers, her names, how she looks, what she wears, thinks, feels, etc. See her in your mind's eye with as much clarity and detail as possible.

This spell should be cast three times, at the new, full, and dark of the moon.

Ingredients:large piece of parchment paper; pen; two purple candles; Moon Oil; power incense; a small moonstone.

Arrange your altar. Carve moons into your candles and anoint them with oil. Anoint yourself as well, on brow, heart, and hands. Seat yourself comfortably and light the candles, saying:

With this flame I awaken the Witch within me.

Light the incense. Close your eyes and breathe deeply for a while; relax and let go. Bathe yourself and your aura in white light. Keep breathing deeply and slowly as you begin to sway and weave, letting your body move in a circular motion. Empty yourself of all distractions and anxieties. When you feel flowing and peaceful, let your imagination fill up with images of your inner Witch. Take up the parchment and pen and make a sketch of her, or you can use the Witch tarot image provided. (Don't worry about style or quality; the simpler the better.) Write your impressions and ideas beneath the drawing. Set this up between the candles so that it is facing you. Take the moonstone and clasp it to your heart. Keep breathing and weaving as you fill yourself with the image on the parchment.

Draw the Witch image into yourself, see her multiplied a thousand-fold, vibrating in every cell of your body. Repeat the following incantation three times:

I am willing to be different and strong
I am willing to be different and beautiful
I am willing to be different and free
I am willing to be different from patriarchy
For this difference
Is the same

Sameness
With the Non-Linear
World of Magic
The Goddess
Her forces
My dreams
The moon
My feelings
My creativity
My passion
My deep love
Of all creation . . .

And the only con-forming
I need to do
Is Forming Creation
For I am form
And I am forming
To universal law
And therefore
Must survive . . .
And even though
I may at times
Feel alone
And misunderstood
I will remember
That I have sisters out there
Who are learning to be free
Like me
And that I am not alone
But All One
And one with the all . . .

And that once free women
Were respected
And loved
And will be again
And will be again
And will be
I will to be
I will it to be
And so doth it be

Forever
And ever
So be it
Blessed be . . .

As you repeat this chant let your words flow rhythmically as you weave and sway. Let your voice create melody. Improvise, make new words if you feel inspired.

When you feel complete slip your parchment beneath the altar cloth. Give thanks to the Goddess and snuff out the candles.

The moonstone is to carry at all times. Keep it in your pocket, under your pillow, or wear it in a pouch. Whenever you feel the need, hold the stone and rub it with your thumb in a circular motion. Think or say:

I am safe
I am me
All is well
Blessed be.

Tell no one of this spell until it has come to fullness. Even as you feel your powers strengthen, it may be best to maintain silence. Be discreet about sharing your magic.

May the goddess give wings to the witch within you! So be it.

The Witch's Star

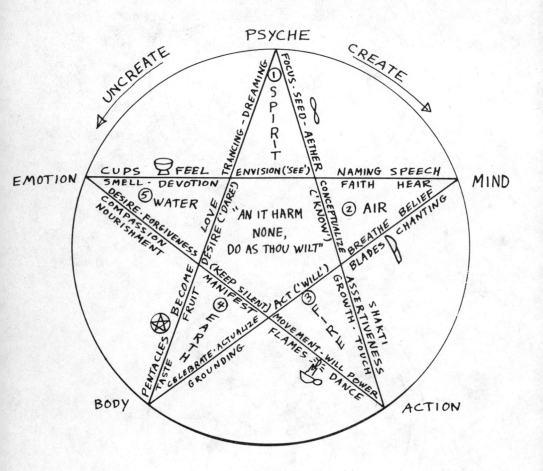

Suggested Projects

1. Select one of the spells provided in this Cycle, and cast at an appropriate time of the moon. I especially recommend the Spell to Strengthen the Witch Within, if you are feeling a need for deepening and reinforcing your magic, your powers as a woman, or your identity as a witch. This one can be adapted for group workings too. The meeting can begin with a discussion on the issues raised in the preliminary text, as well as any others that come up for each woman. Then members can spend some quiet time pondering and making sketches of their inner witch. An altar can be made with these, in the center of the circle, as well as other appropriate power objects. Everyone can participate in the incantation, weaving and improvising together.

2. In your *Book of Shadows*, explore in detail the nine powers of magic discussed in this Cycle. Reflect upon how each of them may have appeared in your life in some capacity, and what you have learned from them. See if you can discover other magical powers and expand upon these as well. (Examples: Love, Community, Myth, Awe, Dreams, Feelings, Inspirations.) Make up a ritual or spell, with the nine or more powers in mind. Perform it at your altar by yourself, or with sisters. Afterward, write about or discuss the uses you made of the powers, how well they worked, or how you could work more effectively.

3. Make a protection charm based on the five elements of the Witch's Star as shown on page 278. Find five small stones or crystals, and charge each one with an image representing its element. Stones are charged by breathing into them and sending the mental images you wish them to carry and project. On five slips of parchment or paper, write an incantation for each stone and its element. For example: "Spirit Stone, please guard my soul, Keep my psyche safe and whole. Air Stone, Please guard my mind, Filled with images divine. Fire Stone, please guard my deeds, turn them to my truest needs. Earth Stone, please, my body keep, that I be grounded in the deep. Water Stone, my feelings seal, please keep them loving, clear and real." Wrap each stone in its parchment prayer, chanting it aloud as you do so. Tie each one off with a sturdy thread and make three magical knots to seal the spell. Place all in a velvet pouch and wear close to your skin or store on your altar, under your pillow, or any other appropriate place.

4. Expand the principles of the charm described above, by turning it into a rite for protecting your space. Imagine that your territory is sitting on a large pentacle, with the five points extending to its boundaries, all surrounded by a sealing and protecting circle. Instead of tiny stones, find five large ones, and charge them up in the same

manner as above. Bury them at the five points of the large pentacle, each with its respective parchment and any other appropriate power objects. Make this a processional ceremony as you move from point to point, chanting, ringing bells, burning rosemary, sage, cedar and thyme. If you live with other people, invite them to participate and share ritual responsibilities. Or invite your circle of sisters.

5. Make a copy of the Witch's Star chart on page 278, big enough to include all the information, plus any new material you would like to add. Color the points of the Star appropriately; for example: blue for Air, red for Fire, green for Earth, purple for Water, silver for Spirit. In the center place an image of yourself, to represent your harmony with all the elements and their powers.

6. Make a series of pentacles, each to be used for a different type of meditation. For example, a Grounding Pentacle could be colored all in earth tones such as rust, brown, tan, green, dark red, black. Point the Earth arm downward and stand it on your altar facing you. Or a Fire Pentacle, for raising energy, can be colored in reds, yellows, orange, sand, and gold, with the Fire arm pointing upward. A Water Pentacle for getting in touch with your feelings with the Water arm uppermost, can be colored blue, purple, dark green, grey and turquoise. An Air Pentacle for aiding communication or mental activity can be colored pale blue, lavender, pink, white and pale grey. A Spirit Pentacle can be colored silver, gold, purple, indigo, and black.

7. Study the Rites of Kore section of this Cycle and read it aloud to yourself or your sisters. Let yourself go into a deep state of relaxation and imagine yourself creating a similar ritual with other women, with as much detail as possible. Then write it up in your *Book of Shadows*, adding more ideas as you go along. Share this with your women friends and ask them if they would like to help create it.

Questions to Ponder

1. Did you feel enchanted by the Rites of Kore? Did the scene feel familiar to you at all? Can you recall having participated in such a ceremony in this life, or perhaps another lifetime?

2. How do you feel about the calling of the directions for circle-casting? What purposes do they serve, in your opinion? How many directions would you like to include, and why? How would you go about doing this? Write down any incantations for calling the directions that you would like to have recorded for future use. Can you think of any alternative ways for casting or closing the circle?

3. Have you found any words or images of power that work for you? List and/or describe these, and make sketches of your images. Discuss the times that you have

used them, how they came to you, and how effective they were. Write about possible future uses of them as well.

4. Do you use awareness of the five senses in your rituals? Write about this in detail, and make records of any useful sense-memory exercises you have found or created. Write a ritual that emphasizes the senses, then perform it alone or with friends.

5. Do you feel safe about doing magic and being a witch? If so, what do you feel has helped in this regard? If not, why not? If not, what can you do to remedy this? Have you done protection magic before doing this study? Describe any protection spells that have worked for you, or that you would like to try.

6. Do you think there is a difference between rituals and spells? If so, what are they? If not, how are they the same? Define each of these terms.

7. How do you feel about casting spells? Performing rituals? Do you prefer one more than the other? If so, why? If not, why not?

8. Do you think rituals and/or spells are important? If so, why? If not, why not?

9. What rituals and/or spells do you perform in your own life? Describe in detail. Do you like to create ceremonies for the Eight Holy Days? For different phases of the moon? Do you do political magic, for instance banishing oppression or visualizing peace in the world? Do you perform rites of passage for yourself or others; for example: first bloods, giving birth, having a birthday, moving to a new home, death and dying, recovery from an illness?

10. Do you feel good about using and developing your magical powers? What ways do you foresee using them in the future?

Reading and Other Resources

Z. Budapest, *The Holy Book of Women's Mysteries*, Vols. 1 and 2.
Anne Cameron, *Daughters of Copperwoman*.
Ann Forfreedom, Julie Ann, *The Book of the Goddess*.
Shakti Gawain, *Creative Visualization*.
Ann Grammary, *The Witch's Workbook*.
Ann Kent Rush, *Moon Moon*.
Diane Stein, *Casting the Circle*.
Valerie Worth, *The Crone's Book of Words*.

Nett Hart and Lee Lanning, *Ripening* and *Dreaming*, almanacs of lesbian lore and
, vision, published by Word Weavers, Box 8742, Minneapolis, MN 55408-0742.
"The Witch's Star," article by Shekhinah Mountainwater. Send $2 to P.O. Box 2991,
Santa Cruz, CA 95063.

Resources:
The song "Free Ticket to Heaven" is available on my tape, *Songs and Chants of the
Goddess*, Volume 2.

CYCLE 11

Plant Magic

A child of plants am I
With vines of ivy twining through my hair
Waters bubble at my step
Whisper in my ear . . .
A daughter of earth am I
shaggy and vulnerable
I am all the things you call me
Witch-Goddess-Angel-Hippie-Spirit-Mother-Music-Woman . . .
I am all the things you make me
A daughter of Goddess am I
Passing through the doors of evolution
Swinging off earth's lever
Into light

I have been falling in love with my garden. When I first moved to this house I didn't care for it very much. Having lived the previous five years in the redwood forests, I was accustomed to a wild environment. My new home felt linear and dull, the garden surrounded by concrete and fences. True there were apple trees, and a place to grow strawberries and herbs, and it was nice to have some garden space. But over the years this garden has become a place of magic and beauty, and in many ways has been my teacher.

I am probably one of the most unconventional gardeners you will ever meet. I am unmoved by trim, controlled yards with mowed lawns and everything planted in straight rows. While everyone else on the block has such yards, mine is wild and lush. I allow the grass to grow as it will, pulling up the dried corpses in late summer. The apple trees are splendid, dripping with fruit in late summer and fall. A passion vine inundates the far fence now, blessing the once ugly view with its deep foliage and startling red-orange blooms. There are several rose bushes, offering up their magnificent, sweet flowers on and off throughout the year. A wonderful herb circle greets me at my door with rosemary, sage and thyme. The strawberries stretch out from the herb circle, yielding delicious fruit every spring. Beyond the circle are more herbs: yarrow, pennyroyal and comfrey. Only one corner still has the old feel of sterility, where a small peach tree has met her end. This tree was ailing when I moved in, and no amount of prayers, songs and hope could save her. Now the passion vine has reached a tendril her way, and I have visions of this vicarious life encompassing the dead tree. In the meantime, she still serves as a place to dry wet garments and hang wind chimes and other lovely things.

My red cat, Angus, comes into his own in the garden. Like a tiny Rousseau lion he is adorable amidst the tall grasses, crazy and silly amongst the tree branches. His fur, beautiful anywhere, takes on a deeper luster in the green surroundings, catching the sunlight and glowing with life.

Often I have felt the disapproval of visitors, as their eyes scan my wild little world. Long ago I learned to say no to their offers of "help," which amounted to wanton killing and disregard for the precious beings who live there. I am sure they meant well, but most humans seem to have a peculiar lack of sensitivity to the life and consciousness of plants.

It is wonderful how many of these innocents appear here on their own. Mallows, good for salad and nourishment, often crop up. A new kind of grass is spreading that never seems to die, never grows very tall, and so never needs to be cut—the ideal lawn! Flowers I know not the names of come and go, startling in their loveliness. A fine fennel bush has taken up residence near the fence. Wild onions with their tousled lavender heads have appeared among the herbs. Morning glories, once started on the front wall of the house, now drape themselves graciously here and there.

There is even magic behind the house, where once only cement and emptiness reigned. The honeysuckle vine from the garden next door has decided to expand herself, sending deliciousness into my bedroom window, and tendrils across the ground. I have hopes that these will keep climbing until they cover the sterile stucco of my back wall. Mint, started by a former housemate, has now multiplied in rich abundance.

I have never been into heavy-effort gardening or intensive planting or weeding. For the most part, I am open to those who appear here on their own and feel blessed by their presence. I plant occasionally, when a special being draw me, or is given to me. Each is a responsibility and a relationship. I spend more time communing with all of these friends than digging or cutting or controlling them. They are people to me, and deserve the same respect and autonomy as myself. I always thank them when I take their fruit or blossoms or leaves, and give water, love and respect in return. I weed only when absolutely necessary, and feel that weeds are people too. They are only called weeds because people haven't yet found a use for them.

Perhaps some of you reading this will think that I am a lazy and negligent gardener. But I am certain that these methods are in harmony with magic and the goddess. Understanding the use of herbs is not so much heavy labor or long memorization of lists of facts, as it is the deep relationship one has with them. The magic works because of the symbols and feelings one associates with a given plant, and the way the plant feels toward the magician. This process takes time, just as in any rewarding relationship.

In the patriarchal world of obligatory harvesting, the work ethic, and profit orientation it takes some determination and courage to garden this way. The conventional approach is to huff and puff, turn out great numbers of plants, cut the grass at least once a week and generally exhaust oneself maintaining a conventional garden. Even in the current herbals I have noticed a propensity for quantity, rather than quality. I have found that true magic is incredibly simple, and like many truths and wonders, will go unnoticed because of this.

Years ago, when I lived in Los Angeles, my house looked out on a residential street with no front yard. There was a tiny strip of earth just under the porch, where growth was discouraged by the grime and traffic of the neighborhood. One day a mysterious shrub began to grow and burst upward with astonishing rapidity. I was delighted, of course, until I received complaints from my neighbors. They said it was blocking the sidewalk. The corner store owner was afraid criminals might hide in it! (It was far too skimpy for this). A policeman was sent to ask me to cut it down.

On Being Forced By My NeighborsTo Trim My Bushes
At my front door the Goddess grew Her hair,
And all the city neighbors came to stare,
So green and soft and lovely, She stretched and preened . . .
"Get rid of those weeds," the city neighbors screamed.

Obedient and mournful (not wishing for a scene),
I sliced and trimmed with cold metal so obscene
Something inside me is hurt and bleeding too
O Mother Earth, forgive me, forgive us for killing You . . .

All over Your body the plants and creatures die,
Trees choke and wither beneath your stained sky,
Your sacred clear waters are soiled and brown,
And still the people cry, "It's in the way! Cut it down!"

O Mother, Sweet Lady, my heart aches full sore,
I fear for Your life each day lost a bit more,
When will the gods rise up from Your caves with mighty roar
And put an end to this destruction forever more?

Miraculously You come poking through my front wall,
And sprouting in at windows like a green waterfall,
Bursting through my faucets in a gushing joyous stream,
I'm full of joy at Your presence, exulting in Your green . . .

I dreamed a dream today that the Earth again was green,
That all the skies had cleared and the waters they were clean,
And all the plants and people could at last communicate
Let it be so, sweet Goddess; let it not yet be too late . . .
—*Los Angeles, late '60s*

At the Findhorn community in Scotland much work is done, but with apparently little effort. Peter Caddy, one of the founders, says, "This whole community is based on the Law of Manifestation! It depends and runs on its principles. It operates in complete faith that all of our needs will be perfectly met!"

This same principle applies to harvesting. Every year my apple trees pour out their bounty, and every year someone comes by and complains about the "waste." There are so many apples for me, so many for friends and neighbors, some for the birds, worms and insects, and some to go back into the earth. This seems an equitable and perfectly natural arrangement to me. But no, cry the voices of convention, you must serve the "obligatory harvest." Life is not to enjoy and flow into, but for sin and suffering, redeemed only by hard, uninspired work.

All forms are the results of thoughts. This is the true meaning of paradise, and the Garden of Eden. The earth was meant to be our place of creativity and play. The split between these and labor afflicts us, just as those between male and female, flesh and spirit, life and death. There is a place of sublime effortlessness known to mystics and healers, where much work is achieved. But it is inspired work, not dreary chores.

Yes there is a place for hard work in the world, and this will always be an important aspect of human nature. But in their zeal to be efficient, people have made gardening a soulless task, and have forgotten that the living beings that spring from the earth have spirits, thoughts and feelings. Moderate pruning and weeding is healthful, but it is more important to talk to plants than to control them.

Another thoughtform behind the obligatory harvest is the scarcity myth. "You're wearing down the earth!" cries Lucy in the Peanuts comic strip, when her friends run by. We have been hoodwinked into believing that there is never going to be enough of anything, and so we make it true. Yet Mother Nature is so infinitely abundant. When one thinks of the incredible number of seeds produced by one tree; how lavish She is in Her overflow! As we get into the flow, we come to realize the endless overflow.

In the last of C. S. Lewis's Space Trilogy, *That Hideous Strength*, the story centers around the battle between those forces that would destroy the earth and those that would preserve her. Those representing destruction have a hideous goal, to "shave the planet." Plants are just a nuisance to them, something to be gotten out of the way.

Often we don't realize how very much we all depend upon plant life for our survival. Our shelters, clothing, food, medicines, oxygen, musical instruments, transportation, paper (and therefore literature, education, communication, business) and many chemicals come from our plant friends. How generously they give of their bodies and their lives, and how blindly we use them! Just the fact that people refer to plants and the earth as "it" shows how far we have distanced ourselves from our sources.

The wonderful film *The Secret Life of Plants* conveys the consciousness of these beings. Scenes that show plants communicating, plants making music, plants being upset or excited leave no further doubts; plants are people too. To be aware of their living spirits requires the same kind of tenderness that makes us value all of life and each other as well. One's heart must be open and vulnerable, able to feel the joys and sorrows of involvement. We must recognize the habits of indifference and insensitivity that make us ignore or cut ourselves off from our kindred beings. This is the basis of any true knowledge of herbal magic.

We have removed ourselves so far from our psychic connections with Mother Nature that now we are on the brink of total annihilation of ourselves and our planet. We are forcing ourselves to go back, to look at our roots and get in touch with Her again; it will be this or death. One can only go without air and water and sunlight for so long before withering. Our spirits wither without loving contact with the spirits of nature.

And so the rise of Goddess awareness occurs once again, and we see people everywhere who are returning to the herbs. Homeopathy, herbal universities, flower remedies, and so on show that even among the most "scientific" minded it is becoming clear that there is something happening here, something we cannot live without.

But it is only the beginning. Still, when one reads up on the subject, one finds for the most part only medicinal information. Magic makers are reluctant to give out their secrets and it is considered subversive to discuss even the healing properties of herbs. For example, in Z. Budapest's *Holy Book of Women's Mysteries*, minimal information is given. I can only guess that Z did this deliberately, not wishing to endanger her credibility, nor to expose secrets that should not be given lightly.

Yet this reflects the split we are dealing with in the world of medicine. If we look at the word "medicine" the way the Native Americans do, we will see that it describes the psychic as well as the physical aspects of healing. The split between these is the same lack of awareness that blinds us to the aliveness of plants. Love is what heals us. Love energy, passing between plant and magic-maker is the essence at the base of the transformation. Through our interaction with the plant ally we contact—the thought-forms and emotions we exchange—the healing or magic takes place. Our myths, our faith, our compassion, our ideas and perceptions of reality . . . all take part in the act. Knowing that Morag went forth one morning with spiderweb in her handkerchief, beat a rowan stick upon a rock, threw it into a river and thereby started a storm . . . gives us an association with the rowan tree. Knowing that this tree is associated with the second moon of the Celtic year also tells us something about that being.

Our kindred plant folk of the earth are not as different from human beings as we might think. The basic form of root, stem and branch is in us too. Our bloodstreams, nervous systems, lymphatic passages and psychic energies flow the same way, becoming finer and more complex as they extend visible and invisible tendrils of contact into the elements of earth and air. Our bodies and limbs, fingers and toes are shaped like trees. Plants are often sexual, and breathe as we do, bringing one vapor into their cells and substance, taking nourishment and transforming it, sending it in new form back out into the biosphere. Plants give out energy and consume energy, and are sometimes even carnivorous! (For example, the venus flytrap, who feeds on living insects.)

We know from feminist writings that the art of healing was originally practiced by women who understood and believed in the properties of herbs. Gradually the old ways were replaced by the male medical profession, and the credibility factor shifted. In the process, the visible became more real than the invisible, the physical cure more real than the story behind it. Now we are more prone to faith in the little plastic bottle on our bathroom shelves, with its shiny artificial looking pills, than to faith in the inherent organic power of herbs. These pills might even be made of herbs, but we will still believe in the one more than the other, because this is what we have been conditioned to believe. We are therefore more likely to be healed by swallowing a pill than by drinking a fresh herb infusion.

In divining the magic properties of herbs, I do a lot of extrapolating. Finding the traditional meanings is helpful, especially if you can find the same plants as listed in books. However, we must each adapt to our own areas, neighborhoods, and accessibility of plants and information. Remember that we create our own realities, and at bottom it is our thoughts and feelings that count the most. To some extent we rely on tradition because this gives more substance to a thoughtform. On the other hand, many traditions have been lost, and we are in a time of creating new ones for future generations. Therefore, banish all self-doubt and let your associations flow. Go out into your garden or walk about in the nearest natural area you can find. Sit and "grok" a tree or plant and ask her to tell you what she is about.

Some of us do not have garden space and may have to buy many of our herbs. In such circumstances, I suggest you create a magic garden in flowerpots or windowboxes, or perhaps on the roof of your home. Think about the kinds of spells you expect to be casting; select a few basics such as love, money, and healing. An effective witch may have only two or three herbs in her garden, but she will do powerful work with them because of her relationship with those beings. Not that one shouldn't grow as many herbs as one wishes, and learn the millions of things there are to know, but this is meaningless without that essential quality of communion.

I feel that the most effective herbal magic is done with living plants with whom one has developed a relationship. If you are unable to grow anything at all, however, please don't be discouraged. Today many high quality wildcrafted herbs are available for purchase. These herbs have been tended by a new generation of devoted herbalists. Adding your vibrations to these can create powerful magic. I have heard that dried herbs keep their potency for about one year.

My three main herbs are rosemary, sage and thyme.

> Are you going to Scarborough fair?
> Parsley, sage, rosemary and thyme,
> Remember me to one who lives there;
> She once was a true lover of mine.
> > —*traditional*

I associate these with the three aspects of the Goddess, and so use them in that context. For a spell concerning the threefold goddess, wear a bit of all three in your pouch.

Thyme

Thyme is connected to virginity, youth, freshness, sweetness, beginnings, and therefore, the Maiden Goddess.

> In my garden grew plenty of thyme
> It would flourish by night and by day
> Oe'r the wall came a lad
> And he took all I had
> And he stole my thyme away . . .
> > —*traditional*

Remember that in the old days virginity did not mean chastity, but selfhood. A virgin was a woman who "belonged to no man," though she may have had as many lovers as she wished. With thyme you can cast a spell for preserving your autonomy, giving you courage for new undertakings and risks, starting new projects, and so on. Traditional writings say use thyme beneath your pillow to dispel nightmares; crush and breathe in fresh thyme to cheer yourself up when melancholy. Refresh and renew yourself with a magical thyme bath.

Rosemary

Rosemary is a Mother herb, giving protection, purification and love. This is one of the most powerful herbs, always found in a witch's garden, growing beside her door.

> . . . for all the trees of divine power rosemary is the most potent in driving away evil, and few gardens were planted without it. Upon the journey to Egypt Mary threw her blue cloak over a rosemary bush, turning the white flowers to the blue of her mantle,

and when she returned to Nazareth she would spread her Son's little garments to dry on a rosemary bush after she had washed them. Rosemary, Dew of the Sea, freshest and sweetest-smelling plant in the world, is steeped in the mercy of Christ. Froniga's tree stood just under six feet high and had not grown at all since she had lived here, which proved that at her coming it had passed the age of thirty-three years, for rosemary never grows after the age when Christ died and never passes the height of Christ while He was a man on earth ... She greeted her tree and curtsied to it. That it was a living personality she was convinced.

—from *The White Witch* by Elizabeth Goudge

Spells suitable for using rosemary and associated with the Mother Goddess are abundance, fertility, support, healing, nurturance and beauty. Womb-related spells are appropriate, such as to ease blood flow or encourage pregnancy. Rosemary has medicinal powers as well, and can be used as a tea for coughs and colds. However, she is extremely potent and can be deadly in overlarge amounts. A crown of rosemary can aid the memory. Hung over the door, she will keep thieves away. Her tiny, delicate blue flowers are great for beauty and love spells of all kinds. A few sprigs in any bouquet or sachet lend beauty and cheer for all occasions.

Sage

Because of her association with wisdom, I have given sage to the Crone. Sage offers psychic protection as well as healing and prosperity. Native Americans treasure this herb, using it frequently in their "smudging" ceremonies. Smudging is the art of using the smoke of burning herbs as an incense and purifier. Pass sacred objects through the smoke of sage for blessings and consecration.

Other Crone spells are: transformation, purification, cleansing, banishments, bindings, endings, easy passage at death, communication with spirits, mind-altering, dream teachings and spells for wisdom or understanding. Wear sage in your pouch, sew it into a dream pillow, drink it in a mild tea, scatter her dried leaves on the floor for rituals, burn and use her smoke for incense. Divination is the province of the Crone, so sage can be used for insight in a tarot reading, crystal-scrying, and so on.

Since there is so little information available on the magical uses of herbs, we can look for hints in what is know of their medicinal properties. For instance, chamomile is known to be a soothing and relaxing herb, great for upset stomachs. Her soft fluffy yellow flowers are used in a tea. The stomach chakra is said to be the power center in esoteric traditions. Our ability to influence and control circumstances and to cooperate with others emanates from this chakra. Disturbances of the power chakra show inequities such as dominance and submission patterns. Good flow means equality and cooperation and power from within. It follows that chamomile would be a good herb in helping to balance one's power. Wear it in a pouch, sleep with it, burn the dried flowers, and so on. Raspberry leaves are great for womb ailments and aid in childbirthing; one could therefore use them in a magic spell to promote pregnancy or menstrual flow.

Comfrey and golden seal are all-around cleansing herbs, used for removing infection and killing bacteria. Golden seal is a powerful being and must be used very conservatively. Comfrey is famous for her healing properties. As a tea she cleanses the entire system, the blood, tissues, and organs. She also speeds up the healing of broken bones. As a poultice she is used to draw infection out of wounds, blisters, etc. These herbs fight off evil, in other words, and can be used for protection and healing spells. Every witch or herbalist usually has plenty of comfrey around.

In her book *The White Witch*, Elizabeth Goudge says that the visual appearance of a plant serves as an indication of its use. Toothwort, for example, has white, tooth-like flowers, and is used to stop toothache! This kind of wisdom is very trusting and childlike, and we must be careful not to let our scientific sophistication stand in our way. On the other hand, we do have to be careful. When experimenting with herbs for healing purposes, start with tiny amounts and see what they do. I cannot be responsible for any medical mishaps and this must be your own concern. From the shamanistic point of view we know that body and soul are intimately connected, and the split between healing and spells is arbitrary and patriarchal. So use good sense and poise yourself delicately between childlike trust and healthy skepticism. Here are some more of my own extrapolations:

Cover grass—blanket, protection
Wild onions—spice things up, energy, excitement
Morning Glories—to wake up happy
Chokeweed—for binding
Passion vine—for passion
Honeysuckle—for sweetness, to lift the vibrations
Lemon leaves—purification, cleansing (also makes a great tea!)
Gum arabic—stick-to-it-iveness
Eyebright—vision, insight
Sprouts—Maiden energy, youthfulness, beginnings, innocence
Prickly cactus—keep enemies away
Wandering Jew—endurance, strength in times of hardship
Prayer plant—enhance prayers, spells, incantations, good beside or on altar
Celery—to break addictions
Cinnamon—love, seduction, magic
Clove—communication
Red clover—healing, protection, prosperity
Ginseng—healing, rejuvenation
Gotu kola—rejuvenation, intelligence, wisdom
Hops—rest, relaxation
Seaweed—ocean magic, safe journeys over water, contacting the deep mind

Lavender—beauty
Narcissus—self-love
Nasturtium—shelter, hearth spells
Olive—longevity, integrity, end of troubles
Pulsetilla (Anenome or windflower)—for strength in adversity
Pussy willow—warm fuzzies, cuddles, affection, gentleness
Snakeroot—raising kundalini

Some Magical Herb Traditions

The Rose

> In June there was the red red rose
> And that was the flower for me
> O often have I plucked that red red rose
> 'Til I gained the willow tree . . .
> *—folksong*

The rose has long been known as the flower of love and desire. White roses connote spiritual love, pink and yellow mean affection, and the deep red rose is for lovers' passion. The form of the rose is based on a five or pentagram. You can see this in the five-leafed form at the base where stem and blossom meet. This makes her especially sacred to the Goddess. Use roses in all love spells and spells of desire. To desire is to wish, and therefore roses can help make all wishes come true. Send the fresh petals in a letter to your loved one, dry and burn them for a delicious incense, wear them in a love amulet pouch. Rose candy can be made by dipping the fresh petals in melted sugar or honey and setting them to harden—food for lovers. Rose tea can be made of the dried petals. Roses are appropriate flowers for Summer Solstice, Aphrodite's day, and can be used on altars, for garland crowns, etc. For a fantastic ritual drink, float a few blossoms in red wine or rose water and pass the bowl around during the ceremony. As you drink, the flowers caress your face, and the scent fills you.

The rose appears in many legends and stories. In *Beauty and the Beast* it is a white rose Beauty wants more than anything, while her sisters demand riches and jewels:

> O bring me neither gold nor jewels
> Nor gowns of silk so fine, o
> But bring to me one white rose
> To show your love is mine, o
> To show your love is mine.

When Beauty's father plucks her rose in the Beast's garden, it is the signal of his doom and the Beast's appearance. The plucking of a rose often means something other-worldly is about to happen. In the story, Burd Janet seeks her lost love, Tam Lin, who has been stolen by the fairies. He makes his appearance as she picks the blooms of love.

Magic wands can be made of rose branches and used for directing the will. Rose hips and leaves can also be carried in pouches.

Ancient peoples worshipped the rose as symbol of the holy vulva with its soft folds and layers of petals. The string of beads called a rosary was originally used for goddess prayers. Though the Christian church attempted to repress these origins, the rosary eventually became standard ritual equipment, and to this day is especially associated with Mother Mary. Suggestion: Make a rosary of miniature roses by stringing them while still fresh, and allow them to dry. A string of 37 beads can be used to represent the Goddess as source of all, the Maiden, Mother and Crone, the five elements, the seven directions, the eight solar holy days, and the thirteen moons of the lunar year.

There are more amazing revelations about the rose in the *Women's Encyclopedia of Myths and Secrets*. The simple game of Ring Around the Rosy, for example, has surprising pagan origins. The use of roses in religious symbolism, legend and song all go back to the worship of the sexuality and beauty of the goddess.

Some more traditional herb magic:

Apples—The Goddess' fruit of immortality, wisdom and fertility. Avalon means "apple land." Cut crosswise and see the pentacle formed by the seeds. Long before the so-called "sin" of Eve, apples were the fruit she offered humanity as Hueva, Hebrew Mother of All. The wild apple gives poetic immortality and is the fruit of Olwen, Welsh love goddess.

Beans—Romans believed that the spirits of the dead resided in beans. Men were forbidden to eat them, lest they commit murder! A woman could become impregnated by eating a bean inhabited by a ghost. Witches were later thought to ride on beanstalks.

Cherry, Peach, Pomegranate, Apricot—all fruits of sexuality, the vulva, beauty and love. Persephone ate of the pomegranate—symbol of death and transformation—on her sojourn in the underworld. Pomegranates ripen in the fall season and are excellent ritual fruits for Kore and Hecate's holy days.

Laurel—tree of inspiration and poetic frenzy. Priestesses would chew on the laurel leaves to induce trance and psychedelic states for ritual. Daphne, when chased by Apollo, was changed to a laurel tree to protect her virginity, making laurel a maiden herb. Later, male heroes were crowned with laurel to give them honor.

Fig—also a yonic symbol and fruit of sexuality and fertility.

Corn—sacred to Kore and the Corn Mother. Kore represents the fate of the grain as she descends into the underworld and rises up again in the spring. All grains can be used in rituals celebrating Kore.

Holly—tree of death and resurrection. From such names as Hohle, Holle, Hole, and holy . . . all referring to the goddess. Magic wands were made of its branches. Protects and defends.

Willow—a crone herb. Associated with death and sorrow; use for spells of mourning and closure. Also a tree of inspiration and the Muse.

Oak—strength, endurance, longevity.

Primrose—for wantonness; fairy flowers.

Damiana and *Lobelia*—used to help remember dreams; also Artemisia or Mugwort. I once nibbled a leaf of mugwort and had one of the most vivid dreams of my life that night. These herbs are often sewn into dream pillows.

Yarrow—to heal a broken heart.

Vervain—for love.

Fern—leads to Elfland, seeds make invisible.

Elder—where mortal and fairy kiss; gives fairy woman power over mortal man.

Ivy—tapping on window, portends death.

Herbs for the Holy Days

Lucina—Evergreen.
Aradia—Snow Drops.
Kore—Wheat, Corn.
Diana—Thyme.
Aphrodite—Roses.
Habundia—Pears.
Persephone—Pomegranate.
Hecate—Sage, pumpkin.

Uses of Herbs

Herbs can be used in many forms. As a tea, infusions can be made with water or wine. Oils can be prepared. Herbs can be powdered. The dried leaves, stems, flowers, roots and seeds can all be used. The seeds can also be used fresh. Burn for incense, dried or fresh; wear in pouches; sew into clothing. A pot of growing herbs can be placed to create desired vibrations: Place herbs over doors and windows; sew into dream pillows; sprinkle tea or powder. Rinse clothing in oils or teas for rituals. Float herbs in your ritual bath. Herbs can be tucked or hung or placed in various nooks and crannies in your home.

The smoke of burning herbs can be used to cleanse the aura, to sanctify objects such as your witch's blade, magic wand, or a specific candle to be used for a spell. Amulets or talismans and crystals can be recharged or blessed in this way. Smoke can be used to invoke the air goddesses, as it is often seen as a symbol of the air element.

Eat a leaf or petal as you affirm and chant your spoken invocations.

Drink dream tea before sleep.

Drink a tea of herbs with divining properties before doing a reading.

Bless the members of your circle with herbs; touch their brows or the cardinal points of their bodies with a rose, for example, or a sprig of thyme.

Cleanse the aura by waving a chosen flower or branch in a sweeping motion around the person. This is also good for placing thoughtforms and images into the aura.

Sprinkle fresh petals and leaves in your ritual space for scent and the vibrations you wish to maintain.

Cast a circle of herbs.

Herbal Literature

Here are some of the few writings I could find on the magical uses of herbs:

Magical Herbalism, by Scott Cunninngham
This is a powerful little book, though at first glance might not seem so. The information is clumped into blocks and categories, giving it a rather matter-of-fact, even dull, appearance. This type of book is part of the commercial occult movement, and is, in some ways, patriarchal. However, there is so little of this type of information available that this book is of great value. By reading slowly and pondering individual sentences and paragraphs, it is possible to extract some very useful knowledge.

Assigning deities, planets and elements to various herbs rings of tradition. Of course, I would prefer to invoke female deities, in keeping with my woman's mystery orientation. Cunningham agrees with me about love spells and is careful to say so in no uncertain terms (that it is wrong to manipulate another person for love or any other reason). He includes many juicy facts in addition to his Witches Herbal, which lists herbs by use, deity, gender, and basic power. There are instructions for making your own oils and incenses, what magical equipment to use, and how to start a magical garden.

We mustn't forget, however, that magic is slippery. No matter how firm and believable a piece of information may seem, it can fall flat on its face without the extra pizazz of the individual witch. If it doesn't ring for you, it may not work. The craft by nature abhors stuffy rules, though it does adhere to gigantic principles or laws. In all spell-casting there must be an element of surprise, a sense of wonder and the unexpected. This is why the poetry and myths related to an herb are so important, for they arouse the imagination and inspire the magic-maker. One of the reasons many witches do not publish their secrets is that such information can lose its potency when it becomes common knowledge.

The White Witch, by Elizabeth Goudge
This is a surprising book, as its author is now known for such magical subjects. Her spiritual passion is real and moving, and makes itself felt in the story told here. Set

in England during the Puritan uprisings, it paints a poignant picture of Froniga, its heroine, and various other characters. Froniga is part gypsy and part aristocrat, and possesses a wild and proud temperament. She is talented with herbs and works as a healer in the surrounding village where she lives. Her garden is magnificent, and Goudge describes it with obvious love and sensitivity. Woven throughout the story are a number of herbal spells and medicines. Here are a few:

Basil—to create affinities, for love, prosperity, sensuality. Prepare when the moon is in Scorpio. Plant on graves to assure the soul's resurrection.

Violet—for beauty.

Parsley—the sower rules the house.

Licorice—Soothes sore throats, cleans the teeth (I therefore consider it useful for spells of communication, negotiation, diplomacy, group harmony. Licorice aids the effectiveness of other herbs.)

Mullein—to draw power, leadership, harmony in groups or families; stalks are used for wands.

Froniga says that herbs bear the sign of what they heal (as in toothwort, mentioned before). For example: Hawthorne draws out thorns and heals blisters, the purple iris is good for bruises, spotted cowslip removes spots!

For wounds—milfoil, to cleanse; samile, to heal; and bugle to open.

Lettuce—pound to a mash for a soporific (tranquilizer), take internally or apply to soles of the feet.

Herb of the moon—honesty.

Harebells—Our Lady's Thimbles.

Thyme, woodsorrel—used in bedstraw stuffings to enhance dreaming.

Lavender, germander, pennyroyal and *rosemary*—used for strewing at special ceremonies.

Mint geranium—leaves placed between pages of special books.

Rosemary wood—made into a box—open lid and inhale the scent; preserves youth.

Marigold—"good for the spirits"; cheering, lifting the mood.

Marjoram—good for the stomach.

Broom—used in a base of jell or fat, applied to the feet for gout.

Lilies of the valley—for weakness of the heart, headaches.

Thyme, mint, and *lavender*—to bring a lover.

Melrosette—a drink made of rose leaves boiled in honey, for comfort in times of distress.

Apples—for wisdom.

Elderberries infused in well water—for convulsions.

Candlewick—for chest ailments.

Broom across the back door—protection.

Christmas roses at the front door—protection.

Rosemary melted into homemade candles—for scent, protection.
A cordial of roses and violets in white wine—for a tender conscience.
Rosemary—strengthens the spirit.
Cowslips—strengthen the nerve.
Marjoram—planted on graves that the dead may rest in peace.
Angelica—for plague, flatulence (farting); chew the root or make a tea with leaves.
A cordial to ease a sad heart—Boil in white wine with sugar or honey: borage, bugloss, calamint, harts-tongue, red mint, violets, marigolds, saffron.
Elderflower—for fever.
Borage flowers steeped in oil of almond for pain, comfort for weakness—soak cloth, wring out and apply to heart and stomach.
Grief tea—rosemary for heartache, chamomile for sleeplessness, lavender for swooning, lily-of-the-valley for headache, clove gilliflower for weakness . . . steep in white wine with honey and egg-white.

> "The scent of a flower is its spirit."
> —*The White Witch*

Star Girl by Thelma Hatch Wyss
This is a beautiful book, written for children. Star Girl, a young woman of the Bannock Indian tribe, ascends a magic birch tree into the sky. There she finds another tribe of people, much like her own. Their medicine healer is Wind Woman, a wise and kind teacher. Star Girl lives with Wind Woman and learns many secrets.

One of the things I appreciated in this book was the manner in which Wind Woman stored her herbs. She used various pouches, identifying their contents with beads, bone, feathers, and so on. These were hung 'round the walls of her tepee along with many bunches of drying herbs. Most of her plants were ground into powders and stored this way.

Here is some of the herbal lore that *Star Girl* has to offer:

Birdnests—dainty white blossoms on slender, twisted spikes—root used for stomachache and fever. Also makes dreams come true!
Blazing Star—roots used for backache and stiff knees. Chew the strings of the root.
Indian Poke—tall with green flowers. Poisonous; causes madness and melancholy (can also be an antidote for these).
Blue gentian—fever.
For deep wounds, mix for a poultice—windflower root, prairie ground cherry, root of the hop vine.
Jack-in-the-Pulpit or Indian Turnip—headaches, for people who talk too much.
Red Turnip—the root is nourishing.
Black Turnip—leads to the shadow worlds.

Tansy—make a tea for sore muscles.
Elderberry juice—used to make wine.
Crinkle-root—for toothache.
Windflower root—"little buffalo medicine" for wounds.
Hawkweed or Snakeroot—for snakebite.
Dandelion tonic—for coughs.
Bloodroot—for love.

> Says Wind Woman:
> "I go by night, unseen on my way
> Then am I holy
> Then have I power
> To heal the sick."

Magiculture by Diane Warburton

This is a charming, in fact, delicious little book that mingles quaint lore, exquisite poetic quotes, spells and common sense, with lovely sketches of a medieval character. Warburton affirms my theory that one can divine the magical uses of plants from knowledge of medical uses. For instance: "... periwinkle, which staunches the flow of blood, to garland the thigh of a woman to prevent infertility and the necks of those who in darker times were on their way to execution. The first was the means of ensuring the perpetuation of the body, the latter that of the Spirit."

Warburton suggests feeding strawberries mouth-to-mouth for love magic, or making a tomato preserve to serve one's lover. Tomatoes were often called "love apples," due to their sensuousness and color. The implication is that anything that nourishes the blood for health purposes, quickens the blood for purposes of love. Some of her love spells, however, seem manipulative to me, and I do not recommend them beyond pleasurable musing. (Thanks to Peny Prestini for sending me this delightful book.)

Clan of the Cave Bear by Jean M. Auel

This is an important and outstanding book, and I recommend it enthusiastically. Ayla is a terrific role model for women today, and her story teaches us many things about patriarchy, nature and society. For me the best parts were those concerning the lessons of nature and survival. As in *Star Girl*, Ayla is apprenticed to Iza and learns the ways of herbs, later to become a healer herself. Throughout the story are tidbits of useful lore, and I found this book one of the best practical resources of herbal medicine. Unfortunately, the split between magic and medicine is rampant in the Clan, with Creb in charge of the former. His secrets were carefully guarded and there is little or no information given regarding the herbs. In the Clan women were not considered eligible to know magic, and in fact were horribly oppressed in many ways. Ayla transcends these limitations, bringing much upheaval and the ultimate downfall of that culture. There is a sequel to this book, called *Valley of the Horses*, but I found it disappointing after the monumental proportions of its predecessor. However, the second volume does provide wonderful survival information. Its hero, later to become Ayla's mate, comes from a goddess-worshipping tribe, and his reverence for women is most refreshing.

This is elecampane, Ayla," Iza said. "It usually grows in fields and open places. The leaves are large ovals with pointed ends, dark green on top and downy underneath . . . It's the root that's used . . . best to collect it the second year, late in summer or fall, then the root is smooth and solid. Cut it into small pieces and take about as much as will fit in your palm, boil it down in the small bone cup to more than half full. It should cool before it's drunk, about two cups a day. It brings up phlegm and is especially good for the lung disease of spitting blood. It also helps to bring on sweating and to pass water . . . The root can be dried and ground as a powder, too.

In Cunningham's book we find that elecampane also has a magical tradition, used in love spells with mistletoe and vervain.

From *Ballad of Ayla and the Clan*, a work in progress
Come children of the ages
And listen to my song
Of Ayla tall and golden
A woman sweet and strong
She lived in times forgotten
When Mother Earth was young
When people lived more simply
And spoke with hand and tongue

Born unto one people
Yet to another flung
Her coming wrought great changes
In the ages yet to come
Like the falling of one petal
Or the shifting of the sand
One woman's touch and footstep
Rearranged the human plan

She was but a tiny daughter
When the earth split open wide
Crushing her dear family
And her people all inside

So little Ayla wandered
Forlorn and all alone
Crying for her mother
And the love and peace she'd known

Long and long she rambled
Through lands she did not know
Her body weak with hunger
Her spirit filled with woe
Til a lion cruelly struck her down
And hurt her body sore
She fell into a swoon so deep
And scarce could rise no more

O Ayla little Ayla
She might have died that day
But the coming of the strangers
It frightened death away
For along their weary journey
There came the Cave Bear Clan
Driven by the earthquake
To find a safer land

Their bodies bent down to the ground
Their brows were dark and low
Their ways were strange and ancient
Old secrets they did know
But the ones who knew most deeply
Of the spirits and the land
Were the elders, Creb and Iza
The wise ones of the clan

Old Creb was bent and twisted
And he only had one eye
But in heart and mind he was powerful
His truths would never die
Though the Cave Bear Clan was fading
And their ways would soon pass on
He was keeper of their magic
And the spirit world beyond

Old Iza was a woman

Who worked with herbs and hands
She knew the plants and potions
She was Healer of the Clan
It was she who took sweet Ayla
Into her loving arms
It was she who helped and taught her
And protected her from harm . . .

In a lovely little book called *Wildflowers* by Hilarion, an elemental system for understanding the properties of plants is offered. Using a four-element system of earth, water, air and spirit, he associates earth with the roots of the plant, water with the stem, air with the leaf and spirit with the flower and scent. I of course, being into five elements, would add the missing element of fire, and apply it to the growth and energy aspect of the plant. Using this system we can cast spells addressed to those aspects of ourselves that the elements represent. A physical ailment could be healed by burning or carrying the root, for example. Emotional spells would employ the stem. Mental pursuits would correspond with the leaves and spiritual matters with the flowers. To slow down use a gentle, slow-growing plant. To enhance or increase energy use a vigorous, fast-growing plant, and so on.

I also wish to recommend Jeannine Parvati's correspondence course, *Hygieia*. (This is also the name of her women's herbal, a truly beautiful book.) Parvati points out the importance of myth in understanding herbs. For example, when Kore is carried off by Hades (in the patriarchal version), she is plucking the narcissus bloom. When she returns from the underworld in the spring, the purple crocus emerges from the earth with her. These flowers have a numinous association with the mysteries; one portends death and winter, the other birth and renewal. Knowing such poetic facts helps us in creating spells with nature's creatures.

Parvati says she learned about herbs in relation to the signs of the zodiac, and so passes her knowledge on in this way. For example, comfrey, garlic and ginger are designated Capricorn herbs; basil and licorice are Taurus; and lavender, parsley and sage are given to Virgo; all related to the earth element. This can be a very helpful way to memorize, particularly for those who are familiar with the zodiac.

There are so many approaches to herbs that it is evident we are dealing with another variety of grids or systems. Since patriarchy has crept into all of them, we need to go deeply within and find our own. The Maiden, Mother and Crone categories offer a viable female alternative that resonates in women's psyches; also using the five elements instead of four helps to keep our forms circular and flowing.

Magical herbs are associated with deities most of the time: love herbs with Aphrodite, Olwen, Erzulie; protection with mother goddesses; divination with crone goddesses. When doing spells we can invoke the patron deities to add potency and support our workings.

A Note On Healing: Sometimes people need their illnesses. This may seem like a strange idea at first, but if we think deeply about the symbolic aspect of sicknesses, we realize that the body is usually trying to tell us something. In preparing to concoct a healing spell for someone, it is important to grok what purposes and causes there may be on the psychological or psychic levels. Often this process alone can effect the cure.

Psychedelics

These are among the most potent and transforming plants of this earth, belonging to the Crone Goddesses. The Crones guide us between the worlds, and mind-altering substances are often a part of Her rites of passage. Down through the ages psychedelics have been an important part of native ceremonies. At Eleusis in Greece when the Myth of Kore was reenacted, ergot was passed out to the congregation. In Mexico there are still shamans using peyote or mescalito. Marijuana is used among some Native American tribes. The *Tibetan Book of the Dead* gives us instruction on what levels of consciousness one may expect to encounter on a psychedelic journey, and how to deal with them. Actually, all magic is mind-altering to some extent, which is how the spell is cast. Psychedelics are especially powerful, and open doors that milder herbs rarely touch.

In the 1960s we witnessed a wave of the use of psychedelics in our own culture. It caused great expansion and social change, and in some ways was a catalyst for dissolving oppression. It also caused problems, and in a few cases, even suicides. This is because of the lack of sacredness, a blight of patriarchy. Along with sex, birth, death, music, and art, psychedelics have been reduced by some to mere function, relegated to the world of science and analysis and by others to the world of taboo.

In traditional cultures, psychedelic rituals were special and set apart, and were not meant to be incorporated into daily life. Primitive ceremonies usually included wild dancing, music, and love-making. The frenzied state was considered holy and was revered as a form of worship or being "possessed" by deity. Even alcoholic beverages were once used only for this purpose. Psychedelics were used with great respect, dispensed by priestesses or shamans, and never treated abusively.

Humans have a peculiar trait, referred to by some as the "forbidden fruit" syndrome. Having once decided that a thing is immoral or illegal, it becomes appropriate to indulge in as a form of rebellion. We see this in the world of pornography, which is obviously a reverse or flip side of puritanical repression of sexuality. Since the "good guys" are authority figures, they become the "bad guys" and being bad becomes good. This is the kind of patriarchal doublethink we are dealing with when attempting to assess the value of powerful things like sexuality and drugs.

All such potent forces are part of the deep mysteries of the universe. They can be used or abused, like magic itself. Since most of our role-models abuse them (i.e., porn filmmakers, heroin addicts, crack dealers), the tendency of the average person is to judge them evil and avoid them altogether. For myself, I find the veil approach best. When Salome danced, she wore seven veils, lifting each in turn at the proper moment. Imbibing psychedelics is a matter of timing, appropriateness, and ritual. It should be done with great care and reverence, in safety, and with proper guidance. When used correctly it can be a tremendously healing and exalting influence. Used incorrectly it can become dangerous and destructive. These are Crone lessons indeed, and like the Crone, require a renewal of respect and attention.

Storing Herbs

Experts seem to agree that the best way to retain the potency of herbs is to dry them and store them in brown glass jars, preferably in a dark place, not too hot or too cold. Their essences can be preserved in oils if you add a preservative to the brew. Some people use alcohol or wine for this purpose. Cunningham suggests adding a few drops off benzoin tincture. Olive oil has been used for centuries as a base for making magical oils, as it is said to last for years.

As in most things, I am an independent type when it comes to storing my magical materials, and usually tend to do what seems most appealing to my intuition and poetic sense. I keep most of my dried herbs in various pouches, baskets and bags, or simply hanging upside down in all their loveliness. One great old Granny bag contains a hodge-podge of dried leaves, flowers and stems, accumulated over the years. I love to save garlands and altar flowers, or any herbs that have been used in rituals. These contain psychic "charge" from the energy that has been around them, and are great for burning in castings or ceremonies. I also have many jars in dark cupboard shelves, filled with a number of teas and leaves. There are lots of goodies tucked around and beneath my altar, continually soaking up psychic energy, and lending their own as well. I often dry them first in pretty baskets, setting them out for all to see before tucking them away. It is helpful to have a supply of wide, flat types of baskets on hand for this purpose. Bowls with lids work well too, particularly for current mixtures or potions one is working with.

It is helpful to consult sources for this kind of information, but ultimately, I am sure you will find that your own storage ideas will come to you naturally. Don't be afraid to work with what you have, and to use your creative imagination freely. The main thing is to maintain good energy between yourself and the plants you work with. Say a little prayer when you bottle or put them away, take them out, pick them, and so on.

CRONE OF EARTH

MEDICINE WOMAN

The Earth Crone is wise in the ways of herbs and contacts them for both magic and healing. She is a knower of earth's mysteries, a weather worker, and gardener of souls.

Suggested Projects

1. Start an herb file of your own. Get some large index cards and alphabetized cards, and make a pretty box for them. For each herb that you wish to categorize, have two cards, one for the magical uses and one for healing uses. Add more as your information accumulates. You can color-code these if you wish—I use green ink for the healing information, and purple for the magic. Label your cards by the plant, and cross-reference them by spell, ailment, cure, myth, holiday and any other relevant categories. Include deities, signs of the zodiac, elements, uses, and recipes.

There's no need to fill up your file with a zillion facts right away. You can consider this a long-term project, something you will use over the years as your magic grows. Record information as it comes to you, and has meaning and use in your practices. You can start with the information in this Cycle, just to get the file going. This file will grow with time and serve as a reference for much magical knowledge. It will put information at your fingertips, and your friends can look things up too— that is, if you wish to share! Some witches prefer to keep such matters secret. Eventually your file can be handed on to your children or other women, and become part of the new legacy we are building in Goddess-lore.

2. Make yourself a witch-kit, filled with the basic necessities for altar work, healing, and magic. Find some attractive jars with tight-fitting lids for your incense powders and other loose materials. Label these with names and magic symbols. Pouches can be used to store fresh herbs, stones, and other delicate materials of a magical nature. Include a spoon or scoop for powders and crumbly dried herbs, an incense burner, matches in a metal container. Magical oils in small vials can be packed into their own special pouch, box or basket. You can also keep a folded altar cloth in your kit for those times when you want to do magic away from home, and a candle or two in small, self-contained holders. Add an image of the goddess and any other special items you would like to include. Be sure all is packed with care and well-protected. A sturdy, decorated box or a lidded basket can make fine witch-kit containers. Some of these can also double as portable altars. Use your imagination and have fun with it.

3. Go out into the wilderness and grok a wild herb. To "grok" means to enter into a state of communion with something, to take it in deeply and discover your thoughts and feelings about it. Ask permission of the plant to take a cutting. Plant her in your garden or in a pot. Research her medicinal and magical qualities, as well as information on how to harvest and care for her. Add any new information you find on her to your herb file. Over time you can do this with many herbs. If access to the wild is a problem, make do with store-bought plants, or start by planting the seeds.

4. Discover and acknowledge your plant ally. Perhaps you have more than one, or perhaps you have allies among different species of plants such as trees, flowers, herbs, grasses or shrubs. There are a number of ways to find your plant allies. You can brew yourself some dream tea (see dream herbs listed in this Cycle) before retiring, and ask the Goddess to send you this knowledge during sleep. Keep your *Book of Shadows* and a pen beside your bed, so you can record your discoveries as soon as you awaken. You can say prayers at your altar asking the Goddess as Lady of the Plants to show you a sign indicating the identity of your plant ally or allies. Sometimes this information comes intuitively, or becomes apparent simply by thinking it over and looking back on your life. You can also go on a guided psychic journey into subconscious realms to find your plants. It helps to spend time with plants, look them up in books and gaze upon their images, read about them in stories, make up stories about them.

Once you have found a plant ally, get involved with her. For example, I discovered that the willow is my special tree. I made myself a willow crown with some fresh wands that had fallen in the rains of early spring. They were still wet and easy to bend into any shape I wished. As the willow is a tree of inspiration, I like to wear my crown when I am doing muse-oriented work, such as making music or composing poetry, or rehearsing a magical play. I also burn dried bits of willow twigs for an inspirational smudge. Research your plant ally, find out her stories, her mythic and magical associations, her magical and practical uses, when she blooms or fades, which parts of her have powers, whether it be her roots, leaves, stems, blossoms, or fruit. Plant her in your garden or somewhere nearby and visit with her often. Ask for her assistance in your spells and rituals, and be sure to thank her. Sleep with a bit of her under your pillow and ask her to visit you in your dreams and give you her teachings.

5. Make an herbal charm. Use the guidelines for making a love charm in Cycle 12, only substitute different themes and appropriate herbs. For example, you can use rosemary in a protection charm, comfrey in a healing charm, celery seed in a charm to break addictions.

6. Plant a magical herb garden. You can use the guidelines in Scott Cunningham's book *Magical Herbalism*, or variations thereof. Decide which herbs you would like to plant and what sort of design you will use in your planting arrangement. Scope out an appropriate spot in your garden, and clear it for this purpose both physically and psychically. Bless and sanctify the area with appropriate rites, and ask the Goddess to give Her blessing. Plant in harmony with the cycles of the moon and sun. Make an altar and a place to sit in our near your herb garden, so you can do magic there. Go to a nursery and to books where you can find out the necessary information for successful planting. Fill your garden with herbs that you particularly love and that you plan to use in your rituals and spells. Sing songs and say prayers at each stage of

the work; when you prepare the soil, sow the seeds, water and weed, harvest and use—or simply when you wish to commune.

7. Do an ecology ritual, alone or with friends. Cast a circle and invoke plant Goddesses, spirits and devas. Wear greens and flowers on your body and in your hair. Make an offering to the earth by pouring spring water or some of your moonblood. Visualize a global cleansing of the soil, the air, and the water, and then visualize images of healthful growth. See the trees returning to the Emerald Forest, the hole in the ozone layer being mended, the air fresh and sweet, and the waters running pure and clear. If you have feelings or sadness and grief, let them come up and then release them. See the threat being lifted from endangered species, and their populations increasing once again. Imagine yourself out in space gazing down on Mother Earth, and see Her glowing with health and vitality, with people everywhere cooperating to create lifestyles that are ecologically sound. When you close your circle send the raised energy back into the Mother and imagine it helping to make your visions real. Follow up the ritual with some concrete action, such as cleaning up at a nearby beach, or starting a recycling movement in your neighborhood.

8. Perform a psychic healing ritual in a circle of sisters. Cast a circle and call upon Hygieia or other Goddesses of healing. Have each woman take a turn lying in the middle, while everyone else works on her with chanting, visualization, and laying on of hands. Use herbs in your rite. Cleanse the aura of each woman by waving a branch of fresh healing herbs over her in spiraling motions; burn herbal smudges, sprinkle fresh herbs over the ritual site, give each woman a healing herbal charm to wear as she arises from the circle's center.

Questions to Ponder

1. Have you ever communicated with a plant?

2. Do you feel an affinity with plants? Any in particular?

3. Think back to the plant episodes in familiar stories from childhood, such as Beauty's rose, Jack's beanstalk, Snow White's apple, Cinderella's pumpkin. What other plant stories can you recall? What influence, if any, did these have on you while growing up?

4. What is your relationship with plants today? Do you take care of any plants, or plan to?

5. Does this Cycle excite your interest in herbs? Do you see yourself making herbs

and their magical uses an important part of your life?

6. What do you know of the healing properties of herbs? Do you work with herbs for healing purposes? How do you feel about this approach, as opposed to standard medical practices?

9. After reading this Cycle, how do you feel about the "obligatory harvest," the work ethic, and other conventional approaches to farming and gardening? Would you consider having a wild garden? (Note: The Federal Government now has a program for encouraging the development of small wildlife preserves in people's private yards. Contact the magazine *Mother Earth News* for information on this.)

10. Do you think about ecological issues and the current threat to plant life on our planet home? Any ideas on what to do about this?

Reading and Other Resources

Jean M. Auel, *Clan of the Cave Bear.*

Jeannine Parvati Baker, *Hygieia.*

Paul Beyerl, *Master Book of Herbalism.*

Scott Cunningham, *Magical Herbalism* and *Cunningham's Encyclopedia of Magical Herbs. Magical Herbalism* is the most complete work I have found on the magical uses of herbs, and I urge you to get a copy if you can.

Louisa Francia, *Dragon Time: Magic and Mystery of Menstruation.*

Elizabeth Goudge, *The White Witch.* I found this one in the public library under fiction.

Robert Graves, *The White Goddess.* This book has many mythic herbal references and tree lore.

Hilarion, *Wildflowers—Their Occult Gifts.*

Jethro Kloss, *Back to Eden.* This is a venerable work on the medicinal aspect of herbs, by one of the pioneers of the health food movement.

Tim Leary, Ralph Metzner, Richard Alpert, *The Psychedelic Experience.* I recommend this highly.

Jeanne Rose, *Herbs and Things.*

Richard Evans Schultes and Albert Hofman, *Plants of the Gods: Origins of Hallucinogenic Use.*

Diane Stein, *All Women Are Healers* and *The Women's Book of Healing.*

Barbara G. Walker, *The Women's Encyclopedia of Myths and Secrets.* This book has mythic herbal references.

Diana Warburton, *Magiculture.* This book may be hard to find; try magic shops or metaphysical bookstores. If you can't find it, write the publisher: Prism Press, Stable Court, Chalmington, Dorchester, Dorset, DT2 OHB, Great Britain.

R. G. Wasson, A. Hofman and C. A. P. Ruck, *The Road to Eleusis.*
Susan S. Weed, *Wise Woman Herbal for the Childbearing Year* and *Healing Wise: The Second Wise Woman Herbal.*
Thelma Hatch Wyss, *Star Girl.* Look in the children's library for this one.

Resources:
Susan S. Weed, author of the *Wise Woman Herbals*, calls herself a Green Witch and offers workshops, weed walks and healing intensives. Write for her brochure. Susan S. Weed, P.O. Box 64, Woodstock, NY 12498.

There is now a correspondence course on herbs being offered through the Temple of Danaan. It is composed and taught by two members of their clergy, Grey Cat and Michael Ragan. I have had a delightful correspondence with Grey Cat for a number of years now, and recommend her with pleasure. If you are interested in finding out more about the course, you can inquire about Herbs for Magick and Medicine, c/o Grey Cat, Box 181, Crossville, TN 38557.

CYCLE 12

Aphrodite

The Myth of Psyche

In ancient times there lived a woman who was beautiful and good, and her name was Psyche, or Soul. She was the youngest daughter of a great king, and was adored by the people as though she were the Goddess of Love Herself. But such adulation can be a mixed blessing, for while she enjoyed the exaltation, it also isolated her from ordinary love. Her older sisters found sturdy husbands and royal households of their own, while Psyche remained unwed, to the consternation of her father.

Meanwhile, in the numinous realm of the gods, Aphrodite, Goddess of Love and Beauty, was angered. "How dare they worship this mortal woman in my stead!" she complained. And she sent for her son Eros. "Fly to Earth, my son, and pierce this human upstart with one of your magic arrows. Cause her to fall in love with a beast of the fields, or some such absurdity." And Eros flew off in all his splendor, to obey his mother's command.

As Fate would have it, however, Eros himself became enamored of the beautiful Psyche. While preparing one of his arrows, he pierced himself by accident, as he gazed upon her, and fell deeply in love.

In the world of mortals the king was becoming more and more concerned about the welfare of his daughter. He betook himself to the oracle, a priestess or sibyl in the nearby temple caverns. "Dress your daughter in black and blindfold her. Form a funeral procession and leave her at the top of the hill. You must perform the rites of the dead and release your Psyche forever from this world."

The king was overwhelmed with grief, but he did as he was bidden. He and the entire household garbed themselves in black robes, with Psyche in their midst, and took her to a hilltop in the wilderness. Psyche wept and moaned, but to no avail, as her father, family and friends left her forever.

And then a wondrous thing happened. She felt herself lifted and carried by the wind spirits, who murmured comforting words in her ears.

> You sent for me on the wind, on the wind
> You sent for me on the wind
> And though I was young and blind, and blind

I followed your voice in the wind . . .

Psyche was carried for some time, whither she knew not, and then gently set down. She removed her blindfold and beheld a magnificent palace set like a jewel in a tiny green valley. Invisible hands led her within, disrobed and bathed her, and dressed her in a gorgeous flowing gown. Then they guided her to a golden table where a sumptuous feast was spread. When she had eaten her fill the mysterious servants guided her once more, this time to a soft and luxurious couch, where she lay down to peaceful sleep and dreams.

> You made me a house of gold and light
> You made me a house of light
> And deep and deep in the velthmyn* dark
> You gave me my heart's delight . . .

In the middle of the night, Eros, the god of love, came to her. They melted into glorious passion and were lovers from then on. But Eros whispered warning in her ear—that she must never look upon him nor know who he truly was. "For if you see me, all this magic will disappear, the spell will be broken, and I must leave you forever."

Time passed and Psyche was at first content. She had everything she could possibly need in the way of comforts and luxuries, and the magnificent love of the god consumed her each night. But it was inevitable that she would grow lonely for the companionship of those she had known. She began to plead with Eros to allow her to see her sisters once more. At first he was adamant; no one must come to this secret place, for if his mother should find out, her wrath could be terrible. But in the end he gave in to Psyche, for he loved her, and knew that her need was genuine.

And so a day arrived when Psyche's two sisters were brought to the same hilltop where she herself had been left for dead, also at the instructions of the sibyl. They too were lifted by the zephyr winds and carried to Psyche's golden house. They embraced one another in joy, and Psyche eagerly showed them the riches and beauty of her new life. But her sisters were filled with jealousy, and instead of celebrating her happiness they planted seeds of doubt and suspicion in her mind.

"Who is this godlike husband of yours?" they insisted. "How is it that you can live like this without ever seeing him or knowing who he is? What if he is some sort of monster, come to devour you at some appointed time?" And they importuned her to light a candle that night, and see who her mysterious lover might be.

After they left Psyche was filled with anguish and conflict. She hated to betray her promise to Eros, and at the same time she feared that perhaps he truly was a monster or some other evil being.

And so one night, Psyche lit a fateful candle. And there in her bed lay the beautiful winged god of love himself. But as she gazed in wonder upon him, her hand faltered and some of the melting wax dripped from the candle and onto his naked skin. Eros awakened with a great cry, flew out the window, and was gone!

> Why did you fly from me, my love?
> Why did you fly from me?
> For when dazzling flame unveiled my eyes
> I saw the Goddess in thee . . .

Psyche was devastated. She had betrayed his trust and lost the beauty and wonder of their love. As she gazed about her the light and magic of their home began to fade. It grew cold and dusty and she felt emptiness overtake her heart.

> O tender flesh of my sweet lover
> Singed so unexpectedly
> O this starting up from velvet slumber
> This anguished cry: Alas!
> The spell is broken,
> And I must fly!

> And O this open window of my soul
> Where you are vanished,
> Flown so soon . . .

> Where o where can I regain thee, love?
> Why East of the Sun, of course,
> And West of the Moon . . .

> You speak to me on the wind, on the wind
> You speak to me on the wind
> And though you have flown beyond the sky
> I follow your voice in the wind . . .

And so Psyche set forth to find her true love. She went to a temple of Aphrodite and begged the goddess to come to her aid. Aphrodite was furious and at first would do nothing in Psyche's behalf. But when she saw her son pining away in his bed, she relented. "There is a path to immortality and reunion with your lover," she explained to Psyche, but it is filled with trials and obstacles." Psyche bravely agreed to undertake the journey.

The first task Aphrodite set Psyche was to sort out a vast pile of mixed seeds and grains, each into their own individual piles. Psyche began with a will, but soon became exhausted and overwhelmed with the enormity of so many tiny grains. She lay down and wept for frustration, finally falling into fitful sleep. While she slept a colony of ants came by, and taking pity on the lovelorn Psyche, they sorted the grains, each and every one. When Psyche awakened she found each allotted to its own pile.

The second task Aphrodite set Psyche was to gather some of the golden fleece from the magical rams of the sun. This was an assignment fraught with danger, for the rams were mighty and aggressive and spent most of their time in violent combat. For the tender Psyche to go among them was to risk harm and death. Again she fell into despair, and this time was helped by the Whispering Reed, who spoke to her in a dream. It instructed her to take the fleece by night from the surrounding bushes while the great rams slept.

The third task Psyche was commanded to perform was to fill a crystal flask with water from the turbulent cascading stream of life that flowed from the highest mountain and down into the underworld. The water was wild and unapproachable, surrounded by great boulders and sharp, slippery rocks. When Psyche attempted to approach she slipped and fell, nearly tumbling into the stream and losing her life then and there. But an eagle flying overhead saw her distress, and flying down to her, took the goblet from her hand and filled it.

"And now for your final task," Aphrodite spoke to Psyche. "Take this casket to the Goddess of the Underworld, Persephone, and ask her to fill it with Beauty. Then bring it back to me. You must not stop to help anyone, no matter how eloquently they may plead, nor must you under any circumstances open the casket, for you would be overcome by Beauty's power."

Psyche was drowning in hopelessness. She thought Aphrodite wanted her to die, and climbed a tall tower to throw herself from its heights and end her suffering forever. But just as she was about to do so, the tower itself spoke to her! "Don't despair, now, sweet Psyche, for you are nearly at the end of your trials." And it gave her instructions on how to reach the underworld.

Psyche took the casket and descended into the world of shadow. She successfully obtained Beauty from Persephone. She remembered not to talk to anyone along the way, and to close her ears to the pitiful cries of those who sought her aid. But when she at last reached the upper world again, temptation overcame her, and she opened the box of Beauty to see what was within. A powerful vapor enveloped her, and she fell into a deathlike swoon.

It was here that Eros found her, for he had regained his health and strength and flown forth in search of his love. He lifted her up and bore her to his country, where Psyche was given the cup of immortality. The lovers were wed and bore a beautiful daughter, whose name was Pleasure.

> Love is as strong as the golden corn
> That grows beside the sea,
> Yet love is as new as a babe unborn
> And old as the bitter withy.*

Nothing in this life can surpass the beauty, the mystery, the power of the experience of falling in love. Aphrodite (Isis, Ishtar, Lilith, Rhiannon, Venus, Euridice, Eurynome, Olwen, Abtagigi, Adamu, Xochiquetzal, Var, Urvasi, Hathor) is a force in our psyches. We weave and unweave our destinies according to the ways in which we love. When the goddess of love is aroused (or our passions within) something is always born, something always dies. We are enchanted, under a spell. There is a sense of timelessness, of immortality. We feel we have known our beloved before, perhaps in another life. We feel caught up in something larger than ourselves.

> With her venom
> Love
> That loosener of limbs
> Strikes me down . . .
> —*Sappho*

It is significant that the state Aphrodite creates is so rarely discussed. As my mother says in her own personal "Sex Code":

> . . . an aspect of sex which is not overadvertised, nor in fact advertised at all. I refer to the dizzying, exquisite thrilling of the autonomous nervous system for which we have no word in English, and which occurs, often mutually, when fortunate lovers touch, or when they exchange glances, or even just when they think of one another in sexual remembrance or anticipation. This powerful and glorious phenomenon is not mentioned in our dreary, necessary sex education courses with their cautious impersonal exposure of reproductive plumbing. It is absent from the recent spate of how-to-do-it sex books. It does not enter into the clinical therapy for our countless sexual cripples and sexual zombies. Yet all but a pitiable few experience it at one time or another, and we all know it's what we're seeking. —*Frances Witlin*

It is this "powerful and glorious phenomenon" that I refer to as Aphrodite. I believe that when she is present there exists between lovers a connection that is physical, mental, emotional, and spiritual. Classical scholars have named her Eros, but this is a masculization, as Eros was Aphrodite's son. His familiar form appears to us most often as the cherub with bow and arrow, who shoots unwitting lovers with a blindfold over his eyes. This childlike, blind, male symbol is a perfect representation of passionate love in patriarchy. By reclaiming the symbol of a strong female figure with clear, open eyes, we can take the first step toward healing some of our deepest personal and social problems.

Understanding and respect for the force that Aphrodite symbolizes is essential for success in doing magic. The energy that we feel when we fall in love is the same energy that is generated in all ecstatic rituals and spell-castings. It is tremendous and can move mountains, cause revolutions, make things come into being and destroy as well. The ancients in their wisdom personalized such forces, giving them names and faces, so that we might have a way of relating to them more easily. This gives us a poetic approach that awakens reverence and touches our spirits.

But Aphrodite is elusive. She does not care for cages. Routines are anathema to her. She is a wild force, untame.

> A free society will have its day
> When Aphrodite has her way . . .

In many ways the patriarchal status quo is maintained by the restrictions it attempts to place on Aphrodite. It is in the interests of male dominant power to define passion in accordance with its tenets of right and wrong. Actually, there is very little room for true passionate love in today's society. Lovers are expected to marry, and it is taken for granted that the magic and intensity of their love must die and be replaced by routine and efficient work habits. Meanwhile the media portrays all manner of sexual and passionate encounters, leading us to believe that love lies around every corner, if only we will use the right make-up or buy the best deodorant. We are like donkeys with the proverbial carrot of love forever dangled before us, never attainable. In reality, there is a horrific scarcity of true love, and most people are starved for what should be abundant nourishment and a natural birthright to all.

Women are taught to surrender totally, to give up their power and autonomy for someone they love. Men are taught to keep themselves invulnerable, to be conquerors and controllers of their women, and to "marry well," meaning their wives should be good status symbols and help to gain respect and access to social rewards. Women are property or "chattel," and love has become a commodity to be bought and sold. A woman who maintains her freedom and her passion is considered a whore and must live outside the pale of respectable society. A wife is expected to be a sort of nun, discarding passion and sensual fulfillment, denying all her needs and living for the fulfillment of the needs of others.

Because patriarchal interests require control of women's bodies, we have lost freedom in our wombs, in our bleeding, in our sexual pleasures, in our sense of beauty and attractiveness. Footbinding, a brutal tradition that mutilates the feet of women in the name of "sexual attractiveness" still goes on in China. (See Andrea Dworkin, *Our Blood and Woman Hating*.) In many parts of the world young girls still have clitoridectomies to restrain them from taking too much pleasure in love. Older women are advised to have hysterectomies as soon as menopause arrives. We are made to feel ashamed of our blood, encouraged to hide it and even get rid of it with "extractions." And we are denied the right to abortions, a natural function of the Crone.

I do not mean to sound careless about abortion rights. All womb-related matters are holy, and must be dealt with in the deepest reverence. I have seen abortions given in cold indifference, with no sense of sacredness or the preciousness of life. This is just as bad as the habit of refusing women the right to all abortions. Whether life is taken or given it must be done with sensitivity, love and care. But my main message is that women must reclaim all our ancient birthrights: our bodies, our souls, our goddesses, our access to the earth, our choices regarding birth, love and death as well, and our magic. We must do so responsibly, and with love for all concerned, and in many ways, Aphrodite is the key.

In the 1960s we saw the "sexual freedom" movement, which brought some relief from the archaic patterns named above, but also introduced other problems. Anything goes became the password, and women were the targets. Love in most cases was even separated from sex. Now women could be expected to give of themselves without any social or moral considerations at all, and we found out that this so-called sexual freedom was less free than ever. With the backswing of the pendulum in the '70s and '80s, we are seeing a reversion to the old forms of patriarchal marriage and control of reproduction, along with a rise in rape and battering.

These are very general statements however, and I don't mean to invalidate the progress that has been made. Largely through the efforts of the women's movement we have begun to see more respect for our sexual choices, and more attempts at equity in lovers' relationships. But I feel we still have a long way to go before understanding of the sacredness of Aphrodite's powers is integrated on a large scale.

We must realize that patriarchy is kept intact by the ways in which people choose to love, or not to love. Men wanted control of society through the blood lines of inheritance and children, and so heterosexual marriage became the means of access to the source of production and reproduction. Women and children and land have become the property of the man, trained to submit, "staked out," and "fenced off." In many cultures brides are still openly bought and sold. All the ways that women are kept under control—the rapes, as "spoils of war," the mastectomies, hysterectomies, the guilt trips about sex and pleasure, the ban on abortions or forced sterilizations—all are signs of the patriarch's interests being kept intact. Witch trials and interrogations were notorious for their sexual nature. Women were accused of having sex with the devil, and were raped and tortured.

Our sexual freedom, therefore, is a basic threat to the system. A woman claiming the right to love whom and where and when and how she chooses directly undermines the social set-up as we know it. Because of this it is important to understand that the ways we choose to love have a political side. If in any way we give up our freedom or our power for the sake of love, we may be, however unwittingly, supporting a system we oppose.

There are countless illustrations of this in history and literature. Take for example, the story of Morgaine as told by Marion Zimmer Bradley in *The Mists of Avalon*. It takes place during a period of history when the last of the Old Religion was being supplanted by the new Christianity. Her personal loves and choices had a pivotal part to play in the changeover. To begin with, she performed a rite of sacred love with Arthur, and bore him a child. In the ancient religion, this type of hieros gamos (sacred marriage) was basic, and the child was expected to carry on the bloodlines of the priestesses and priests who birthed her/him. But because King Arthur was Morgaine's half brother, she spent much of her life in shame and regret over this union. This type of shame over incest was a purely Christian sentiment and was unheard of in the Old Religion.

Though Arthur was the one who truly loved and appreciated Morgaine, and was also committed to supporting the old faith as well as the new, Morgaine gave her heart to Lancelot, who turned his back on the goddess' ways. Tied in to her rejection of the old style ritual union with Arthur, was Morgaine's rejection of her role as priestess at Avalon, the ancient seat of the goddess religion. She was one of the last in the line of priestesses, and her neglect of her sacred trust was instrumental in bringing about the downfall of that tradition. She spent the better part of her life in the patriarchal world and in the royal courts, letting the magical isle of Avalon slip further and further into the mists of oblivion. Interestingly, Morgaine had a brief love encounter with Raven, one of Avalon's other priestesses. One cannot help but wonder where the Goddess religion would stand today if those two had become committed and faithful lovers!

Another outstanding example is Isadora Duncan, the mother of modern dance. Isadora lived through her passions and danced the beauty and poetry of myth. It was said that her performances literally lifted people from their seats, so powerful was her dancing. Yet the myths she enacted were male-identified, and she devoted her primary passions to men that took her away from her children, her art, and ultimately her life. She was killed in a dreadful accident while motoring with a lover. What if Isadora had danced more woman-identified myths, and her children had danced with her? What if the woman friend who was her devoted support and companion (and whom Isadora cruelly rejected) had been her lover?

And then there was Sappho. Like Morgaine, Sappho lived in a time of transition between religious traditions. According to the matriarchal traditions, young women would attend schools such as Sappho ran, to learn all the goddess' ways . This meant cultivating themselves in the arts, in poetry and dance, learning about beauty, music, and all the attributes of the Goddess of Love. And it included, at times, becoming lovers with their woman instructor. "The matriarchal tribe utilized adolescent homosexuality to create a powerful educational bond in which a girl's basic sense of her woman identity was founded on love of her own sex. This love was the sexual love of a powerful and honored adult woman—who was also a priestess and thus incarnated the Goddess herself." (From *Life on Lesbos*, by Jeanne Gallick.)

It is difficult for women of today to understand the morality of matriarchal times. Sappho lived at the end of this period, but she was still basically a free woman in her passions and sexuality. She also gave herself to men and bore a daughter, Cleis. But patriarchy was on the rise, and most of her young women were torn from her to ·be sent into marriage and servitude to men. Traces of what she suffered can be found in her poetry:

. . . my silent tongue is broken,
and a quick and subtle flame
runs up beneath my skin.
I lose my sense of sight, hear only drumming in my ears.
I drip cold sweat,
And a trembling chases all through me.
I am greener than the pale grass
And it seems to me that I am close to death.

Most of Sappho's poetry has been lost to us, for it was deliberately destroyed by those who found it immoral and threatening to the new male-dominated ways. All we have are fragments, most of them recorded in the journals or writings of contemporaries and friends. And yet she will never, never be forgotten, for the power of the goddess—her deep and magnificent passions—shines eternally.

These were all incredible women who have become immortal through their unforgettable talents, strengths, integrity and beauty. They can be our role models in many ways, and goddess knows, there are few enough of these! And it is here that Aphrodite triumphs after all, for the passions of these women have kept them alive in our hearts and minds.

But as long as patriarchy remains intact, we as witches and women must examine these lives with a critical eye. Beyond this, we can learn from them, and apply these lessons to ourselves. I wept bitterly when I read of Morgaine's grief and suicidal feelings when she finally came to realize her mistakes and the effects they had. She saw that she had forsaken the Goddess, forgotten the magic, the rituals and practices, and lost her skill. And in doing so a whole nation of the Little People, who were counting on her to maintain the temple, was virtually annihilated. I realized that I have made similar mistakes in my own life, and resolved all the more firmly to avoid them from then on. The death of Isadora's young children (drowned in a locked car that had rolled into a lake) still grips me at times; I can feel her remorse, guilt, anger and dreadful, numbing grief.

Not that we should ever lay the entire blame on ourselves or any individual woman. True blame must be directed at the perpetrators, the social forces that oppress and harm the goddess on every level. But we must look to our own choices and see where we have participated, and how we can change that. For women do hold up half the sky as the feminists say; we must hold ourselves accountable for the myriad ways that we uphold and support the patriarchy.

To do this we need to come to an understanding of the ancient morality of Aphrodite. "Freedom does not mean license," says A. S. Neill in his classic book *Summerhill.* Aphrodite does have a morality. She is the most demanding combination of fleeting and everlasting, and requires of us the most exquisite kinds of discipline.

The Mammalian Prerogative

... From a biological point of view, patriarchal religion denied women the natural rights of every other mammalian female: the right to choose her stud, to control the circumstances of her mating, to occupy and govern her own nest, or to refuse all males when preoccupied with the important business of raising her young.

... Patriarchal religion declared war on pagan societies where motherhood was once considered the only important parental relationship; where women owned the land and governed its cultivation; and sexual attachments were made and unmade at women's discretion.

—From *The Women's Encyclopedia of Myths and Secrets*
(the Introduction) by Barbara G. Walker

Aphrodite as the ecstatic Mother Goddess

The female-dominated Greater Mysteries of Eleusis were marked by hallucination through narcotics, by androgynous and incestuous symbolism, and by nocturnal, liminal behaviour. They confronted and flouted the artificiality of the antithesis between sexuality and maternalism that was upheld in all public cults in the male-dominated society. In modern terms, we would say that the focus of the Mysteries was on the mystic union of the complexes of sexuality and maternalism, of Aphrodite and Demeter-Persephone. Precisely because of this they were under such a categorical and successful taboo ...

—hypothesis by Paul Friedrich in *The Meaning of Aphrodite*

The beginning of Patrimony

... these Romans counted their lineage through the male line, rather than sensibly through the mother; it was silly, for how could any man ever know precisely who had fathered any woman's child? Of course, these Romans made a great matter of worrying over who lay with their women, and locked them up and spied on them. Not that Igraine needed watching; one man was bad enough, who would want others who might be worse?

—from *The Mists of Avalon*, by Marion Zimmer Bradley, p. 7

The new all-male pantheon; the Goddess made evil

... said the Merlin, sitting very erect, "but the followers of Christ have chosen to say, not that *they* shall have no other Gods before their God, but that there *is* no other God save for their God; that he alone made the world, that he rules it alone, that he alone made the stars and the whole of creation."

..."They believe," said Viviane, in her smooth low voice, "that there is no Goddess; for the principle of woman, so they say, is the principle of all evil; through woman, so they say, Evil entered into this world; there is some fantastic Jewish tale about an apple and a snake."

—from *The Mists of Avalon*, p. 11

The sacred marriage

... The way of the tribal festivals was more honest, that man and woman should come together with the sun tides and moon tides in their blood, as the Goddess willed; and only if they wished, later, to share a home and rear children was marriage thought upon.

Sex separated from holy passion

... And he did not seem to mind, it seemed to him that this was the way it should be, so that they were both pleasured ... as if nothing mattered but their bodies, that there was no greater joining with all of life. To the priestess, reared in Avalon and attuned to the greater tides of life and eternity, this careful, sensuous, deliberate lovemaking seemed almost blasphemy, a refusal to give themselves up to the will of the Goddess ... still in his heart he hungered ... for some woman he could have without giving more of himself than this empty touching of skins ...

Sexuality and passion for the Mother seen as sin, dishonor

... he had said, *I do not want to hurt or dishonor you*, as if he truly believed there could be something wrong or dishonorable in this coming together. . . . At last he said, almost choking, "The sin seems to me more deadly, I suppose, than it is—I would you were not so like my mother, Morgaine—" . . . It was like a blow in the face. . . . In Avalon this could never have come to pass—those who came to the Goddess in this way would never have so refused her power . . .

—From *The Mists of Avalon*, pp. 323-326

The Rites of Beltane

..."There was a day," said Accolon, "when the queen of the land was the Spring Maiden, and the Harvest Lady as well, and *she* did that office in the fields, that the fields might have life and fertility." . . . said Uriens hastily, "but the past is past ... and it is no longer needful that the queen should bless the fields in that way." ...*No*, thought Morgaine. Now all is sterile, now we have priests with their crosses, forbidding the lighting of the fires of fertility—it is a miracle that the Lady does not blight the fields of grain, since she is angry at being denied her due.... "So tomorrow the fields are to be blessed (said the King) ... and perhaps we should be grateful we live in a civilized land, and the king and queen need no longer bless the fields by lying together in public ..." ... Morgaine sighed ... Accolon had roused in her an anguished memory of her years in Avalon—the torches borne to the top of the Tor, the Beltane fires lighted and the maidens waiting in the plowed fields ... and tonight she had had to hear a shabby priest mocking what was, to her, holy beyond holiness. . . .

—From *The Mists of Avalon*, pp. 577-579

Incest made sin (Morgaine finally wakes up!)

"I am his father's wife and of all women I am the one most forbidden to him. I am more forbidden to him, in this Christian land, than I was to Arthur.... What has come to me again and again?" . . . Every man she had desired had been too close kin to her. . . . "But they are too close kin to me only by the laws made by the Christians who seek to rule this land ... to rule it in a new tyranny; not alone to make the laws

but to rule the mind and heart and soul. Am I living out in my own life all the tyranny
of that law, so I as priestess may know why it must be overthrown?"

—From *The Mists of Avalon*, pp. 583-584

The ancient morality of Aphrodite

"Even as we lay together under the stars that Midsummer, I knew that what we had
done was not so much lovemaking as a magical act of passionate power; that his
hands, the touch of his body, were reconsecrating me priestess, and that it was her
will . . ."

—From *The Mists of Avalon*, p. 588

For behold,
All acts of love and pleasure are my rituals . . .

—From *The Charge of the Goddess*

The morality of Aphrodite is based upon the preciousness of all life and
creatures. Coming together with a lover is an expression of the life force in action,
and as such is immanently sacred. Aphrodite does not pay heed to the patriarchal
attempts to draw lines between lovers. She will arise between the old and the young,
the rich and the poor, between men and women, between women and women,
between men and men, among two or three or more, between those who are supposed
to be of different class or enemy camps . . . in truth she is basically indifferent to
patriarchal morality. But she demands allegiance to the sacredness of her energy.
Making love to Her is an act of worship, an acknowledgment of the power and beauty
and wonder of all creation. Thus, when we violate this, we violate all that is holy to
her. Sex without love is such a violation. Sex performed without a sense of ritual,
performed without reverence, as a ploy for power or money, as a way to manipulate
or control another . . . all are violations to Aphrodite.

Passion as a force in our lives is as necessary as rain. With it we are filled with
inspiration and joy. Without it we wither and become as empty shells. We need it not
only in our loving of one another, but also in other aspects of our lives—in our work
and in our communities. A free people is a passionate people. True revolutions are
always based in passion. True, creative work is always based in passion. Happy,
loving families and communities are imbued with passion. Truly, the Goddess
Herself creates everything out of passion, her great and abiding love. The forces of
patriarchy, in their attempts to restrict and deny Her, deny of the force of Life itself.

The Goddess smiles upon all true lovers, regardless of species or gender. She
accepts all forms of union, in infinite variety. Though patriarchy would have us
believe that male-over-female is the only natural and acceptable form, careful
examination of nature's ways will reveal the lie. The amoeba loves herself and life
so much, she simply divides into two! The male seahorse carries the child to term.
The anemone fish, born as a male or female, goes through both male and female
stages in later life. If the dominant mother anemone fish dies, the largest male changes

into a female in order to take her place, and can then lay eggs. The *acarophenax tribolii*, a type of mite, never births its male offspring. They remain within the mother's body, where they mate with their sisters and eventually die. The male anglerfish, tiny in comparison to the female, mates by attaching himself by the mouth to a protuberance on her body. He then dissolves, losing his original form, and merging almost entirely. Parthenogenesis (birth without sperm), is far more widespread than most people realize. It has been found that a certain percentage of women's eggs are self-fertilizing; that is, they begin to divide spontaneously, thus resulting in the formation of an embryo. University of Illinois ecologist Michael Lynch has discovered that many species have acquired the capacity to reproduce without mating. Virgin births occur in frogs and mice, in human beings, and countless other species. It is clear that the Goddess delights in all forms, and all are variations on a single theme—She Herself.

We must therefore realize that the taboos and restrictions placed upon love in our society are false. They were created for one reason alone, to keep the power in the hands of selfish and controlling males. Our fears of sensuality, of pleasure, of homosexuality, of love outside of marriage are nothing but brainwashing and social conditioning, deliberately implanted through the generations, and reinforced by religious institutions.

History and literature abound with examples of the suffering caused by patriarchal suppression of passionate love. *Romeo and Juliet* is a prime example. Only in death could those lovers find one another at last. *The Thornbirds*, a recently televised dramatic series, is another example. The leading characters, a Catholic priest and a young, aristocratic woman, love one another passionately, but are forbidden ever to consummate their feelings. Celibacy and suffering are made a virtue, and when the two finally give in to their longings, they are victims of guilt and self-loathing for the rest of their lives.

What a blight has been laid upon us by the cruel and vengeful god of the patriarchs, who makes of love a sin and a crime, and abstinence therefrom a prime virtue! The effect is to send people into bitterness, cynicism, guilt and pornography, violence, frustration and rape. Separating their sexuality from love and the spirit, their pleasures are taken in secret perversion, twisted into abuse and sadism. Aphrodite has been made ruler of a terrible and ugly world consisting of pornography and prostitution, robbed of all beauty and spiritual value.

>Oh patriarchs
>Your maiden goddess
>Is a Playboy bunny
>Your mother goddess
>An emaciated cow
>Jumping over the moon
>And your crone—

Where is she?
Wreaking havoc
In the underground . . .

An important aspect of Aphrodite's expression is woman-loving-woman. The very fact that this arouses shock and suspicion in the mainstream society is a sure sign that the Goddess is at work. Lesbian love is the Goddess loving Herself, is woman loving herself, is sister loving sister in the deepest way possible. There have always been same-sex lovers, contrary to the repressive attitudes of the current system. For women to open to this kind of love is to heal ourselves profoundly, and also to heal all of society. Although not everyone will seek expression in this manner, its existence is nourishing to all. For it nourishes the life-stream, sending a reflection of the goddess-loving-the-goddess-loving-the-goddess through time, space and psyche. The ultimate revolution is to love women, ourselves and each other, not only sexually, but in all ways. For patriarchy is built upon the hatred of woman and rejection of the feminine forces. This is why lesbian love is so threatening, and why it will ultimately bring about the necessary changes.

In many ways lesbians today are developing the frontiers of consciousness. They are learning new ways to survive, to relate, to worship, to work and to play. They are developing new myths, new philosophies, new kinds of families, new kinds of language, art and creative expression. No matter what our sexual orientation, we must all look to the woman-identified movements for information and guidance. These women are making inroads into a new universe because they are the farthest removed from the old one. Not that they are perfect, and I do not mean to say that we should swallow all that they say and do in entirety. We are all in this century, and we all have conditioning to undo, lessons to learn. I have seen some lesbians that I consider more patriarchal than some men I have met! But we have to start somewhere, and healing love is an excellent place to begin.

Womanlove is one of the great initiations. It is a passage into the mystery of the Self. When women bond as lovers they embody the anciently new myth of the Goddess' love. In many ways a lesbian spirituality is an antidote to the ills of this world. Love of women, of women's bodies, of female pleasure and ecstasy, of the mythic symbolism implied in vulva, breasts, soft and curving flesh—these are essential healings. It is an affirmation of the Goddess' ability to re-create Herself endlessly. It is an affirmation of a woman's autonomy, and her right to live as she chooses, fulfilling herself in all her potentials.

Patriarchy insists that only one kind of loving is acceptable, that of male-over-female. Dissolve the heterosexual imperative and men lose control of inheritance, women and children. Hence we are trained to believe that the natural varieties of love are sin. And yet, in Nature, the variety is incredible! Even among humans we see amazing variation—men who are small and delicate, women who are muscular and hairy. It is now known that men actually have vestigial wombs! Aphrodite does not draw the distinctions of male-centered dualistic morality. To Her all forms of true love are divine rites of passage, as long as they are true love.

One pattern that must be overcome is the tendency to perpetuate the dominant-submissive expressions modelled for us by the patriarchal standard. This is a power-over dynamic, with one person oppressing/controlling and the other submitting as victim. This model is at the root of all our power-over institutions, from the most private couples to nations controlling nations. We must learn to love as equals, to share power, to take turns making decisions, initiating passion, being assertive and being receptive. We need to replace pyramids and hierarchy with circles of equality, where the energy flows around and around and all participants can benefit. As women who have been most often trained to submit, we must work to undo our tendency to be too passive, to look for authority and power outside of ourselves. At the same time we need to learn how to reclaim our power and autonomy in a female image, rather than imitating the macho male model of power. This awareness applies not only to lesbians, but to all lovers.

As discussed before, a good archetype to help us with this is the five elements of the Witch's Star. We are each of us a five-pointed star; we each have in our personalities airy (mental), fiery (active), watery (receptive), earthy (physical), and spiritual (psychic) qualities. Regardless of gender, it is possible to express freely through all arms of the star. Attractions in this context are based on the elemental pulls of fire to water, earth to air, spirit to earth, air to water, and so on. Since we all naturally tend to be more developed in some elements than others, we will be magnetically drawn to those who have the other qualities. (For more information on this, see my essay, "The Witch's Star.")

One issue that many people are torn by is the "monogamy versus non-monogamy" controversy. On the one hand, we need love, and sturdy, lasting relationships. On the other hand, we need freedom and room to grow. "Monogamy" supporters often seem to stifle and restrict themselves, while "non-monogamy" advocates often sever valuable ties. This is another either/or trap, created by the illusion that we must select only one, and that there are no alternatives.

The solution, I believe, is the eternal quality of Aphrodite. Both monogamy and non-monogamy are concepts based in patriarchal tradition. One is the conventional marriage, born of male control of inheritance and reproduction. The other is male conquest of women, the more the merrier. How many men do you know that are capable of lasting passion? Though there may be a few, they are rare. Most are trained from a very young age to turn off such tendencies in themselves.

True love never dies. It may change in its form of expression, but its energy goes on and on beyond space and time. In order to allow this force to flow in our lives we must learn to be free, and we must learn to love ourselves and one another unconditionally. Aphrodite is timeless, immortal. She does not concern herself with how few or many lovers we may have; she is concerned only that we honor her. Herein lies the exquisite discipline I mentioned before, for we must learn to be fluid

APHRODITE'S STAR

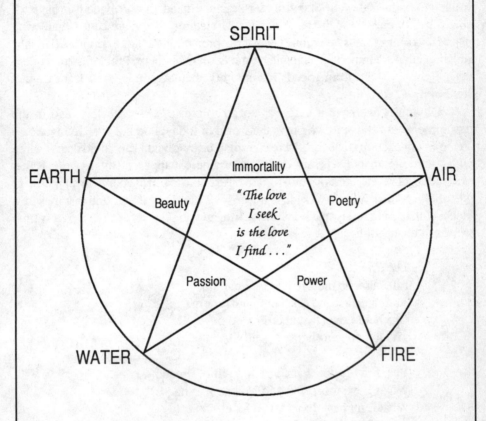

SPIRIT

EARTH

AIR

Immortality

Beauty

Poetry

*"The love
I seek
is the love
I find . . ."*

Passion

Power

WATER

FIRE

THE ATTRIBUTES OF TRUE LOVE

and independent, while at the same time maintaining eternal commitments to those we love.

A good model of a society based on this sort of life-style is depicted in Marge Piercy's *Woman on the Edge of Time*. In her utopian community everyone has their own space—a small house, dome, or treehouse set off from the rest, and private. People enjoy their solitude and are protective of their time alone. They form relationships based on their feelings for one another, visiting one another for as long or as short periods as desired. There are "hand friends" and "heart friends," and strong community links as well. Stability and practical needs are provided through all channels, not only through one-to-one lover relations. There are central gathering places and dining areas; everyone takes turns preparing the large communal meals. Relationships are important, and much time is spent on them. Problems are worked out, often with help from friends, community members, and even from trained counselors.

Obviously we have a long way to go to create such a society, and in the meantime we must live as we can in the world of today. I do not wish to invalidate any love-connections that you, the reader, may be involved in and hold dear. I agree with Aphrodite, that love is sacred, no matter where it appears. But my hope is that as a student of magic and as a woman that you are able to fulfill your own magnificent potential, and that your life is such that true love can flow. If you find that these are blocked, that you have no passion in your life, and no power, then perhaps it is time to start to change this.

> *The Choice*
> Life came to me while I lay dreaming
> And in each hand She bore a gift for me
> One held Love, the other Freedom
> "Which do you choose?" said She
>
> Yes, I'm the one that chose the gift of Freedom
> When Love was offered in Life's other hand
> What right have I to cry I'm lonely
> When I can walk unbound through man's wasteland?
> "You've chosen well," She said, and bent to kiss me
> "For now I can return to you again
> "And when I come, two gifts I'll bring you
> "But then the Two will be in one hand . . ."

Aphrodite and Magic

Aphrodite's energy is Shakti in motion, the awakened kundalini, which the Hindus say is the female stuff of which all matter is composed. When we fall in love we feel this energy vibrating through our entire beings. She sends all of our chakras whirling, from root to crown, and beyond. This state has been called "samadhi," or "nirvana," and has also been experienced by Western saints as an exalted love of God. Heroic warriors of Celtic tradition were said to have their battle fever upon them when the chakras were aroused. But these are merely the patriarchal attempt to twist the powers of love to the perverted expressions of asceticism and war. "Make love, not war," is a truer saying than most realize!

The awakened forces of Aphrodite can be channelled for magical purposes. The desire lovers feel for one another can be directed, with affirmation, focus and visualization, to create a chosen end. This is why it is so important that we redirect the forces of love for peaceful purposes that nourish the earth, the community, and honor the sacred life force in every creature. True love causes all the chakras to vibrate at an intense and harmonious pitch. When coveners fall in love their energy can amplify the magic for the entire group. Making love and making magic are really the same thing, though in the latter case we work to arouse kundalini through techniques and meditations. When Aphrodite appears She "turns us on" automatically, with no effort on our parts. In both cases, however, we need the same openness, vulnerability, receptiveness, trust, and trustworthiness; this is the ecstasy of the orgasmic state. Out of this we can birth circumstances, form, ideas, creations, children, power connections. The possibilities are infinite.

The ancients understood these things far better than we. They knew that aroused kundalini affects the universe and all creatures who are near. Hence the orgiastic rituals in the ploughed fields beneath the full moon, to nourish the community and the crops.

Though Aphrodite is wild and has rhythms of Her own, it is possible to invite her in with magic. My favorite way of doing this is with ritual theater, as described in the Rites of Kore at the beginning of Cycle 10. Aphrodite loves beauty and inspiration, and She loves stories that are danced and poetically uttered in Her honor. This is the same principle used by lovers when they set the scene for love-making, with candlelight, soft music, sensuous food, clothing, ritual baths. These are all ways of inviting Aphrodite in. Often She will make her appearance through music, especially when played and sung in the Sapphic style with poetry and passion.

> . . . O how my spirit yearns
> For that clear pure strong place
> Shared with my lover
> Continuing the chakra connection
> Up through heart, throat, third eye and crown

Song soaring, spinning out and through us
Muse bringing us together in ecstasy

And then, to make love
So intense and beautiful
Melting
Warm
And infinitely sweet . . .

To Make A Love Charm

Cut a circle of red fabric, about five inches in diameter. In the center place fresh herbs like lavender, mint, thyme and rosė petals. On a small pieces of parchment write: *Aphrodite of the sea, send my true love unto me.* Fold this into a tiny triangle and place with herbs. Gather up the cloth so that contents remain bunched at the center and fabric flares out from this like a skir.

Wind with a scarlet thread until firmly held, and tie off one end. Leave the other end long enough to make a necklace; tie this off as well. You can wear the charm under your clothing and keep it under your pillow at night. Bless it by passing it through incense or herbal smoke. Hold it aloft in your cupped hands and call upon Aphrodite. Ask her to empower the charm, and place your visions into it. Hold it to your heart for awhile. Repeat this ceremony from time to time.

Ethics and Protection

Remember, it is wrong to interfere with the free will of any individual, unless in exceptional situations where banishing or binding may be acceptable. (See the Crone Cycle.) Love magic must be done with this in mind. You can ask for love, or send a suggestion to someone you desire, but always leave the final decision to them. If you are already bonded to a lover and have mutual consent, charms can be made to strengthen and nourish your love. Feel free to adapt the form to suit your needs and circumstances. Also, don't forget that silence is the fifth rule of magic!

By this time it must be clear to you that magic really works. As Viviane says in *The Mists of Avalon*, be careful what you ask for; the Goddess may grant it to you. As women we may be particularly vulnerable, many of us are not trained in the Amazon qualities of self-defense and care of our own interests. This can make us prey to unworthy or exploitive lovers. As witches this is doubly true, for a magical approach to Aphrodite necessarily makes us open to the depths of our being. It is essential that we open ourselves only to love that enhances us and is in harmony with our magic. While I am the first to extol the beauty and the power of love, and to express my conviction that we need a society based in Her, I must caution you never to make yourself a slave to Aphrodite.

When we connect in passion to another being, there are strong invisible cords that hook up all our chakras, head to head, heart to heart, and so on. When energy flows back and forth along these connections it is total bliss. But if for some reason there is a block to these energies it can be agony, and it can be dangerous too. It is likely that many of you reading this have suffered in this way, and are familiar with what I am talking about. Often it will be trivialized as "mere jealousy," or dismissed as unrequited love. But such painful situations are no light matter, and should be carefully avoided. Aphrodite is very powerful, and her energies can kill as well as heal. Most people do not see the damage that can be caused, because the energies operate inside us, in our hearts, stomachs and wombs, and psychically. But those who suffer in love are many, and are the walking wounded of our society.

> Love leaves coal in the eye sockets
> ashes for hands,
> the smell of flesh burning,
> smoke for a person.
>
> Love creates corpses and earthquakes
> Collapses friendships and forests
> Love compels our attention like fire.
>
> Afterwards we cool to rock.
> —From *The Shining House*, by Jean Erdman

This is what I call the inner holocaust (or holy cost), often caused by sacrificing Aphrodite to repressive social mores. It is better to be alone than to open ourselves to such damage. Better that we protect ourselves to begin with, than become the hard and cold cynic described in the poem above, who can never love at all.

Love is power is magic is power is love is power . . . when you give passion to a lover, you are giving them your power. This is as it should be, and wonderful when your beloved returns in kind. But if she/he does not, then beware. Protect yourselves my sisters. You are a temple; your heart, your mind, your womb—these are sanctuaries, precious and worthy of respect. Any being who enters therein should be worthy, whether the connection is to be a passing thing, or an intimately committed bonding.

Aphrodite is not averse to passing connections, which can be approached as the hieros gamos (sacred marriage). This was once a tradition, offered by priestesses of the goddess in the temples. A total stranger could connect deeply in a sacred rite of love and pass on, never to be seen again. The experience can be empowering and healing for both, as long as it is approached with ritual and understanding of its passing nature. In such rites the personalities of those involved recede, and they embody the life force. For a deeper, ongoing bond, however, it is necessary to have more personal affinities. Make sure your lover is in harmony with you in each arm of the five-pointed star—your body, mind, emotions, activities, and spirit. And in both cases, make sure that anyone you connect with as a lover has respect for the sacredness of the act.

Aphrodite And Myth

The primordial image of Aphrodite's beginnings shows Her arising out of the sea. Her ascension was known as the *anados* in pre-patriarchal Greek legend, reminiscent of the rising of Persephone from the bowels of the earth, or Pele from the flaming volcano. While earlier myth depicted these goddesses as self-propagating, our more familiar tellings of Aphrodite's origins are patriarchal. Every high school and college mythology course will insist that Aphrodite was born from the severed genitals of Uranus, who had been castrated by his son. This probably symbolized the overthrow of an older male order by a newer male order, both of which undoubtedly borrowed Aphrodite from an even earlier, female order. (We have already discussed the subject of male blood sacrifice in the Goddess' name . . . see Moon and Muse Cycles.) This myth said that the bloody members were tossed upon the ocean waves and mingled with the foam, out of which Aphrodite was born. She was transported to land on a scallop shell, blown to shore by the zephyrs or wind spirits, who cloaked her dazzling nakedness with beautiful robes. "Foam born," and "Queen of the Sea," are some of her names . . . Even in a male context the images of this birth are female. The woman delivered out of wind and water, naked and lovely, emanating from nature . . . this is ancient imagery of the immanent goddess. I like to think that she was the child of the love between the Ocean and the Air, who heaved and rolled in might orgasm as they exchanged their cosmic passions, and birthed the lovely Aphrodite, gifting her to the Earth, their sister . . . The breasts of Aphrodite were said to shine silver, like the Moon.

The ocean—the many-mooded sea, now turbulent, now calm—seems a fitting image as the Mother of the Goddess of Love, for love itself is known to run the gamut of all emotions. Whether matriarchal or patriarchal, Aphrodite was always virgin, that is, a free and independent woman who made love as she chose, but remained ever whole unto herself. Herein lies the meaning of the thorns among her sacred roses, for no matter how deeply we may unite in the flames of passion, we must return ever and again to Self; the wave must die that it may always be reborn. Thus Aphrodite is a transformative goddess and encompasses Maiden, Mother and Crone. She is Attraction, Union, and Separation, the Scent, the Rose, and the Thorn, a never-ending cycle of love through birth and life and death . . .

This concept is corroborated nicely in Barbara G. Walker's *Women's Encyclopedia*:

Often dismissed as a "Greek Goddess of love," Aphrodite was really much more than that. Like Kali, she was a Virgin-Mother-Crone trinity. She was once indistinguishable from the Fates (Moirae); her old name was Moira, and she was said to be older than Time. She governed the world by *ius naturale*, the natural law of the maternal clan . . . Cyprian Aphrodite was like all other manifestations of the Great Goddess: ruling birth, love, death, time, and fate, reconciling man to all of them through sensual and sexual mysticism.

The dark side of Aphrodite was not only expressed as the ocean but also as the ocean's creatures, both natural and fantastical. She is often seen as a mermaid, sometimes with two thrashing tails, symbolizing the birth and the death of Her affections. These images remind us of the instinctive quality of Her energy that comes from a deep, unconscious part of ourselves. We can see echoes of this in the fish emerging from the cup in the tarot, symbolizing a message from the deep. In the *Song of the Wandering Angus* by William Butler Yeats, the Celtic god of Love and Music goes into the hazel wood to catch a silver trout from the magical stream. He finds the fish transforming before his eyes into a beautiful woman:

> I went out to the hazel wood
> Because a fire was in my head
> And cut and peeled a hazel wand
> And hooked a berry to a thread,
> And when white moths were on the wing
> And moth-like stars came flickering out
> I dropped the berry in a stream
> And caught a little silver trout . . .
>
> When I had laid it on the floor
> I went to blow the fire aflame
> But something rustled on the floor
> And someone called me by my name
> It had become a glimmering girl
> With apple blossom in her hair
> She called me by my name, and ran
> And faded through the brightening air . . .

The thrashing fish, the writhing serpent, the aroused kundalini, the heaving ocean, the storming winds, all of these images call up Aphrodite. Her dance is the undulant belly-dance, the spiralling womb that gives blood, life, and pleasure. When Aphrodite moans in her passion, the mountains moan with her. When she weeps the seas swell and weep with her. Her surrender to ecstasy is the pull of the moon, the magnetic power of the soft and vulnerable aspect of woman. Her myths and her symbols are her thealogy, they are guidelines for understanding her Mysteries.

Greek myth tells us that Aphrodite could be called upon for assistance in finding true love. Though primarily known as a Moon Goddess, she also had a solar aspect as the Golden One. Homeric hymn describes a magic charm which she gave to Hera:

> She spoke, and from her breasts unbound the elaborate pattern-pierced
> zone, and on it are figured all beguilements, and loveliness
> is figured upon it, and passion of sex is there, and the whispered
> endearment that steals the heart away even from the thoughtful.
> She put this in Hera's hands, and called her by name and spoke to her:
> "Take this zone, and hide it away in the fold of your bosom.
> It is elaborate, all things are figured therein. And I think
> whatever is your heart's desire shall not go unaccomplished."

The more one finds out about Aphrodite, the more all-encompassing She becomes. She is the passion everyone longs for, the missing life-force that has left our communities starved, the mystic union that every soul seeks. She slips elusively away from us, like the slippery silver fish that slithers from our grasp, and overwhelms us in sudden, thunderous embrace. In many ways the quest and struggles of woman are her search for union with this cosmic love.

There are very few myths that give a "heraic" guide for women, though more are now being written. Lynn Andrews has given us *Medicine Woman* and *Flight of the Seventh Moon*, which depict her own shamanic quest for power and wholeness, or "medicine." Though limited by its exclusively heterosexual resolution and its tendency to sound a bit contrived at times, this tale is a stunning saga and very inspirational. We are in sore need of such legends that show the mythic levels of our own struggles and give examples of solutions, goals achieved, battles won.

One very outstanding heraic myth has survived—that of Eros and Psyche, retold at the beginning of this lesson. Jean Shinoda Bolen, M.D., a feminist and Jungian therapist, discusses this myth from a psychological point of view in her excellent book *The Goddess in Everywoman*. She interprets Psyche as the "Aphrodite woman," meaning a type of woman in today's society who is primarily influenced by this archetype. Aphrodite is a goddess set apart in Bolen's book, with traits in common with all the other Goddess archetypes. She encompasses and yet transcends them all, and Bolen appropriately calls her the Alchemical (transformative) Goddess.

Bolen's goddesses are patriarchal. She has drawn upon patriarchal myth and real case histories of her experiences in therapy. Thus her goddesses are the adaptations of real women caught between genuine archetypal forces and the demands of a male-dominated system. Yet in this context they are wonderfully described and most accurately portrayed. I highly recommend this book. But in order to find true liberation and make any real changes in this world, I am certain that we must go back, back, farther into the past and deeper into ourselves to find the pure and original archetypes that take us beyond male-identified roles, beyond intellect and "psychology," to the Goddess Herself.

Some patriarchal myths contain female symbolism that we can extract and use for our journey. Such a one is the myth of Psyche, which we also find echoed in the familiar fairy tales of *Beauty and the Beast* and *East of the Sun and West of the Moon*. All of these tales show a woman's mystic union with her lover, who is numinous and divine, at once a deathly and frightening force and a force of beauty and union. Once she comes to know his nature, she loses him, and then must perform a variety of tasks in order to regain him. Inherent in the symbolism of the tasks are psychological and spiritual messages. Bolen and other Jungians have made some inroads into discovering the meanings of the various tasks of Psyche.

The Sorting of the Grains: Years ago, when I used to act out this story with my children, it occurred to me that the grains represented thoughts, for what else appears within us in such profusion and can be so hopelessly entangled? Bolen corroborates my theory: ". . . when a woman must make a crucial decision, she often must first sort out a jumble of conflicted feelings and competing loyalties . . . an inward task, requiring that a woman look honestly within, sift through her feelings, values, and motives, and separate what is truly important . . ." The ants, says Bolen, represent the work being done on an instinctive, intuitive level. Psyche sleeps while the work is accomplished; she allows instinct to take over. In an age of rational thought and achievement through effort, this is an important message for us. It is easy to see a strong resemblance between this mythical approach to problem-solving and the approach of the five-pointed star. The sorting of seeds is a lovely metaphor for the work done in the air element of the star—the cutting and separating and organizing of mental process, and especially, the Naming.

Finding the Golden Fleece: Bolen says that the Fleece represents power in this world, and that feels right, except I would add to this the meaning of power in the other worlds as well. Psyche learns to circumvent the danger by receiving the power "indirectly" or at night, when the dangerous rams of competition and conflict are at rest. As a matter of fact, she achieves all of her ends indirectly, if you think about it, leaving the problem to instinct, or the deep self. In this way she can keep her sweetness and her softness, and maintain her gentle, compassionate nature. I would connect the Golden Fleece with the Fire arm of the star, for it grows on the great Rams of the Sun. The male macho way of getting power is to fight and clash one's antlers and attempt to subdue an enemy. But the ancient feminine way is to gather and weave and spin and wait, gather and weave and spin the power in . . . Truly Aphrodite and Athene and Arachne must be one!

Capturing the Waters of Life: This turbulent stream is the great heaving tide of passion, of emotions and all the ups and downs our feelings can take us through . . . And yes they are beset at times with danger, slipperiness, the risk of drowning. Psyche gains control of this force by employing the overview of the eagle's detached perspective. In witch's language she balances the water with the air, the emotions with analysis and understanding.

The Descent into the Underworld: Bolen suggests that Psyche's main lesson here is learning to say "no" to those who would take her energy by appealing to her sympathies at a time when her own journey is the priority. Another fairytale comes to mind, about the young woman who must climb a mountain to get the treasure at the top. All along the way are stones who cry out to her for help; they are actually people who were turned to stone by a wicked wizard. Once she reaches the treasure she is able to free them all, but if she stops to help anyone on the way, all will be lost and she will become a stone herself. This is wonderful wisdom for today's soft, giving women; often we become trapped in helping others at the cost of liberating ourselves. It seems natural that Psyche's trip into the underworld be aligned with the Spirit and Earth arms of the star and the mysteries thereof.

To me the most important aspect of Psyche's story is the Love that she feels, seeks, and wins. One wonders if there was not an earlier version of the story in which her union is with Aphrodite, the Goddess of Love Herself. Aphrodite's anger and jealousy must come from the more recent patriarchal mythos that engenders competition and hatred between women over the allegiances of men. Yet even in this tale the goddess' powers are undisputed. Psyche must cooperate and win her favor in order to find the love that she desires. As a force of passion and desire, Aphrodite definitely has her needs and makes her demands. Perhaps earlier versions of Psyche's tasks referred to the novice priestess' initiation into the Goddess' temple of love.

All the goddesses Bolen describes in such winning detail can be found in the old triad of Maiden, Mother and Crone, but not broken up into so many parts. The very number and the conflicts between them reveal fragmentation that we must heal. It is true that Bolen is also concerned with healing, and the last part of her book is devoted to finding harmony among the goddesses within. I salute her for a landmark study and a truly intelligent and loving approach to finding solutions. The danger of this book, however, is that we may be led to accept these versions of the goddess as authoritative. Our real healing can begin here, but eventually must take us beyond. All goddesses are one goddess, and returning to this awareness is the ultimate healing.

An important aspect of this is the link between Aphrodite and the Mother. Patriarchy separates the Mother and the Lover, a habit which has proven devastating for women. Mothers are cast aside, especially when they begin to show signs of age. Even during the child-rearing years mothers are widely rejected as lovers. Only young maidens are considered eligible. Aphrodite *is* the Mother; this is the lesson that we must learn. She is the full moon, pregnant with life, overflowing with fertility, nurturance, and passion. These things were never meant to be separated. Nowadays if a lover tells a woman, "You remind me of my mother," it is the voice of doom, and means the end of passionate feelings. In ancient times a woman was Whole. Her Maiden, Mother, and Crone aspects were equally adored, respected, appreciated. All of her life stages, from growth to bloodflow to pregnancy to birth to lactation and menopause were recognized as part of the endless and miraculous cycles of life. To be in love was to be in love with life and Her . . . and so we come to realize that the

Goddess is truly One and all her aspects go back to this ultimate oneness. The Patriarchal myths show Her fragmented, thereby diluting Her powers. The Nine Muses were once a single Muse, the Mountain Mother of Helicon. The Moon, though she goes through her many phases, is still One Moon. We urgently need to redeem the ancient unifying oneness of the Goddess, our source, creatrix of all. In so doing we redeem the concept of woman as lovable and worthy of passion at all the stages of her life. Only then will Mothers and Crones cease to be rejected, blamed, and cast out.

In realizing this, I have come to feel that Aphrodite is the Goddess Herself. A woman who is influenced by the Aphrodite archetype suffers much from the oppressive mores of this world. Her strong sex drives are considered shameful, and her independence a threat. Yet just the fact that she is the object of so much disapproval and/or exploitation is a sign of her numinous power. If we had a society that honored the Aphrodite qualities, we might truly see what peace on earth is like.

Aphrodite is Passion. Aphrodite is Connectedness. She is powerful, yet can be gentle and yielding as well. She is vulnerable and can "disarm." She is beauty, ecstasy, inspiration. She inspires religious devotion and a passionate regard for the life force. Her love is unconditional and lasts forever. She *is* the life force, bringing birth and manifestation, sustaining all creation. Aphrodite is the primordial original Goddess force. Hers are the missing qualities in the violent, harsh and alienated world of today. Therefore, let us bring back Aphrodite in all Her splendor, the Golden One who will heal us!

The Goddess of Love fills us with Her magnetism and ecstasy, awakening our kundalini or Shakti fire. She connects our chakras in passion, teaching us the mysteries of union and separation.

Suggested Projects

1. Write a pact or set of promises to the Goddess of Love. You can use the one in the Summer Solstice ritual provided in Cycle 8, adapt it to suit yourself, or create a new one. Address such issues as spiritual versus non-spiritual sexuality, sex with or without love, casual sex, playful sex, the gender of lovers, the number of lovers, commitment, exploitation, motivation, and so on. Take your time; such promises are not lightly made. Sign your pact ceremoniously with moonblood or any other red liquid that has been consecrated to this purpose.

2. Create and perform a ritual in honor of Aphrodite or any other love Goddesses you prefer. Use the Summer Solstice ceremony in Cycle 8 as a model, or create one of your own. Include the signing of your pact, as outlined above. Write up the experience in your *Book of Shadows*, and save it for future rituals.

3. Create and perform an Aphrodite ritual with your lover. You can use the Ritual for Lovers in Cycle 10, page 269. Write about this one too.

4. Cast a spell to bring love into your life or to strengthen an existing love relationship. You can make a love-charm as outlined on page 328 of this Cycle. Make a special Aphrodite altar with red draperies, roses, rose-pink candles, dried rose petals for burning, and an image of a love Goddess. Full moon is a good time for love magic. Carve the candles with winged hearts for love and freedom, and anoint them with rose water or rose oil. When all is ready, cast a circle and call upon Aphrodite to come and bless your workings and grant your requests. Bless your love charm by passing it through the smoke of the burning petals, then place it 'round your neck with appropriate visualizations and incantations. If there are obstacles to your loving, you can banish these. Take a black stone and project visions of all the obstacles into it, then plunge the stone in a bowl of water to clear it. Replace all that you have banished with visions of love. Embellish this ceremony in any way you wish, then give thanks to Aphrodite and bid Her farewell until next time. Open the circle and snuff out the candles whenever you feel the time is right. Keep and wear the love charm continuously, until you feel the spell has come to fruition.

5. Do some research on love Goddesses around the world. Find out what their stories are, their powers, attributes and deeds. Learn their names and memorize them so that you can chant them easily in rituals and spells. Contrast the qualities of different Goddesses from different cultures. See which ones have parents or children, and which do not, and what sort of relations they have with them, if any. Some good books

to start with are *The Women's Encyclopedia of Myths and Secrets*, by Barbara G. Walker, *The Book of Goddesses and Heroines*, by Patricia Monaghan, *Jambalaya*, by Luisah Teish, and *The Greek Myths*, by Robert Graves.

Questions to Ponder

1. Do you identify with Aphrodite, or some other love Goddess?

2. Do you fall in love easily?

3. Have you been hurt in your passions?

4. Have you been fulfilled in your passions?

5. Have you been blocked in your passions?

6. Do you experience lovemaking as spiritual?

7. Do you feel confident of your own beauty?

8. Is there a steady flow of passion in your life?

9. If so, are you able to maintain your selfhood?

10. Can you identify with the tasks of Psyche? What do they mean to you? Have you experienced any of them in your own life?

11. Have you, or anyone else you know, ever been put down or ostracized for having passionate feelings? How do you interpret this?

12. Do you understand the link between love and magic? How are they the same? How different?

13. If you identify as a witch, is this compatible with the loves in your life?

Reading and Other Resources

Lynn Andrews, *Medicine Woman* and *Flight of the Seventh Moon*.
Apuleius, *The Golden Ass*, a translation by Robert Graves.
Mary Barnard, *Sappho*.
Jean Shinoda Bolen, M.D., *The Goddesses in Everywoman*.

Anne Cameron, *Daughters of Copperwoman*. This has a wonderful story about a bear that falls in love with a woman.

Kim Chernin and Renate Stendhal, *Sex and Other Sacred Games*.

Mary Daly, *Gyn/Ecology*.

Andrea Dworkin, *Our Blood, Woman Hating*.

Dione Fortune, *Moon Magic* and *The Sea Priestess*.

Elsa Gidlow, *Sapphic Songs*.

Robert Graves, *The Greek Myths* and *The Song of Songs* (translated by Graves). Also see the original *Song of Songs* in the *Bible*.

Esther Harding, *Woman's Mysteries*.

Jane Ellen Harrison, *Prologemena*, *Themis* and *Epilogemena*.

Karl Kerenyi, *Goddesses of Sun and Moon*.

C. S. Lewis, *'Til We Have Faces*.

Kate Millett, *Sexual Politics*.

Marge Piercy, *Woman on the Edge of Time*.

Charlene Spretnak, *Lost Goddesses of Early Greece*.

Other Resources:

The Beltane Papers' Octava: Spiritual Feminist Gazette for the 8 Feasts. Octava, P.O. Box 8, Clear Lake, WA 98235.

Jeanne Gallick, "Life on Lesbos," Published in *Matrix Women's Newsmagazine*, 108 Locust, Santa Cruz, CA 95060.

For background on parthenogenesis, see:

Gina Covina and Laurel Galana, *The Lesbian Reader, An Amazon Quarterly Anthology*.

Elizabeth Gould Davis, *The First Sex*.

Helen Diner, *Mothers and Amazons*.

Special thanks to Bonnie Reitz for providing information on biological varieties.
*Note: Velthmyn is a word I coined—a combination of velvet and mythic. Withy means willow.

CYCLE 13

Return

May the circle never be broken
May the earth always be whole
May the rattle ever be shaken
May the Goddess live in my soul . . .
                                     —*Circle of Hecate*

You come to the last passageway, the final cavern deep in the darkening earth. This one is line entirely with rose quartz, the love stone of Aphrodite. In the center is a round altar, made of the same rosy stone. Two rose-pink candles are aglow, filling the space with warm gold. At the altar's center a crystal fountain of pure water murmurs.

You sit for awhile and give honor to the Goddess of Love. She is the first and last mystery, the ecstatic impulse of desire. You dip your fingers in the cool water, anoint your heart chakra, womb and brow, then fill cupped hands and drink. How sweet and clear are her waters. You find a censer filled with dried rose petals, and light them for an offering. The scent of roses breathes into you, as you gaze around this cave, glowing with the warm love-light of Aphrodite. Somewhere there is music playing, and a woman softly singing. Your three companion Goddesses come and sit with you, caressing you and holding you tenderly. It is so peaceful and beautiful here; you could stay forever.

"It's time to start back," says Themis gently, ever the practical one. Idea jumps up and tugs at your hand. "Come! The world is calling." Mnemosyne hands you the silver ball of thread. "Time to rewind," she smiles.

You rise and take the thread. It is smaller now, its endless strand unwound and stretching with a soft gleam back and back, back and back into the space and times you have visited. As you begin to re-wrap the silky gossamer, it grows taut and gently tugs at the ball, pulling you. Mnemosyne is right beside you, whispering in your ear. "Just let it take you," she instructs, "back through the chambers for review, back toward the entrance, where we will pause to prepare you for re-emergence into the world."

Your feet move of their own volition, becoming light as air, and the walls and caverns slide by, as if in a dream. Back and up you travel, relaxing into the tug of the silver ball in one hand, rewinding the thread now swiftly, now slowly, with the other. You are drawn to a special chamber of green and golden citrine crystal, the stone of teachings and new ideas. Upon one wall there turns a great Wheel, a mandala filled with many beautiful designs. Idea leaps across the gleaming floor, and turns a somersault of delight. This is one of her favorite caves.

Upon the Wheel is encapsulated all the thealogical Goddess principles you have been shown by following the thread. "Belief creates reality," says Themis, "and our own symbol system gives us the power to decide what that reality shall be. Imagine yourself inside the Wheel, standing at the center. Know that all the parts of the patterns are parts of the universe as well as yourself."

"Memorize the design," says Mnemosyne, and it will always be with you, giving you a reality to model yourself upon, a truth to rely on. Whenever you have need of it, you can remember the Wheel, and it will help you to create ritual, to heal, to recall old visions and discover new ones. Learn and memorize my sister, memorize and learn . . ."

At the core of the Wheel is Goddess, source and center of all. This is the foundation stone upon which all the rest is built, the Goddess/Self of all creation and of every individual being. She births and contains all the myriad forms of Her making, sends them forth and draws them back into Herself in eternal transformation. She is the One from which emanates the Many, the primal form that sculpts Herself in endless variation. Women and men are Her children, equally sacred in Her sight, as are all the animals, plants, insects, rocks, elves, fairies, angels, devas, grains of sand . . . She is like the first ripple at the center of the pond when we throw a pebble into the water. From Her all ensuing, spiralling ripples evolve.

This oneness is particularly significant in re-evaluating our ideas of gender and duality. Instead of viewing our universe in terms of two opposing forces mutually manifesting all, we are placing pairs within a larger, central perspective. This allows us to view both woman and man as kinfolk with a common source, basically the same and not necessarily opposite. Within this context all variety of loving and relating are acceptable and normal. By seeing ourselves as equals within the loving embrace of our Mother, we can move beyond the hierarchical structures on which the present society is based, and into more cooperative forms of interaction.

Placing the Goddess at the center of all things not only relieves us of polarizing splits and authoritarian hierarchies. It also gives us a new model of authority, that of Mother and Child, or the principle of nurturance. She or he who nurtures, who cares for the young, the old, the infirm, is the true authority. In the authentic matriarchies the mother was the center (not the top!) of the tribe. Her authority was based on love and concern for those she nurtured, and this gift was held in reverence. Social order was based on this Mother-type authority. Nowadays we see a widespread hatred for the authority of the Mother, and mothers themselves often discard it and emulate the power-over forms of patriarchy.

A WITCHES' WHEEL

FOR A GODDESS-CENTERED REALITY

Begin at the Center, and travel the spiralling line....

The Witches' Wheel: Key to Subjects Represented
(Beginning at the center)
1) Goddess/Self/Within
2) Maiden/Mother/Crone
3) Five-Pointed-Star (Spirit, Air, Fire, Earth, Water)
4) Eleven Directions
5) Eight Holy Days/Women's Mysteries/Chakra-Runes
6) Thirteen Tree-moons
7) Thirteen Planets
8) Zodiac
9) Womanrunes

Hatred of the authority of the Mother is based on the anger and jealousy of the younger male race who overthrew Her. Natural authority sustains life, as when a mother seizes her child from in front of an oncoming car. This has been replaced with authoritarianism, or power-over authority based on control, class differences, intimidation, scarcity, and status brainwashing.

The authority of the nurturer is like that of any good mother, whether it be as teacher, sustainer or facilitator; that is, it is an authority that ultimately phases out. Nurturing parents try to be sensitive to the growth phases of the child. They sense when the child is ready to walk and no longer needs to be carried. They know when the child is ready to take on more responsibility and when the child is ready to take wing. Understanding parents let go and encourage the child on her/his way. A good teacher knows when to say, "I have taught you all I can, now let's be friends or move on . . ." It is my hope that those of you who decide to become teachers of the craft will practice this nurturing model of authority so that you will not be helping to propagate a society of mass groupies, but one of self-empowered individuals.

During the period when the receiver is depending on that authority, it should be respected and honored. For this is the Goddess incarnate as Mother, She who sustains through Her wisdom, Her skill, Her commitment, Her taking of responsibility, Her supportiveness. It is essential for the healing of our world that we begin once again to value this type of Mother authority, as was done in the ancient matriarchies. We must also realize that the nurturers need to be nurtured; Mother Earth Herself needs our love, and human mothers need our care too.

These Goddess-centered concepts dissolve another major split—that between the Self and the Other. When every individual is valued and embraced, we can see that there is no contradiction between these two. It is, in fact, simply another circle which I have chosen to name Me/Us/You. A view like this makes an equalitarian society possible.

The next section of the Wheel is the threefold expression of the Goddess, Her manifestation as Maiden, Mother, and Crone. Maiden/Mother/Crone teaches us the Great Round of Being, the endless cycles of birth and life and death on every level of experience, from the most personal to the most universal. Everything can be seen as doing Maiden/Mother/Crone, Maiden/Mother/Crone, around and around, again and again. Matter itself blinks in and out of existence continually, as physicists and Eastern mystics have found. Everything has a beginning, a middle, an end, and a new beginning. The Moon is doing Maiden/Mother/Crone as she cycles through her dark phases and her light phases. The seasons are doing a prolonged MMC cycle. Our days can also be seen as having a birth, a life, and a death, or morning, noon, and night.

When we understand cycles we are assured of eternal renewal and our own immortality, for a new birth always follows a death. As the Native Americans say, there is no "death," only a change of worlds. Maiden/Mother/Crone teaches us about the cycles of our own lives as women and the mysteries of our passages through Birth,

Bleeding, Passion, Childbirth, Aging, Death, Learning, and Rebirth. And Maiden/Mother/Crone provides us with a flowing model that can take us out of the either/ors of patriarchy. When stuck in a conflicted two, we can search for a third and mediating factor, place it in the middle and set up a flow. Three is a circle; two is a line. All opposites are connected, and dependent on one another for their existence. Attempts to exalt one and deny the other only cause pain.

The circular model can be applied to every aspect of human society: economics, politics, assemblies, schools, ceremonies, the shape of buildings and cities, personal relationships, and the many uses of energy and power. Circles are important in resolving all the various forms of scarcity that exist in our society today. In the cosmos all energy flows; stuck energy leads to stagnation, illness, deprivation and eventually death. Hierarchies are often maintained by scarcity. The worker must bow to the will of the boss because he needs money; the renter must bow to the will of the landlord because she needs shelter; the student must bow to the will of the teacher because she needs credit, and so on. We can see this scarcity principle used in personal relationships as well. For instance, the parent who controls the child by threatening to withhold love. By moving from this linear form of interaction to a circular, flowing form, we can create abundance of all things for all people.

For example: sit a group of people in a circle and have them pass a rattle. Each person has a turn to speak while everyone else listens attentively. This form creates an abundance of communication. Everyone is heard, seen, acknowledged and supported; no one is left out. The symbol of the rattle can be translated into many human interactions. Even when we are not literally sitting in a circle we can understand that on a larger scale we are part of a circle of friends, communities and nations. If each member gives and takes energy—love, recognition, communication, support, fuel, food, money, attention, whatever it may be, and sends it 'round, there will always be a flow. In fact, there will be an overflow. Buckminster Fuller taught us about synergy: combine the energies of a group and you get more than the sum of its individual parts. This is synergy—more than enough; the next thing beyond energy.

The circle is also the magic circle, that special realm we create when we leave the routines of daily life and waking consciousness. And it is the circle of our own personal qualities that Maiden/Mother/Crone so beautifully represents. Maiden/Mother/Crone helps us to "take back the night," in every sense, for it helps us to accept and affirm our dark sides. Women taking back the night are women taking back their magic, the dark realm of the moon and the unconscious, symbolized by the Crone and the Dark Maiden. This is the realm where we cast our spells and project the visions that create our chosen realities. This is the place of mystery, the dark of the moon, the dark of the womb, the hidden side of us that has been so repressed, the undulating, swooning, pulling, sensual, watery and oh so sensitive side . . . the power to pull, as the moon pulls the tides, a very great power indeed. Today we see few images to affirm it, except for weak and evil ones such as cruel and beautiful witches, or meek and submissive Mary. But if we delve into past mythologies we find powerful images of women being openly sexual, openly magical, strong, self-confident, respected. To reclaim the dark is to reclaim our psychic powers and take back the privilege of thinking our own thoughts and projecting our own images. It is to end the brainwashing and scripts taped into our minds that tell us what to think, what to believe in. It is realizing that we are women and we are powerful when we hold a common vision of our own liberation.

This is what the witches knew and were feared for, burned for, raped for. This is why many women are seeing themselves as witches today, because we are realizing that we once had the power to heal and invoke spirits and bring good weather and nourish and keep the community peaceful. Now we have priests who say they are the keepers of our sacred mysteries, and teachers who say they are the knowers of our history and the guides of our children, and doctors who say they are the makers of health, and police and soldiers who say they are the keepers of the peace. But when we look at the world they have made we can only wonder—where are the goddesses, where are the mysteries of woman, where can the children learn of the history of woman? "Without a sense of history there can be no sense of self." Here we can see another circle—the circle of time and history, and the truth that must ever re-emerge to heal us.

The next segment of the Wheel is also a circular form. It is the five-pointed star of the witches, which symbolizes the elements of air, fire, water, earth and spirit. All natural forms and creatures, the animals of the earth, the birds and insects of the air, the creatures of the water, the beings that dwell in fire and the inner planes, can be included in this symbol. Humankind encompasses all these zones and interacts between and among them to varying degrees. We are each also a small universe of the elements, containing within us the fires of action and will, the waters of emotion, the earth of our bodies, the air of our minds and thoughts, and the spirit of our psyches. There are endless levels of meaning in the witch's star, some of which we have already discussed, many of which you will undoubtedly continue to discover.

In addition to the oneness of the Goddess-centered view, and the cycle of Maiden/Mother/Crone, the five-pointed star is extremely useful and liberating with regard to gender. With the star we can go into this subject in more detail, and deal with the qualities traditionally assigned to the male and the female. As Andrea Dworkin so eloquently puts it:

> One basic principle of reality, universally believed and adhered to with a vengeance, is that there are two sexes, man and woman, and that these sexes are not only distinct from each other, but are opposite. The model often used to describe the nature of these two sexes is that of magnetic poles. The male sex is likened to the positive pole, and the female sex is likened to the negative pole. Brought into proximity with each other, the magnetic fields of these two sexes are supposed to interact, locking the two poles together into a perfect whole . . .

The male sex, in keeping with its positive designation, has positive qualities; and the female sex, in keeping with its negative designation, does not have any of the positive qualities attributed to the male sex. For instance, according to this model, men are active, strong, and courageous; and women are passive, weak, and fearful. In other words, whatever men are, women are not; whatever men can do, women cannot do; whatever capacities men have, women do not have. Man is the positive and woman is his negative.

. . . This diseased view of woman as the negative of man, "female by a certain *lack* of qualities," infects the whole of culture. It is the cancer at the gut of every political and economic system, of every social institution. It is the rot which spoils all human relationships, infests all human psychological reality, and destroys the very fiber of human identity.

—From *Our Blood*, the final chapter: "The Root Cause"

It is so important, I feel, that we find an alternative model for understanding the natural energies of men and women that places us in positions of equality. All subjections originate with the subjection of women. Change this essential corruption, and all other healings must follow naturally, through all levels of society. Dworkin goes on in her article to propose the androgyny theory, but I think the five-pointed star is even better (many thanks to Debra Kaufman, who first led me to this idea), for it transcends dualism and gender roles altogether. Now instead of seeing male and female as items on two lists such as passive-aggressive, light-dark, and so on, we can envision such qualities as earthy, airy, watery, spiritual, and fiery, without having to genderize or linearize them in any way. No longer do we have to be a society divided against itself, or individuals divided against ourselves. Now we can see whole communities of whole people each true to their own natures and capable of loving in any form they may desire.

The five-pointed star is also a guide for doing magic, for casting spells and enacting rituals. It reminds us of the powers we all possess: visioning, naming, willing, loving, and manifesting. This is the magical process, from imagination to manifestation. The Witch's Star helps us to remember our tools of magic: the cup of emotions, the blade of penetrating mind, the flame of our will and actions, the pentacle of our earthy bodies, the infinity sign or spirit-guide. This star is in itself a medicine wheel and can be used in any number of ways. It can spin, so that emphasis can be placed in any particular arm or arms of the star as appropriate. Point the fire arm upward to raise energy, for example, or the earth arm downward for grounding.

The next aspect of this Witch's Wheel is spherical: the seven directions Before, Behind, To the Left, To the Right, Above, Below, and Within, or North, South, East, West, Above, Below, and Within. Here we move from the level of form to that of time and space, setting ourselves within the larger universe. The directions help us to orient ourselves so that we can find our center and know where and when we are placed. In casting a circle they help us to create a mini-universe where we are protected on all sides and can contain the power we are generating. The directions give us stability, and therefore security, as explained in Cycle 10.

Many witches and magic makers cast a circle of four directions and four elements. As explained before, I feel this sets up a linear and oppositional view of reality. I have noticed that these traditions that propagate a foursquare universe are often earmarked by gender duality, usually with male over female, sometimes subtly, sometimes overtly. I have also seen a propensity to "command" the elements, deities, and forces. Phrases like "let all the elements do my will," or "do my bidding . . ." or the idea that Morgaine "commanded" the mists to lift or descend over the lake of Avalon are common. These are power-over concepts and often go hand in hand with dualistic and square grids. The idea of a human being controlling nature is inherently patriarchal, and is the basis for this type of magic. It goes along with hierarchies and dominant/submissive relationships.

As my friend Julie says, you don't command the elements or gods, you *ask*. We must return to a respect for the tree will of all conscious beings, to a respect for the forces of nature, for only then can our own free wills be honored. We must learn to ask the goddesses to appear because they want to, to ask for abundance because we have given it, to see this as a flow, based on mutual regard.

In conjunction with these foursquare grids I have notice the use of words like "lord" and "queen," "Master" and "Mistress." I have seen liturgies and ritual plans where much bowing and scraping goes on; the goddess or god appears and we must bow before her/him. I feel we should question this kind of approach to religion for it may serve to perpetuate the very system that is harming women, the earth, and all of us. Cooperative models are based on the simple idea that all beings are divine and equal, that none should be subject to the will of another, except within the natural nurturer/child dynamic, as explained. This is why, in my Rainbow Cone invocation (page 29) I say, "My legs bend to kneel beside thee," and not "before thee." To kneel together is to bend together, to allow oneself to surrender and share power, without making oneself more or less than another. This does not mean we cannot feel the inspiring awe of the Goddess' incomprehensible greatness, nor that we must puff ourselves up with false ego; but it means that we can worship without in any way diminishing ourselves.

Since I first developed the concept of seven directions, I have found four more: North-West, North-East, South-West, and South-East. I have added these into the Wheel, because they bring into alignment the eight holy days and the five-pointed star. Spirit is in the North, because that is the part of the sky we see at Winter Solstice. This is the most spiritual time of the year, because manifestation has gone "underground." Aradia aligns with North-East, Kore with East and the element of Air. South-East lines up with Diana and the element of Fire, as the year heats up and the Goddess bleeds and takes Her power. Aphrodite or Summer Solstice is South, partaking of the elements on either side, Fire and Earth. South-West is aligned with Habundia (or Lammas), and the element of Earth. This is the most manifest time, when the first harvests come in and the Goddess nurtures us with Her milk and honey. Persephone, time of aging and descent, is aligned with West and the element of Water. She dissolves and flows back toward Spirit as She becomes menopausal and goes into the dark. And Hecate, day of Death, is in the North-West. Above, Below, and Within are a bit awkward to include on a two-dimensional design, so I ask you to use your imagination. If the wheel were in three dimensions, and you were standing in the center as Mnemosyne suggests, Above would be over your head, Below would be beneath your feet, and Within would be within you.

Still, when all is said and done, I find all concepts of the directions debatable. For example, much of this information would have to change in the Southern Hemisphere. When we begin to think globally, everything must be re-examined. In my daily practices I rarely call the directions, though I am keen on creating flowing, circular, and spherical safe space. Perhaps the directions are like training wheels, something we may need for a time until we get our bearings, and the ability to define sacred space becomes more automatic. I know that some of the most powerful women's circles I have experienced had no mention of directions. These circles were soaring, exalting, filled with love, poetry, magnificence, and joy. And yet they were well defined and contained by the bodies, minds, energies, hearts and spirits of the women. Circles where everyone walks to the four corners and recites invocations for each are lovely in their own way too. It's fun to do all the gestures together, and some of the words are beautiful. But these circles, in my experience, do not soar or fly or swirl or spin out into that "other" zone which is so hard to describe.

My friend Carol laughingly comments, "Just as we have a Goddess of Ten Thousand Names, so do we have a religion with ten thousand opinions!" Yes this is true, and it may be one of the healthiest aspects of our movement. And so I offer these new ideas about the directions in that spirit, leaving you to decide what feels best. My main concern is that women's mysteries may not always coincide with the larger stream of mixed male-and-female mysteries, and can get lost in the shuffle. In many ways patriarchy puts us in boxes. Let us be sure that our religion helps to free us, rather than creating new traps to get stuck in.

After the directions comes the eight seasonal holy days of the solar year. This is Maiden, Mother, and Crone broken down into more parts, and represents the stages of the goddess' life, the life of the year, of individual woman, of the light and the dark tides, the planting and the harvest, and so on. Each of the Holy Days is a passage, a mystery, a birth and a death, and is especially relevant for community ritual and for the sharing of magic as culture. Thus with this segment of the Wheel we move from the individual perspective to that of the community. With the holy days we can mark time together and come together to empower one another, to cast spells for mutual abundance, support and peace. At the same time the passages of the year can be seen as deeply personal, for we all experience them in our unique and individual ways. As the seasons of the world go round, so do we each experience our personal lights, multicolors, and darks. As the seasons of our individual lives come round—our births, bloods, deaths, trystings, passages from child to adult, from adulthood to old age, our moves from one home to another—all of these can be understood as our inner "seasons."

The eight-fold year also gives us eight Names of the Goddess which we can learn and use for spells of power. These rituals take us beyond religious expression, for they are an endless fountain of culture. The poetry, art, foods, life habits, stories and traditions to be passed on, inventions that come out of planning and setting up rituals, history to be unearthed and remade—these are just a few examples of how religion becomes culture, and vice versa. Observing the Holy Days is so essential, giving shape and equilibrium to our lives, keeping the magic flowing, ever deepening our understanding of the mysteries, helping us to cope with the psychological and emotional stresses. They give us myths to live by, thus giving us power with all aspects of our lives, each other's lives, the life of the community, of nations, of the planet. Alignment is bliss on all levels of being . . . community is the ultimate healing.

As a priestess of the Goddess I have encountered many responses from students with regard to the Holy Days. Some are so turned off by their alienating experiences with Judeo-Christian celebrations that they have discarded all such observances. Others are enthusiastic and eager to join in the new traditions. It is my hope that more and more people will begin to observe nature-oriented holidays around the world, as I feel they are essential for propagating a healthy civilization.

As a Jewish woman, I have observed the strength and vitality such ritual observances can bring to a people. Though I didn't appreciate them very much as a child, and still feel turned off by their patriarchal aspects, I have come to see how important community celebrations have been in keeping the Jewish identity alive. One of my most outstanding memories is of the yearly reminder at Passover (which is near to Spring Equinox) that we as a people were oppressed, and that we escaped. The Jews are among the few groups I know who have kept some semblance of tribal consciousness—and responsibility to its members with a sense that one stands by one's own. I have seen an aliveness, a warmth, a joi de vivre that is often lacking elsewhere. I think this happens among any people that maintains its ethnicity, its culture and its rituals. As witches we are especially denuded of such traditions, having been so oppressed and fragmented for so many centuries. As women we have been divided into as many camps as there are patriarchal communities; we are a lost tribe. Nothing works to oppress and destroy a people so well as the destruction and dismantling of its culture and its rituals. We have seen glaring examples of this in our own country as the white man conquered the red race, made their religious practices illegal, forced their children to attend their schools, wear their clothes, observe their holidays.

The next segment is thirteen-fold, applying to the yearly cycles of the Moon. Although I have discovered that there are not always exactly 13 moons for every "solation" (solar year), it is fitting that we include them all on our wheel so as to have the information for all time.

Connecting with the moon, as we have said, is one of the essentials of witchcraft. In learning to keep time by Her cycles we can free ourselves from much of the structure of patriarchy. The moon gives us a clock that measures the time and the tides both within and without. She gives us miniature seasonal passages and keeps us in touch with the different aspects of ourselves—physical, emotional, and psychic. Luna gives us support and guidelines for the performance of spells and rituals. She enhances our ability to go into trance, to surrender, to be wild and spontaneous, to open up emotionally, to connect with the psyche of humanity, the planet, and of all the universe. She teaches us through her phases of crescent, full, and dark, the perennial wisdom of cyclicity, periodicity and immortality, as well as the phases of our own lives and personalities as we cycle through interaction, commitment, and withdrawal. For women the moon is especially connected to our blood, and so links us to all the mysteries of birth and life and death. The moon connects us with the trees and their stories and uses, as each of her cycles is named for one of these living kinfolk of the earth. In a society based on solar concepts and imagery, Luna is especially helpful in attuning us to the dark side and the many qualities associated with the deep self.

With the final segments of the wheel we move from the innermost to the outermost and discover the relationships between them, taking our consciousness out into space to encompass all the universe. We see our connections to the stars and planets, the interaction and shared consciousness of all created forms. The signs of the Zodiac and the planets of our Solar System give us clues to human personality, like the witch's star and the tarot. There are very convincing theories about a thirteenth sign of the zodiac, and so I have opted to incorporate Arachne, the Spider Woman, between Taurus and Gemini. I have also given the bodies of the solar system thirteen spaces, to include the Sun, the Earth, the Moon, and the newly discovered Chiron and Lilith. In addition I have provided some goddess names for these beings.

Whenever humans discover another being or phenomenon out in space there is a direct corresponding expansion of consciousness here on earth. Outer space and inner space are really the same, and comprise the next frontiers. It is natural that the migration into one will correspond with a migration into the other. When we went from seeing the Earth as flat to round, from seeing ourselves as earthbound to star travelers, our awareness of who and where we are in relation to one another and to the universe expanded accordingly. Thus it is appropriate that a modern witch's reality-grid would include these dimensions.

Finally, I have added an outer circle of runes, giving us a series of symbols that can be applied to the many details of our lives. Who knows what further circles may be added to the Wheel in times to come. But ultimately, it is the Circle of Women or Sisterhood that encompasses all.

PREPARATION FOR RE-ENTRY
Unraveling the Dilemma of Patriarchy

Now as we come to the end of our cycles together, and the Thread guides you back to the entrance of the cave, let us consider the world you will re-enter, and what it will mean to come into it with the information and experiences you have gained.

Goddess-centered spirituality is based upon a circular view of reality. It teaches us to take example from all the wheels of life and creation, and learn to flow ourselves, in circular harmony. We know, however, that modern society is built not upon circles, but upon lines, squares, oppositions, and staircases. On every level the cutting apart of the female and the male breaks circles: the circle of wholeness within the self, the circle of the five elemental qualities, the circle of intimate relationships, the circle of human relations with animals and nature, and the circle of human exchange and cooperation.

At the center of all circles, I believe, is the Goddess, She who creates Herself from nothing, then reproduces Herself through all infinity. Out of the process of birth and rebirth comes all the ensuing forms and creatures of Earth and the Universe. Life first takes a female form, then produces male form.

In other words, man is the younger race. This is the inescapable reality of biological fact. Woman is His parent, the older race against whom He rose up in rebellion. Virgin birth is fact; the male is not always present in the perpetuation of the human species. All original ritual was "ritu" (from a Babylonian word meaning "to menstruate"), the cere-mony (ceres, cereal, the Goddess' gift of grain) of woman's yonic powers of blood, birth, periodicity, and pleasure. Out of the products of her body woman created magic, life, science, agriculture, community, and religion. The life source or "god" is female.

Men wanted the power. In many cases men were insanely jealous of the power. The stories of their horrific revenge abound in anthropological, historical and present day sociological data. The Australian Aborigines, for example, cut their penises lengthwise and hold them against their stomachs in ritual imitation of "the one with the vulva." In the Jewish "bris" or circumcision, the tender newborn genital is brutally mutilated as a "covenant with God." The ancient "Castrada" or young priests of Greece severed their testicles and offered them to their deity.

Men began by taking revenge on themselves, on their own bodies. Later they turned this violence on women. Priestesses old and young were systematically slaughtered in Crete. Temples and their officiates were annihilated in Israel. Witches were tortured, burned, raped and mutilated all over Europe for hundreds of years. Today women are still raped, battered and subjected to clitoridectomies, mastectomies, hysterectomies . . . not to mention all the more subtle forms of control under which they are kept.

The old Goddess of Life, Hera, was supplanted by the new god of war, Hera-cles, or Her-cules, as worth shifted from the gentle bleeding of the vulva to the violent, pain-wracked bleeding of the cut male body. To quell an enemy was the new icon, replacing the old love of mother-flesh. Blood sacrifice was yet to follow, then war, a legacy we still face today. Patriarchy is basically a great cut.

To consolidate the cut, man came up with an ingenious belief system. He separated himself from the female and declared that henceforth man and woman would be opposite to one another. Man would be strong and woman would be weak. Man would be wise and woman would be stupid. Man would be the Self and woman would be the Other. Man would be clean and woman would be unclean. Man would be objective and in control, woman would be out of control, a slave to her emotions. Man would be hard and woman soft.

Men introduced this belief system into the minds of succeeding generations, first by killing off those who believed differently, then by "educating" the remaining populations. At first he did it in the name of the Goddess and later in the name of his male gods. Today we are witnessing the death-throes of the society he has produced out of this insanity. All over the world people are starving, fighting, doped up, struggling, dying. Many species have already been made extinct. The Earth herself is out of balance. The atmosphere is so damaged we have begun to wonder if there will be enough air to breathe in the next hundred years. Children are born deformed; people are dying of cancer. Nuclear threat hangs over us all . . . the horrors are too endless to name. In severing himself from the female and all that she represents in nature and psyche, man has brought us to the brink of total destruction.

What is the solution? First of all, men and women both need to come to terms with the truth. Woman is older, but this does not mean better. Men need to look at their own fear, the deep and ancient fear of being extraneous. Then we all need to work together to heal this fear by helping men to feel a part of things, to see that they do have an essential and sacred role to play in the stream of life. Our dilemma is man's biology and his suppressed fear of it. Because of this unacknowledged fear he casts a shadow back on woman, naming her evil, lesser, etc. It is his own terror of being "less" that makes him strive to be "more." The solution is for him to learn to surrender and accept, make peace with his origins. Only then can he integrate and become them. Women can help, not by coddling his false ego, but by nourishing his true self and his "female" qualities, beginning with education of the boy children.

Men need to reclaim their womanness, in other words. They need to stop dividing themselves, suppressing all those aspects of themselves that were made anathema to "maleness." Equality of all beings must return to this planet with no more hierarchies and no more enforced heterosexuality.

What is this "womanness"? It is, first of all, the power of nurturance, the tender care of babies, children, the old and the infirm. It is loving life and taking care of it in all the ways that this can be done. It is the ability to be vulnerable, to swoon with ecstasy, to fall in love. It is the power of pull, of the moon and the tides. It is the ability to connect with all things and to feel the sacredness of being. It is the ability to be sensitive, to have feelings, to care, to cry, to be upset, to be filled with joy. It is the ability to be intuitive, to "sense" things, to be psychic. It is the ability to dream and to believe in dreams. It is the ability to make poems and songs, to be creative, inspired. It is to see sense in "nonsense," in the mythopoetic, non-rational view of reality. It is to go into trance, to surrender, to walk on hot rocks without being burned. It is the ability to recognize the soul and the eternal, to know that we have been here before, and will be again. It is to feel the cycles, the shifts of light and dark, the seasons, life and birth and death and transformation. It is the desire to celebrate and align oneself with these patterns alone and with one's community. It is the ability to be passionate, and compassionate, to be there when someone cries or is hurting, to give solace and comfort instead of scorn and the label of "loser." It is the ability to cooperate instead of competing, to form coalitions instead of opposing "teams," nations, worlds . . .

All human embryos are female first. The male Y chromosome is a broken X. Man is female. Scientists have discovered that the male womb and vagina exist inside the penis. Men have breasts; male babies are sometimes born with milk flowing. Men have cycles or tides, though not as visible as women's. Men can feel and cry. When boy babies are born they are just as tender and sensitive as the girls until they get trained out of it and "toughened" up. Men have the capacity to be all the things named above until they become socialized and suppress them. There are also many women with so-called "male" traits—women who are more hairy, deep-voiced, muscular. The truth is that we are not evenly divided into two distinctly different and opposite forms at all; we are all variations of the original form of woman.

Thus we can connect once again with our source, when we can learn to love Her and love her deeply, return to the Goddess in Her ancient and powerful oneness, all splits will be joined, all inequities balanced, all atrocities will cease. It is the one hope that we have—that people will catch on quickly enough to prevent total annihilation.

In the everyday sense this takes the form of loving woman and loving everything that has been deemed womanly. It is taking care of ourselves. It is taking care of our mothers. It is taking care of the earth, for one cannot take forever without giving back. It is enjoying the talents and powers and the fulfillment of every woman who walks this earth and celebrating her participation in every aspect of the community, both public and private. It is listening to what women have to say, or sing, or write, giving them a voice. It is learning to operate collectively instead of hierarchically, banishing forever the power-over forms of authority. It is learning to share everything—money, love, attention, recognition, food, and so on—allowing all of these things to flow evenly so that there is enough and more than enough for all. It is replacing jealousy with happiness for one another's successes, and the knowledge that we each have successes of our own.

It is becoming well known that thoughts are things, that we create our reality with our images and symbols. It follows that we need new and more wholistic symbols in order to change the world. Circles and cycles are natural. The whole universe is run on them. The human consciousness is already beginning to embrace them. People are meeting in circles, building round houses, seeking non-linearity (as in quantum physics), holograms, and spirals. It is time for the change, and it is already begun.

Many of us have experienced the cycles of growth and adolescence, adulthood and old age in our own lives. We have seen how we have a need to rebel against our parents, to separate ourselves from them for a time. Often we go through a period of resentment, even hating them. It seems that they have so much power and we resent their control of us. We feel our identity threatened with annihilation because we are so much like them, and our secret longing for re-submergence intensifies the threat. And so we push them away for a time, go off to develop our own reality, our own identity.

Then we grow up (hopefully!). We become sure and strong in our own identities. We look at our parents and realize that we love them. We are no longer threatened by their power nor offended by their human failings. They are people like ourselves, and we can accept our likenesses and our differences with equanimity. Now that we have seen more of the world and the struggles of being, we can understand better what they do and believe. It is now possible to have an equal, adult relationship with them, to reconnect with the life stream through the generations.

This is what must happen between the parent and child races of woman and man. It is time for man to grow up. His destructive adolescence must end, for if it does not, we will all be destroyed.

This writing is not to cast blame or point an accusing finger at one segment of the population. Women also must look to themselves for their responsibility in the scheme of things. We have been the oppressed, but we have also taken on the beliefs and assumptions of that oppression. Let us all look to see what ways we can change, and for loving solutions that bring us together in peace and harmony.

> Sisters
> Invoke the power of the spoon
> Stir up the cauldron
> Raise raise the warriors . . .
> Let confrontation be our sword
> Compassion be our shield
> A call to arms
> (Loving arms)
> But selfhood never yield . . .

When we Goddess-lovers attempt to explain our views we are often misunderstood. The assumption is that we are proposing another hierarchy, simply reversing the old male-over-female to female-over-male. This is because most people are still thinking in linear oppositions, and have not yet made the leap into circular forms. Opposition thinkers sometimes "flip their grids," or reverse the poles, thinking they are seeing an alternative. Hence we get the "radicals versus the establishment,"

GODDESS-CENTERED
MATRISTIC VIEW

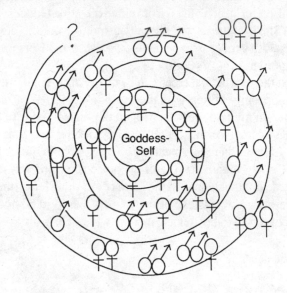

PATRIARCHAL DUALISM

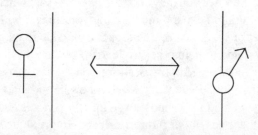

Beneath, Behind	Above, on Top
Negative	Positive
Weak	Strong
Dependent	Provider
Receptive	Agressive
Emotional	Intellectual

These images show the contrast between Goddess-centered reality
and the linear or polarized either/or view of patriarchy.

syndrome, in which rebels oppose those in power at one stage of the game, but invariably revert and become themselves the power-over controllers at a later stage. This is why linear revolutions have not changed the essential power-over structures of society.

The illustration on page 355 is my attempt to explain the unexplainable, and to show how very different linear reality is from circular reality. Goddess-centeredness is not hierarchical. She is at the center, not at one end of a pole! No one is beneath or above anyone else. All gender arrangements co-exist within Her embrace, equally sacred, equally important.

In this context the idea of "balance" can be misleading, for it often implies the adjustment of two opposing entities, as in the well-known Scales of Justice, held by the Goddess Athene. In my tarot deck I changed the scales in the Justice card to a spinning crystal pendulum. Now instead of looking to see if two ends of a scale are balanced. we look to see if there is a stuck place or wobble in the flow. And so, in moving from God-Goddess dualism to the all-encompassing Goddess-Centeredness, we move from the ideal of "balance" to the ideal of "equilibrium," the harmonious flow of cycling energies. Now instead of viewing the world in polar opposites, we can heal the split between all opposites and thus we will begin to unravel the dilemma of patriarchy.

Groups, Power, and Priestessing

In addition to political consideration, I want to encourage you to look to future directions for your magic. Some of you may choose to work as solo witches, but some of you may feel a natural urge to expand into sharing your magic with others.

There are a number of ways that one can reach out to share magic. You may wish to become a teacher, and to help others to learn. You may wish to find a few friends to do rituals with and share support. Some of you may be inspired to go at it in a big way and organize public events, a witch's newsletter, start a church, or organize a political lobby. Others may choose to go into the schools and bring magic to the children, who are the seeds of our future world, or simply share with children what they know. All of these are valid ways to spread the energy. I do not wish to put any pressure on, however; just being a witch and living your life can be enough in itself, and sometimes difficult. Whatever path the goddess takes you on must be the right one for you.

In case you should decide to get involved with a group, I am providing a few guidelines gleaned from my own experience as a priestess and feminist activist. Perhaps they will be of some use to you at a future time.

Passing the Rattle: I have found it wonderfully whole-making to sit in a circle with a group of people of good will, and pass a rattle or some sacred object that designates the turn to speak. She who holds the rattle holds the power, in more ways than one. I'll never forget my early experiences with this process in '60s feminist consciousness raising groups. A topic would be selected, such as our experiences with marriage, children, other women. Each woman would talk for ten minutes or so, giving time to say a little about what she had been through. It was always staggering to me how transformed everyone in that room would be by the time we had gotten around the circle. We learned and saw things we had not seen before. We saw how much we had in common, that our oppressions were shared oppressions. For me it was the budding of sisterhood, and an abiding love for women, and the beginning of my liberation.

Since then I have learned so many things about communication and power and human beings through the process of passing the rattle. I have come to see that every voice must be heard before the whole story can be told and that the truth resides not in one person but in the center, in the agreed-upon truth of all present. From this I learned the incredible power of agreement—that it can move mountains.

Together we can do anything.

Passing the rattle is a way for every member to take responsibility, to participate fully in whatever may be happening. It is also a way for everyone to get support, for we all need to share our heart-songs, our ups and downs, our successes and struggles with someone who cares and is interested. Passing the rattle takes us out of isolation into a safe and empowering intimacy. It gives us the advantage of many points of view. It is an excellent form for dealing with conflicts, making decisions, balancing communication, verbalizing visions, planning rituals and casting group spells.

Creating Safe Space: Doing magic together requires love and trust. Success in this is dependent upon all participants coming together in a spirit of sisterhood. People may disagree, but no one should be mean or antagonistic toward another. People should like each other and enjoy each other for a group to do well together. Sometimes it is best to keep groups small, so that there is room for close friendships to grow. There must be an honesty, a willingness, to tell the truth about oneself, and a promise not to repeat such revelations elsewhere. A woman feels safe in a group where she knows everyone there is glad to see her, interested in what she has to say, concerned if she is in trouble, happy when she is happy. A safe group is one you can turn to when the going gets tough, for healing, insight, and the wonderful wisdom of woman. It is a place where you can expect honesty, but rot put-downs, where you know you will always be able to speak your mind freely.

Common focus: I have found that group sharing is the most rewarding when there is a shared focus. Random focus is nice for parties and other social occasions, but when a small group comes together to do magic, there is a need for some time to be spent when everyone's attention is on the same things at the same time. What these things are should be agreed upon to begin with, whether it be a shared vision, a poetic reading, a chant or teaching. Attention is a great power; we know from magic that whatever we pay attention to will eventually exist or manifest. When we synchronize this power in a group situation we get a synergy of magic power. I think it is important for people to learn how to put their synchronized attentions together, without being coerced or talked down to or having to play "audience." When people have a common focus you can feel the energy of it . . . there is a glow, a tingle in the air. It feels good! We are taken out of ourselves, as our energies merge into a unified purpose.

Commitment: Over the years of teaching women's groups I have gone the gamut from year-long commitments, to lifetime, to no commitment at all, to nine months, to three months. I have found that those who make the greatest commitment to the Goddess usually get the most rewards. However, people are varied and are pulled in many directions. Sometimes their spiritual process will take them elsewhere. I have found I must strike a compromise between their needs and mine. As teacher I found that drop-in groups, where there was no commitment at all, became draining on me. I was there, week in and week out, keeping the energy going, while everyone else came and went. It was impossible to get any continuity, to get information out or plan rituals and such. I realized that some commitment on the part of students was necessary for the group energy to flow well. It takes at least three months, meeting once or twice a week, for a group to form a bond and feel like everyone knows each other. Many witches say that a year and a day is a good amount of time for studying the craft with an eye to initiation. I like that amount of time myself, and am overjoyed when people show their readiness for this. However, I don't think this necessarily a rigid rule, and no one should be pressured or made to feel obligated.

Respecting varying viewpoints: One of the reasons I like the Neo-Pagan movement is because of its respect for the differing beliefs of its members. For a successful group mutual regard and basic human warmth are necessary. It is not necessary for everyone to agree on religious doctrine. I am pretty straightforward in my view that Goddess is the center, but I have had sisters in circle with me who see God in the center, or the God and the Goddess together, or even a life source that is neutral and nameless. Groups can be torn apart by bickering over what is *the* truth. Though I prefer to cast the seven directions or create a cone or sphere and declare it sacred space, some women prefer to cast four directions with four elements. Ritual can still be high and happy-making for everyone present, with each sister's magical views honored. The main thing is that we are together and sharing ourselves. We can enjoy one another's ideas and honor our own as well. We can even debate them in a spirit of enjoyment and learning. But when we forget that human love, sharing, and an appreciation for the power of individual choice are central, we can lose the very purpose we began with.

Leadership: One of the best models I have found for successful group leadership is the mother/child model discussed on pages 341 and 343. This is a hairy topic and women especially have much to learn (myself included!) about giving and receiving leadership. I won't go into it extensively here, except for a few brief guidelines. The most successful groups are where everyone feels empowered and a part of the decision-making process. A good leader is one who facilitates this, rather than simply imposing her own preconceptions on everyone. However, there are times when people need a strong person to take the energy and direct it for them, especially when they are new to the subject and to one another. When I direct groups I usually make more decisions and initiate more of the format in the early stages, and try to phase out my leadership as the members learn to take these responsibilities themselves. The better people know one another, the more sensitive people are to one another, and the less leadership is required. It is important to realize that leader/follower is another circle, that both are equally powerful and depend upon one another to exist. I cannot lead you if you don't want me to, nor do I wish to. Therefore, should you decide to become a group leader, I suggest you have very clear agreements with each member right from the start. Make sure there is mutual consent on all sides and that way no one feels they are being coerced. I have found it useful to begin each new group with individual interviews. This way there is time for each person to state her needs and expectations, and to let each other know what we wish to give. I have found it to be a pitfall to assume any of these things without discussing them first. *Mutual consent* and (remembering that) *leadership is a service* (not a coercion), are good phrases to remember.

(Note: Starhawk has some fine material on group dynamics in her books *Dreaming the Dark* and *Truth or Dare*. She also has written on this subject in the newsletter *Reclaiming*, which comes out of the collective she helped to create.)

Problems in Groups

The oppressor smiles smugly and rubs his hands with glee
When he sees the women fighting . . .
He still keeps the ring of power in his pocket
Because we the people
Haven't learned how to share it . . .

I first began leading women's circles back in the early '70s. I was quite naive about it at the start, of course, and had much to learn about group dynamics. I ran into pitfalls and patriarchal programming I had no idea existed. I jumped in eagerly, with innocence, my heart open to women. I thought we were all perfect and that once we got together everything would be wonderful and we would "turn the world around," as Pat Parker says. I have experienced glory and healing, and I have also experienced hurt and disillusionment. I want to share these thoughts with you, not only so that you will be better prepared, but also because you may be able to avoid some of the difficulties I encountered. After all is said and done I want to let you know that I have no regrets . . . I am glad I made the plunge, felt the pain and learned the things I learned because the process was growthful for me and for many of the women I have worked with. Despite the problems we learned many things and moved a few inches closer to creating the world of our hearts' desires. I am committed to working in groups of women, more so now than ever before. The joy of seeing women flower and take wing, discover the goddess in themselves, form bonds of understanding and love—these experiences are worth a great deal. And besides, with all the issues I have dealt with under my belt, I am better equipped to do it successfully.

Community is the ultimate healing, and magical community is the best of all. In a world that keeps us in isolation, suppresses women, divides us, perpetuates scarcity of love, economic flows and community support, we urgently need to break down the barriers. From a magical point of view, banishment is a helpful way to look for solutions. Remember the three steps to banishing: Naming, Dissolving, Replacing. What follows are names for some of the Demons that can be destructive to groups:

Splits: In circular theory, what seem like oppositions are ultimately connected, mutually creating, dependent on one another to exist. Splits are usually caused by people taking sides on each end and refusing to see the other point of view. It is a cutting of the circle and hence a breaking of the connection, and is a frequent cause of divisions among people.

Scapegoating: When one person, or a smaller group of persons become the focal point for the venting of rage, frustration, hostility, and so on, by a larger group, community, or nation. The witch-burnings and Nazi holocaust are outstanding examples of large-scale scapegoating. Smaller-scale scapegoating occurs within groups, where one person, or a smaller group of persons are accused, punished, ostracized, blamed, etc., for the ills that many may be suffering. Individuals can often scapegoat one another on a one-to-one basis, when they perceive one person as representing/containing the "enemy" or the oppressor.

The Staircase: The staircase is an insidious demon that attacks many groups. Everyone feels like she is on one step and trying to get to the highest or next highest. Those higher up are struggling to keep those lower down from climbing up, and those lower down feel inadequate, and hate themselves. Everyone is always comparing themselves and each other, deciding who is most worthy or less worthy of approval. Jealousies and competitions flourish, and usually the persons at the top get more powerful, while those at the bottom get more crushed. Like scapegoating, examples of the staircase effect can be found internationally, within groups, and between individuals. The caste or class system is a staircase. "God over Man over Woman over Child" is a staircase. "Man over nature" is a staircase. The United States over "underdeveloped countries" is a staircase. Staircases exist in most conventional forms of human interaction, from the school to the workplace to the church.

Pecking Orders: These are an extension of the staircase, where several members join up on one step, others on another step, and so on. They give one another clout, support one another in the conflict with all those other people on those other steps . . . they also give an illusion of oneness within the order and help members to forget their connection to the whole. These in-groups generally rally around a leader whom they use to represent them and whom they eventually sacrifice and topple from the pedestal.

The Pedestal: This is a modification of the staircase based on an either/or relationship between the boss/martyr and the slave/dependent. The pedestal is mutually created by both members. It is invariably exploded when the underling rebels and overthrows the person she has placed above her, dividing both people, who in the pain of it all, flee from one another in rage, neither seeing how she has helped to create the game.

Discrimination: This is when a person or group is rejected by another because of—you name it—race, size, class, gender, religion, age, sexual preference, disability, or just being "different."

Communication Breaks: Interruptions can be oppressive when less assertive people don't get to have their say. Some people are louder and get heard more often. Decisions can only be made on the basis of what was communicated, and unspoken perceptions can go by the wayside. "As I have the strength to take the rattle, so do I have the understanding to pass the rattle on." "She who holds the rattle holds the power." The power comes from the attention given to the one who is speaking. Aggressive people tend to jump in freely, which is good, but they sometimes forget to pay attention to those who are more quiet. Quiet people often suppress their ideas, and don't take the responsibility to speak up.

Scarcity: When some members feel there is not enough time, attention, support, interest, etc. for themselves.

Personal Insecurities: There are uncountable numbers of these, but one of the most effective in dividing groups is the personal fear of being strange, weird, different or unacceptable in some way. People who feel this way usually are afraid to contribute, and eventually disappear. Another is the illusion of powerlessness—that the group is being created by "them" and "I" have no effect on its decisions, qualities, etc.

Having named these demons, the next step of the banishing would be to send them away. This can be done with ritual, using all the magical techniques as outlined in previous Cycles. Here are a few ideas on what forms could be used to replace the banished ones:

Splits can be replaced by *Circles* and by *Mediation.* When caught in a conflicted two, find a third factor, look for the good or truth on either end, discard what is false and set up a flow. Also, remembering that we are all connected and divine is very helpful in preventing disagreements from becoming splits. If none of these things work, separation might be the best thing after all. We don't have to feel imprisoned with one another; there are always new patterns forming in the future, new connections to be made and lessons to be learned.

Scapegoating can be replaced by knowing who the true enemy is—the real perpetrators of oppression. Instead of casting blame on one person or a small group, it is important to realize that this only plays into the hands of the oppressors, keeping us divided and blaming one another. Those who have been scapegoated, such as Jews, black people, witches, gay people, women, fat people, poor people, etc. can band together in mutual support, instead of remaining divided. If we find ourselves wanting to pick on one person, let us look inside ourselves and see what old pain and anger we may be projecting, and realize that we all have faults, that no one has to be perfect, that we are not one another's enemy.

The Staircase can be replaced with the Circle of Equality, seeing that every person is beautiful, valuable, divine and essentially good. The circle of equality means that we each honor ourselves as well as one another, that no one is made more or less than another, that everyone has something precious and beautiful to give.

Pecking Orders would probably not even exist in a group where people feel equal. However there is sometimes a genuine need for people to pair off or meet in smaller clusters, and this can be very nourishing and positive, when based on good feelings rather than for purposes of gossip or consolidating divided power. Divided energy can be prevented by smaller groups sharing their experiences with the larger group.

The Pedestal can be replaced by cooperation and dividing the responsibilities evenly, as well as the rewards.

Discrimination can also be replaced by the circle of equality, like the staircase.

Communication Breaks can be replaced by attentiveness and sensitivity to one another, or by the rattle process, which symbolizes this.

Personal Insecurities often take prolonged work and healing techniques, but we can begin by giving one another and ourselves "strokes." This means telling ourselves and each other how wonderful we are, affirming this, letting ourselves believe and enjoy it.

Scarcity can be replaced by *abundance*, created by all members giving from whatever stores of energy they have, and by all members allowing themselves to receive.

The Goddess Ministry

"Our religion is powerful, but it must never
get too organized, or the magic will be lost . . ."
—Guess Who

It is clear to me that a widespread Goddess Ministry is badly needed in the world and that more and more people will be searching for this as the next decades progress. They will be looking for someone to turn to for spiritual support, someone who can offer this in a feminist context, someone who reflects their belief in the Goddess. Religion is the ultimate politics, for it reaches people "in their mysteries," as Z.

Budapest says. Social reality stems from the symbols and beliefs of people. In a world where women are hated, raped, robbed of their individuality and rights over their own bodies, denied an image of themselves as divine, made to feel that their sexuality, their bleeding, their emotions and passions are sinful and dirty . . . where the mysteries of birth and life and death are robbed of their numinous, sacred power . . . where the Earth herself is daily raped and torn . . . the myth of a beautiful, strong, powerful and loving Goddess is perhaps the most essential key to universal healing. The real soldiers, says Z., are the myth-makers and poets, the real battleground is cultural.

Those women who put themselves out as leaders, teachers and spiritual guides in the Goddess movement can find themselves in a vulnerable position. If, on the one hand, they present themselves as bosses or having power over those they lead, they can rightly be accused of patriarchal behavior. If, on the other hand, they deny their own gifts and powers of insight and bury their lights, many needed changes are lost to everyone.

As a teacher of Goddess mysteries over the past 15 years, I have run the gamut between these extremes, and have continued to seek for a working alternative. At first people would put me on a pedestal and later knock me down. In other words, they would adore me at first, but later resent me and have to find fault with me in order to redeem their own self-respect, because they had made themselves less than me. This can be a very painful situation for all involved.

When I realized what was happening I went to the other extreme. I said okay, there's no leaders here, let's do everything by consensus. But this didn't work either. Everything was chaos and nothing got accomplished, because no one wanted to take responsibility or make commitments and decisions. I felt frustrated and unfulfilled (the endless dilemma of women in patriarchy!) because the visions and insights I had to share were buried, as well as those of everyone else in the group. I made myself less than I was, because I felt intimidated by those who resented me taking power, and found myself repressing my own expressions.

These issues are basic because the resolving of them is crucial to social change. As we look at history we can see that revolutions have always been the replacement of one hierarchy with another. On the other hand, we the people can never take power as long as our energies are scattered. This means that the current hierarchy remains intact, because it is organized and we are not.

On page 364 are three sketches of the realities I am trying to describe. On the right is the hierarchical staircase of patriarchy. At the top is the leader, teacher, president, star, father, god, or whatever—the head honcho. The lines drawn between him and those on the lower steps represent attention, communication, and energy. As you can see, all of this energy is directed only to the top. The people below have no contact with one another, and all the energy moves in one direction. In other words, the respect, love, attention, money, power and support all go to the top. Some of these hierarchies are more benevolent, in which case there is a trickle-down of these essentials to those beneath. There is more to the higher steps, less to the lower. The

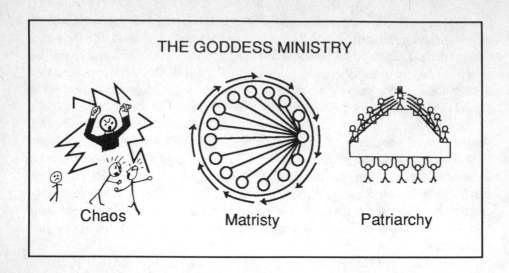

THE GODDESS MINISTRY

Chaos   Matristy   Patriarchy

more tyrannical the set-up, the less trickle-down of energy. In both situations the top-dog still gets most of the goodies, and must carry most of the responsibility. This model can be found at every level of patriarchal society, from the nuclear family to the classroom, to the church and state.

On the left hand is what seems to happen when people get fed up with the staircase. It is a hodgepodge of random energy, with some people fighting, some people controlling by being the loudest or most self-righteous, some submitting by being passive or intimidated, others leaving in disgust. Communication lines are scattered and decision is in conflict. Cliques of two or three or more form on the sidelines, adding to the embattled atmosphere, until they go off to form their own hierarchies. Some members become lone-wolf types and decide that all groups are a lost cause. Everyone loses and such groups generally fall apart, and guess where its members end up—in some old "respectable" hierarchy. At least they are organized and some form of survival is provided, despite the fact that those at the bottom are often being abused.

In the center is my proposed alternative. All members of this group are seated in a circle, which symbolizes total involvement of every individual. All are seen, and the energy flows around the circle. At the moment, one person has the rattle. In other words, she is speaking, singing, telling her story, making decisions, proposals, facilitating ritual, or whatever the situation requires. All are giving her power by lending their respect and attention, honest feedback, and so on. When she is finished she will pass the rattle to the next person, and the energy will continue around the circle until all have had their turn. Each person is supported and the needs of the group are met equally.

This system works in small groups, but it requires a responsibility from all present to give and take power, each at the appropriate time. I have found that most people either take too much or not enough, give too much, or not enough. Taking power is speaking out when your turn comes, singing your heartsong, telling your story, making your decision, granting yourself the right to be heard and seen. Giving power is acknowledging the next person, giving your support, your undivided attention and honest feedback when requested. Both require a basic recognition of the divine in each person. It is a sensitive balance between the needs of the self and the needs of the other. The person with the rattle can be the teacher for a time, the priestess, the facilitator, or just someone being heard. Her position is given by the mutual consent of the group, based on the awareness that this is beneficial to all present. But it in no way means that she is higher or better than any other woman present. We can all teach, lead, or follow. If one person is to hold the rattle for a prolonged period (say to teach a class), arrangements can be made for the other members of the circle to give her energy that supports her, so that the flow is still happening and the needs of both teacher and learner are being met.

This form can work at any level, from the most practical business to the most psychic or spiritual rituals. It is cellular, like biological organization, and by necessity, decentralized. It allows for intimacy, time and space for everyone, and individual freedom. Its best glue is simple affection! It allows things to get accomplished, decisions made, rituals performed, while maintaining equality among all present. Such groups can stay intact for as long as is agreed upon . . . a day, a few months, a year, a lifetime . . . When it is happening and everyone understands, the most amazing and wonderful miracles can occur.

Unfortunately, people whose minds are still caught in the staircase image often confuse the woman-with-the-rattle with the head honcho. Sometimes, no matter how carefully I explain, how many diagrams I wave, there will be people who are ready to bow down to me and demean themselves in the process, and there will be people who resent my taking power and will feel threatened. It is very difficult to be free and equal in a society that is based on inequality and scarcity. All I can tell you is to keep trying. If a person is attacking you for taking power, you have a right to protect yourself from them. If a person is lowering themselves to learn from you, you can try to help them to see a new way, to take power themselves. Perhaps the information I am providing here will prevent some of the heartaches and struggles I have had to go through to learn it; I sincerely hope so. Through the years I have learned much and have grown stronger too. Looking back I can say that the joy and glory have far outweighed the difficulties, and that it has been more than worth it.

As I finish writing this final cycle, I listen with half an ear to some of the Sunday morning TV ministers. I think how much joy and fun it would be to pour out my soul that way and share my love of goddess, my spiritual insight more directly, with living, present, flesh-and-blood human beings . . . and I think of all the differences between my beliefs and those propagated on the screen. I think of Goddess and how that very word changes all such possibilities.

A woman calling herself Reverend Terry comes onto the screen. I don't know much about her but am impressed by her progressive contributions to the spiritual tube. She speaks to us of how the world is full of love and that we are loved, telling us how wonderful we are. She says that we are powerful and wonderful and precious. Terry talks about safeness and abundance and how we can create heaven or hell with our thoughts. When she asks for money she makes you feel so good about giving, telling you that this will "prosper you." She wants you to have all that you can have, be all that you can be, and it is obvious that she has claimed all of this for herself as well, without shame. She explains that jealousy happens when we deny another the right to have and be, because we are inwardly denying ourselves these things—out of guilt, bad self-image, etc. In my mind Terry becomes the embodiment of nurturing love, the love once universally received from a Mother Goddess. I learn some things from Reverend Terry—she helps me to feel good about myself, to accept myself, to give myself permission to be all that I wish to be.

Jimmy Swaggart, on the other hand, makes people feel bad about themselves with his emphasis on sin. He attacks many groups and ideologies and sees his way as the only way. (Reverend Terry says if you do not attack you will not be attacked.) I feel as though his congregation is composed of many sheepish, guilty people, who think they must be punished and brow-beaten before they will be able to forgive themselves for whatever crimes they have committed. Though glaringly bigoted, hierarchical, and patriarchal, the Jimmy Swaggart show gives me food for thought. I am struck by the powerful stream of archetypes included in a song a woman sings. The words of the chorus are: "He died of a broken heart," referring to the sufferings of Christ. The "blood of mercy," the "love that never lets go," the forgiveness of humanity, the suffering, the cry for forgiveness—these are the old emblems of the Great Mother in disguise: Her blood which came in bliss, Her unconditional love which came in Her sweet embrace, Her life that came in abundance and fulfillment. The blood of Jesus is connected to suffering. The death of Jesus gives no hope of return. His compassion is linked to self-denial and suffering. The Mother offers us all of these things—her blood, her love, her forgiveness, her life, her abundance—without pain and sorrow, but in joy and well-beingness. Yet the old archetypes continue to resonate, for as Jimmy Swaggart aptly says, "This is not an atheistic nation."

Both of these ministers are sincere and truly inspired by their visions, I believe. Both have eager, supportive followings. I thought how many people are searching, and how there are thousands of ministries and everyone sort of gravitates to the one that works for them at the time. How I did this myself for many years, and looked into all kinds of teachings. How I learned from each some truth that has always remained with me. How they all eventually led me to the Mother . . .

For a moment, on mainstream TV, I see the Goddess come through Reverend Terry and through the woman who sings of the sufferings of Jesus. In this moment, these women are my sisters, and they become channels of truth and love. I think, well, perhaps it doesn't matter in the end how one names or genderizes one's deity, as long as the love is there and people are empowered and healed.

And I reflect on how Jesus himself has evolved into a kind of suffering mother with his bleeding heart and flowing robes and moist, compassionate eyes. Part of me feels patient and compassionate with his followers.

But then I realize that all of these TV spirit healers are working for the patriarchy, for they still say "God" and "Christ" with no mention of the Goddess. I recall the end of Morgaine's story in *The Mists of Avalon*, when she visits the little church and worships the goddess through the statue of Virgin Mary enshrined there. She says in essence, oh well, they still have Mary . . . as if to resign herself to the patriarchy and this watered-down version of the Goddess. And I think of how much hatred there is toward mothers on earth today, how women are still made to feel unclean, unworthy, and inferior. I think of the poverty that exists in the world, while the prosperity preachers seem to propagate riches with no accountability to this. And then a part of me rises up in protest and cannot accept quietly the TV ministries of God, even those that are well-meaning and progressive.

Will there be a day of Goddess radio and TV? I have long predicted that there will. We can see some small beginnings with the creation of Z. Budapest's cable series "13th Heaven" and Donna Reed's film series "The Goddess Remembered." It will be interesting to see how these things develop. Now I find myself in a ministerial position, in that people are reaching out to me, want to hear what I believe, are finding hope and healing through this communication. And I fantasize being on the tube at midnight, when the channel signs off, giving words of the Goddess, images of the divine female, music of poetic and passionate ecstasy, rituals of women . . .

Even closer to my heart are visions of gatherings of live people, going around the world, talking, sharing, doing rituals together, helping women to affirm their own power, giving joy to their spirits with music, poetry and myth . . . I see many priestesses, many and varied forms of worship.

A goddess ministry would perhaps contain some of the elements of other ministries, but it would have to go beyond them in essential ways. It would have to remain de-centralized, with no main pope or expert or authoritarian figure. It would have to be female-oriented, and supportive of the divinity of all that is female. It would be such that individuals would be empowered at the grass-roots level. Gradually, quietly, it would become apparent that people are embracing Her way, not because it makes a good sales pitch, not because the boss dictates it, not because a preacher or priestess insists on it, but because it has bubbled up from deep within the souls of many individuals. A Goddess ministry would have to be accountable to the inequities of patriarchal society, and would go hand in hand with the changing of those inequities. Any true priestess or priest of such a ministry would have to be able to spread the word as the one-who-holds-the-rattle for a time, and not as the "head honcho."

This is how I see my own priestessing—as a spark to others, a light that passes on, to be replaced by other lights, and later to be remembered. I hope that in writing all of this I will be of some inspiration to you to join the wave. I think any true priestess of Goddess will be accountable to issues of power, and will not seek to set herself above anyone. Eventually I would like to see great priestess pow-wows where the rattle is passed and energy is raised around the world. When priestesses stand by one another, nothing, nothing will be able to stop us!

Together we can do anything.

Finale

"Now," he said, "now we're away, now we're clear, we're clean gone, Tenar. Do you feel it?"

She did feel it. A dark hand had let go its lifelong hold upon her heart. But she did not feel joy, as she had in the mountains. She put her head down in her arms and cried, and he cheeks were salt and wet. She wept in pain, because she was free.

What she had begun to learn was the weight of liberty. Freedom is a heavy load, a great and strange burden for the spirit to undertake. It is not easy. It is not a gift given, but a choice made . . .

—From *The Tombs of Atuan*
by Ursula Le Guin

Being a witch is not always easy. It is a path of freedom and self-directedness. There are times when, as witches, we have no one to turn to but the Goddess Herself. There are times when people around us, at the place we live, work, or go to school, will not understand our religion. There will be times when we feel like outcasts, especially when we see the latest film on psychic evil, or the latest sensational television commercial for some "hot" occult product, or hear the latest bigoted invective against our faith.

But the rewards are tremendous. When we can get beyond our own doubts and fears we find that the Goddess is truly there for us in every way possible. If we feel afraid or lonely or unsupported, we can do magic and ritual to change these circumstances. If we need abundance, we have but to call upon Her to help us to create it. Our freedom gives us a strength that can never be taken away from us, that can never be matched by the dependency-producing hierarchical faiths. As more and more of our numbers grow, as we each find our inner strengths and come together to share them, we will find that being a witch in today's world will become easier. And we will know that we are instrumental not only in our own healing, but in the healing of all the world.

The thread has guided you to an ante-chamber, located near the entrance to Ariadne's cave. Here is where Ariadne resides, ready to welcome new initiates and help to midwife them across Her thresholds, both in and out of the labyrinth.

This cavern is softy draped and lit with many candles. A great stone altar, carved in the likeness of Gaia, is part of one wall, facing the arched exitway. A high ledge near the vaulted ceiling runs 'round the entire chamber. On it are placed many statues of goddesses from around the world. You recognize Isis with Her great wings lifted, Arachne, weaving Her star-spangled web, Oceana, whose watery gown seethes with wave and foam, Demeter, offering fruit and grain from Her great golden cornucopia, Cerridwen, stirring Her pearl-rimmed cauldron, Ariadne's twin Persephone, who extends a hand as if to lead you back again, into the depths. There are many couches and comfortable cushions placed around the room. You catch a glimpse of bookshelves lined up behind the velvet draperies. This is a place of learning, as well as repose. In one crystalline alcove there is a pool of warm water, where you bathe and wash away your tiredness. It has been a long journey.

You move to the altar and seat yourself, to commune with this great ancient Mother. "Oldest of Deities" She has been called. Her crown of leaves and flowers is embedded with lapis lazuli, green aventurine, amethysts and opals, rose quartz and rich red garnets. In the crooks of both elbows she cradles her many children—babies of varying shapes and sizes who snuggle against Her, climb up to nuzzle Her neck or search for the nipples of Her great, luscious breasts. Her face is powerful, yet serene. Her hands are carved so that they can hold candles between the massive fingers. There are two placed there now, tall and white, engraved with pentagrams and images of women, but not yet aflame.

Ariadne appears. She is robed in blue and silver, and Her dark eyes are filled with a deep and abiding love. Her slender crescent crown still rests on Her brow, and you can see the little golden snake peeking out from the folds of Her gown, looking at you curiously, and flicking its thread of a tongue. Ariadne kneels to embrace you, smiling and congratulating you for having made this great journey. She smells of musk and amber, and there are tiny silver bells sewn into Her garments that ring softly whenever She moves.

Idea bounces into the chamber, all dressed in rainbows and laughing happily to see Ariadne again. Themis returns as well, robed in velvets of rust and brown and deep wine red. She smiles in Her slow, dignified way, and comes to sit beside you and take your hand. In Her other hand She holds a parchment scroll. Mnemosyne wafts in from somewhere, shimmering in pearlescent clouds of pale blue and dove grey. Her face shifts and changes; now She is a young maiden, now a mature woman, now a wrinkled crone. All the Goddesses come to be with you before the altar, and together you form a sisterly circle.

Ariadne rises and lights the two tall candles in Gaia's hands. She fills a censer with sweet dried rosemary, sage and thyme, lights them as well, and chants:

> "Hail to Thee Great Mother, Goddess of all Goddesses
> We honor and welcome Thy presence
> And ask You to bless this circle of initiation.
> So Be It."

She returns to the circle with a rattle made of woven willow, filled with fragments of shells from the sea. You all converse for awhile, reflecting upon the recent adventures, and the possibilities to come. Then Ariadne leads everyone in a group breath to clear your minds and center yourselves. She starts the rattle 'round, and the Goddesses formally ask you Nine Sacred Questions:

Idea takes the rattle first:
"Answer truthfully and well, dear sister, and if you say yes we will pronounce your Passing. Do you feel and know that the Goddess has always been present in your life, and always will be?"

And you respond: _____

All affirm your response: "Blessed Be!"
Idea: "Are you aware that you are divine, and yourself a Goddess?"

You reply: _____

All affirm: "Blessed Be!"
Idea: "Do you understand that all that lives is sacred?"

You: _____

All: "Blessed Be!"
Idea passes the rattle to Themis:
"Do you see your mortality as well as your immortality? Do you know that you have been here before, and will be again?"

You reply: _____

All affirm: "Blessed Be!"
Themis: "Do you take pride in yourself as a woman?"

You: _____

All: Blessed Be!"
Themis: "What are the Eight Passages of the Goddess year, and how are they like unto your own Birthing, Living, and Dying?"

You respond: _____

All: "Blessed Be!"

And Themis passes the rattle to Mnemosyne:
"Can you feel your connection to all things and beings in the great web of life and spirit?"

And you answer thus: _____

All: "Blessed Be!"
Mnemosyne: "Do you know that there is consciousness in all Beings and Things in the universe?"

You: _____

All: "Blessed Be!"
Mnemosyne: "And last, but not least of the Nine Sacred Questions—do you feel the universal Love of the Goddess enfolding you?"

And you answer thus: _____

All affirm: "Blessed Be!"

(Assuming that you have answered in the affirmative) Ariadne begins to sing a song of blessing and celebration. All the Goddesses join in, then rise and lift you to your feet, still singing:

> We thank you Goddess for this woman
> Who has traveled deep and well
> We thank this woman for her presence
> And the tale she comes to tell . . .

Each of the four Goddesses embraces and kisses you, sharing Her special acknowledgments. "You are a woman after my own heart," laughs Idea, with a warm hug. "When the world is filled with such women," says Themis, placing Her two hands firmly on your shoulders, "it will be a very different place!" Mnemosyne looks deep into your eyes, smiling softly in eloquent silence.

Ariadne pulls a small flask of liquid amber from the folds of Her cloak and anoints you on your brow, throat, heart, solar plexus, womb, feet, hands and crown, speaking spells for each:

Brow: May the Goddess be ever in your thoughts.
Throat: May you speak and sing Her names.
Heart: May your heart be ever filled with Her love.
Solar Plexus: May your powers flow freely.

Womb: May your womb-fires rise up at your desire, in pleasure and divine creativity.
Feet: May you ever walk in the ways of the Goddess.
Hands: May you do the work of women and the Goddess in joy.
Crown: And when your time has come, may you return to me.

She takes your hand and leads you to the altar, then helps you up to be seated in Gaia's generous lap. Mnemosyne, Idea, Themis and Ariadne all gather 'round and give you praises and adoration, for you too are the Goddess. "Hail to thee sweet Goddess," they cry in unison. They ask you to tell your tale and speak your heart and mind about all that you wish to share of your wonderful journey.

Then each Goddess produces a parting gift for you to take with you into the world. Mnemosyne has a velvet bag of runestones, so that you will always be able to find answers to your questions. Themis gives you the parchment scroll, which is your Inscription of Initiation. It pronounces your accomplishments and names you Wise Woman. Each Goddess puts Her mark upon it as a seal and witness to your transformation. Idea gives you a new blank book made of old parchment paper, and bound with a lush brocade. "For the magic and ideas yet to come," she grins. Ariadne goes to the laurel tree at the entrance to the cave, unties the silver thread and snips a length of its endlessness. She winds it into a crown for your head. "So that you will always be connected to us, and to this place. Come back when you are ready to deepen further."

She takes your hand once more to help you down, and walks with you slowly to the entranceway. "Be blessed and safe back in the world." She makes the pentacle sign of protection over you. All the Goddesses surround you and hold you, kissing you farewell. "May the circle be opened, but never broken."

You look down to see that the silver ball of thread has rolled to your feet. You pick it up and hand it back to Ariadne. She smiles and tucks it into a fold of her robe, then steps aside. You look out from the labyrinth into the world once more, and step through the opening . . .

This is an image of ideal communication, a circle of women where the rattle is passed and every voice is heard. In this process, a symbol of true community can be found where the potential exists for mutual empowerment, consciousness raising and solidarity.

Suggested Projects

1. Design and perform an initiation ceremony. Feel free to use any of the elements of rituals provided in the Cycles, including the circle of Goddesses described in the last scene. Or you may prefer to compose from scratch, or simply improvise something out of spontaneous inspiration. For a statement of commitment to sisterhood and goddess ways, you might like to use some or all of the "Pact to Build the Temple of Trust" (see page 378), and sign this as part of your ceremony. Also provided is a sample "Inscription of Initiation" (page 379) which can serve as a pronouncement of your new level of development. Both documents can be copied by hand on special paper, decorated as the Muse inspires, and signed in moonblood or any consecrated red liquid such as: wine, ink, fruit juice, hibiscus tea, beet juice. Use a magic pen; in other words one that you have blessed and consecrated to such purposes. If you are sharing this ritual in a group, everyone can sign and witness each others' statements. You can dress up as different Goddesses and enact their parts as outlined, or create new and additional roles.

2. Make a copy of the Witch's Wheel on page 342, or create a mandala of your own design. Include it in the principles as discussed in Cycle 13. If you have not yet made a calendar wheel, you can emphasize the material on solar and lunar time (see Cycles 7 and 8). Add any concepts that you feel are relevant or important to you. Color the wheel, giving thought to the meanings of colors. (See page 361 in Cycle 10 for suggestions on these.) If you make your wheel large enough, you'll have room for additional symbols, runes and other decorations such as trees, Goddesses, seasonal scenes, and so on. If done on paper, you can mount it on wood or cardboard to make it sturdy, perhaps apply a coat of protecting varnish or artists' spray. Bless and consecrate your Wheel for use as a magical tool. This can be done as part of your initiation ceremony, as suggested above, or as a separate ritual.

3. "Rewind the thread," as Mnemosyne suggests. Go backward through the Cycles, taking notes in your *Book of Shadows* as you go. See how many new insights you can discover. Write down any questions you may have, any additions or revelations. These can be explored in your circle, in future studies, or as your magical life develops. Look to see which Cycles are your favorites, and why.

4. Make yourself a Witch's Rosary, as described in Cycle 11 on Herbs. You can actually use small dried roses on a string, threading them while they are still soft and fresh. (One student of mine dipped her roses in paraffin wax to preserve them, and strung them with tiny rose-quartz beads in between. Beautiful!) Have one rose-bead

for each of the aspects of the Witch's Wheel, starting with the Goddess for the first bead, moving to Maiden, Mother and Crone for the next three, and so on. This rosary can serve as a magical necklace to wear at ceremonies, and can be used as a mnemonic device for all the messages it imparts. You can also include a blessing and consecration of your rosary in your initiation ceremony. If done in circle, women can put them on each other with appropriate incantations.

5. Start a project that will help bring the ways of the Goddess into the world. Form a coven with others, or a Goddess support-group, or develop a women's spirituality event in your community. Get involved with ecology efforts, animal rights, peace actions, projects to help women, children, aging people, homeless people, or people in need of healing. Form neighborhood associations and have "town meetings" where the rattle is passed and everyone's voice is heard. Publish a home-style newsletter and collect writings and art from women you know. Apply for grants from organizations with money, to help provide real support for such activities. There are a million ways to get involved; think about and research such possibilities.

Questions to Ponder

1. How did you like working with *Ariadne's Thread*? What gave you pleasure? What didn't you like?

2. Do you feel that you know more about: The Goddess, Magic, Rituals, Holidays, Herbs, Power, Sisterhood, Feminism, Belief, The Moon, Blood, Sexuality, Herstory, Women, Yourself? What have you learned and how do you feel about these things?

3. Do you feel motivated to continue on the path of Goddess spirituality and/or magic? If so, how will this take form? (Covening, solitary practice, study, political action, creative pursuits such as writing goddess-related materials, creating magical crafts, or . . . ?)

4. Do you feel drawn to any particular path such as Dianic, Druid, Faery, Gardnerian, Goddess-Centered, etc.? Will you prefer to create your own approach, or an eclectic combination? What elements attract you in current traditions, what don't you like? Have you changed in this regard, or do you see yourself changing in the future?

5. How do you feel about your participation in this course? Did you give it as much devotion as you might have? Would you like to go through it again more deeply? If you went through it with a teacher or group, would you like to try doing it alone? Vice versa?

6. Do you think about becoming a priestess—that is, one who facilitates ceremony

and teaches about the Goddess? How would you go about developing this?

7. Do you feel called to develop magical talents such as psychic healing, divination, poetry-writing, spell-casting, myth-making, ritual-making, other? How would you go about pursuing these?

8. Do you feel that this study has changed your life? In what way? Has it helped you to grow or heal or to open up? To be more assertive or receptive? Has it made you more or less spiritual, more or less political? Has it created any conflicts in your present life-style or relationships? If so, how will you resolve these?

9. How do you see your life unfolding in the future? Do you feel inspired to work toward changing society? What changes would you make? How would you go about doing this?

10. Do you feel there is hope for the future of our planet? For women, children, animals, old people, young adults, artists? What is your idea of a happy, sane, goddess-oriented society? What does it look like; how do people live, work, relate?

11. What cosmology now makes sense to you? Do you view the universe as Goddess-centered? God/Goddess? Neuter? Other?

12. How do you explain gender? Do you feel motivated to explore this subject further? How do you feel about homosexual love? Heterosexual love? Celibacy? Sexual love between more than two? Marriage? Love outside of marriage? Incest and rape? Trysting? (See *Casting the Circle* by Diane Stein for an account of some trysting ceremonies.)

13. Now that you have completed this course, do you identify as a witch? What effect, if any, does this have on personal relationships? Professional relationships? In your current life-style can you be "out" as a witch? If not, would you consider ways to change this? After all the experiences you have been through with the Thread, what is your definition of the word witch?

Readings and Other Resources:

Cerridwen Fallingstar, *The Heart of the Fire.*
Janet and Stewart Farrar, *The Witches' Goddess.*
Jade, *To Know.*
John Rowan, *The Horned God.* This is a book on men's mysteries, pagan men's feelings and pain about their role in patriarchy. It is about taking responsibility, working to heal the split.

For anthologies of writings by contemporary priestesses, see:
Caitlin Matthews, editor of *Voices of the Goddess: A Chorus of Sibyls*.
Diane Stein, editor of *The Goddess Celebrates: An Anthology of Women's Ritual*.

Newsletters:
Of A Like Mind magazine. An excellent spiritual/political resource for women. Box
6021, Madison, WI 53716.

Note

The Pact to Build the Temple of Trust on page 378 was composed collectively
by a women's circle called Hecate, several years ago. It is the distillation of pacts
composed by several other circles. We wanted to state our ethics and the promises
we felt should be made to solidify the new reality we were creating.

I have found that the Hecate pact has stood the test of time. I usually re-sign it
each year at Aradia, occasionally adding a new phrase or two. Because of the poetic
language I find that the meanings continue to unfold, making it especially beautiful
and moving.

I invite you to adopt this pact for your own, if you so desire, or adapt it to fit your
beliefs. You are invited to use it in your closing ceremony, to join the many women
who have signed it before, and to have it in your life as a constant guide and
companion to your magic.

Pact to Build the Temple of Trust

Ariadne, Hecate, Demeter, Diana, Arachne, Persephone, Selene, Cybele, Aradia, Kore, Tiamat, Amaterasu, Iris, Gaia, Wakanmah, Athene, Aphrodite, Medusa, Themis, Ea, Astarte, Adame, Ashtorah, Kali, Isis, Artemis, Elphame, Oceana, Oshun, Ondine, Ngame, Yemanja, Paige, Shekhinah, Melissande, Psyche, Sappho, Isadora, Danu, Elfroot . . . (add goddess and/or women's names as desired).
Goddess of a thousand names
Thou who bore us
And thou to whom we will ever return
I pledge my heartfelt vows to thee:
I trust myself to fill myself
For thou art the self I see
As I create a beautiful vision of thee
So is my faith ever renewed
And so am I empowered . . .
As I welcome the Maiden into my arms
So do I become Her
As I welcome the Mother into my heart
So do I become Her
As I welcome the Crone into my soul
So do I become her . . .
As thy energy flows through all life forms
Bringing balance to all things
So doth my energy flow in harmony . . .
As I celebrate thy womb which sends forth all life
So doth my womb, and the blood of my womb be celebrated . . .
All children are thy children
Brought forth from thy sacred womb
As we send them forth empowered by Thee
So do they bring forth revelation . . .
As I respond to the sacredness of my body, and thy body, the Earth
So am I filled with life and health and ecstasy . . .
As I know thine infinite abundance in matterful things
So do I ever have enough for my needs
And enough to share with my loved ones
As the Muse whispers her songs to me
So do I sing them
As I listen to thy voices in the wind and trees
In the ocean and thunder
And from the throats of all thy creatures
So doth my voice be heard
With strength I speak thy truth
And so am I trusted
Let confrontation be my sword
Compassion be my shield
And as I ever have the strength to take the rattle
So do I have the understanding to pass the rattle on . . .
As my own sacred space is honored
In thy physical and psychic realms
So do I honor my loved ones' sacred space . . .
As I honor the gifts of my loved ones
So are my own gifts honored . . .
As my own well of energy is replenished by others
So do I fill my loved ones' well . . .
As I honor the eternal quality of thy love
So am I loved forever.
So be it!
Blessed be!

Here is the *Inscription of Initiation* used by me and my students when we work through the mail. Teachers can use this or something similar, solitary students or teams and groups can adapt or create an appropriate document.

Inscription of Initiation

I call upon the Goddesses of Spirit, Air, Fire, Earth, and Water. I call upon the Maiden, the Mother, and the Crone. I call upon The Great Goddess Who births us all, and to Whom we all return.

to please support and witness here:
the Initiation of

_____
(student's name)

Who, having completed the 13 cycles of the Mysteries of the Goddess studies, now proclaims herself to be a true witch.

_____ , I name thee Wise Woman.
(student's name)

And therefore let us rejoice in the rebirth and transformation of this beautiful woman-soul!

So Be It   Blessed Be

Signed this _____ day of the _____
(moon-date)   (tree name)

Moon of Our Lady, _____ , by
(year)

_____
(teacher's name)
Priestess of Women's Mysteries

AFTERWORD

I am a lover, a mother, a daughter, and a sister of women. I am a priestess, a teacher, a writer, an artist, a scholar, a musician, tarot and runemaker, reader of tarot and runes, a craftswoman, a ritualist, a healer and a changer. I am a wild and watery woman, a magical mystical poet, a woman-identified witch, a lesbian, and weaver of song and myth. I am a founding mother of the women's spirituality movement, one of the first to channel Goddess revolution in our times.

I first received the Goddess in the early 1970s, when Her present returning wave was just beginning. At that time I felt that Goddess-awareness would sweep the planet, that it was the solution to all the world's major problems, and that women especially would be Her devotees. I still feel this way, but I didn't know how long it would take, nor how difficult it would be.

In those early years I met and worked with many women who, like myself, were falling in love with the Goddess, with each other, with themselves, with the earth. It was an ecstatic honeymoon period, and few of us were prepared for the struggles and shattering that would follow. At that time I was the only teacher in my area offering women's goddess-study groups and rituals. It wasn't until the mid-'70s that I found out there were a few others like myself, scattered here and there around the planet. I learned of Z. Budapest, who was living in Los Angeles, California at that time, beginning to generate women's spiritual groups there, as I was doing up in the mountains of Santa Cruz. I met Ann Forfreedom; at that time she was posted in Sacramento. Ruth and Jean Mountaingrove were up in Oregon, producing *Womanspirit* magazine, a kitchen table treasure-trove of women's earliest contributions in poetry, articles, letters and art, from all around the world. Back in those innocent and isolated times, *Womanspirit* was to become one of the first important links in the Goddess chain.

Why was it such a struggle? The patriarchal system in many ways is an overwhelming obstacle to the ways of the Goddess. While Goddess women seek to connect and create mutual support, the system teaches us to cut off and compete. While feminists seek to liberate women, the system is built upon maintaining women's subservience. While women-loving-women seek to bond with one another, the male-dominated system seeks to ensure that all women will put men first. While Goddess-reality is about propagating abundance and more than enough for all, patriarchal economics depends upon scarcity and wage slavery. While Goddess sisters seek to share and take turns with power, the system pushes us toward dominance and submission. All of these and many other factors served to tear sisters apart, not only through external circumstances, but also through our own unconscious programming. We still have much healing to do, and a long way to go.

But times have truly changed since those beginning years. Now feminist spirituality is all around us, and growing by leaps and bounds. Where once you might be able to dig up a few dusty books in the library, now there are dozens of books available on shelves in every bookshop. Where once *Womanspirit* was a lonely voice in the night, now there are hundreds of pagan and goddess-oriented publications. In place of the occasional circle of women are multiple circles, groups and festivals around the world. Church groups are beginning to accept the Goddess, and there are women's spiritual studies in many universities. Goddess products abound in the marketplace, and Goddess-loving women and men are everywhere. The other day I decided that the world has really changed, when I saw a shiny new red truck with a bumper-sticker that said "Goddess is alive, magic is afoot." We who were the pioneers of this awakening, managed to hang in there through the hard times, and the new ways have taken hold.

Now in this current era of success and growth, our movement confronts new questions. How can we sell Goddess products and images without "selling out?" How can we build a common base for cooperation, rather than competition? How will we develop agreement on ethics, philosophy, thealogy, without creating dogmatism? How will we make sure our religion doesn't become another power-over institution, or "just another commercial fad," instead of a lasting way of life that can help to heal our world? How will we make sure that Goddess-reality is nourishing to women's lives, and not just another means for absorbing them back into oppression?

These are great questions, not easily answered. Perhaps some of the thealogical concepts and forms I have created will be of help.

My training was somewhat unorthodox, and I hope this will not be a deterrent to those of you seeking information. While I am not an academic, and cannot boast of the usual credentials, I have done much studying on my own. My education began at the side of my extraordinary mother, who taught me to love learning, nurtured my art, and gave me culture in my childhood years. I studied theater in high school and college, and subsequently made my living as a folksinger on both the east and west coasts. I sang the exquisite ballads of high poetry and haunting melody, particularly those that migrated from the British Isles. My music has been Ariadne's thread for me, taking me ever deeper into the mysteries. Discovering trance and writing mythic songs led me to the ecstatic ancient journey of shamans. Discovering the Goddess roots in male-centered esoterica and folklore led me to create many new systems: tarot, runes, calendars, rituals, ethics, holidays, myths. Women came to me for teachings and so I have become an educator as well.

Readers will find many thealogical principles here, due to my efforts to find new symbol systems that can help to propagate a woman-loving reality. Perhaps some of them will ring true, perhaps not. I am aware that the Goddess loves freedom and independent thought, and a movement true to Her ways would necessarily resist conformism or dogma. At the same time, I believe there is a common thread of truth which arises spontaneously in many individuals, yet bears messages that are universal. The Maiden Goddess loves freedom, but the Mother Goddess builds strong and lasting forms, and the Crone reveals the inescapable verities that have always been with us. Such concepts as circularity, immanent spirit, the sacredness of all life, the primacy of the female, the divinity of women, shared power, the aliveness of Mother Earth, and the consciousness of all beings and things in the universe are not my invention. They are part of a reality we are all discovering on some level.

A recent ritual, performed by a local coven here in Santa Cruz (called The Web), exemplifies these principles:

Several women arrive at the beach to celebrate the spring. Each has been invited to come dressed up as her favorite Goddess. One woman is Gaia, the Earth Mother, and another is Kore, the newborn Maiden. Another is dressed as Kali in Her death aspect, all in black with rattling bones. The Maiden explores and discovers, exclaiming in wonder at the newness of everything. "Who are you?" she inquires of Gaia. "I am your mother, maker of your blood and bones. I am the ground you walk upon, the air that you breathe, the water that you drink. You are my hope for the future, the continuation of my dreams." Maiden and Mother hold and adore one another. Kali rolls upon the ground, writhing and screaming. "Aieee! Aiieeee!" everyone cries, "It is the death of Winter . . . !"

This enactment is improvised and completely spontaneous. The women open themselves to the moment and let themselves flow, allowing whatever thoughts or movements or expressions they wish to come through. And yet, in their unique way, they are enacting the Myth of the Kore, the universal principles of spring coming out of winter, of birth coming out of death, of Maiden-coming-out-of-Mother-coming-out-of-Crone. Their process is equalitarian, yet there is gentle leadership and structure. Each woman goes away feeling energized, affirmed and empowered.

The woman who came as the Kore, Biddy Remick, has been my student for quite some time now. She brought to the ritual the knowledge she has found with me, as well as the flowering of her own inner knowing. Biddy works part time for the Nuclear Freeze, helping to bring peace to the earth. In our circle we did many magics to help her find "right livelihood." Next week she will be in spring ceremony with me, enacting my version of the Myth of the Kore. Another member has been leading and priestessing women's circles for many years. She has her own business as a seamstress, and says she loves repairing and saving garments that would otherwise be thrown away. A newcomer to the group brought her experience as a performer at renaissance fairs. Some of the women will continue to circle together, others will come and go. "I'm so happy," Biddy exclaimed joyously, when she told me about the ceremony on the phone.

So our movement grows, and I feel satisfied that I am doing my part. May the works I have offered here to you, dear reader, be a continuation and an expansion of this wonderful process. So be it. Blessed Be.

May 7, 9991 Alder Moon, Day 23

The Crossing Press publishes a full
selection of feminist titles and the
Celebrating Women's Spirituality Calendar.

To receive our current catalog,
please call—Toll Free—
800/777-1048.